THE LOST RIVER

The Lost River

On the Trail of the Sarasvatī

MICHEL DANINO

PENGUIN BOOKS

An imprint of Penguin Random House

PENGUIN BOOKS

USA | Canada | UK | Ireland | Australia
New Zealand | India | South Africa | China | Singapore

Penguin Books is part of the Penguin Random House group of companies
whose addresses can be found at global.penguinrandomhouse.com

Published by Penguin Random House India Pvt. Ltd
4th Floor, Capital Tower 1, MG Road,
Gurugram 122 002, Haryana, India

Penguin
Random House
India

First published by Penguin Books India 2010

Copyright © Michel Danino 2010

Page 340 is an extension of the copyright page

12 11 10 9 8 7 6 5

ISBN 9780143068648

Typeset in Sabon by Michel Danino
Printed at Repro India Limited

www.penguin.co.in

MIX
Paper from
responsible sources
FSC® C047271

To the many archaeologists,
noted or forgotten,
who have diligently dug India's soil

To my parents,
with deep gratitude

Contents

Contents

Preface

The Lost River: On the Trail of the Sarasvatī attempts to popularize, in the best sense of the term, the present state of research into the legendary river. Understandably, the Sarasvatī has often burst its scholarly banks to spill out into the public arena. To tell my tale, I have used a lay person's language as far as possible, but I have rested my case on the most authentic findings from a variety of disciplines.

Detailed references for all quotations—which, let me stress, do not necessarily present the whole viewpoint of the quoted author —are found at the end of the book. (They are referred to in the text by Arabic numerals, while footnotes are referred to by asterisks.) My interpolations are within square brackets, which means that any parentheses are those of the quoted author. Except when indicated, the English translations of French texts are mine.

As the lay reader may find diacritical marks for Sanskrit words bothersome, I have only indicated long vowels, except for current geographical names: thus 'Yamuna' is today's river, 'Yamunā' is the one in Harappan or Vedic times (in quotations, the author's usage has been left unchanged). Indian place names, once rendered into English, are often spelt with disconcerting variety; I have chosen the most common spellings, preferably official ones, mentioning alternatives when possible. For dates before the Common Era, I have used the now standard abbreviation BCE instead of BC, and CE instead of AD. Maps are important in this book; in those drawn by me, international boundaries, when they appear, are as close as possible to those found on maps approved by the Government of India, yet should be regarded as only approximate, not authentic.

While writing this book, I often felt that the Sarasvatī's story has the potential to captivate non-Indian readers too; I hope the brief explanations I have inserted to enable them to follow details of India's geography and history will be excused by those familiar with them.

The motif at the end of each chapter, a bunch of three pipal leaves, is found on Harappan pottery.

*

I wish to thank the Archaeological Survey of India for its gracious permission to reproduce many photographs in this book. I am grateful to a few distinguished archaeologists, including Prof. B.B. Lal, the late Dr S.P. Gupta, Dr V.N. Misra, Dr R.S. Bisht, Prof. K.V. Raman and Dr R. Nagaswamy, who, over the course of a decade, generously shared their vast experience and patiently answered my nagging questions on various aspects of India's protohistory. Many Indian, American and French friends helped me gather the materials for this book or drew my attention to new findings; some of them are acknowledged in the Notes at the end of the book, but I cannot fail to mention here Dr S.P. Gupta, Dr K.N. Dikshit, Prof. R.N. Iyengar, Dr Kalyanaraman, Vishal Agarwal and V. Karthik.

I am greatly indebted to Ravi Singh, chief editor of Penguin India, for his warm interest in the story of the Sarasvatī; my thanks, too, to R. Sivapriya for her guidance and to Debasri Rakshit for her careful editing. The book could not have been written without the support of my parents, my companion Nicole, and a few close friends whom I need not name; they know my debt to them. Finally, I owe a special debt of gratitude to Dr Nanditha Krishna for her precious advice on the conception and plan of the book, and for her constant encouragement.

Prologue

India loves myths; they people every literature and every oral tradition of the land. By 'myth', I mean a complex, multilayered legend that weaves together heroic deeds and divine miracles, and, through powerful symbols, imprints a set of values on the mind of a people. The myth becomes, in turn, inseparable from its people's customs and traditions. Certain tribes of India's Northeast enact till today scenes from the Mahābhārata or the Rāmāyana, the two great Indian epics, even if it means substituting bamboo huts for glittering palaces. The message is what matters, not the décor.

And whether or not a myth has some historical basis, it is 'true' as long as it lives—and works—in the minds it has shaped. The great flood, the churning of the ocean, the descent of Gangā, the construction of a bridge to Lanka by an army of monkeys, or Krishna's lifting of the Govardhan hill are, in that sense, true. Whether they are 'facts' in our limited sense of the term is irrelevant: myths are something greater than facts. As long as we live life like a burden on our shoulders, Gilgamesh will pursue his quest for immortality, and Sisyphus will keep pushing his boulder uphill only to see it roll down again. Myths of creation, of origin or identity, myths of conquest and heroic defiance, all fulfil precise social, cultural and spiritual functions. Whether or not a myth has grown around a historical seed, it is a maker of history.

Our modern mind cannot easily grasp the role and impact of myths in ancient or traditional societies, whether Greek, Polynesian or Indian: today's societies are 'mythless' ones; for better or

1

2 The Lost River

worse, we have depopulated our inner worlds. In a bizarre reversal of meaning, the very word 'myth', which originally meant 'word' or 'speech' in Greek (much like the Sanskrit *vāch*), has come to evoke a web of lies, a concocted fable or a collective delusion.

*

Our story starts with a 'mythical' river that makes its appearance in the Rig Veda, the most ancient Indian text—'her' appearance, rather, since the Sarasvatī was also a goddess, a mother, and soon came to embody sacred speech, the Word. Multi-layered, as I said. Later texts, including the Mahābhārata, described the Sarasvatī as a 'disappearing' river, until she became 'invisible', meeting Gangā and Yamunā at their confluence; by then, she was the goddess, as we know her today.

As it happens, this myth is rooted in more than a vague historicity: we will discover how the Rig Veda's 'mighty river' has been identified by most experts with the now dry bed of a river that once flowed through northwest India,* in a course roughly parallel to the Indus, a little to the south of it. The story of the quest for the 'lost river' has never been told in full, and there is a frequent misconception that the Sarasvatī's rediscovery is a recent one to be credited to satellite photography. Rather, we will see how, in the early nineteenth century, British geologists, civil and military officials started surveying the region, which today includes parts of the Indian states of Haryana, Punjab and Rajasthan and the Cholistan Desert of Pakistan; the river's bed apart, they found its banks strewn with countless ruined settlements, mute evidence that this desolate landscape had once known better times. Indeed, by the 1850s, Indologists were in no doubt about the location of the 'mythic river'. Decades later, hundreds of those sites were found to have belonged to the Harappan or Indus civilization, which we will visit at some

---

* When referring to ancient times, like most scholars I will use India as synonymous, in a geographical sense, with the Indian subcontinent.

length. We will discover, in particular, considerable evidence that much of its culture survived the collapse of its cities, some of which is still surprisingly alive today.

At this point, we might expect a relatively simple story—as simple as, say, the rediscovery of Troy by Schliemann and its correlation with Homer's Iliad—since the ancient literature also refers to numerous sites along the Sarasvatī. But the river got embroiled in a thorny issue, that of the Aryan invasion or migration theory, leading a few scholars to locate the Vedic Sarasvatī elsewhere, or deny its physical existence altogether. We will hear diverse viewpoints, learn from every one of them, and I will present my own, while weighing and trying to reconcile inputs from a variety of disciplines, including geology, climatology and archaeology. In the Indian context, a synthesis of archaeological and literary evidence has generally proved so elusive that archaeologists have often given up the attempt as a bad job, while scholars of literature rarely try to integrate archaeological data into the picture they construct from the texts. I hope to show that in the case of the Sarasvatī, we find a surprising number of echoes reverberating between the two disciplines, and can venture to exploit the correlations beyond what has been done so far.

Whatever perspective my readers will choose to adopt in the end, I will be rewarded if they feel enriched by insights on the dawn and early development of the Indian civilization—a civilization watered not only by the Indus and its tributaries, but also, in the view of most archaeologists, by a second river system that has since vanished.

Let us set off on our journey, attentive to every clue on the trail of the lost river.

Part 1

THE LOST SARASVATĪ

'The trace of the ancient riverbed was recently found, still quite recognizable, and was followed far to the west. [This discovery] confirmed the correctness of the tradition.'

Louis Vivien de Saint-Martin, 1855

'Although the river below the confluence [with the Ghaggar] is marked in our maps as Gaggar, it was formerly the Saraswatī; that name is still known amongst the people.'

C.F. Oldham, 1893

Part I

The Lost Sarasvati

The trace of the ancient riverbed was recently found, still quite recognizable, and was followed far to the west. [This discovery] confirmed the correctness of the tradition...

Louis Vivien de Saint-Martin, 1855

Although the river below the confluence [with the Chaggar] is marked in our maps as Gaggar, it was formerly the Sarsuti; that name is still known amongst the people.

C.F. Oldham, 1893

The 'Lost River
of the Indian Desert'

A few years ago, the BBC ran a story on what it called 'India's miracle river'. The Sarasvatī river's dry bed, it announced, had been traced in the Rajasthan desert, and there was 'startling new evidence that it may not have been a myth after all'.[1] Such articles had been regularly appearing in the Indian press since the 1990s, prompting the public to believe that this 'mythical river' had just been rediscovered. While some of the evidence in question is indeed two or three decades old, in reality the search for the river goes back almost two centuries.

The British Raj may rightly be blamed for many sins, but not for a lack of thoroughness in documenting the features of the newly acquired 'jewel of the Empire'. From the latter part of the eighteenth century onward, surveyors, geologists, naturalists, educators, administrators and army officers criss-crossed the Indian land mass and produced a commensurate mass of reports, papers, gazetteers, thick tomes and treatises, many of which remain invaluable documents of the time. From the humblest herb to the highest peak, little escaped their painstaking inventories.

We have, thus, a few early accounts of explorations of the region that concerns us: in the east, the Himalayan foothills known as the Shivalik Hills, with an altitude of 900 to 2300 m; moving westward, we cross India's states of Haryana and Punjab, the northwestern fringes of the Rajasthan desert, its Pakistani counterpart called the Cholistan Desert, finally reaching the Indus river

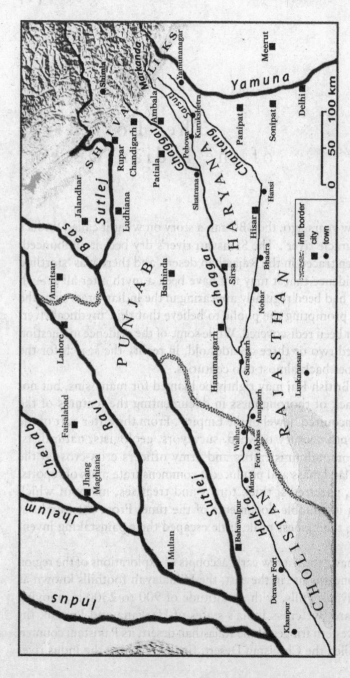

Fig. 1.1. A portion of the Northwest, with today's cities, towns and rivers. Note that unlike the Indus and its tributaries, the Ghaggar-Hakra system is now dry, except for a meagre seasonal flow in its upper reaches.

system (Fig. 1.1). Most of the scenes in this book will unfold in this setting, a vast and largely arid plain that was the theatre of many historical developments—and protohistorical ones, as its explorers soon realized.

FIRST SURVEYS

With the collapse of the Maratha confederacy in 1818, the Rajput chiefs, who had placed themselves under its protection, were forced to accept British suzerainty. One of the agents in that collapse was Lieutenant Colonel James Tod, who in 1812 had been deputed as the East India Company's 'political agent in Rajpootana' (today's Rajasthan). When he was not busy gathering intelligence, the post gave him ample opportunity to explore this vast region and meticulously document its geography, history and culture; he would also send emissaries to remote parts if he could not personally visit them. Tod's interest in the culture of the land was not a mere eyewash; he became something of an 'Orientalist' and an amateur numismatist. From the eleven folio volumes of notes he submitted to the Company, he extracted a two-volume *Annals and Antiquities of Rajasthan*, which remains a reference in the field. Tod died in 1835 at the age of fifty-three, three years after the publication of his work, and perhaps exhausted by it, as a side remark he wrote on his poor health suggests.

The part of interest to us is titled 'Sketch of the Indian Desert'. In Tod's description, the 'Marusthali',* as it was then called, consists of 'expansive belts of sand, elevated upon a plain only less sandy, and over whose surface numerous thinly peopled towns and hamlets are scattered'. He also records 'the tradition of the absorption of the Caggar river, as one of the causes of the comparative depopulation of the northern desert'.[2] This tradition was transmitted in the form of a 'couplet still sung among

---

* In Sanskrit, *maru* = desert, *sthala* = region. The name can also be taken to mean 'land of the dead' or, as Tod calls it, 'region of death'.

Rajputs, which dates the ruin of this part of the country back to the drying up of the Hakra.'³ Although Tod could not recall the exact text of the said song, he acknowledged 'the utility of these ancient traditional couplets'.⁴ 'Folk history', as we would call it today. A little later, we will meet a young Italian scholar who also got prodigiously interested in the bardic lore of Rajasthan.

But what are these 'Caggar' and 'Hakra' rivers? They are, in fact, one and the same (with a few variants, such as Guggur, Sankra, Slakra, Slakro, etc.) and had been marked on British maps since 1788 at least, when James Rennel, Surveyor General of Bengal, published his *Memoir of a Map of Hindoostan*.⁵ The first name, today spelt 'Ghaggar', refers to a largely seasonal river that rises in the Shivalik Hills near Dagshai and touches the plains close to Pinjore, some 20 km northeast of Chandigarh; it then flows north of Ambala, through Sirsa in Haryana, and Hanumangarh and Suratgarh in Rajasthan. The Ghaggar crosses today's Indo-Pakistan border near Anupgarh and continues, under the name of 'Hakra', through Fort Abbas, Marot, Derawar Fort (where it is also known as Wahind,* Sotra, etc.), until it loses itself in the sands of the Cholistan Desert—its bed, rather, since its waters never reach that far; although they occasionally flowed down to Hanumangarh till the early twentieth century, today the monsoon-fed river exists only in its upper course, and, even there, is never more than an average stream. Yet, James Tod finds worthy of mention a tradition alive in the 1810s that blames the region's 'depopulation' on the Ghaggar's 'absorption' or disappearance; he even notes how 'the vestiges of large towns, now buried in the sands, confirm the truth of this tradition, and several of them claim a high antiquity.'⁶ This tradition can only mean that the river once had much more abundant waters than in Tod's time—but let us not anticipate.

The etymology of the word 'Ghaggar' is interesting (and there are several rivers in India bearing kindred names, such as the Ghaghara or Gogra flowing through Ayodhya). We find a few

---

* Interestingly, 'Wahind' means 'river (*wah*) of India (*Hind*)'.

candidates in Sanskrit texts: the word *gargara* occurs in the
Atharva Veda (4.15.12) in the sense of a stream or a water body;
the Mahābhārata (12.59.111) mentions a *tīrtha** on the banks
of the Sarasvatī called 'Gargasrota', where Garga, a yogi versed
in astronomy, lived; 'Ghargharikā Kunda' is the name of a *tīrtha*
in the Brahma Purāna (25.64).[7] In the same line, we find the word
gharghara, of obvious onomatopoeic origin: it is cognate with the
English 'gurgle', and the river's music must have suggested it.

Major Colvin is our second witness. In 1833, as Superintendent
of Canals, he submitted to the government a report 'On the
Restoration of the Ancient Canals of the Delhi Territory', a title
that aptly summarizes his mission. In order to suggest how best
to revive some of those 'ancient' canals, generally dating to
medieval times (such as the Western Yamuna Canal), Colvin first
had to document every important watercourse and channel,
natural or man-made, in the region extending from Punjab to
northern Rajasthan. He followed the bed of the Chitang (or
Chitrang, today generally called Chautang), a small river flowing
alongside the Yamuna at first, then veering westward and continuing south of the Ghaggar before uniting with it a little above
Suratgarh in Rajasthan (see Fig. 1.1). But it is a junction of riverbeds only, since 'the *Ghaghar* river . . . does not in the heaviest
season pass in force beyond *Bhatnir*[†] . . . and the period when
this river ceased to flow as one is far beyond record, and belongs
to the fabulous periods of which even tradition is scanty.'[8] Those
'fabulous periods' will be the subject of our own exploration.

Some of Colvin's careful observations of the region deserve to
be noted in some detail:

> What the country about and west of *Raneah* [Rania, near
> Sirsa in Haryana] . . . has been, may be inferred from the
> numerous sites of towns and villages scattered over a tract,

---

* A *tīrtha* is a sacred site or place of pilgrimage, often associated with a body
of water.
† Variously spelt Bhatnir, Bhatnair, Bhatner or Bhatneer, this fortified town, once
a stronghold of the Bhatti Rajputs (hence its name), is now part of Hanumangarh, on the northern tip of Rajasthan (in the erstwhile Bikaner state).

where now fixed habitations are hardly to be met with. I
allude only to the vicinity of the bed of the *Ghaghar*, with
which I am personally acquainted;—when the depopulation took place, I am not prepared to say; it must have been
long since, as none of the village sites present[s] one brick
standing on another, above ground,—though, in digging
beneath it, very frequent specimens of an old brick are met
with, about 16 inches by 10 inches, and 3 inches thick, of
most excellent quality: buildings erected of such materials
could not have passed away in any short period. The evident
cause of this depopulation of the country is the absolute
absence of water . . .

It is striking that Colvin should agree with Tod (whose work
he seems to have been unaware of) on two crucial points: the
region was once ('long since') populated, as ruins of 'towns and
villages' show, and it ceased to be so when the Ghaggar somehow
lost much of its water.

Those two observations were corroborated a decade later
by Major F. Mackeson, 'Officiating Superintendent on Special
Mission to Seersa and Bahawulpore'. His 1844 report on the
route between those two cities (Sirsa in today's Haryana and
Bahawalpur on the Sutlej, now in Pakistan) makes it clear what
this 'special mission' might have been: it had to do with commerce and, probably more so, with military preparations. Both
required a more direct route between Delhi and what is today
Pakistan's southern province of Sind: 'Whether viewed with
reference to the march of troops, or to the dispatch of military
stores from the heart of our Upper Provinces at Delhi to Scindh
[Sind], or to a direct line of *dāk* [station on a post route] from
Delhi to Sukkur [on the Indus, in Sind], the advantages of the
new road are too obvious to require to be dwelt on. The saving
of time in marching troops by this road [between Sirsa and
Bahawalpur] instead of by Ferozepore [that is, through Punjab]
would be ten days.'9

At the time of Mackeson's exploration, the British had not yet
acquired control over Punjab in the north; they would do so a

few years later, taking advantage of the disarray that followed Maharaja Ranjit Singh's death in 1839. Access to Sind, which had just been annexed, was therefore limited, and a new route could prove useful in case of turmoil there. In addition, the Bolan Pass, at the top of Sind's Kachi plains, offered access to Afghanistan via Quetta; in fact, with Ranjit Singh refusing passage through Punjab, that was the pass the British had had to use in 1838, when they launched their first and disastrous onslaught on Afghanistan, after years of playing cat-and-mouse with Russia (the famous 'Great Game').

But how could Mackeson's 'new road' to Sind be so advantageous when it ran through what appeared to be an arid and hostile terrain?

Fig. 1.2. A 1950 view of Bhatner's massive fort in today's Hanumangarh, on the bank of the Ghaggar river. The fort was built by the Bhatti Rajputs, probably in the twelfth century. (© ASI)

Between Sirsa and Suratgarh, Mackeson, like his predecessors, found that 'the country bears traces of having once been well inhabited. At no very distant period, the waters of the Guggur [Ghaggar] river reached as far as Sooratgurh, and old wells are numerous as far as Bhatner [Hanumangarh]'.[10] Moving further westward, he noted 'one remarkable feature in the country traversed to Bahawalpore, which is the traces that exist in it of the course of some former river'. And 'it is to the forsaken bed of this river that we are indebted for the opening to us of a road through the desert'.[11] Indebted because only along this 'deserted channel' was there 'a continuous line of villages . . . for the reason that wells dug in it are generally found to have sweet water, while the water of wells dug at a distance from it either North or South, is usually brackish'.[12] This important observation has since been corroborated by scientific studies.

In fact, Mackeson opined that beyond Anupgarh, which today stands close to the Indian side of the international border,

> the breadth to which the bed of the Slakro [Hakra] attains in this part of its course is such as to favour the idea that it was a larger river than the Sutlej . . . Ages have elapsed since this river ceased to flow, and I shall leave to those who care to prosecute the inquiry to establish the permanency or otherwise of its character, merely observing here, that . . . I traced to my entire satisfaction the deserted course of a large river as far as the Kalipahar* wells . . . From that point its course was reported to me to continue . . . passing Delawur [Derawar Fort] and other forts in the desert, built on its channel . . .[13]

What mattered to Mackeson was that the route was not only clear, it was serviceable. Indeed, should the need arise, 'camels may march by it fifty abreast on either side of a column of troops'. And although, as he noted above, 'ages have elapsed since

---

* Probably today's Kalepar, in Pakistan's Cholistan Desert, about halfway between Fort Abbas and Derawar Fort.

this river ceased to flow', they would have no worry on account of water: 'the present supply of water from wells would suffice for the passage of a *kafila* [caravan] of three hundred camels, and we have only to increase the number of wells on the road to admit of large bodies of troops moving by it.'[14]

This strategic angle apart, Mackeson dwelt at length on the promising trade openings the new route would offer, and ended with a zealous expression of his 'sanguine hopes of one day seeing the neglected rivers to the North West of the Indian Continent vie with those to the East, as channels of commerce and civilization'.[15] In that order, if you please.

Major Mackeson might have been surprised to learn that his proposed 'new road' was not that new. It lay precisely in the Multan–Delhi alignment, and many an invader with an eye on Delhi had used it in past centuries. So had Masud I, son of Mahmud of Ghazni, when in 1037 he decided to expand his empire beyond the Punjab, reaching Hansi (on the Chautang) and conquering its fort before pushing on to Sonipat and beyond.[16] Or Timur who, leaving Samarkand in 1398 on his Indian expedition, rode through Afghanistan and crossed the Jhelum below its confluence with the Chenab; from Multan, Timur's army reached Bhatnir, whose population of 10,000 it massacred; the scene was soon repeated at Sarsutī (today's Sirsa, also on the Ghaggar), at Delhi, and all along Timur's northward thrust to the Shivalik Hills and on to Jammu.[17] If we can disregard the macabre side of the invaders' chronicles, we will note, at least, that the Ghaggar–Chautang interfluve was then more populated and richer than at any time thereafter: six decades before Timur left his trail of devastation, the well-known Arab traveller Ibn Battutah, reaching Delhi through the same route, had found the region abounding in paddy fields,[18] and even earlier it was renowned for its sugarcane. In contrast, the *Gazetteer of Western Rajputana*[19] of 1901 noted that in the stretch from Anupgarh to Hanumangarh, less than one-tenth of the land was under annual cultivation.

A FRENCH GEOGRAPHER BUTTS IN

About the same time as Mackeson was surveying his promising 'new' route, a very different kind of exploration of Indian lore was going on, which would soon get entangled with our explorations of the topography of the Northwest.

In the eighteenth century, European travellers to India, especially French ones such as A.H. Anquetil-Duperron or Antoine Polier,[20] had been hunting for a copy of the mysterious Rig Veda—a text which, they were told by their Indian informants, contained the oldest records of the Hindu religion. Their quest for this oriental Grail was in vain, though otherwise fruitful of precious travelogues and testimonies. Unknown to them, and with a wholly Indian irony, the object of their pursuit was all along patiently waiting in Paris, in the form of a full manuscript received by the Royal Library (today's *Bibliothèque Nationale*) as early as in 1731.[21] With no one knowing Sanskrit at the time, the manuscript could not be identified, much less deciphered, and soon fell into oblivion.

Half a century later, a few British scholars, including the famous William Jones, finally managed to master the sacred language. This newly acquired knowledge soon spread, and so did the first translations of Hindu and Buddhist texts: in just a few years, a new yet tantalizingly ancient world opened up before a bemused Europe. In Paris, the *Collège de France* opened Europe's first chair of Sanskrit in 1814. In 1830, the first excerpts of the Rig Veda were published in Latin by Friedrich A. Rosen, a German Orientalist, followed posthumously eight years later by his translation of the first of the Rig Veda's ten books (*mandalas*). Sitting in Oxford, the formidable German linguist and Orientalist Friedrich Max Müller, whose path we shall cross again, started publishing his monumental edition of the Vedic text in 1849; the following year, H.H. Wilson released the first volume of his complete English translation.

Across the English Channel, a French scholar who had pored over Tod's, Colvin's and Mackeson's accounts was now going through those translations (including French ones) with the keenest interest. Louis Vivien de Saint-Martin had been a founder member of the prestigious *Société de Géographie* in 1821, when he was just nineteen; through maps and travellers' accounts, he explored the sources of the Nile and other parts of Africa, the Caucasus and Mexico, eventually becoming a much-published geographer, author of atlases as well as historical studies of the progress of geography in many parts of the world. His *History of Geography and Geographical Discoveries from the Remotest Past to Our Times* (1873) is a landmark of the genre. In 1864, Vivien de Saint-Martin sponsored the admission of his friend Jules Verne to the *Société de Géographie*; the latter readily acknowledged his debt to the great geographer—by making him a principal character in his novel *In Search of the Castaways*: Jacques Paganel, the erudite but absent-minded 'Secretary of the Geographical Society', was drawn on Vivien de Saint-Martin's model.

Whether the real-life geographer was flattered or not, we do not know, but in his work he was anything but absent-minded. Inspired by a programme proposed in 1849 by another learned society, the *Académie des Inscriptions et Belles-lettres*, for 'the reconstruction of India's ancient geography from the most primitive times to the epoch of the Muslim invasion',[22] Vivien de Saint-Martin planned a series of twelve major studies of India's geography. He was aware of 'the immensity of the task' and wondered 'whether I am destined to fulfil it. Human life is brief, and its necessities often painful; the number of days we are granted is rarely sufficient to the realization of the projects nurtured by our mind with the greatest love'.[23] He completed three of the planned volumes, all of which had a considerable influence on generations of scholars. The last two, published in 1858, dealt respectively with Greek accounts of India's geography and with Hsüan-tsang's* travels through Central Asia and India.[24]

The first of these three thick tomes is the one of interest to us here: *A Study on the Geography and the Primitive People of*

---

* 'Xuanzang' in Pinyin spelling.

India's North-West, According to Vedic Hymns proposed the first-ever synthesis between the Rig Vedic hymns and British surveys of their newly acquired territory. Presented to the *Académie des Inscriptions et Belles-lettres* in 1855 (and published in 1860), it was awarded a prize. In his introduction, Vivien de Saint-Martin explained how 'our first labour had to be dedicated to Sanskrit geography, a truly immense field of investigation, which we found to be almost virgin. Ten years of almost uninterrupted diligence hardly sufficed to explore every part of it. Nevertheless, we dare hope that historical and archaeological researches will henceforth find solid support in the very extensive work we dedicated to India's ancient geography'.[25]

His hopes would be fulfilled. Among the many riddles his book delved into, while trying to match the Veda's locales with the Northwest's geography, was that of the Sarasvatī. Where should the lost river be located on the map? Vivien de Saint-Martin's approach to the problem that concerns us was straightforward. He observed, correctly, that the Sarasvatī river is 'the one which the hymns mention most frequently, whose name they utter with the highest praise and predilection'. It was also 'the first river wholly belonging to the Veda's historical arena'.[26] And it was, according to tradition, on its banks that the Vedic hymns were collected and compiled by Vyāsa into the four Vedas.[27]

He then noted the existence of today's stream called 'Sarsuti, . . . a rather insignificant river . . . which rises at the foot of the last steep slopes overlooking the plain [that is, the Shivaliks] in the rather narrow corridor between the Djemna [Yamuna] and the Satledj [Sutlej].'[28] That is also correct: there is indeed today a seasonal stream called 'Sarsuti', an obvious corruption of 'Sarasvatī' (we saw above how the city of Sirsa was also 'Sarsuti' in medieval times); the stream had been noted by Rennel in 1788 and marked on his 'map of Hindoostan' as 'Sursooty (or Sereswatty)'.[29] The Sarsuti, then, rises in the Sirmur hills that are part of the Shivaliks; it touches the plains near Ad Badri,* flows past

---

* Also spelt 'Adh Badri' or 'Adi Badri', some 15 km north of Bilaspur, on the

Thanesar and Kurukshetra, receives the waters of the monsoon-fed Markanda near Pehowa, and joins those of the Ghaggar near the village of Rasula, close to today's Haryana–Punjab border—to be precise, halfway between the towns of Kharak (Kaithal district, Haryana) and Shatrana (Patiala district, Punjab). Fig. 1.3 shows a map of 1862 clearly marking the bed of the Sarsuti (nowadays, most maps simply call it 'Sarasvatī'*). Till recently, maps of the Survey of India marked the stream as 'Sarasvati Nala' or 'Sarasvati Nadi', probably because the same names are still found on decades-old rail and road bridges crossing the dry bed, as a team from the Indian Space Research Organization (ISRO) noted.[30]

Vivien de Saint-Martin showed a geographer's insight when he remarked, 'The ancient designation of Sarasvatī very much appears to have embraced, apart from the chief watercourse flowing far to the west, the totality of the streams flowing down from the mountain close to each other before they unite in a single bed.'[31] In other words, he regarded all the streams we have seen so far—from west to east, the Ghaggar, the Markanda (and we should add the Dangri or Tangri between these two), the Sarsuti and the Chautang, and their smaller tributaries—as being, collectively, the relic of the Rig Veda's Sarasvatī. (The Chautang, as we will see, was later identified with the Vedic Drishadvatī river.)

Vivien de Saint-Martin added the Veda's description of the Sarasvatī as a river 'flowing to the sea', which, to him, indicated that 'its course then extended through the now arid and water-less plains extending between the Satlej and the gulf of Kotch.[†]

Haryana–Himachal Pradesh border; it is a pilgrimage centre with temples to Narayana, Kedarnath and Mantra Devi. (This Ad Badri is not to be confused with the pilgrimage centre of Adi Badri located in the Chamoli district of Uttara-khand, one of the Panch Badri shrines.)

* But I will always use the spelling 'Sarsuti' when referring to today's stream above its confluence with the Markanda.

† The Rann of Kachchh (older spellings include Kach, Kutch, Cutch, etc.) is a vast marshy and salty expanse in Gujarat, north of the island of Kachchh and south of the Indo-Pakistan border (see maps in Figs 1.5, 1.7 and 4.2).

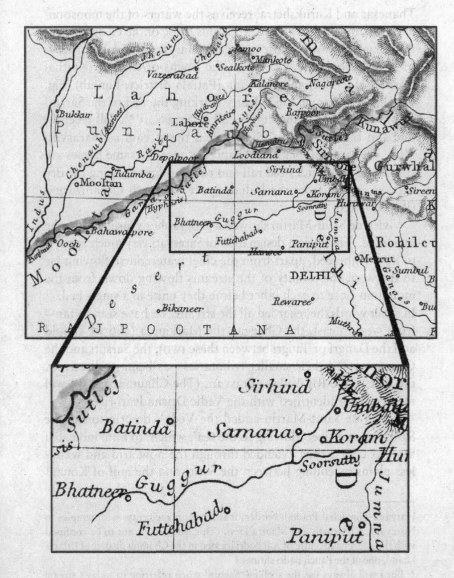

Fig. 1.3. A detail from an 1862 British map of India.[32] (Bottom:) The Sarasvatī region: south of the Sutlej, the 'Guggur' (Ghaggar) flows past 'Umballa' (Ambala) and beyond 'Bhatneer' (Hanuman-garh); note its tributary the 'Soorsutty' (Sarsuti).

The study of the region fully confirms the Vedic piece of information. The trace of the ancient riverbed was recently found, still quite recognizable, and was followed far to the west',[33] a reference to the explorations of Tod, Colvin and Mackeson. Vivien de Saint-Martin summarized their findings, which, to him, 'confirmed the correctness of the tradition'.[34] His own conclusion was, 'This positive recognition of the locale is crucially important for a full understanding of Vedic geography',[35] a clue later scholars made ample use of.

He was probably the first scholar to spell out the problem in such clear terms: the Rig Veda refers to a mighty river called Sarasvatī, and the topography of the Yamuna–Sutlej interfluve is scarred by a now dry river system, one of the streams of which still bears the name of Sarsuti (Sarasvatī). Can the two be equated? His answer in the affirmative was accepted by generations of Sanskritists and Indologists, some of whom we will talk about in the next chapter.

PUNJAB'S 'SACRED RIVER'

The same answer soon made its way into the gazetteers published by the colonial powers. In 1885, under the entry 'Ghaggar', the encyclopaedic *Imperial Gazetteer of India* described the river's course, and noted: 'In ancient times the lower portion of the river seems to have borne the name of its confluent the Saraswati or Sarsuti, which joins the main stream in Patiala territory. It then possessed the dimensions of an important channel . . . At present, however, every village through which the stream passes has diverted a portion of its waters for irrigation, no less than 10,000 acres being supplied from this source in Ambala District alone . . . During the lower portion of its course, in Sirsa District, the bed of the Ghaggar is dry from November to June, affording a cultivable surface for rich crops of rice and wheat.'[36]

Let us turn to the entry 'Saraswati (Sarsuti)', defined as a 'sacred river of the Punjab, famous in the early Brahmanical annals'. We learn that the river rises 'in the low hills of Sirmur

State, emerges upon the plain at Zadh Budri [Ad Badri], a place esteemed sacred by all Hindus', and, before joining the Ghaggar, 'passes by the holy town of Thanesar and the numerous shrines of the Kuruksetra, a tract* celebrated as a centre of pilgrimages, and as the scene of the battle-fields of the *Mahabharatha*'. The *Gazetteer* repeats, 'In ancient times, the united stream below the point of junction appears to have borne the name of Sarsuti, and, undiminished by irrigation near the hills, to have flowed across the Rajputana plains ...'

Correlating geography with early literature, the *Gazetteer* adds, 'Some of the earliest Aryan settlements in India were on the banks of the Saraswati, and the surrounding country has from almost Vedic times been held in high veneration. The Hindus identify the river with Saraswati, the Sanskrit Goddess of Speech and Learning.'[37]

We will come to the reasons for this identification in due time; for the moment, we must turn to fresh explorations of the region's topographical features, which sought to pinpoint more precisely how the river came to be 'lost'.

CHANGING COURSE

Richard Dixon Oldham, a British geologist, joined the Geological Survey of India (GSI) in 1879 at the age of twenty-one; it ran in the family: his father, Thomas Oldham had been the GSI's first director. But scientific posterity remembers the son more than the father: apart from reference works, memoirs and numerous research papers on India's geology, R.D. Oldham specialized in seismology; when a terrible earthquake struck Assam in 1897, destroying Shillong (which was then part of that state), his study of the seismographic records led him to deduce the existence of the earth's molten core. Ill-health forced Oldham to leave the GSI and India at the age of forty-five, though he continued to contribute to the discipline from his retreat in England and later southern France.

It is his lesser-known research that concerns us here: his upstream

---

* 'Kurukshetra' was originally the name of a region, not just a town as it is today.

would be of anything like so great a range as that just found, a range from maximum to minimum of about 11 per cent. of the mean heating effect.

———————

XVIII.—*On probable Changes in the Geography of the Punjab and its Rivers: an Historico-Geographical Study.*—*By* R. D. OLDHAM, A. R. S. M., *Deputy Superintendent, Geological Survey of India.*

[Received 30th September ;—Read December 12th, 1886.]

(With a Map—Pl. XIX.)

Introductory.—Of all the problems with which we are brought in contact when we try to unravel the ancient geography of India, none surpass in interest or difficulty those connected with the rivers of the Punjab and Sind. Both interest and difficulty result from the fact that, previous to the advent of the English, all civilization and every invader have entered India from the North-West, and their difficulty from the changes that appear to have taken place in the courses of these rivers during the last three thousand years. It cannot be said that this subject has been neglected by previous writers on the ancient geography of India, but their efforts have mainly been addressed to the identification of towns or countries, and their references to the rivers are often marked by an ignorance, or neglect, of the fundamental principles of physical geology ; yet the matter is one on which the geologist must be heard as well as the scholar, for, whatever dependence may be placed on history or tradition, the conclusions that are drawn are only valid so long as they are possible, and no one that has not studied the mode of action of rivers on a geological basis can decide whether any particular change in the course of a river, of which there appears to be historical indication, can or cannot have taken place.*

* Throughout the following paper, I am largely indeb..d to the author of an anonymous essay in the Calcutta Review, on the "Lost River of the Indian Desert", (vol. lix, pp. 1—29, understood to be by Surgeon-Major C. F. Oldham). I am indebted to this writer for having first drawn my attention to the subject, for having suggested most of the opinions supported in the following paper, and for many of the references given below. I have, however, except where the contrary is expressly stated, verified them in every case ; and, to save wearisome repetition, I must request all who wish to see how little I diverge from the opinions expressed by the writer referred to, and to what extent this paper goes beyond the matter he has treated of, to compare the two, promising that the perusal of the article in the Calcutta Review will prove anything but a waste of time.

Fig. 1.4. The first page of R.D. Oldham's paper of 1886 in the *Journal of Asiatic Society of Bengal.*

(rather, 'upbed') survey from the Bahawalpur region to the Hissar district, in his capacity as deputy superintendent of the Survey. Understandably, his professional competence gave him an edge over his military predecessors.

Writing in 1886 in the *Journal of Asiatic Society of Bengal*[38] (Fig. 1.4), he rejected theories of the days that attributed the loss of the Sarasvatī to diminished rainfall, pointing out that this would have affected all rivers equally. Instead, he proposed that the 'Lost River of the Indian Desert was none other than the Sutlej, and that it was "lost" when the river turned westwards to join the Bias [Beas]'.[39] This explanation has been broadly endorsed since then, especially in view of the Sutlej's sharp westward bend near Rupar (or Ropar, or Rupnagar, in India's Punjab, not far from Chandigarh), and the existence of a palaeobed that connected it long ago with the Ghaggar, which flows hardly 50 km away to the east.

Oldham also believed that part of the Yamunā's waters might have flowed into the Ghaggar–Hakra bed in Vedic times: 'It may have been . . . that the Jumna [Yamunā], after leaving the hills, divided its waters . . . and that the portion which flowed to the Punjab was known as the Saraswati while that which joined the Ganges was called the Yamuna.'[40] In his opinion, that double desertion of the Sarasvatī, by the Sutlej and the Yamunā, which brought about 'a considerable change in the hydrography of the region',[41] was caused by the well-known waywardness of north India's rivers. As a more recent example, he cited the case of the Brahmaputra changing its course in the early nineteenth century, a little upstream of its confluence with the Ganges (in today's Bangladesh). That waywardness is nothing but the effect of the very flat flood plains of the entire Indo-Gangetic basin: here, the phenomena of erosion and sedimentation, which would hardly be noticeable in the Deccan's rivers, get greatly amplified and trigger frequent shifts in the watercourses.

In fact, Oldham might have just as aptly quoted Strabo, a Greek savant of the first century BCE whose *Geography* of the ancient world remained unsurpassed for centuries. For his description of northwest India, Strabo relied on the work of several Greek historians, among them Aristobulus who had accompanied Alexander the Great on his campaign to India. Strabo noted, for instance:

> He [Aristobulus] says that when he was sent on some business, he saw a tract of land deserted which contained more than a thousand cities with their villages, for the Indus, having forsaken its proper channel, turned itself into another on the left much deeper, into which it burst like a cataract, so that it no longer watered the country on the right, from which it receded, for this had been raised by the inundations not only above the level of the new channel but even above that of the new inundations.[42]

What could have uplifted this strip of land on the right bank of the Indus? Strabo shrewdly assumed that 'India is liable to earthquakes as it becomes porous from the excess of moisture and opens into fissures, whence even the course of rivers is altered'.[43] While the explanation for earthquakes is, of course, fanciful, Strabo's assumption that northwest India's seismic activity might cause changes in the course of major rivers was surprisingly prescient; in fact, this phenomenon has been invoked by geologists in recent years in the context of the Sarasvatī (and witnessed in the case of the Indus).

At this point, it is worth stressing that the three currently minor rivers that we have focused on—the Ghaggar, the Sarsuti and the Chautang, along with their tributaries such as the Dangri or the Markanda—flow down from the Shivaliks in the strip of land between Chandigarh and Yamunanagar, which is hardly more than 80 km in breadth. A few more kilometres to the west, we find the Sutlej flowing towards the Indus and the Arabian Sea; and a little to the east, the Yamuna winding her way to the Ganges and the Bay of Bengal. In other words, these seasonal rivers are located on a narrow and fairly flat* watershed between

---

* The average gradient is roughly 300 m over 1000 km, that is, an imperceptible 30 cm/km or 0.03 per cent. (300 m is the average altitude of the plain below the Shivalik Hills, and 1000 km the approximate distance to the Rann of Kachchh.)

the two vast river systems of the 3000 km-long Indus and the 2500 km-long Ganges: it is easy to visualize how a slight uplift of the sort reported by Strabo, or else erosion caused by powerful spates, could have triggered the diversion of the Sutlej or Yamuna waters westward and eastward, respectively, away from the Ghaggar–Hakra system, a diversion cogently explained by Oldham for the first time.

That explanation apart, R.D. Oldham's work was valuable because it established that the landscape of today's Punjab and Haryana must have been radically different at some remote time.

THE RANN

Five years later, a monumental paper on the hydrography of the Indus basin appeared under the pen of Henry George Raverty, a British major of the Indian Army who had acquired first-hand knowledge of the Punjab during the military campaigns that culminated in the subjugation of the state. But there was a scholarly side to this army officer, as he authored in 1849 a gazetteer of Peshawar, perhaps India's first district gazetteer. He also learned the Pashto language of Afghanistan so well that he went on to author a grammar book and a dictionary of it, and translated into English selections from Afghan poetry.

Our poetic major's paper, published in 1892, dealt not with the Sarasvatī, but with the identity of the 'Mihrān of Sind', a river reported by the eighth-century Arab invaders to be flowing east of the Indus in a course parallel to it.[44] We need not go into Raverty's intricate analysis of historical evidence and discussion of the relative shifts in the beds and confluences of this river system, especially as many important details remain disputed.[45] It will be enough for our purpose to highlight some of his conclusions: 'Sursuti [Sarsuti] is the name of a river, the ancient Saraswatī ... Sutlaj [Sutlej] was a tributary of the Hakrā or Wahindāh', which was nothing but the bygone Mihrān, and flowed down to the vast salty expanse of the Rann of Kachchh through the Eastern Nara. The Nara (see Fig. 1.7), now a dry channel, has often been assumed to have been an ancient outlet of the Indus, whether a perennial or a seasonal one; it splits into two channels on either side of the Rohri Hills of Sind, and is the eastern branch that would have received the Hakra's waters. The Hakra's drying up, which according to Raverty took place in the fourteenth century CE, 'reduced a vast extent of once fruitful country to a howling wilderness, and thus several flourishing cities and towns became ruined or deserted by their inhabitants'.

Raverty also traced the name 'Hakra' to the Sanskrit *sāgara* or 'ocean', an etymology that has been largely accepted and explains variants such as Sankra and Sankrah, terms used in Islamic chronicles.

Raverty's work in the lower reaches of the Hakra was supplemented by that of Robert Sivewright, an officer from the Public Works Department (PWD), who spent a few months exploring the Rann of Kachchh and its geological features, trying in the process to reconstruct some of its history from the days of Alexander's campaign in the Indus Valley to the Arab conquest of Sind in the eighth century and beyond. In 1907, having retired and returned to Britain, Sivewright presented a paper on 'Cutch and the Ran' at the Royal Geographical Society, a lecture which R.D. Oldham also attended.[46]

One of Sivewright's important observations on this forbidding region was the 'silting up of the Greater Ran by the Hakra';[47] in his opinion, this silting caused the gradual build-up of the Rann, which, he observed, was still navigable even for some time after the Arab conquest.[48] But a tectonic uplift of the region may well have been a contributory factor to the drying up of the Rann, as a 1967 study of the uplift of the nearby Makran coast suggests.[49]

Be that as it may, Sivewright's conclusion that 'the Ran is the delta of the Hakra, the lost river of Sind'[50] is of greater relevance to us. Sivewright thus agreed with Raverty that the Hakra river kept its name all the way to its estuary north of the Rann, and his map (Fig. 1.5) makes this even more explicit.

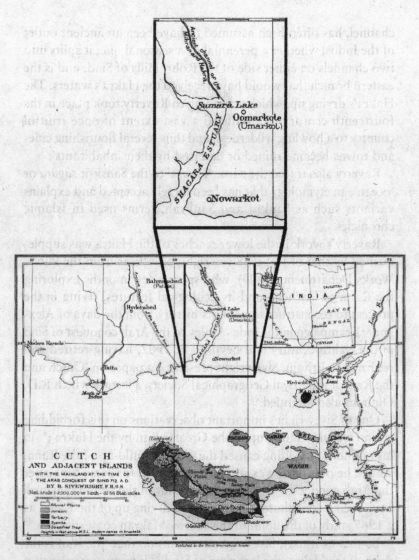

Fig. 1.5. Robert Sivewright's map (1907): 'Cutch and Adjacent Islands, with the Mainland at the Time of the Arab Conquest of Sind 712 A.D.' On the Rann's northern shore is the Shāgāra Estuary, that of the Mihran and Hakra (see enlarged area). Note also the 'Karir Island' (today spelt Khadir), where the Harappan site of Dholavira will be discovered in 1966.

'RUINS EVERYWHERE'

In his 1887 paper, R.D. Oldham had frequently referred to an article published anonymously in the *Calcutta Review* (Fig. 1.6) thirteen years earlier,[51] from which he borrowed the idea that the Hakra–Nara had been the Sutlej's original bed. The anonymous paper's author, Oldham informed us,[52] was a namesake (though probably no relative): C.F. Oldham, a surgeon-major in the Indian Army. The surgeon-major distinguished himself by medical notes (on malaria in particular), but, like Raverty, is remembered for his varied scholarly interests: among them, the origins of serpent worship in ancient cultures, including India's, and the Sarasvatī river.

In 1893, almost two decades after his anonymous article, C.F. Oldham examined the whole issue afresh in a comprehensive and erudite paper entitled 'The Saraswati and the Lost River of the Indian Desert',[53] which included a detailed map (Fig. 1.7). He also started off with mentions of the Sarasvatī in the Rig Veda, and noted that one of its hymns clearly places the river 'between the Yamuna and the Satudri [Sutlej] which is its present position'.[54] After a brief description of the present course of the Sarasvatī, Oldham stressed that even after its confluence with the Ghaggar, 'it was formerly [known as] the Saraswatī; that name is still known amongst the people . . .'[55] He had no doubt, therefore, that the lost Rig Vedic river flowed in the bed of today's Ghaggar. And he added valuable details:

> Its ancient course is contiguous with the dry bed of a great river which, as local legends assert, once flowed through the desert to the sea.
>
> In confirmation of these traditions, the channel referred to, which is called Hakra or Sotra, can be traced through the Bikanir and Bhawulpur [Bahawalpur] States into Sind, and thence onwards to the Rann of Kach.
>
> The existence of this river at no very remote period, and the truth of the legends which assert the ancient fertility of the lands through which it flowed, are attested by the ruins

THE
CALCUTTA REVIEW.

№ CXVII.

ART. I.—NOTES ON THE LOST RIVER OF THE INDIAN DESERT.

THE large blank space marked "Great Desert," in the north-west of the map of India, is probably familiar to most people. Some, however, may not be aware that a considerable portion of this tract was once cultivated and prosperous, studded with towns and villages, and inhabited by powerful tribes.

No doubt a great part of the desert has undergone little change since pre-historic times. Its ancient name of Marus-thali (region of death) proves this. But with regard to the lands of Nair and Kadal—the Ramala of the Arab geographers—the truth of the legends which assert their ancient fertility is attested by the ruins which everywhere overspread what is now an arid, sandy waste.

In confirmation of the local traditions which ascribe the deso-lation of this once flourishing country to the drying up of the stream by which it was fertilized, the dry bed of a large river may still be traced from near the Himálaya, through Bhat-tiána, Bikanír and Bháwalpur, into Sindh; and thence onwards to the Rann of Kach (Runn of Cutch).

This old channel, which is more than six hundred miles in length, is known in different parts of its course as Naiwal, Sotra, Hakra, Wahind, Dahan, &c. The names Sotra, Hakra and Wahind are those most generally used, the others being more local.

In Kiepert's map of Ancient India,* the Sotra or Hakra is represented by a dotted line as a continuation of the Gaggar; and as joining the Indus a little below Uchh. The true position of the channel is, however, forty miles south of that city; and it is plainly traceable onwards into Sindh.

Major-General Cunningham, R.E., has, in his Ancient Geography of India, laid down the course of the Hakra correctly from longitude 74° to longitude 70° (Maps V, VI and IX) as Noudras

* In illustration of Prof. Lassen's Indian Antiquities.

A

Fig. 1.6. The first page of Surgeon-Major C.F. Oldham's anonymous paper of 1874.

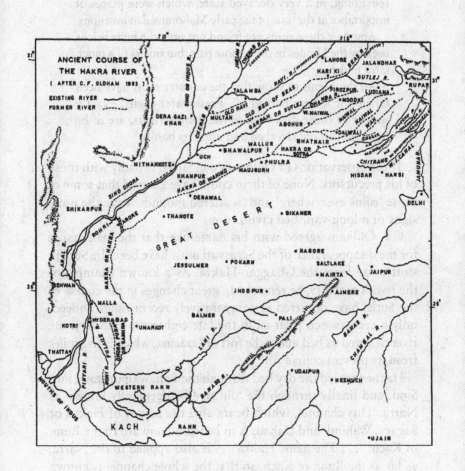

Fig. 1.7. C.F. Oldham's 1893 map 'shewing courses of Hakra'.[56]
Existing rivers are drawn in continuous lines, and former rivers
in dotted lines. The Sarasvatī is shown as a tributary of the
Ghaggar; further downstream (above Sirsa), we read 'Gaggar
or Old Saraswati R.', and below, 'Chitrang or Drishadwati R.'

which everywhere overspread what is now an arid sandy waste.

Throughout this tract are scattered mounds, marking the sites of cities and towns. And there are strongholds still remaining, in a very decayed state, which were places of importance at the time of the early Mahommedan invasions.

Amongst these ruins are found not only the huge bricks used by the Hindus in the remote past, but others of a much later make.

All this seems to show that the country must have been fertile for a long period . . . Freshwater shells, exactly similar to those now seen in the Panjab rivers, are to be found in this old riverbed and upon its banks.[57]

These observations of Oldham's concurred broadly with those of his precursors. None of them could have guessed that some of those 'ruins everywhere' and 'scattered mounds' were the mute signs of a long-vanished civilization.

C.F. Oldham agreed with his namesake that the main cause for the disappearance of the Sarasvatī must have been the Sutlej's shift away from the Ghaggar–Hakra. As a known example of the river's mobility, he remarked, 'great changes in the course of the Sutlej have occurred in comparatively recent times. Indeed, only a century ago [that is, in the late eighteenth century], the river deserted its bed under the fort of Ludiana, which is five miles from its present course'.[58]

He then traced the dry bed through the Bahawalpur state, into Sind, and finally through the 'old riverbed generally known as Narra. This channel, which bears also the names of Hakra or Sagara, Wahind, and Dahan, is to be traced onward to the Rann of Kach[59] . . . The name Hakra . . . is also applied to the Narra, as far as the Rann of Kach, so that the whole channel is known by this name, from Bhatnair [Hanumangarh] to the sea'.[60]

According to C.F. Oldham, there was thus a single river from Rajasthan to the Arabian Sea, bearing a single name Hakra. This view finds confirmation among Raverty and Sivewright, both of whom, as we saw, used the name 'Hakra' for the river's terminal stage north of the Rann of Kachchh. Let us also note here another tradition recorded by C.F. Oldham in his earlier article: 'a tradition prevalent, on the borders of Bikaner,* to the effect that the waters of the Hakra spread out in a great lake at a place called Kak, south of the Mer country'.[61] The Mers were a tribe formerly living to the north of the Rann of Kachchh, a clue that the 'great lake' of Kak was nothing but today's Rann of Kachchh.

Again, a local legend narrated by Oldham evoked the time when the Sutlej 'flowed southwards from the Himalāya . . . and onwards, through Sind, to the sea'—until, for some reason, a prince-turned-ascetic named Puran, a hero of many Punjabi legends, cursed the river to leave its bed and move westward. 'The stream, in consequence, changed its course more and more towards the west, until, six hundred and fifty years ago, it entered the Beas valley . . .', which would take us to the thirteenth century CE; but leaving aside the date, the consequence was 'a terrible drought and famine in the country on the banks of the Hakra, where [large] numbers of men and cattle perished. The survivors then migrated to the banks of the Indus, and the country has ever since been desert'.[62]

In Oldham's judgement, this tradition—the same, he assumed, as the one James Tod had recorded decades earlier—made perfect sense on the ground. He also noted that 'the traditions of all the tribes bordering upon it [the Rann of Kachchh] agree that this expanse of salt and sand was once an estuary',[63] the combined estuary of the Indus in the northwest, the Nara–Sarasvatī in the north and today's Luni in the northeast, of which only the last still flows there. It must have been a huge delta, as its topography bears out.

The view held by the two Oldhams and by Raverty that the Sutlej earlier flowed into the Hakra was endorsed by the *Imperial Gazetteer* in its 1908 edition: 'In the year A.D. 1000 it [the Sutlej] was a tributary of the Hakra, and flowed in the Eastern Nara

---

* Bikaner, a city of northern Rajasthan, was then the capital of a Rajput princely state of the same name. In 1949, it was integrated into Rajasthan.

... Thus the Sutlej or the Hakra—for both streams flowed in the same bed—is probably the lost river of the Indian desert, whose waters made the sands of Bikaner and Sind a smiling garden.'[64]

This view became, in time, the standard one, though with some variations. In the meantime, C.F. Oldham was satisfied that

> The course of the 'lost river' has now been traced from the Himalaya to the Rann of Kach . . . We have also seen that the Vedic description of the waters of the Saraswatī flowing onward to the ocean, and that given in the *Mahabharata*, of the sacred river losing itself in the sands, were probably both of them correct at the periods to which they referred.[65]

What is this 'Vedic description of the waters of the Saraswatī flowing onward to the ocean', and how does the Mahābhārata come into the picture? We must now turn to those and other ancient texts, and extract whatever information they can give us on what brought ruin to this region—a region which, far from a desert, was regarded in Vedic times as teeming with life.

2

The Mighty Sarasvatī

We have seen what early topographic surveys and local traditions have to say on the evolution of the watershed dividing the two great river systems of north India, those of the Indus and the Ganges—the homes of India's first two civilizations. A third stream of evidence comes to us from early sacred texts, and although much of it flows through a jungle of myths (again, in the true sense of the word), we are faced with a surprising internal consistency.[1]

THE BEST OF RIVERS

In forty-five of its hymns, the Rig Veda showers praise on the Sarasvatī; her name appears seventy-two times, and three hymns are wholly dedicated to her. She is often invoked in the company of two sister-goddesses, Ilā and Bhāratī. Sarasvatī's waters are lauded as a 'great flood',[2] she is 'great among the great, the most impetuous of rivers', and was 'created vast'.[3] 'Limitless, unbroken, swift-moving', she 'surpasses in majesty and might all other waters'[4] and 'comes onward with tempestuous roar'.[5] Sarasvatī, indeed, is the 'mother of waters' or of rivers (*sindhumātā*[6]). At least one of the Vedic clans, the Purus, is said to dwell 'on her two grassy banks'.[7]

Many Sanskritists take the word *sarasvatī* to mean a 'chain of pools' or 'full of lakes' (*saras*), and draw various conclusions regarding the river's initial condition; but the word *saras* originally means 'water' or 'flow' (from the root *sr*, 'to flow'), and the river's name may equally be rendered as 'she of the stream, the flowing movement',[8] to quote Sri Aurobindo's translation. Both renderings are legitimate, so it would be hazardous to attempt a physical description of the Sarasvatī on the basis of its name alone. (Both renderings may even be correct: a flowing river, especially if its plain is fairly flat, may form oxbow lakes when it abandons a meander.)

From being an impetuous river, Sarasvatī acquires a powerful image in Vedic symbolism, embodying the flood of illumination or inspiration. She is the 'impeller of happy truths' who 'awakens in the consciousness the great flood and illumines all the thoughts'.[9] Sarasvatī is 'the best of mothers, best of rivers, best of goddesses',[10] and we see here the origin of the traditional deification of rivers, from Gangā to Kāverī. A few centuries later—in the Yajur Veda, to be precise—Sarasvatī, additionally, becomes the goddess of speech, the Word (vāch or vāk).

Some scholars have wondered why this particular river—not the Indus or the Ravi—came to embody inspiration and speech. A few found a simple explanation in the geographical location of the Vedic poets on its banks, with the river gurgling past their ashrams: its sounds, poetically described in the Rig Veda, were soon taken to a metaphorical level. Others observed that right from the beginning the river was praised as an 'inspirer of hymns',[11] which makes the connection with speech natural. Developing this line, Catherine Ludvik, a Canadian Indologist who recently authored a fine study of Sarasvatī as a 'riverine goddess of knowledge',[12] highlights the goddess's constant association with dhī or inspired thought. Speech and inspiration being the vehicles of knowledge and learning, the river's transformation is complete— although not quite: somewhere along the way, Sarasvatī became the 'mother of the Vedas' and Brahmā's consort (sometimes daughter), added the arts to her field, and entered the pantheons of Buddhism and Jainism: to Jains, Sarasvatī is the chief of the sixteen Vidyādevīs or goddesses of knowledge, and a special festival, Jñāna Panchamī, is dedicated to her. The river-goddess then burst her Indian banks to flow to Southeast Asia and as far

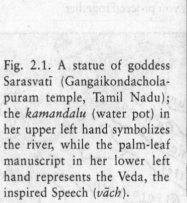

Fig. 2.1. A statue of goddess Sarasvatī (Gangaikondacholapuram temple, Tamil Nadu); the *kamandalu* (water pot) in her upper left hand symbolizes the river, while the palm-leaf manuscript in her lower left hand represents the Veda, the inspired Speech (*vāch*).

as China and Japan (she bears the names of 'Thuyathadi' in Myanmar, and 'Benten' or 'Benzaiten' in Japan).

To return to her Vedic origins, the Sarasvatī's early symbolism clearly rests on a physical fact: the existence of an actual river. The Rig Veda makes this clear in one of its very rare geographical descriptions, the *Nadīstuti sūkta*, a hymn (*sūkta*) in praise of rivers (*nadī*), which invokes turn by turn nineteen major rivers of the Vedic world. Let us hear its fifth and sixth verses (*mantras*), with each river's modern name in parentheses when it is not in doubt:

Imám me gange yamune sarasvati śútudri stómaṃ sacatā párusṇy ā́ |
asiknyā́ marudvṛdhe vitástayārjī́kīye śṛṇuhy ā́ suṣómayā ||
ṭṛṣṭāmayā prathamáṃ yā́tave sajū́ḥ susártvā rasáyā śvetyā́ tyā́ |
tváṃ sindho kúbhayā gomatíṃ krúmum mehatnvā́ sárāthaṃ yā́bhir
íyase ||

(10.75.5–6)

O Gangā, Yamunā, Sarasvatī, Shutudrī (Sutlej), Parushnī (Ravi), hear my praise! Hear my call, O Asiknī (Chenab), Marudvridhā (Maruvardhvan), Vitastā (Jhelum) with Ārjīkiyā and Sushomā.

First you flow united with Trishtāmā, with Susartu and Rasā, and with Svetyā, O Sindhu (Indus) with Kubhā (Kabul) to Gomati (Gumal or Gomal), with Mehatnū to Krumu (Kurram), with whom you proceed together.

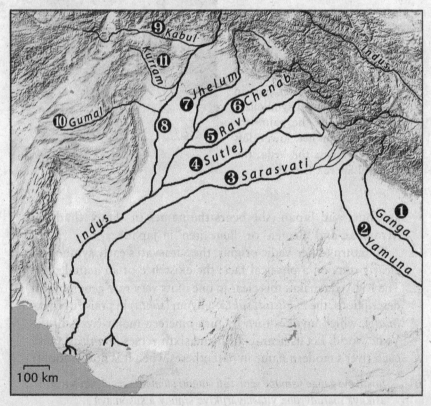

Fig. 2.2. The chief Rig Vedic rivers, numbered in their order of appearance in the *Nadīstuti sūkta*. The land between the Indus and the Sarasvatī was the 'Land of the Seven Rivers', *Sapta-sindhava*. (Note that the rivers are shown here in their present courses, but some of them have shifted their beds since Vedic times.)

Table 2.1: Principal rivers listed in the *Nadīstuti sūkta*, with their
respective Greek and English names.

Sanskrit	Greek	English
Gangā	Gange/Ganges	Ganges
Yamunā	Diamouna/Jomanes	Yamuna
Shutudrī (later *Shatadru*)	Zaradros/Hesudrus	Sutlej
Vipāsh	Hyphasis	Beas
Parushnī (later *Irāvatī*)	Hydraotes/Hyarotis	Ravi
Asiknī	Akesines	Chenab
Vitastā	Hydaspes	Jhelum
Sindhu	Indos	Indus
Kubhā	Kophen	Kabul

This remarkable hymn thus starts from the Ganges and moves
westward to the Indus and three of its tributaries flowing down
from Afghanistan through the Sulaiman mountain range—a
bird's-eye view sweeping across more than a thousand kilometres,
which, at the very least, reveals the poet's intimate knowledge of
the region's geography (Fig. 2.2). Even Max Müller, who made
a virtual dogma of the 'savage phase of thought which we find
in the Veda', was compelled to grant that in this hymn, 'the rivers
invoked are . . . the real rivers of the Punjāb, and the poem shows
a much wider geographical horizon than we should expect from
a mere village bard'.[13] We may wonder what the said village bard
would have thought of this left-handed compliment . . .

However, of central interest to us is the hymn's plain statement
that the Sarasvatī flows *between the Yamunā and the Sutlej*—
precisely the region where our British explorers found a wide, dry
bed and ruined cities, the region where local traditions assert that
a large river flowed once upon a time. A picture is certainly taking
shape.

We can glean a few more clues from the Rig Veda. The Sarasvatī is 'seven-sistered' or 'one of seven sisters',[14] which, if not purely
metaphorical, would indicate that she had several tributaries; this

is also hinted at in a hymn that invokes her as 'the seventh'.[15] Once, she is mentioned in conjunction with another river, the Drishadvatī.[16] She 'breaks through the ridges of the mountains with her strong waves',[17] which points to a mountainous origin; this gets confirmed when, besides being 'unbroken', the Sarasvatī is hailed as 'pure in her course from the mountain to the sea'[18] (*giribhya ā samudrāt*). This was the verse that C.F. Oldham had in mind when he spoke of 'the Vedic description of the waters of the Saraswati flowing onward to the ocean'.

THE RIVER'S DISAPPEARANCE

The other three Vedas (Yajur, Sāma, Atharva) do not significantly add to the Rig Veda's descriptions of the Sarasvatī, except for a mention, in the first, of the Sarasvatī having five tributaries,[19] an echo of her 'seven sisters'.

However, something must have happened before the next generation of Vedic literature, the Brāhmanas.* In a few of those ancient texts,[20] we read for the first time that the river disappears at a place called *Vinashana*, a word meaning 'loss' or disappearance: the Sarasvatī's previously 'unbroken' flow to the sea was no longer so.

Some Brāhmanas locate the river's source near a place called *Plakshaprāsravana*,[21] named after a giant fig tree (*plaksha*) that grew there.[22] The Mahābhārata makes it clear that this spot was somewhere in the Shivalik Hills.[23] The distance from this spot to the river's point of disappearance is stated to be forty-four *āshvina*s, or days on horseback, but there is a hitch: even at a slow pace of 40 km a day, the distance would be more than from the Shivaliks to the Arabian Sea! In reality, the Pañchavimsha Brāhmana makes it clear that the stated distance is notional and

---

* The Brāhmanas are long commentaries on the Vedas that include detailed instructions for conducting rituals, apart from important legends. (*Brāhmana* derives from the word *brahman*, whose primary meaning, in the Rig Veda, is 'prayer' or 'inspired hymn'.) Several centuries at least separate the Vedas (the *samhitā*s or collections of hymns) from the Brāhmanas.

not to be taken literally, for it adds, 'This is the same distance as from the earth to the heaven.'[24]

Indeed, it seems as if this place where the river disappeared or became invisible (*Vinashana* is also called *Adarshana* or 'invisible') came to be looked upon as a metaphor for the transition from the physical to the non-physical. *Vinashana* thus became a sacred spot: the same text and several later ones[25] report how consecration rites were conducted at *Vinashana* at the start of a pilgrimage, which consisted in following the Sarasvatī upstream, crossing on the way its confluence with the Drishadvatī. The last detail is of importance: Sanskritist O.P. Bharadwaj, author of a series of erudite papers on the Sarasvatī,[26] showed how, in later literature *Vinashana* moved eastward, eventually reaching Kurukshetra in the Bhāgavata Purāna. This can only mean that the river's drying up was gradual, not a sudden vanishing act—a significant point that archaeology will bear out.

The Sarasvatī, as Bharadwaj again demonstrated, appears in the Rāmāyana as 'the sacred Ikshumatī, Brahmā's daughter', which messengers from Ayodhyā cross on their mission to fetch prince Bharata.[27] But it is the Mahābhārata that best illustrates the drastic change alluded to in the Brāhmanas. Although it gives prominence and sanctity to the Ganges (which figures only twice in the Rig Veda), the Sarasvatī remains important, all the more so as she flows through the Kurukshetra plains, the arena of the terrible war that forms the core of the epic. Vyāsa, the legendary compiler of the Vedas and traditionally the Mahābhārata's author, lives in a forest near the Sarasvatī. When the five Pāndavas go into exile, 'performing their ablutions in the Sarasvatī, the Drishadvatī and the Yamunā', they keep 'travelling in a westerly direction'[28] and finally take refuge in a forest near the Sarasvatī. The *rishi* (seer) Vasishtha has his 'high abode' at a *tīrtha* on the river's 'eastern bank',[29] while his irascible rival Vishvāmitra dwells on the opposite bank; as a result, the poor river gets caught in one of their famous confrontations—but that is another story.

What we must note for now is that several of the epic's descriptions of the river are direct echoes of the Rig Veda. For instance, the Sarasvatī 'of swift current flows from the sides of the Himavat [Himalaya]'.[30] It has seven forms, reminiscent of the Veda's 'seven sisters'; those forms are actually named (the one appearing at Kurukshetra being the Oghavatī), and they 'mingled together at . . . that *tīrtha* known on earth by the name of *Sapta-Sarasvatī* [the seven Sarasvatīs].'[31] The Drishadvatī is once again paired with the Sarasvatī: 'They that dwell in Kurukshetra which lies to the south of the Sarasvatī and the north of the Drishadvatī, are said to dwell in heaven.'[32] And in a significant passage, goddess Uma, prompted by Shiva, explains, 'The sacred Sarasvatī is the foremost river of all rivers. She courses towards the ocean and is truly the first of all streams.'[33] Elsewhere, the river again 'mingles with the sea'.[34]

SARASVATĪ GOES TO THE DESERT

Thus, we still find a river flowing 'from the mountain to the sea', as the Rig Veda puts it—but with a crucial difference now: 'In some parts (of her course) she becomes visible and in some parts not so.'[35] As in the Brāhmanas, at the spot known as *Vinashana* the Sarasvatī became 'invisible': it 'disappeared'[36] and was 'lost'[37] —rather broke up into separate segments, since the places of her reappearance are named and regarded as especially sacred.

The Mahābhārata does not miss the opportunity to weave a few legends around the theme of the Sarasvatī's disappearance. In one of them, the wife of Utathya, a rishi, was snatched away by god Varuna while she was bathing in the Yamunā. In order to pressurize Varuna, who dwelled in the waters and ruled over that element, to return his wife, Utathya caused 600,000 lakes of the region to disappear, and commanded Sarasvatī 'to become invisible', to 'leave this region and go to the desert'.[38] The epic never expects its readers (or listeners) to take its numbers literally, whether those of arrows flowing from Arjuna's bow or of elephants standing on the battlefield; nevertheless, this legend, if it rests on a fact, seems to hark back to a time when lakes dotted the region. And at any rate, the Sarasvatī did 'go to the desert'.

And curiously, an astonishing number of names of towns and villages in western Rajasthan (the heart of the Thar Desert) have names ending in the word 'sar', such as Lunkaransar, with 'sar' meaning 'lake' (from the Sanskrit word *saras*). I counted over fifty of them on an ordinary map,[39] and there must be many more. Why should all those places be named after non-existent lakes? An unwary tourist reading a map of western Rajasthan might as well assume that the region is some kind of a Lake District!

The Mahābhārata also recounts in some detail Balarāma's pilgrimage along the banks of the Sarasvatī. Balarāma, Krishna's brother, started from Prabhasa (a *tīrtha* near what is today Somnath in Saurashtra) and proceeded upstream, that is, 'towards the east, and reached, one after another, hundreds and thousands of famous *tīrthas* . . . [located] along the southern bank of the Sarasvatī'.[40] While ritually bathing in every one of them, he exclaimed, 'Where else is such happiness as that in a residence by the Sarasvatī? . . . All should ever remember the Sarasvatī! Sarasvatī is the most sacred of rivers!'[41] Indeed, 'the whole region seemed to resound with the loud Vedic recitations of those Rishis of cleansed souls, all employed in pouring libations on sacrificial fires'.[42] At length, Balarāma reached a spot where 'although the Sarasvatī seems to be lost, yet persons crowned with ascetic success . . . and owing also to the coolness of the herbs and of the land there, know that the river has an invisible current through the bowels of the earth'.[43] This 'coolness' of the vegetation is significant, and we will return to the invisible current—also to a great drought of twelve years' duration, which, the epic tells us,[44] occurred in the vicinity of the upper Sarasvatī, and afflicted even the rishis, causing them to wander about.

FIRE AND WATER

While the Rig Veda did not explicitly define its own territory, late Vedic literature used *Vinashana* as a natural westernmost frontier of the Vedic world. Savants like Baudhāyana, Vasishtha (not to be confused with the Rig Vedic rishi) and Patañjali, who lived some time between the fifth and second century BCE, define *Āryāvarta*, the 'Aryan land', as the region east of *Adarshana*, west of a certain 'black forest' (located near Haridwar), south of the Himalayas and north of the *Pāriyātra* mountains, which were a part of the Vindhyas.⁴⁵ A similar territory is the *Madhyadesha* ('middle country'), the land south of the Himalayas, north of the Vindhyas, west of Prayāga (what is today Allahabad) and east of *Vinashana*.⁴⁶ A third, more limited geographical entity is the region between the Sarasvatī and the Drishadvatī: 'That land, created by the gods, which lies between the two divine rivers Sarasvatī and Drishadvatī, the (sages) call *Brahmāvarta*,'⁴⁷ says the *Manusmriti*. What matters in these definitions is that all of them adopt the Sarasvatī and its western frontier as a major reference point.

The Purānas, those encyclopaedic texts that constitute an important ingredient of Hinduism as we know it today, also have their say on the Sarasvatī, negatively at times: the Vishnu Purāna, for instance, does not mention the Sarasvatī at all in its lists of rivers, which suggests that it had become too insignificant to be noted. On the other hand, the Mārkandeya Purāna⁴⁸ enumerates all the rivers flowing down from the Himalayas, beginning with 'Gangā, Sarasvatī, Sindhu'—in other words, from east to west, just as we saw in the Rig Veda. Other Purānas provide long lists of the holy places to be visited along the Sarasvatī, from the Shivalik Hills to today's Gujarat.

The Padma Purāna narrates an intriguing legend: a reluctant Sarasvatī was persuaded by her father Brahmā to carry to the western sea an all-consuming fire that was threatening to engulf the whole world; after a halt at Pushkar (near Ajmer in Rajasthan), she proceeded, finally reached the ocean, and safely deposited the fire in it. Could this 'all-consuming fire' represent a severe drought that afflicted the whole region?

The Sarasvatī's disappearance left a deep imprint on subsequent literature and traditions. In *Meghadūtam* (the 'Cloud Messenger'), India's divine poet Kālidāsa (probably living in first century BCE), entreats a cloud to visit various spots of the northern plains and in the Himalayas, and invites it, after a visit to Kurukshetra, to go and taste the purifying waters of the Sarasvatī.[49] But in *Abhijñānashakuntalam* (the famous play *Shakuntala*, which so moved Goethe), the despondent king compares his fruitless life to 'Sarasvatī's stream lost in barbarous sandy wastes'.[50]

Much later, in his encyclopaedic treatise, the *Brihat Samhitā*, the renowned sixth-century savant Varāhamihira gives us an overview of India's geography, in which he refers to 'the countries bordering the Yamunā and the Sarasvatī'.[51] From this reference, we may legitimately assume that there was still some flow in the river's upper reaches at least in the sixth century CE.

We get an unexpected confirmation from Bāna, the celebrated author of *Harshacharita*, the chronicle of Emperor Harsha-vardhana who ruled over much of northern India in the first half of the seventh century. When Harsha's father, the king of Sthānvīshvara,* passed away, the people 'bore him to the river Sarasvatī, and there upon a pyre befitting an emperor solemnly consumed all but his glory in the flames'. In a classic ritual, Harsha 'passed on to the Sarasvatī's banks, and having bathed in the river, offered water to his father'.[52] Bāna's frequently ornate style is plain enough here, and these passages (there are a few more) endorse Varāhamihira's geography of the preceding century.

Epigraphy also has its say in the matter: some 30 km west of Thanesar–Kurukshetra is Pehowa, near which, as we saw, the Markanda today joins the bed of the Sarsuti. 'Pehowa' is a corruption of 'Prithūdaka' (named after a legendary King Prithu), and the Mahābhārata[53] refers to a 'highly sacred' *tīrtha* nearby, at the confluence of the Sarasvatī with a river called Arunā, which seems to have been the Markanda or a branch of it.[54] Now, at Pehowa was found an inscription of King Mihira Bhoja of the Gurjara-Pratihāra dynasty, which refers to Prithūdaka in the vicinity of the river *Prāchī Sarasvatī* or 'eastern Sarasvatī'.[55] The inscription, datable to the middle of the ninth century CE, is

---

* What is today Thanesar or Thaneswar, near Kurukshetra.

crucial evidence that a river known as Sarasvatī flowed down to Pehowa at least—a welcome confirmation of the literary references we have seen so far; but the addition of the qualifier 'eastern' suggests a western Sarasvatī, which, I assume, refers to the dry part of the bed, beyond *Vinashana*.

An Islamic chronicle of the fifteenth century, the *Tarikh-i-Mubarak Shahi*, also testifies to the existence of a Sarasvatī river in the region, since it refers to a 'stream that emptied into Satladar [Sutlej]: it bore the name of Sarsuti.'[56] The chronicle adds that the stream emerges from a hill, which fits what we know of the Sarsuti; if it was indeed a tributary of the Sutlej, it can only mean that the latter had a branch joining the Ghaggar. (We will soon return to the Sutlej's complex history.)

What emerges from our brief survey of literary sources is, above all, a sense of consistency as regards the Sarasvatī's location right from the time of the Rig Veda, and the awareness of her disappearance at a certain point of her course. Also, successive texts reflect a gradual evolution in the drying up of the once 'mighty river' and the region it watered.

FOUR SARASVATĪS

The above two-fold recollection was preserved in the popular mind just as well: we have seen how James Tod and C.F. Oldham were struck by the local songs and legends that attributed the ruin of the region to the drying up of the Ghaggar–Hakra. Another testimony comes to us from Alexander Cunningham, an official of the East India Company who, as early as 1843, recommended the creation of an Archaeological Survey of India; as the preservation of India's cultural heritage was rather low on the list of the Company's priorities, it took another three decades before the institution was founded, in 1871, with Cunningham as its first director. He will be remembered, among other contributions, for embarking with stupendous energy on the first inventory of India's countless heritage sites, monuments and inscriptions, some of which received a degree of protection (but others a degree of

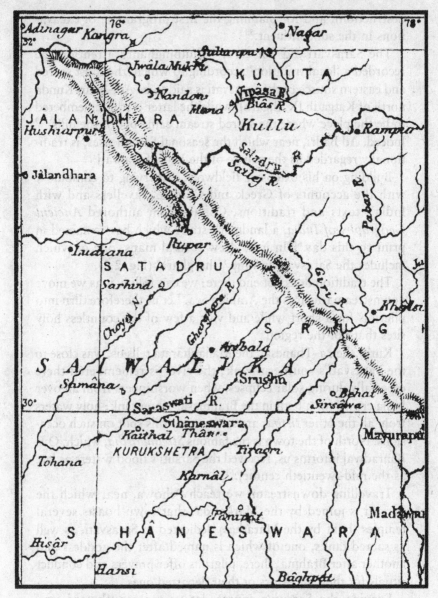

Fig. 2.3. Detail of a map by A. Cunningham showing the Sarasvatī and neighbouring rivers.[57] (Names in capital letters refer
to kingdoms mentioned by the Chinese pilgrim Hsüan-tsang.)

destruction), and for planning the first programme of excavations in the subcontinent.[58]

The Sarasvatī did not escape Cunningham's attention: he recorded a 'local tradition' according to which 'the most sacred and eastern source of the Sarasvatī is said to be Adi-Badri Kunda north of Katgadh [Kathgarh], while the latter is still remembered to be the place where the sacred stream came out of the hills.'[59] Indeed, Ad Badri, near which the seasonal Sarsuti rises, is traditionally regarded as the source of the Vedic Sarasvatī.

Building on his extensive fieldwork and trying to combine it with the accounts of Greek and Chinese travellers and with India's texts and traditions, Cunningham authored *Ancient Geography of India*, a landmark study which has remained in print to this day.[60] In it he drew several maps, one of which includes the Sarasvatī and the 'Gharghara' (Fig. 2.3).

The tradition does not end there: we can follow it as we move downstream towards the Arabian Sea. Let us therefore turn into pilgrims for a short while and visit a few of the countless holy sites that dot the region.

Kurukshetra–Thanesar, the Mahābhārata tells us, was close to the Sarasvatī's southern bank; the river is remembered there especially during solar eclipses, when worshippers from all over India crowd for a bath in the Brahmasar water tank; holy waters from all the other *tīrtha*s are said to visit this spot on such occasions. North of the town is the famous *Sthānu tīrtha*, which, O.P. Bharadwaj informs us, received the Sarsuti's flood waters as late as the mid-twentieth century.[61]

Travelling downstream, we reach Pehowa, near which the Sarsuti is joined by the Markanda; that town boasts several temples (built by the Marathas) dedicated to Sarasvatī, as well as sacred tanks, one of which is named after the goddess and another after Brahmā; there, pilgrims offer prayers and conduct rituals for their ancestors or their departed ones.

Leaving the Sarsuti's course, let us veer southward into Rajasthan. A little earlier, we heard a legend narrating how the Sarasvatī once halted at Pushkar on her way to the ocean.

Pushkar's main temple and its famous lake are dedicated to Brahmā, Sarasvatī's father (and, later, consort) in Puranic mythology. From the lake's waters, the Sarasvatī is said to re-emerge after her disappearance at *Vinashana*. (This is not the course of the river we had followed so far, but let us not quibble over such details now.) Legend has it that Rāma, Sītā and Lakshmana, the protagonists of the Rāmāyana, once came to the lake for a dip in those waters, and every year, large numbers of pilgrims converge on it for the same purpose. Perhaps in remembrance of the Sarasvatī's halt at Pushkar, the upper course of the Luni river, which has its source a few kilometres away, locally still bears her name, and is marked as such on some maps.[62]

If we follow the Luni's southwesterly course, we reach the Great Rann of Kachchh; a little to the south, the Little Rann is joined by a third river that bears the name of Sarasvati. With its source at the southwestern tip of the Aravalli Hills, its full course runs for hardly a distance of 200 km. (It is sometimes called 'Kumari' or virgin, as it does not 'wed' the ocean.) Marked on Fig. 4.2, it is by no means an impressive watercourse, yet on its banks we find several towns that have preserved the memory of the Sarasvatī, notably Siddhapur and Patan, two important pilgrimage centres. Siddhapur is famous for its beautiful, though ruined, Rudramāla temple and its sacred pond Bindusarovar, where Gujarati Hindus often perform rituals in memory of their departed parents or their ancestors. Patan draws visitors to its magnificent stepped well 'Rani Ki Vav' and its impressive waterworks alongside a now dry channel of the river; at the eastern end of a huge reservoir, three small pyramidal shrines draw the eye: they are dedicated to river-goddesses Gangā, Yamunā and Sarasvatī.

Finally, we reach the southwestern tip of Saurashtra to find a small river named 'Sarasvati' flowing down from the Gir Hills to Somnath. In his wide-ranging treatise on India, the eleventh-century Islamic scholar Alberuni recorded the 'mouth of the river Sarsuti',[63] three miles east of Somnath (in Saurashtra). A few kilometres upstream lies the much-visited *tīrtha* of Prabhas Patan (which may or may not be the Mahābhārata's Prabhasa from where Balarāma set out on his pilgrimage). There, three rivers meet: Hiranya, Kapila and Sarasvati.

These four Sarasvatis—the first flowing down from the Shivaliks, the second with its source near Pushkar, the third rising in the Aravallis and the fourth in the Gir Hills—are separate rivers, and very likely were always so. The third Sarasvati must have been so named in memory of the Vedic Sarasvatī's estuary in the Rann of Kachchh. When the Rann turned into a huge marsh, that memory must have been further transferred to nearby Saurashtra for the convenience of worship—that seems to be the most logical way to explain a fourth Sarasvati at Prabhasa, which cannot have been physically connected with the Rann. Such 'transfers' of names are common in Indian tradition. In Rameswaram, for centuries pilgrims walked some 18 km from the central Rāmanathaswāmy temple to the *Agni tīrtha* located at Dhanushkodi on the island's eastern tip. When Dhanushkodi was ravaged by a cyclone in 1964, the *Agni tīrtha* was 'transferred' to a creek near the town centre, a stone's throw from the main temple; today, the average pilgrim probably believes that this has been the *tīrtha*'s location from time immemorial! In the Hindu mind, the symbol or the inner concept always outweighs the physical object.

There are a few more Sarasvatis in other parts of the country, but the above-mentioned four are clearly part of the same tradition originating from the Vedic Sarasvatī. There is, however, a better-known Sarasvatī: the 'invisible' one at the triple confluence (*triveni sangam*) of Prayāga (Allahabad), where the Ganges and the Yamuna meet. But that is a later, Purānic tradition; it does not figure in any Vedic literature. It is another case of 'transfer', and I will later propose a likely mechanism for it.

Tradition lives on in different ways: the Sārasvat Brahmins, one of the five Gowda (or northern) Brahmin clans, are today found all the way from Punjab (and till recently Kashmir) to Karnataka and Kerala; remarkably, they have a long-preserved memory of having lived in the Sarasvatī Valley in ancient times, till they were forced to migrate in several directions after the river dried up.

SARASVATĪ IN THE EYES OF INDOLOGISTS

Let us now cross the oceans: we need to go and pick the brains of European Sanskritists, who formed their own opinions on the vanished river when they started poring over the various texts that mention her.

Possibly the first to comment on the issue was H.H. Wilson, who translated the Vishnu Purāna in 1840. He wrote in his introduction:

> The earliest seat of the Hindus within the confines of Hindusthān was undoubtedly the eastern confines of the Panjab. The holy land of Manu and the Purānas lies between the Drishadwatī and Saraswatī rivers, the Caggar [Ghaggar] and Sursooty [Sarsuti] of our barbarous maps.* Various adventures of the first princes and most famous sages occur in this vicinity; and the Āshramas, or religious domiciles, of several of the latter are placed on the banks of the Saraswatī . . . These indications render it certain, that whatever seeds were imported from without, it was in the country adjacent to the Saraswatī river that they were first planted, and cultivated and reared in Hindusthān.[64]

Wilson thus endorsed without hesitation the identification of the Sarasvatī with the Sarsuti, and placed in its vicinity 'the earliest seat of the Hindus'.

A few years later, in his *History of Ancient Sanskrit Literature*, Max Müller sought to identify the 'Land of the Seven Rivers', which the Rig Veda frequently evokes (*Saptasindhava*[65]). It consisted, in his opinion, of 'the Indus, the five rivers of the Panjab, and the Sarasvatī'[66]—the five rivers in question being the Sutlej, the Beas, the Ravi, the Chenab and the Jhelum, all of which figure in the Rig Veda (see p. 37). Max Müller was convinced that the Vedic Sarasvatī flowed in the bed of today's Sarsuti, though the

---

* The Drishadvatī is no longer associated with the Ghaggar, but with the Chautang, whose existence Wilson was unaware of. The Ghaggar flows north of the Sarsuti, the Chautang south of it (see Fig. 1.1).

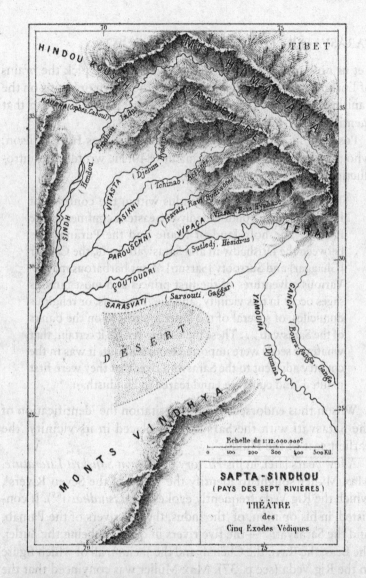

Fig. 2.4. Map of the 'Sapta Sindhu (Land of the Seven Rivers)' published in an 1881 French book, *Vedic India*, with the Sarasvatī identified with the Ghaggar and located between the Yamunā and the Sutlej. (The map adds the rivers' Sanskrit and Greek names.)

latter may be 'at present . . . so small a river'.[67] The Sarasvatī in
the east and the Indus in the west thus bracket the Land of the
Seven Rivers—the Vedic heartland (Fig. 2.2). Indeed, the Rig Veda
rarely mentions any river beyond it: Gangā occurs only twice,
and the Yamunā only three times, despite its proximity to the
Sarasvatī's basin.

The Orientalist M. Monier-Williams, author of a monumental
Sanskrit–English dictionary, endorsed this definition of the *Sapta-
sindhava* in 1875, with the same location for the Sarasvatī.[68]
More scholars of the nineteenth century could be cited who shared
that view, including Weber,[69] Eggeling[70] or Oldenberg.[71] Thus, a
book published in France in 1881, *Vedic India*,[72] which reflected
the views of Indologists of the time, included a map of the Land
of the Seven Rivers, where the Sarasvatī was clearly identified
with the Ghaggar (see Fig. 2.4).

If anything, twentieth-century Sanskritists were even more
emphatic. In 1912, A.A. Macdonell and A.B. Keith, in their
authoritative *Vedic Index of Names and Subjects*, had no doubt
that

> the Sarasvatī comes between the Jumna and the Sutlej, the
> position of the modern Sarsūti . . . There are strong reasons
> to accept the identification of the later and the earlier Saras-
> vatī throughout [the Rig Veda].[73]

A decade later, the British Indologist F.E. Pargiter published a
landmark study of India's ancient history derived from the dynas-
ties listed in the Mahābhārata and the Purānas. Throughout his
scholarly reconstruction, Pargiter placed on the map the ancient
kingdoms mentioned in the texts, and tried to make out the
migrations of the main clans. And he followed his predecessors
in locating the Sarasvatī: 'The river constituted the boundary
between the Panjab and the Ganges–Jumna basin.'[74] Fig. 2.5
reproduces a detail of a map drawn by Pargiter to illustrate some
of his research.

H.H. Gowen, a U.S. Orientalist, also made it clear that he
regarded the Sarasvatī as the eastern boundary of the Vedic

territory.[75] And he began his enthusiastic *History of Indian Literature* (written in 1931) with an image as lovely as it is apt:

> Often enough it seemed as though, like the river Sarasvatī, the lost stream of the old Sapta-sindhavas, the river of Indian thought had disappeared beneath the surface or had become lost in shallow marshes and morasses . . . But, sooner or later, we see the stream reappear, and then old ideas resume their way.[76]

Writing in 1947, French Sanskritist Louis Renou, one of the most respected authorities of his time, painted the Rig Vedic landscape in his unrivalled *Classic India* (co-authored with Jean Filliozat and a few other scholars); listing the Sindhu and its five tributaries (the five rivers of Punjab), he added: 'More important is the Sarasvatī, the true lifeline of Vedic geography, whose

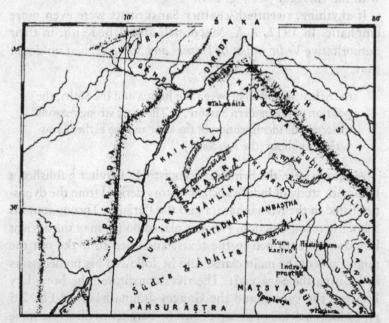

Fig. 2.5. A detail of Pargiter's map of clans in the time of the Mahābhārata. The Sarasvatī is shown flowing south of the Sutlej, and stopping in the middle of the desert.[77]

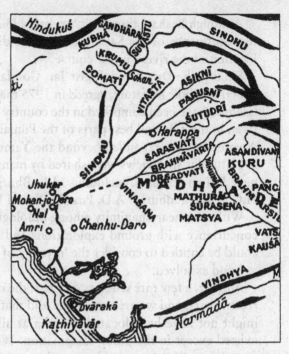

Fig. 2.6. A detail of Louis Renou's map of northwest India in Vedic times, with the Sarasvatī flowing between the Yamunā and the Sutlej.

trace is assumed to be found in the Sarsutī, located between the Satlaj and the Jamnā. With the Indus and its five tributaries, it forms the Veda's "seven rivers".'[78] Renou made the location of this 'true lifeline' clear in several maps; a detail of one of them is reproduced here in Fig. 2.6.

Thomas Burrow, another authority on Sanskrit, plainly stated in 1963 that the Ghaggar is 'the ancient Sarasvatī'.[79] Three years later, the British scholar of Asian civilization, Arthur L. Basham, wrote in his well-known *Wonder That Was India*:

> When the [Rig Vedic] hymns were written the focus of Āryan culture was the region between the Jamnā (Sanskrit *Yamunā*) and Satlaj (*Shutudrī*), south of the modern Ambālā, and along the upper course of the river Sarasvatī. The latter river is now an insignificant stream, losing itself in the desert of Rajasthan, but it then [in Rig Vedic times] flowed broad and strong . . .[80]

Although Basham thought it 'probably joined the Indus below the confluence of the Satlaj', he at least did not question the location of the river's upper course.

Finally, the Dutch Indologist Jan Gonda, an acknowledged expert on Vedic literature, agreed in 1975 that most of the hymns 'seem to have been composed in the country round the Sarasvatī river, in the hilly and best parts of the Punjab . . . To the east the Aryans had not expanded beyond the Yamunā.'[81]

Naturally, such views were shared by many other equally eminent Indian scholars, including M.L. Bhargava,[82] B.C. Law,[83] H.C. Raychaudhuri,[84] A.D. Pusalker[85] and D.C. Sircar.[86]

With such near unanimity among Indologists and such a close concurrence with ground explorations and local traditions, we could be entitled to consider the 'mystery of the vanishing river' as good as solved.

And yet, a few rare scholars differed; the dissent has grown in recent years, and we are sometimes told that the Vedic Sarasvatī might not have been located in India at all, or perhaps never existed except in the poets' imagination. What prompted them to swim against the current, we will examine in Chapter 11.

For the moment, we must complete our picture of the Sarasvatī with a survey of recent findings from a variety of scientific disciplines, each of which will enrich our understanding of the lost river.

3

New Light
on an Ancient River

Understandably, the quest for the Sarasvatī has captivated researchers of all fields: an opportunity to pull a 'mythical' river out of the mists of time does not come your way too often. In fact, the amount of data that has accumulated during the last three or four decades is so enormous that I can only highlight here some of the main findings, even if a lot of minor ones are equally interesting.

I cannot refrain from mentioning, as an example of the latter, the case of the freshwater shells noted by C.F. Oldham (p. 32) along the bed of the Ghaggar–Hakra, 'exactly similar to those now seen in the Panjab rivers'. Six decades later, in 1952, the Indian archaeologist Amalananda Ghosh, who conducted pioneering explorations in the Sarasvati region, also noticed 'a large number of shells, kindly identified for me by the Zoological Survey of India ... Some of these, being freshwater shells, must have got deposited on the banks of the river when it was alive.'[1] So humble shells, too, have a tale to tell.

FROM VASISHTHA TO BALARĀMA

After R.D. Oldham, quite a few geologists have scoured this stretch of land between the Indus and the Gangetic systems. Today a largely arid region, extending southward to the Thar Desert, it was once streaming with water, since one of its peculiarities is a thick layer of fertile alluvium, ranging from 5 to 30 m,

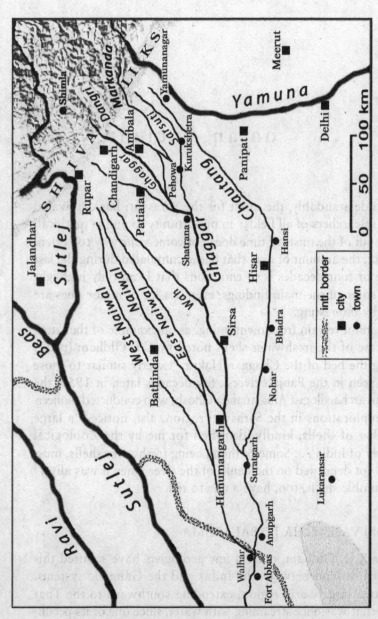

Fig. 3.1. A closer view of the ten main channels in the Ghaggar system (their seasonal waters are today largely diverted to irrigation).

often buried under layers of sand accumulated by the wind once vegetation started dwindling.[2]

The most recent layers of alluvium date back to the end of the last Glacial Age some 10,000 to 12,000 years ago: as temperatures rose, ice sheets started retreating over much of North America and Eurasia, as did glaciers in mountainous regions such as the Himalayas. The melting ice generated bountiful streams and rivers, and if I were offered a trip on a time machine, my first choice would be 8000 BCE: I would love to watch those waters deliriously roaring down the Himalayas, bouncing on the Shivaliks, as it were, and flooding the plains below. It must have been an exhilarating sight, perhaps a little scary, and certainly scarring for the landscape. Indeed, hundreds of palaeochannels, small and large, abound in eastern Punjab and Haryana, and many have been diligently traced.

Running from west to east across the Punjab–Haryana plains in today's India, we meet four seasonal streams rising in the area between Bathinda and Patiala (Fig. 3.1): the three Naiwal channels (Western, Central and Eastern), almost parallel to each other, join the Ghaggar at two points, just across the international border and near Hanumangarh. Between the Eastern Naiwal and the Ghaggar runs the Wah (also known as 'Sirhind'), and then the Patialewali (or 'Patiala'), which flows through the city of Patiala. Today, being diverted to irrigation through a dense network of canals and weirs, the seasonal waters of the Naiwals, the Wah and the Patiala almost never reach the Ghaggar. Those five streams are often thought to be palaeobeds of the Sutlej, which once branched off near Rupar to connect to the Ghaggar system.

Continuing with the Ghaggar itself, the Dangri, the Markanda, the Sarsuti and the Chautang—we have ten major channels whose waters once flowed together as the Hakra in today's Cholistan Desert. And there are many more minor ones, most of which were converted at minimal cost into canals, or disappeared under sediments or sand blown by the wind.

It would be wrong, however, to imagine crystal-clear, sparkling water streaming from the mountains: it must have been muddy enough, washing along vast amounts of debris from glaciers, rubble and sand. Two decades ago, geologists P.C. Bakliwal and A.K. Grover commented on findings near Lunkaransar, a town in the Thar Desert, south of Suratgarh (Fig. 1.1):

> Recent exploration by the Geological Survey of India reveals the presence of older alluvium with gravel beds up to 90 metres thick in Lunkaransar area indicating the presence of river-borne materials below the sand dune country.[3]

Lunkaransar is over 400 km from the Shivaliks as the crow flies; such a colossal layer of gravel—as high as a thirty-storey building—could only have been accumulated there by a massive flow of water over the ages.

Overlooking the Ghaggar, just upstream of its confluence with the Chautang, lies an important Harappan site: Kalibangan. In 1968, as excavations were nearing completion, US hydrologist Robert Raikes drilled a few bore holes in the Ghaggar's bed just north of the site, and found 'at a depth of about 11 metres below the present floodplain level, a coarse, greyish sand very similar in mineral content to that found in the bed of the present-day Yamuna. It extended over a width of at least four times that of the bed of the present-day Yamuna and down to a depth, at one point, of 30 metres.'[4] In his opinion, this 'wide buried bed of coarse sand' was the result of 'an immediate post-glacial Yamuna, much enlarged by Himalayan ice-melt, flowing to the Indus system'.[5] Above this greyish sand were layers of 'silty clay' alternating with 'shallow beds of a fine silty sand still containing the grey granite-derived material that occurs in the Yamuna'.[6] Raikes explained this alternation by 'a series of alternating captures [of the Yamunā] by the Indus and Ganges systems',[7] which fitted neatly with various protohistoric and historical stages of occupation and abandonment of the area, but this explanation has not found much acceptance among other experts; on the other hand, the geological connection of the Ghaggar with the Yamunā, which R.D. Oldham had already proposed (p. 24), has since been endorsed by many.

Indian geologist K.S. Valdiya is one of them; in his brief but rich monograph on the Sarasvatī, he writes, 'The river that caused the diversion of the Saraswati and carried its water to the Ganga via the Chambal, is called the Yamuna. In this manner, the Ganga "stole" a major portion of the discharge of the Saraswati River.'[8]

Balarāma, whom we had followed on his pilgrimage along the Sarasvatī, returns on the stage at this point, with a curious legend. Finding some divine liquor in a forest near Vrindavan one day, he became so inebriated that he was taken over by the fancy to summon the Yamunā to himself so that he could bathe in her. The lady was less than enthusiastic, however, and turned a deaf ear. Furious, Balarāma seized his ploughshare, plunged it into her bank, and dragged her to him: 'He compelled the dark river to quit its ordinary course,' says the Vishnu Purāna.[9] The Bhāgavata Purāna adds: 'Even to this day, the Yamunā is seen to flow through the track (river bed) through which [she] was dragged.'[10] It might be stretching the legend too far to read in it the Yamunā's desertion of the Sarasvatī, but it does show, at least, that people remembered a shift in the Yamunā's course.

And what about the Sutlej, which the two Oldhams had also blamed for the Sarasvatī's disappearance? Geologists (Gurdev Singh,[11] for instance, in 1952) have long identified 'a wide dry channel coming south from the spot near Ropar where the Satluj abruptly swings westward'; that palaeochannel meets the Ghaggar near Shatrana (Fig. 3.1), some 60 km south of Patiala, close to the point where the Sarsuti also joins the Ghaggar. It roughly follows the bed of the seasonal Patialewali. Remarkably, notes Valdiya, 'at the point of confluence, the Ghaggar channel suddenly becomes 6–8 km wide—and remains unusually wide until it loses itself in the sand dunes of the Thar desert, west of Anupgarh'.[12] This sudden broadening of the Ghaggar is the unmistakable sign that it once received some of the Sutlej's waters at this point.

Further downstream, the Wah and the three Naiwals represent more palaeochannels of the Sutlej in its westward migration. Then, shortly after the Sutlej finally moves away into Pakistan, another dry channel runs parallel to the international border on the Pakistani side until it joins the Hakra near Walhar. One more palaeochannel starts some 30 km northeast of Bahawalpur and proceeds southward to meet the Hakra again. And the list is not exhaustive: in fact, geologists have found 'a large number of abandoned channels left by the ever-shifting Shatadru [Sutlej] in the Panjab plain'.[13]

Clearly, then, the Sutlej has had a turbulent history. Something of its evolution is reflected in the ancient literature: named 'Shutudrī' or 'swift-flowing' in the Rig Veda, it became 'Shatadru' in post-Vedic literature, which means 'of a hundred channels', one more sign that ancient Indians were keenly observant and knew their geography; but rather than record it in scholarly accounts in the manner of ancient Greeks, they preferred the medium of 'legends'. Let us hear one more.

The Mahābhārata tells us how the great rishi Vasishtha, sorely distressed when he found that all his sons had been killed by his arch rival Vishvāmitra, wished to end his life. He tried various ways, but the elements always refused to cooperate; the sea or rivers into which he repeatedly hurled himself, bound with ropes or weighed with stones, stubbornly cast him back ashore. Thinking he was a ball of fire, the last river he plunged into 'immediately flew in a hundred different directions, and has been known ever since by the name of the Shatadru, the river of a hundred courses'.[14] Here again, the textual tradition is in accordance with what we find on the ground in the form of the Sutlej's multiple channels.

In 1983–85, an Indo-French mission explored an area of Haryana and Rajasthan between the Ghaggar and the Chautang; experts in geology, hydrology and archaeology were drawn from the Archaeological Survey of India and France's CNRS. I will discuss in Chapter 11 its chief conclusions, which proposed a new perspective on the Harappan environment and agriculture, and challenged generally accepted views on the Vedic Sarasvatī. For the moment, I will only mention French geologist Marie-Agnès Courty's findings, based on a microscopic study of the area's sediments, of 'true grey sands at a depth of over 8 m, identical to those of the Yamuna and the Sutlej'.[15] This is similar to Raikes's mention of greyish sand, suggestive of an ancient connection with the Yamunā, although Courty's chronology differs from his: according to her, 'mighty rivers with their sources in the Himalayas flowed at the end of the last ice age in the Ghaggar's present basin',[16] but those 'Yamuna-like rivers . . . stopped flowing in the study area well before the Protohistoric period',[17] that is to say, well before Harappan times (2600–1900 BCE).

Explorations of riverbeds and their terraces in the Shivaliks have also yielded important results. Overlooking the plains, the west-flowing Markanda and the east-flowing Bata (Fig. 3.2), both of them relatively modest and now seasonal rivers, flow in disproportionately broad valleys, over 1 km for the former and reaching 6 km and more for the latter (before it joins the Yamuna at Paonta Sahib)—widths suggestive of far more copious flows in the remote past.

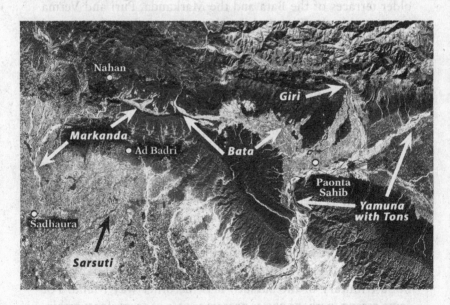

Fig. 3.2. A composite satellite view of the 'Yamuna tear' through which the river, assumed to have previously flowed westward through the Bata and Markanda Valleys, now escapes eastward.

V.M.K. Puri, a geologist and former director of the Geological Survey of India, took part in a worldwide listing of glaciers organized from Switzerland, and identified over 1500 of them in the Himalayas. In 1998, he and his colleague B.C. Verma published their findings based on a study of four terraces in the Markanda and Bata Valleys.[18] In summary, they found that the higher, more ancient terraces abounded in metamorphic rocks and quartzites characteristic of the Higher Himalayas, not of the lower Shivalik Hills. This, they argued, proved that those rocks had been carried there by a river fed by glaciers ensconced in the inner Himalayas. Climbing to an altitude of 4000 to 5000 m, they identified three such glaciers in the Bandarpunchh massif; their meltwaters now meet at Naitwar, high up in Uttarkashi, and feed the Tons, the largest tributary of the Yamuna before the latter reaches the plains (the Tons is, in fact, larger and longer than the Yamuna upstream from their confluence). To explain the Himalayan deposits in the older terraces of the Bata and the Markanda, Puri and Verma assumed that the Tons and the Yamunā once flowed westward into the wide valley of the Bata, and onto the Markanda's. To them, 'all the evidences point to only one conclusion, that the present-day Tons was in fact Vedic Sarasvatī in its upper reaches'.[19]

While the exact evolution of those Shivalik rivers remains to be confirmed, the work of Puri and Verma has shown, at the least, that larger glacier-fed—and therefore perennial—rivers once flowed through those wide valleys, a finding endorsed by Valdiya.[20]

However, it is fair to point out that the small Sarsuti, born on the slopes of the Shivaliks, might never have answered that description, as there is no marked opening connecting it to the Markanda–Bata corridor above. It seems to me that the Markanda itself, with its much longer course in the Shivaliks and its broader valley, is a more suitable candidate to represent the upper course of the ancient Sarasvatī. Technically, in fact, the Markanda is not a tributary of the Sarsuti: it is the other way round. For some reason, perhaps one as prosaic as ease of access for worship, tradition may have transferred the origin of the Sarasvatī in the plains from Kala Amb (or Kalamb), where the Markanda flows down from the Shivaliks, to nearby Ad Badri, where the Sarsuti is said to emerge; the distance between the two being no more than 15 km.

TECTONIC EVENTS

Geologists have long suspected tectonic and seismic events—earthquakes, in plain language—to be responsible for some of the shifting of rivers. The reason is not far to seek: the entire belt formed by the Himalayas, including their foothills and piedmonts, has been seismically active ever since the Indian subcontinent, separating from the Gondwana supercontinent and cruising along in a northeasterly direction at the speed of 15 cm a year, collided with Eurasia some fifty million years ago; forced to slide beneath the Eurasian plate, it uplifted the latter higher and higher, somewhat as Varāha is said to have uplifted the earth. The Tibetan plateau and the Himalayas are the result of this prodigious impact —and the mountain range continues to rise, since India's sub-duction goes on at the rate of almost 6 cm a year. The colossal friction between the landmass of India and that of Asia resulted in ripples (the Shivaliks are one of them) and numerous faults; inhabitants of not only the subcontinent's northern parts, from Pakistan to Bangladesh, but also of the region as far south as Gujarat and Maharashtra, are all too familiar with the destructive earthquakes periodically witnessed along one or the other of those active faults.

Earthquakes in the region that concerns us have left both geo-logical and archaeological scars. Among the latter, Kalibangan, where Raikes explored the Ghaggar's bed, displays a marked cleavage in its lower layers, proof of a strong earthquake dated about 2700 BCE, which is thought to have put a violent end to the city's Early phase.[21] Coincidentally, at the other end of the Sarasvatī basin, Dholavira, a fascinating Harappan site in the Rann of Kachchh to which we will return, suffered considerable damage, including the collapse of massive fortification walls, as a result of an earthquake during the same epoch.[22] Bracketed between five faults, Kachchh has a long seismic history; many will remember how it was devastated by a powerful earthquake on 26 January 2001.

With this context in mind, Puri and Verma concluded that a tectonic event must have been responsible for the opening of the 'Yamuna tear', as it is called (clearly visible in Fig. 3.2), through which the joined waters of the Tons, the Bata and the Yamunā escaped southward, robbing the Sarasvatī of its headwaters. Of course, if an earthquake did cause this tear, it would not have been instantly as broad as we now see it: a small opening and eastward tilt in the slopes would have been enough to funnel part of the glacier-fed rivers through the new gap; erosion would have done the rest in the course of time.

Valdiya reaches a similar conclusion, quoting recent work[23] to the effect that sometime after 1900 BCE, a major earthquake uplifted a riverine terrace near the Yamunā by 20 to 30 m. That earthquake struck along the fault that passes through the Paonta Sahib Valley, a fault still quite active today. Valdiya thus wonders, 'Was this the tectonic event that caused the river to deflect abruptly from its previous westerly course and enter the channel of a river that flowed south ... now known as the Yamuna?'[24] It is certainly a good candidate, at least.

SATELLITE PHOTOGRAPHY

In the West, aerial photography from aircraft was first put to military uses during World War I; soon after the war ended, it was directed to more peaceful areas, geology and archaeology in particular. But only in the 1960s was aerial photography of the Haryana–Punjab region initiated, chiefly to make more precise topographical surveys; as far as I know, its considerable ability to identify potential archaeological sites was not exploited. But the next decade saw a radically new technology upset the field: remote sensing through satellite photography and imagery, which had been rapidly developing since the 1950s in the West, where it served such diverse purposes as mapping, search for oil and other resources, meteorology, or, notoriously, intelligence gathering.

Photographs taken by satellites of the NASA's LANDSAT series, followed by those of the French SPOT series, and more recently the IRS (Indian Remote Sensing) series, were used to study the Sarasvatī's basin. For the first time, the dry bed of the Ghaggar–Hakra was revealed in dramatic fashion (Fig. 3.3). It was, of course, not the bed itself that appeared in the photographs, but the contrast created by the richer soil and vegetation found all along the river's course. Processed by advanced digital enhancing techniques, satellite imagery vividly brought out the numerous palaeobeds that criss-cross the Sutlej–Yamuna watershed, most of which are invisible at ground level. The whole question now was to try and make sense of these Himalayan data, in both senses of the term.

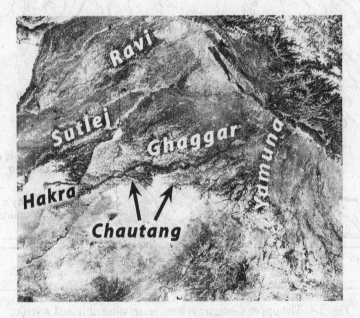

Fig. 3.3. A composite satellite view of northwest India, with a well-delineated Ghaggar–Hakra system.

In 1980, four scientists, Yash Pal, Baldev Sahai, R.K. Sood and D.P. Agrawal, published a paper entitled 'Remote Sensing of the "Lost" Sarasvatī River', based on an analysis of many photographs of LANDSAT satellites; their work soon became something of a classic among such studies. They began by confirming 'the

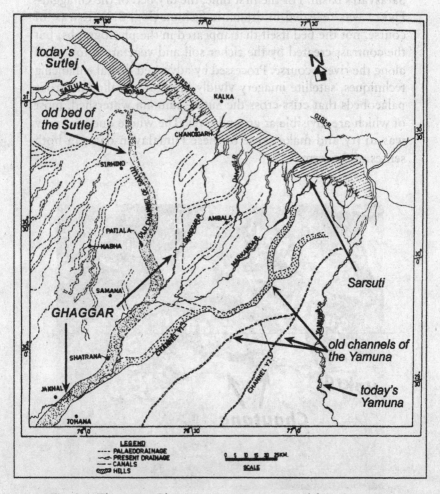

Fig. 3.4. The upper Ghaggar system reconstituted from LANDSAT imagery, with a few of the palaeobeds (adapted from Yash Pal, et al.).

sudden widening of the Ghaggar Valley about 25 km south of
Patiala which is obviously a misfit if we take into account the
considerably narrow bed of the Ghaggar upstream. This sudden
widening can be explained only if a major tributary was joining
the Ghaggar at this place. The satellite imagery does show a
major palaeo-channel joining the Ghaggar here'[25]—the same
channel that we mentioned earlier as coming straight from the
Sutlej's sharp bend near Rupar.

They detected, in fact, not just one, but a 'multitude of small
channels into which the Satluj braided till it found its present
channel'.[26] Shatadru, or 'flowing in a hundred channels', is therefore a most apt designation for this capricious river! Indeed, the
authors themselves remarked how 'the braiding of the Satluj
seems to have been echoed' in the Mahābhārata's legend.

Our scientists attributed the Sutlej's westward migration away
from the Ghaggar to tectonic movements. Downstream, they
found 'a distinct paleo-channel which seems to suggest that the
Satluj flowed through the Nara directly into the Rann of Kutch',
as C.F. Oldham had proposed.

In the east, they traced three ancient beds of the Yamunā, indicative of a gradual eastward migration; one of them coincides with
the Chautang or Drishadvatī.

The paper's conclusions, accompanied by a map (Fig. 3.4), are
quite in tune with previous topographic explorations:

> The ancient bed of the Ghaggar has a constant width of
> about 6 to 8 km from Shatrana in Punjab to Marot in Paki-
> stan. The bed stands out very clearly . . . The vast expanse
> of the Ghaggar bed can be explained only by assuming that
> some major tributaries were flowing into it in the past . . .
> Our studies thus show that the Satluj was the main tribu-
> tary of the Ghaggar and that subsequently the tectonic
> movements may have forced the Satluj westward and the
> Ghaggar dried . . . The other major river system contributing
> waters to the Ghaggar may have been some prior channel
> of the Yamuna. [These two] main feeders were weaned
> away by the Indus and the Ganga, respectively.[27]

Subsequent studies of satellite imagery have delineated more palaeochannels in the Sutlej–Yamuna watershed. As an example, a few years ago, three scientists led by A.S. Rajawat of ISRO,[28] examined the area between Tanot and Kishangarh in the north-western part of Jaisalmer district, Rajasthan, close to the international border. Enhanced photographs of the IRS 1-C satellite revealed, buried under the thick sand dunes of the desert, two

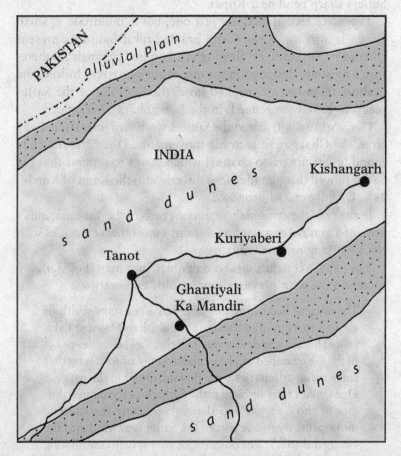

Fig. 3.5. Two major palaeochannels identified in the Tanot–Kishangarh region of Jaisalmer district (adapted from A.S. Rajawat, et al.).

important palaeochannels (Fig. 3.5), broadly oriented northeast to southwest; their width, ranging from 2 to 4 km, bears witness to the existence of a respectable river system in what is today a barren landscape of endless dunes. Since the area is hardly 30 km east of the Hakra, these paleochannels must have been connected to it.

The existence of these palaeochannels has been confirmed by the most recent study in the field, an ambitious attempt to trace the entire drainage of the Sarasvatī. Three ISRO scientists, J.R. Sharma, A.K. Gupta and B.K. Bhadra, presented in 2006 the results of their research based on multi-spectral data from the new generation of IRS satellites.[29] They identified five principal courses, numbered 1 to 5 in Fig. 3.7 (made clearer in Fig. 3.6).

The first, 4 to 10 km wide, is more or less the Ghaggar–Hakra drawn by earlier researchers, except that the branch that runs past Fort Abbas and Marot in Pakistan dies out in the desert and the real course turns south just before the international border, meeting the Hakra a little farther south. A second difference is that its last stretch is not the Nara but a course 40 km east of it, although the authors cautiously suggest that this needs to be verified. The estuary is the Rann of Kachchh, in accordance with earlier studies.

The second course, 4 to 6 km wide, roughly follows the international border up to the Jaisalmer district, where it precisely connects with the palaeochannels identified by A.S. Rajawat and his colleagues in the Tanot–Kishangarh area; it then turns due south up to the Rann.

The third is a minor channel running west of the second. The fourth and fifth courses start south of the Chautang and hug the foothills of the Aravallis; they broadly correspond to the Luni's basin. Those last three courses are fairly narrow—a few hundred metres at the most—in comparison with the first two. In fact, several experts have suggested that the Luni's drainage could have been the most ancient course of the Sarasvatī, which would have drifted westward in stages, all the way to the Hakra.[30] Our three ISRO scientists disagree and opt for the first course (strictly speaking, the second is inseparable from the first). But the two viewpoints are not wholly irreconcilable: the ISRO's own map suggests that through the Chautang (the Hissar–Nohar stretch), a connection between the Sarasvatī and the Luni systems must have existed at some point, probably when some of the Yamunā's waters flowed into the Chautang.

Overall, the ISRO study confirms the existence of numerous palaeochannels and proposes the most likely courses for the Sarasvatī—not as neat as the single line we see on many maps (including mine in Fig. 1.1 or 3.1). It is a welcome reminder of the complexity of the region's history.

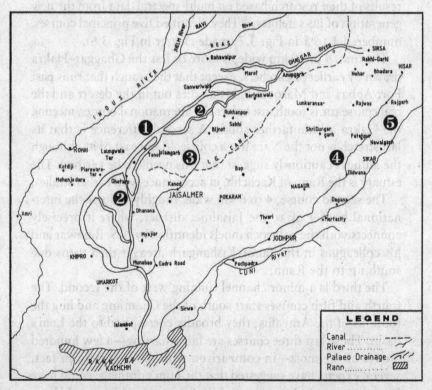

Figs 3.6 (above) and 3.7 (on the next page). The main ancient watercourses identified in the Sutlej–Yamuna watershed by the ISRO team.[31] In the above, simplified map, courses 1 and 2 are regarded as representing those of the Vedic Sarasvatī.

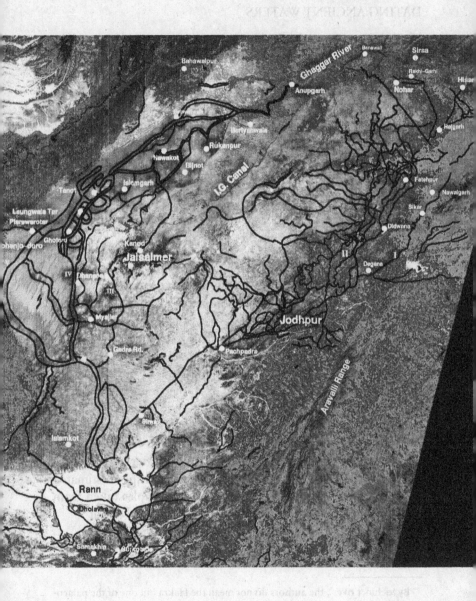

DATING ANCIENT WATERS

The latest entrant in the field is nuclear physics, or rather one of its byproducts: a wide array of dating techniques, from which geology, oceanography, archaeology and other disciplines have benefited immensely. Radiocarbon dating, based on the carbon-14 isotope ('normal' carbon being 12), is the best known of the lot; it is effective for carbon-based material such as wood, cloth or bone, which makes it the favourite dating tool of archaeologists. It even created something of a revolution, enabling for the first time an excavator to obtain absolute dates, instead of relative ones, based on comparison with other sites and ultimately on literary evidence. However, for materials like pottery, stone or metal, which hold little or no carbon, other dating techniques have been perfected.

Water is what interests us here. In 1995, S.M. Rao and K.M. Kulkarni, two scientists from the Bhabha Atomic Research Centre (BARC), drew samples from wells in various parts of Rajasthan. They studied the proportions in isotopes of hydrogen (deuterium and tritium) and oxygen (18, while 'normal' oxygen is 16), in addition to radiocarbon from dissolved carbonate compounds (such as limestone). In the northwestern part of Jaisalmer district, precisely the area where A.S. Rajawat and his colleagues identified two important palaeochannels (Fig. 3.5), they found that 'in spite of very low rainfall (less than 150 mm) and extreme conditions of the desert, groundwater is available at depth of about 50-60 m along the course of the defunct river* and a few dug wells do not dry up throughout the year.' This groundwater is not a static water table; it actually flows subterraneously at a speed estimated at 20 m a year. Their analysis of the water samples taken from shallow wells (typical depth less than 50 m) showed that

> The groundwater in the area is enriched in stable isotope content . . . compared to that of Himalayan rivers . . . The

---

* By 'defunct river', the authors do not mean the Hakra but one of the palaeo-channels visible in Fig. 3.5, which correspond to course no. 2 in the preceding study by ISRO scientists (Figs 3.6 and 3.7).

groundwater samples exhibit negligible tritium content
indicating absence of modern recharge. Radiocarbon dates
suggest the groundwater is a few thousand years old . . .
(uncorrected ages: 4950 to 4400 BP [before present]).[32]

Once calibrated, those dates would be approximately 3700 to
3200 BCE,[33] after which very little recharge took place: the date
of these 'fossil waters' suggests the onset of an arid phase in the
area, or at least a drying up of this watercourse.

In fact, the research of Rao and Kulkarni was part of a broader
project: in collaboration with BARC and other agencies,[34] the
Rajasthan Ground Water Department (RGWD) proposed to explore
reserves of groundwater under the desert sand, with a view to alle-
viating water scarcity in western Rajasthan, especially Jaisalmer
and Bikaner districts. Years earlier, it had noted that 'freshwater
was available in many places of Jaisalmer district, and some wells
never dried up. This aroused considerable interest, for Jaisalmer's
water is known to be saline. Investigations revealed that about
100 m away from the site of the fresh water, the groundwater
was saline.'[35] In some places, freshwater was available at depths
of 30 or 40 m—extraordinarily shallow for such arid areas, con-
sidering that in regions of India where intensive agriculture is
practised, it is not uncommon to find the water table as low as
200 m or more. Moreover, the very presence of freshwater in the
heart of the Thar Desert is revealing: the alignment of freshwater
wells corresponds with subterranean palaeochannels, some of
which, in the view of the scientists involved, formed part of the
Sarasvatī system: 'There are palaeo-channels in all ten districts
of western Rajasthan, and these have been mapped to prepare
the river's ancient course.'[36]

In 1999, a study by four Indian scientists led by V. Soni in the
Jaisalmer region found that even though some of the tubewells
had been in use for up to forty years, their output was stable and
there was no sign of the water table receding: this confirmed that
the underground flow was active.[37] I cannot help recalling here
the 'invisible current through the bowels of the earth', which, the

Mahābhārata told us (p. 43), accomplished sages sitting near the lost Sarasvatī could alone detect.

Regardless of whether there was an invisible current or not, K.R. Srinivasan, a former director of the Central Ground Water Board, estimated in a report that the central Sarasvatī river basin in Rajasthan could sustain a million tubewells.[38] The search for the Sarasvatī can thus have quite pragmatic applications even today. Let us hope, however, that any exploitation of those ancient reserves of water will be accompanied by effective replenishment measures; otherwise, it might be a case of killing the proverbial goose.

Significantly, the same situation prevails in Cholistan, as Mackeson had noted: 'Wells dug in it [the Hakra course] are generally found to have sweet water, while the water of wells dug at a distance from it either North or South, is usually brackish.' (p. 14) This has since received strong support from a 'comprehensive hydrogeological, geophysical, and isotope hydrological survey conducted from 1986 to 1991' by German scientists M.A. Geyh and D. Ploethner in the Hakra's floodplain of Cholistan between Fort Abbas in the east and Fort Mojgarh in the southwest.[39] Their survey revealed a huge body of fresh groundwater, some 14 km wide, 100 km long and 100 m thick; it was unexpectedly shallow, too, at a depth of less than 50 m on average. A tritium-based isotope study established that 'the present recharge of groundwater in Cholistan is negligible',[40] pointing to 'a range of the actual water age from 12900 to 4700 years BP',[41] that is, till about 2700 BCE.

The last date is broadly consistent with that of 3200 BCE, which resulted from the study by the BARC scientists in nearby western Rajasthan, and it is corroborated by a study of 2008, in which a team of British, U.S. and Pakistani researchers directed by Peter Clift conducted field excavations on the Ghaggar–Hakra's floodplain in Pakistan's state of Punjab. They obtained dates of sedimentation by 'radiocarbon dating freshwater gastropod shells and woody material recovered from the pits'. According to their initial but promising findings, 'Provisional age data now show that between 2000 and 3000 BCE, flow along a presently dried-up course known as the Ghaggur-Hakkra River ceased, probably driven by the weakening monsoon and possibly also because of headwater capture into the adjacent Yamuna and Sutlej Rivers.'[42]

Clearly, something radical happened to the river in the third millennium BCE.

A LONG JOURNEY THROUGH THE DESERT

Right from the two Oldhams, the Sarasvatī conundrum never ceased to fascinate observers; at regular intervals, new researchers came along to add their perspectives. We cannot hear them all, but we will end this first leg of our journey of exploration with a few observations from two geographers, the first, Indian, the second, German.

Shamsul Islam Siddiqi's contribution, 'River Changes in the Ghaggar Plain',[43] dates back to 1944. After a mention of seven major dry river channels joining together in that plain, Siddiqi follows the resultant Ghaggar downstream and observes that 'this dry river bed can be traced, fairly continuously, from Jakhal in Hissar [district] to the Eastern Nara in Sind'.[44] In his analysis of the historical evidence, 'the Sutlej was not always a tributary of the Indus . . . It was a late interloper into the Indus system',[45] and before that, the main feeder of the Ghaggar system, proceeding straight to it from Rupar instead of taking the present unnaturally sharp bend westward. 'The Sutlej was the most westerly and the Jumna the most easterly tributary of the Ghaggar and their present courses are of comparatively late acquisition.'[46] A conclusion supported, in Siddiqi's opinion, by 'the Hindu tradition which believes a mighty river, Sarsuti, to have once flowed across the Ghaggar Plain'.[47]

Writing in 1969, Herbert Wilhelmy, a distinguished German geographer, provided a more detailed analysis: having surveyed the topographic and geological findings available in his time (therefore without satellite imagery), he proposed a careful reconstruction of the evolution of the hydrography of the Sutlej–Yamuna

watershed, accompanied by five maps depicting the successive
stages of the Sarasvatī river system.

In the first (Fig. 3.8), which corresponds to Vedic times, the
Sarasvatī flows through the Ghaggar, receives the waters of the
'Veda–Sutlej' at Bhatnir* (Hanumangarh) and those of the 'Ur-
Jumna' or proto-Yamunā (flowing through the Chautang) near
Suratgarh. The second stage sees the Yamunā captured by the
Ganges system in the east, while the Sutlej had veered westward,
meeting the Ghaggar farther downstream, at Walhar; the next
three stages are marked by the continued migration of the Sutlej,
until its final capture by the Beas. The details of these migrations
are not crucial to us at this point; Wilhelmy's general conclusions
are what matters:

> The extraordinary breadth of the Hakra bed, which is not
> less than 3 km over a distance of 250 km and is even 6 km
> in some places, must therefore be due to the flood discharge
> from the big glacial rivers coming down from the Himala-
> yas[48] . . . The small Siwalik rivers would not have been
> enough to supply all the water in the Sarasvatī. In other
> words, the Sarasvatī must have had a source river in the
> Himalaya; the Sarasvatī must have lost this source river
> either due to a diversion or tapping, as indicated by the
> sharp bend near Rupar.[49]

The work of Puri and Verma cited above, which sought to
connect the Sarasvatī's source to glaciers of the inner Himalayas,
comes in support of this view. Wilhelmy continues:

> There should no longer be any doubt that Sutlej water
> flowed into the Hakra at three different places in an earlier
> period[50] . . . In the very distant past, the Jumna [Yamuna]

---

* Wilhelmy prefers this palaeochannel of the Sutlej (which corresponds to the
Central Naiwal) to that identified by Yash Pal, et al. (see Fig. 3.5), which meets
the Ghaggar upstream, near Shatrana. Of course, both channels are valid (and
so are several more), and could have been in use at different times, or even
simultaneously.

> was certainly one of the big water suppliers of the 'Lost River of Sind'. The water flowed through an old 1.5 km wide bed of the Chautang[51] . . .
>
> This dry bed is indeed the holy river 'Sarasvatī' . . .; once upon a time, this was a genuine solitary river which reached the ocean without any tributaries on its long way through the desert.[52]

Such is the picture that all the studies we have surveyed here converge on with a satisfying degree of agreement, whatever differences they may have in terms of data and interpretation, especially as regards the chronology of the main stages in the Sarasvatī's decline and final disappearance.

If we have to postpone till the later chapters a more complete discussion of that crucial stage, it is because it did not merely impact the hydrography of northwest India; it affected millions

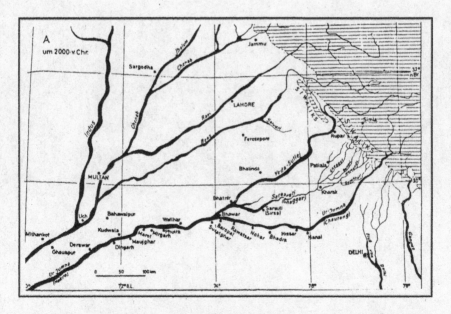

Fig. 3.8. Wilhelmy's reconstruction of the first stage of the Sarasvatī river system, 'around 2000 BCE'.

of children, women and men who have so far not appeared in our beautiful but rather disembodied landscape. We will never fully know their story, but some of them have left us substantial traces of their existence: we have in front of us not just a collection of scattered settlements, but a far-reaching network extending to the Indus and to Gujarat—a whole civilization, the first on Indian soil.

Part 2

INDIA'S FIRST CIVILIZATION

'Several hundred sites [of the Indus civi-
lization] have been identified, the great
majority of which are on the plains of
the Indus or its tributaries or on the
now dry course of the ancient Sarasvatī
River, which flowed south of the Sutlej
and then southward to the Indian
Ocean, east of the main course of the
Indus itself.'

Raymond Allchin, 2004

'The large number of protohistoric settlements, dating from c. 4000 BC to 1500
BC, could have flourished along this river
only if it was flowing perennially.'

V.N. Misra, 1994

4

A Great Leap Backward

Given a chance for a second trip on our time machine, I would unhesitatingly opt for 2700 BCE. Something mysterious was beginning to unfold around that date, complex stirrings that remain poorly understood to this day. For at least four millennia, a few regions of the Indo-Gangetic belt had already harboured settled village communities—settled, but slowly evolving new practices of agriculture, technology (metallurgy in particular), and crafts. Suddenly—over a few decades, at most a century— the Northwest witnessed the explosion of a wholly new category of human settlements: cities. Extensive, planned cities, rising almost at the same time hundreds of kilometres apart, fully functional by 2600 BCE and interacting with each other through a tight network. They thrived for seven centuries or so, declined, and were slowly swallowed by sand and soil. Until . . .

THE PIONEERS

In 1844, Major F. Mackeson, as we saw, pleaded with his superiors for the opening of what he thought to be a new route from Delhi to Sind via the Ghaggar–Hakra. Five years later, however, with the annexation of Punjab, the project lost its *raison d'être*: all that was now needed was to strengthen communications to and through Punjab, which the British promptly set about doing. Telegraph and railways, always projected as bringing 'progress' to India, were, in reality, first and foremost indispensable tools in the delicate exercise of keeping this huge territory under

Britain's 'providential rule'. In the late 1850s, railway lines were laid through Punjab, particularly between Lahore and Multan, a line running south of the Ravi river, and through Sind. But to stabilize a railway line, you need ballast—a lot of it—and in flat alluvial plains, ballast material is not always easy to come by. Unless, of course, you are lucky enough to have an old ruined city at hand, with tons of excellent bricks waiting to be plundered.

That is precisely what happened to a group of huge mounds located near a village called Harappa, in the Sahiwal district of Punjab, on the bank of a former bed of the Ravi, twelve kilometres south of the river's present course. No one could have guessed that this name, 'Harappa', was destined to become world-famous —least of all the engineers of the Western Railways, who had eyes only for the cartloads of bricks they could 'mine' from this bountiful quarry. The cartloads soon became wagonloads, with a light railway laid for speedier extraction. Alexander Cunningham, who had visited the site in 1853 and again in 1856, returned to it in 1872 as the director of the newly formed Archaeological Survey of India (ASI); in his report, he recorded, with some anguish, that the massive ancient walls he had noted during his initial visits had vanished, having been turned into ballast for no less than 160 km of the new Lahore–Multan line.[1]

Who could have manufactured those compact, precisely proportioned baked bricks? Neither Cunningham nor the few of his countrymen who preceded him to Harappa[2] had a clue. Since the Mauryan age then constituted the farthest horizon of Indian archaeology, Cunningham naturally assumed that the site belonged to it—to 'Buddhist times' to be precise, as his eras seemed glued to religious lines (pre-Buddhist times, for instance, were 'Brahminical'—a meaningless term that still lurks around in quite a few Indological studies). Cunningham also thought that Harappa was still a populous town in the seventh century CE when Hsüan-tsang visited the region. And when he came across a black-stone seal from Harappa, on which a bull and a few strange characters were incised, he could only see in them 'an archaic kind of writing of c. 500 or 400 BC'.[3] He was wrong on all three counts—but his curiosity was tickled.

In two captivating studies, historians Upinder Singh and Nayanjot Lahiri recently wove the story of the beginnings of archaeology in India.[4] Cunningham retired in 1885; after him the ASI went through ups and downs—mostly the latter. Nominated India's viceroy in 1899, Curzon lost no time in reconstituting it; his immediate goal was to appoint a new, young and dynamic director, a post which successive financial curtailments had ended up abolishing. Enquiries zeroed in on John Marshall, a twenty-five-year-old classical scholar trained in archaeology in Greece, Crete and Turkey. Reaching India in early 1902, he took up his first assignment: apart from familiarizing himself with a largely unknown land, it consisted in the preservation of many badly neglected monuments, an issue that had much preoccupied Curzon. Given the viceroy's contemptible political record in Bengal, it is good to remember this positive contribution of his: had he not stemmed the rot in the archaeological establishment, India would have lost hundreds of more monuments, ancient and medieval.

Curzon's protégé, Marshall, energetically moved on with his work, encouraging his superintendents and hiring local pundits to spot valuable antiquities, and getting Buddhist and other sites identified, protected and, when possible, excavated. All the while, he kept at the back of his mind the puzzling absence, in the archaeological record then available in India, of Bronze Age sites comparable to those that had come to light in recent decades in Egypt, Mesopotamia or the Aegean islands, such as the Minoan civilization of Crete, where Marshall had worked. It was now understood that the Bronze Age was a stage between the Neolithic and the Iron Age which saw a rapid development of civilization. In India, a few copper and bronze implements had indeed been collected here and there, but no full-fledged site of such a period had so far come to light. The Iron Age was thought to begin around 800 BCE (the date has now been pushed back by a whole millennium in the Gangetic region[5]). Beyond those misty times there was a big blank.

In 1913, Marshall started an ambitious excavation at Taxila in northern Punjab (close to today's Islamabad), a large city of early historical times. Ancient texts referred to it as 'Takshashila' and located an important Hindu–Buddhist centre of learning there; it was founded around 600 BCE and lived on for a millennium till it was destroyed by the invading Huns. Marshall returned there season after season until 1934, long after his directorship of the Survey had ended. Although remarkably extensive in scope ('horizontal', as archaeologists would put it), meticulously performed by the standards of the time, and important with regard to India's historical period, it was not the excavation that would earn Marshall lasting fame. That would be Harappa, to which he deputed assistants in 1909 and again in 1914 in order to assess the potential of its badly plundered yet still impressive mounds— and also to look around for other specimens of the intriguing seal with unknown characters that Cunningham had described (a few more of the same type had since come to light through private collectors). Those brief explorations failed to reveal much of interest, yet it is to Marshall's credit that he persisted with a plan to excavate the site.

World War I and greater financial squeeze delayed it. In February 1917, Daya Ram Sahni, a Sanskrit scholar and epigraphist with a long experience of excavations, and now superintendent of the Archaeological Survey's Northern Circle, paid a visit to Harappa on Marshall's instructions. It took another four years for the necessary acquisition of two of the mounds and protection of the others. Finally, in January 1921, the digging began. In a little over a month, apart from pottery, portions of brick structures, long beads, numerous bangles and terracotta toys, Sahni dug out two inscribed seals and a lot of 'well-burnt bricks of fine texture' of proportions that were different from those of the bricks found in historical sites: Harappa's bricks had, in his words, 'the scientific proportion of two widths to a length, which is the essential condition of good bonding'.[6] (He could have added two heights to a width: in short, height, width and length were in the ratio 1:2:4, 'one to two to four'.) All these artefacts,

thought Sahni, must have belonged to a 'pre-Mauryan' epoch—
how much 'pre' was the question. Excited by the seals and their
'curious pictographic legends',[7] Marshall pressed for deeper
diggings into this huge vertical mound.

A year earlier, in December 1919, Rakhal Das Banerji, another
brilliant archaeologist and superintendent of the Survey's Western
Circle, had, in the course of a tour of Sind, paid a visit to imposing
mounds not far from Larkana, a little to the west of the Indus,
on the bank of an abandoned bed of the river. Locals called them
'Mohenjo-daro',* that is, 'mound of the dead'. Banerji returned
to it three years later with a team of excavators, and soon a few
inscribed seals came to light in the middle of brick structures.
Learning of this find in the spring of 1923, Marshall was, as he
wrote to Banerji, 'immensely interested'.[8] The next year, he sent
Madho Sarup Vats to pursue excavations at Mohenjo-daro; apart
from unearthing more seals, Vats emphasized other important
parallels with Harappa, notably pottery styles and baked bricks
with identical proportions.

Yet, sailing down the Ravi from Harappa, on to the Chenab
and the Indus all the way to Mohenjo-daro is a voyage of no
less than 800 km: if such distant cities belonged to the same
ancient culture, a new horizon was definitely opening up, which
is precisely what a wide-eyed Marshall and his Indian collaborators were now contemplating. A firm chronological anchorage
was, however, missing.

Marshall took the plunge and published a detailed article in the
Illustrated London News of 20 September 1924. Aptly entitled
'First Light on a Long-forgotten Civilization: New Discoveries
of an Unknown Prehistoric Past in India', it began with these oft-
quoted and prescient lines:

> Not often has it been given to archaeologists, as it was
> given to Schliemann at Tiryns and Mycenae, or to [Aurel]
> Stein in the deserts of Turkestan, to light upon the remains

---

* Alternative spellings include Mohenjodaro, Mohenjo Daro and Moenjo-daro.
'Daro' means 'mound' in Sindhi.

of a long-forgotten civilization. It looks, however, at this
moment, as if we were on the threshold of such a discovery
in the plains of the Indus.[9]

The article's *pièce de résistance* was a series of photographs
depicting some of the structural remains that had been unearthed,
pottery items, objects of daily use, and nineteen of the seals found
at Harappa and Mohenjo-daro: for the first time, a wider public
peered at unknown characters overlooking magnificent bulls and
bull-like unicorns. Marshall was not after mere sensationalism;
his hope was to obtain some clues. In fact, the magazine's editors
explicitly invited its 'expert readers' to help 'elucidate the script'.

The response was prompt: the *Weekly*'s very next issue carried
a letter by A.H. Sayce, an Assyriologist, who pointed out that
the seals looked very much like 'proto-Elamite' tablets found at
Susa, the capital of Elam. Elam was an ancient culture related
to the Mesopotamian civilization, located in today's southwestern Iran (see Fig 5.6), and the proto-Elamite tablets were dated
to the third millennium BCE. Sayce, therefore, pertinently wrote
that the discovery of the Harappan seals 'is likely to revolutionize
our ideas of the age and origin of Indian civilization'.[10] The following week, two more scholars attempted to parallel some of
the Harappan signs with cuneiform Sumerian signs; Sumer, the
earliest Mesopotamian civilization, again pointed to the third
millennium BCE (its first cities, in fact, rose during the preceding
millennium). However, such parallels remain conjectural at best.
A third, more tangible piece of evidence came from Ernest J.H.
Mackay, an archaeologist who wrote to Marshall reporting the
recent find of a small square steatite seal at Kish, one of Sumer's
city-states. Mackay had excavated there, and was struck that the
Kish seal looked identical to those in Marshall's article, from the
bull to the signs above it. A single conclusion imposed itself,
however unlikely it seemed at first glance: the citizens of Mohenjo-
daro were in contact with the Sumerians.

AN 'AGE-OLD CIVILIZATION'

Marshall was understandably thrilled. At one stroke, India's protohistory had taken a giant leap into the past: no one had dared to advance a date older than the first millennium BCE for the Indus finds, and now there was talk of 3000 BCE! India could at last take pride in having been home to a civilization that was contemporary with ancient Egypt or Mesopotamia, and one that, in addition, reached out as far as Sumer and Elam (Table 4.1).

Table 4.1. A timeline of the Indus and contemporary civilizations.

Date (BCE)	Egypt	Mesopo-tamia	Iran	BMAC (Oxus)	Indo-Gangetic Plains
1000	▶ Amenhotep III ▶ End of Middle Kingdom	▶ Assyrian Empire ▶ Hittite culture ▶ Kassites control Babylon ▶ Hammurabi's reign	▶ Middle Elamite Kingdom ▶ Elam crushed by Hammurabi	▶ End of BMAC or Oxus civilization	▶ Painted Grey Ware culture ▶ Late Harappan culture moves towards Ganga ▶ Iron in Gangetic Plains ▶ Harappan urbanism ends ▶ The Sarasvatī dries up
2000	▶ End of Old Kingdom ▶ Great Pyramids at Giza ▶ First Pharaoh	▶ Ur's ziggurat ▶ Sargon's reign	▶ Linear Elamite script ▶ First phase of Elamite civilization ▶ City near Jiroft ▶ Proto-Elamite tablets at Sialk and Tepe Yahya	▶ Harappans set up Shortughai in Bactria ▶ BMAC's urban phase ▶ Towns develop	▶ Mohenjo-daro's Great Bath ▶ First break-up of the Sarasvatī river ▶ Emergence of cities in Indus–Sarasvatī Plains and Gujarat
3000	▶ Hieroglyphs ▶ First dynasty	▶ Uruk ▶ Babylon ▶ Cuneiform writing ▶ Wheel-turned pottery ▶ The wheel			▶ Pre-urban elements: weights, Indus-like signs, proportioned baked bricks, trade
4000	▶ Copper metallurgy develops	▶ Copper metallurgy ▶ Irrigation systems			▶ Copper metallurgy in Indus–Sarasvatī Plains
5000					▶ First dates at Bhirrana (Haryana)
6000		▶ Brewing of beer ▶ Agriculture develops ▶ First permanent settlements	▶ Farming communities are established	▶ Agricultural settlements in Hissar (Tajikistan)	▶ Farming communities at Mehrgarh, domestication of animals ▶ Domestication of rice in Central Ganges Plains
7000					▶ Mehrgarh's Neolithic stage

As Marshall himself wrote at the start of an article reproduced in many Indian dailies in late 1924:

> Indians have always been justly proud of their age-old civilization and believing that this civilization was as ancient as any in Asia, they have long been hoping that archaeology would discover definite monumental evidence to justify their belief. This hope has now been fulfilled.[11]

The wide publicity that followed had the happy consequence of loosening the stingy government's purse strings. Daya Ram Sahni resumed his excavation of Harappa while archaeologist K.N. Dikshit was sent to Mohenjo-daro in 1924. Marshall himself joined the latter the next year, recruiting more excavators such as N.G. Majumdar (who was killed by dacoits during explorations in Baluchistan a few years later) and Ernest Mackay, who had left Mesopotamia for the Indus on Marshall's invitation.

While excavations continued off and on at those two sites, Marshall was conscious that there must be more of the kind. Settlements that had been spotted earlier but had not been related to Mohenjo-daro or Harappa were revisited during the following years, such as Sutkagen-dor on the Makran coast, close to today's Iran–Pakistan border, Dabar-Kot and Nal in Baluchistan, Chanhu-daro, some 140 km downstream of Mohenjo-daro (on the same abandoned bed of the Indus), and Amri, closer to today's Indus. Those sites were small and unimpressive as compared to Mohenjo-daro, yet they contributed important data.

Since most of them were found in the Indus basin or its periphery, when Marshall edited a massive three-volume excavation report on Mohenjo-daro in 1931, he titled it *Mohenjo-Daro and the Indus Civilization*. Some of his colleagues preferred the term 'Harappan civilization',* following the tradition of naming a culture after the first representative site to come to light. Both designations remain in use, and we will see later a third which has been proposed more recently.

---

* Which explains that the term 'Harappans' does not mean inhabitants of Harappa, but the inhabitants of any site of the civilization.

BOUNDARIES

At the time of the 1947 Partition, the known Harappan sites numbered about forty; with two exceptions, they were located in newly created Pakistan: more precisely, in Pakistan's Punjab, Sind and Baluchistan. By 1960, the number of these sites had reached about 100. Following a few systematic campaigns, especially on the Indian side, it grew by leaps and bounds, to 800 in 1979[12] and 1400 in 1984.[13] In 1999, the US archaeologist Gregory Possehl, who has excavated Harappan sites and written prolifically on the Indus civilization, published a gazetteer of about 2600 sites.[14] A more recent list adds up to over 3700,* and hardly a week or month goes by without some new settlement being reported. The last two lists agree on a little over 1000 sites for the urban, also called the 'Mature', phase.

As a result, the expanse covered by this civilization has considerably increased since the 1920s. We have already travelled westward along the Makran coast almost as far as Iran. In northern Afghanistan, a small but important Harappan site came to light in 1975: Shortughai, on the left bank of the Amu Darya (ancient Oxus), close to today's border with Tajikistan, across the Hindu Kush range and over 1000 km away from Harappa! Another site was found some 30 km from Jammu, on the Chenab. But the biggest surprise came from India's states of Punjab, Haryana and northern Rajasthan, and Pakistan's Cholistan Desert, which turned out to be studded with hundreds of smaller or larger settlements. This region is precisely the basin of the Ghaggar–Hakra, and we will visit some of these sites in Chapter 7. Gujarat, too, contributed a big crop of Harappan sites. The eastern and southern boundaries of this civilization were finally pushed back, respectively, to western Uttar Pradesh and the valleys of the Narmada and the Tapti. It does seem that to the Harappans,

---

* We will come to it in Chapter 6, and will see that geographically distinct sites (that is, those appearing as separate dots on a map) probably number 2000 to 2500.

the region south of the Vindhyas was largely *terra incognita*, though archaeologists have not ruled out possible sporadic contacts with south India.

Altogether, the area covered by this civilization (Fig. 4.1) was about 800,000 km²: roughly one-fourth of today's India, or, if we make comparisons with contemporary civilizations, ancient Egypt and Mesopotamia put together. This vast expanse must have offered unique opportunities as well as posed peculiar challenges—opportunities in terms of a wider choice of sources for raw materials and a richer store of human skill and experience; and challenges arising from a greater diversity of regional

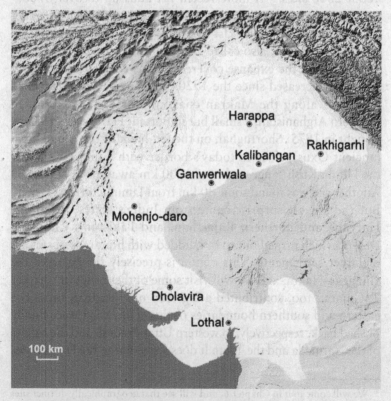

Fig. 4.1. The expanse of the Indus civilization (in white), with some of the principal sites.

cultures which had to be integrated, or at least coordinated, and the sheer extent of communication networks required to keep it all together. For a few centuries, the Harappans appear to have met those challenges with remarkable success, even though many of the solutions they worked out remain riddles as of today.

Let us keep in mind, however, that this territory was not their exclusive preserve; on its fringes and sometimes within it, several regional Chalcolithic* cultures have been identified;[15] these remained based on village life, often interacting with the Harappan cities, but never adopting its most characteristic traits. And of course there were, as there are today, many tribal groups in the hilly areas, from Baluchistan in the west to the lower Himalayan ranges in the north and east, as well as nomadic communities criss-crossing the landscape.

THE MATURE PHASE

Marshall, building on Mesopotamian parallels, proposed that Mohenjo-daro had flourished between 3250 and 2750 BCE. However, since the 1950s, radiocarbon dating from different sites[16] has shown that the first Indus cities appeared around 2600 BCE, and that by 1900 BCE (or earlier for some sites) the urban structure had largely disintegrated.

Those seven centuries represent the Mature phase of the Indus civilization, whose hallmarks include an advanced civic order, standardized brick sizes and proportions, a standardized system of weights, steatite seals inscribed with still mysterious characters, and specific art forms expressed through figurines, painted pottery, ornaments and daily objects.

Less conspicuous aspects were also at work. One, an agriculture that produced enough surplus to feed the cities, regardless of unpredictable rivers or the vagaries of the monsoon. Two, refined

---

* Chalcolithic, meaning copper ('chalco') with stone ('lithic'), refers to the prehistoric period that saw the introduction of copper metallurgy in a Neolithic background.

technologies, particularly in the fields of bronze metallurgy, water management, sanitation and bead-making. Three, such techniques depended on a dynamic internal trade, and sometimes gave rise to an equally dynamic external trade. Four, as we just saw, a large-scale integration of regional cultures, traditions, ethnic groups, and probably languages and dialects, made it possible to have broadly the same urban features or pottery styles across hundreds of kilometres.

For this last reason, the US archaeologist Jim Shaffer, who has contributed stimulating new perspectives on the Indus civilization, proposed the use of the term 'Integration Era' for this Mature phase.*

Mohenjo-daro, whose population has been estimated at 40,000 to 50,000, was probably the most extensive city; its total area, a fifth of which has been excavated, is generally stated to be between 150 and 200 ha (hectares), although the German archaeologist Michael Jansen, who conducted a detailed research on the city's urbanism, leans towards 300 ha,[17] which would make it possibly the largest city of the ancient world. Harappa was about half that size. Other cities and towns (Fig. 4.2) include Rakhigarhi (over 105 ha) and Banawali (10 ha), both in Haryana, Kalibangan in Rajasthan (12 ha), and, in Gujarat, Rangpur (possibly 50 ha), Lothal (7 ha) and Dholavira (48 ha within the fortified enclosures and perhaps as much outside). But quite a few still await the excavator's spade: Ganweriwala, for instance, in the Cholistan Desert, on the Hakra, is thought to extend over 80 ha.

Large cities have a special appeal to lovers of ancient civilizations, but they are not everything. Scattered throughout the hinterlands of Mohenjo-daro, Harappa, Kalibangan and Lothal, hundreds

---

* I will not trouble the reader with the complex debates among archaeologists on questions of terminology. For them, terms such as 'civilization', 'culture', 'tradition', 'city', 'era', 'phase', 'age', etc., have specialized meanings, though unanimity on their usage is rare. I use those terms in accordance with their common acceptance, which is enough for our limited purpose.

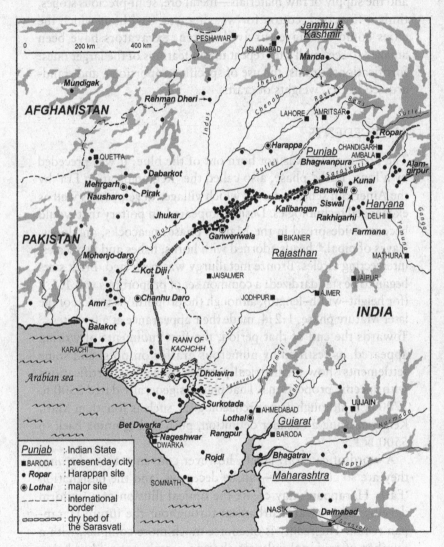

Fig. 4.2. The main sites of the Indus civilization. The Sarasvatī river (in a segmented line) follows the course of the Ghaggar–Hakra. Note the density of sites in the Sarasvatī basin, particularly in the Cholistan Desert of Pakistan.

of smaller towns and villages ensured the agricultural production and the supply of raw materials—metal ore, semi-precious stones, timber, firewood, cotton for weaving, etc.—without which the cities could not have survived. Often, excavators have been amazed to see small sites repeat urban features of the larger ones: fortifications, drains, the use of specific proportions, and standardized bricks, weights or crafts.

ANTECEDENTS

The urban phase was not born out of the blue; it was preceded by a long 'Early' phase, also called the 'Regionalization Era' by the American school, during which villages developed as well as exchanged technologies. Designs appeared on pottery that would become widespread in the Mature phase: peacocks, antelopes, leaves of pipal,* heads adorned with horns, fishes and fish scales, intersecting circles. Bronze metallurgy was perfected. Brick sizes began to be standardized: a common set of proportions was 1:2:3 (for height–width–length), although the proportions typical of the later Mature phase, 1:2:4, made their appearance at a few sites.[18] Towards the end of that period, the first rudiments of writing appeared, as testified by numerous graffiti on pots, and some settlements show geometrical patterns as well as fortifications with specific proportions. That phase is generally dated 3500 to 2700 BCE, although some archaeologists, such as Jonathan Mark Kenoyer, using a broader definition, push its beginning back to 5500 BCE.[19]

A word of caution: labels, however convenient—or *because* they are so convenient—can be deceptive, and the designation 'Early Harappan' may create the optical illusion of a uniform development towards urbanism throughout the future Harappan realm. The reality is of course much more complex, with a number of regional cultures sharing certain traits, but being

---

* Also spelt 'peepal' or 'peepul'. It is *Ficus religiosa*, India's sacred fig tree, commonly found in temples or near shrines.

distinct from each other in many respects: the 'Early Harappan' pottery styles in, say, Cholistan differ from those in Baluchistan, which is why archaeologists prefer to give them their specific names and speak of Amri-Nal, Kot-Diji or Sothi-Siswal cultures, among others. What matters to us is the process of convergence of those regional cultures, which culminates in the urban phase— 'cultural convergence'[20] is indeed the term used for this transition by Raymond and Bridget Allchin, two British archaeologists who have spent decades exploring the subcontinent. Jim Shaffer and Diane Lichtenstein call it 'fusion'.[21]

However valid those two terms may be, there were also striking innovations at the start of the urban phase in every field, from architecture to technologies and crafts. The most radical departure is probably in town planning, and it often seems as if the Mature Harappans wished to start with a clean slate: almost half of the sites were established at virgin locations; elsewhere, for instance, at Kalibangan or Dholavira, older structures and plans were altered to the new standards; and at a few places, such as Kot-Diji, Nausharo or Amri, layers of ash suggest that the old settlement was simply set on fire to make room for the new (as we may assume from the absence of any sign of conflict). 'Change in continuity' is probably the best way to summarize the transition from the Early to the Mature Harappan phase.

But even the 'Early' phase was not the earliest. In the 1960s, the French Archaeological Mission in Pakistan identified an important site in Baluchistan: Mehrgarh, strategically located at the foot of the Bolan Pass, named after the Bolan river, which cuts across the overhanging Kirthar hills, and which probably carried away part of the site in the past millennia. Mehrgarh, spread over some 250 ha, came to life around 7000 BCE, four millennia before the Indus cities. According to Jean-François Jarrige, who directed the excavations, it saw the emergence of agriculture-based communities, and 'a veritable agricultural economy solidly established as early as 6000 BCE'.[22] Indeed, extensive compartmentalized buildings for grain storage speak of a strong community organization controlling harvested grain and its distribution. That was the time when staple cereals such as wheat and barley were domesticated, along with sheep, goats and cattle (also the faithful dog). Importantly, right from the Neolithic epoch, the Indus plains saw the establishment of 'long-distance trade networks',[23] evidenced at Mehrgarh by the presence of exotic materials such as conch shell (fashioned into bangles), lapis lazuli and other semi-precious stones.

Although Mehrgarh is, for the moment, one of its kind, Neolithic antecedents leading up to the Harappan culture may yet come to light elsewhere. The newly explored site of Bhirrana in Haryana, for instance, has produced several radiocarbon dates in or before the fifth millennium;[24] if confirmed, they would open new horizons on the antecedents of Harappan culture in the Sarasvatī basin.

Table 4.2. Chronology of the Indus civilization according to the recent views of a few archaeologists (all dates are BCE).

Phase	Chakrabarti[25]	Kenoyer[26]	Possehl[27]
Early Harappan	3500–2700	5500–2600*	3200–2600
Mature Harappan	2700–2000	2600–1900	2500–1900
Late Harappan	2000–1300	1900–1300	1900–1300

AFTER THE COLLAPSE

Some five millennia thus elapsed from the earliest antecedents at Mehrgarh to the collapse of the urban order around 1900 BCE (Table 4.2). But contrary to earlier assumptions, the Harappan tradition did not vanish overnight; rather, it scattered over hundreds of generally smaller sites, some of which lasted till about 1300 BCE or even later: that is the Late Harappan phase or the 'Localization Era'. (Here again, lumped together under these labels are many regional cultures, such as Cemetery H, Jhukar,

---

* See p. 96 for Kenoyer's initial date for the Early Harappan phase.

Pirak, Lustrous Red Ware, etc.) A few sites even show continuous occupation right into the historical age (first millennium BCE): Pirak, for instance, near Mehrgarh, was occupied from 1800 to 700 BCE; according to Jarrige, again, this site reveals 'a real continuity with the older periods in many fields, but also a number of phenomena clearly marking the start of a new age'.[28]

We will glance at the new age later; we first need to explore further the Indus age in its maturity. Let us turn for a while into citizens of a Harappan city, walk through the busy streets, and indulge in some sightseeing.

5

The Indus Cities

The most conspicuous trait of the Indus civilization—and the one that so struck its early explorers—was the sophistication of its urbanism. Most towns, big or small, were fortified and divided into distinct zones. The acropolis ('upper city' in Greek), often also called 'citadel', usually had larger buildings and wider spaces. In the lower town, houses were more tightly packed together. (In Chapter 7, we will visit a spectacular exception to this neat upper/lower town dichotomy.)

Mohenjo-daro's acropolis (Fig. 5.1), measuring about 200 x 400 m, is majestic by any standard. It boasts the famous complex of the 'great bath' with its central pool used for ritual ablutions, a huge 'college', a 'granary', an 'assembly hall' (or 'pillared hall'), and wide streets carefully aligned along the cardinal directions. We may allow ourselves to conjure up the ruler or rulers meeting in some of those spacious halls along with officials, traders and, perhaps, on special occasions, representatives of the main craft traditions: builders, potters, seal makers, metal workers or weavers. Except, perhaps, for the actual rulers or high officials, the rest lived not in the acropolis but in the lower town, where a much denser network of streets and lanes led to hundreds of houses, with the larger ones often found side by side with the smaller ones (Fig. 5.2).

Harappa presents a more complex picture with four mounds, some of which were surrounded by walls as thick as 14 m at the base, with impressive gateways controlling access to the city. Unfortunately, the site was too badly plundered to give us a fair idea of the overall plan of the fortifications, except in the case

of the acropolis ('mound AB', Fig. 5.3), which interestingly has
the same dimensions as Mohenjo-daro's: about 400 x 200 m.
There are fewer large structures in Harappa than at Mohenjo-
daro, the main one being an imposing 'granary', 50 x 40 m,
consisting of two rows of six large rooms (6 x 15 m each). As
far as excavations have shown, the four mounds were occupied
simultaneously and formed a single city.

One thing to note is that designations like 'citadel', 'college',
'assembly hall' or 'granary' used in the preceding paragraphs are,
quite simply, arbitrary. Most of them were proposed by the British
archaeologist R.E. Mortimer Wheeler. Given the charge of the
Archaeological Survey of India in 1944, when he was a brigadier
in the British army fighting in North Africa, he revived the ASI
and institutionalized a more rigorous stratigraphic method
designed to record a site's evolution period after period. Irascible
but magnanimous, theatrical but hard-working, Wheeler energetically put his stamp on Indian archaeology. But having
received his archaeological training in the context of the Roman
Empire, he transferred its terminology wholesale to the Harappan
cities, which thus became peppered with 'citadels', 'granaries',
'colleges', 'defence walls', etc., when no one, in reality, had a clue
to the precise purpose of the massive structures that had emerged
from the thick layers of accumulated mud.

In recent years, for instance, some archaeologists have disputed
the existence of huge granaries such as those identified by Wheeler
at Mohenjo-daro and Harappa, pointing out that there is no
hard evidence for such an identification, and that in the region,
grain was traditionally stored in bins.[1] Also, it is less than clear
whether the massive 'citadels' and fortifications had a military
purpose, as we will discuss shortly.

None of the larger structures (Mohenjo-daro's 'college' measures
70 x 24 m!) were clearly palaces, either. Unlike in ancient Egypt
or Mesopotamia, where the residence of the pharaoh or king is
conspicuous enough, Indus cities do not seem to have assigned
magnified quarters to their rulers. Rather, a concern for the
ordinary citizen is what impressed the early archaeologists.

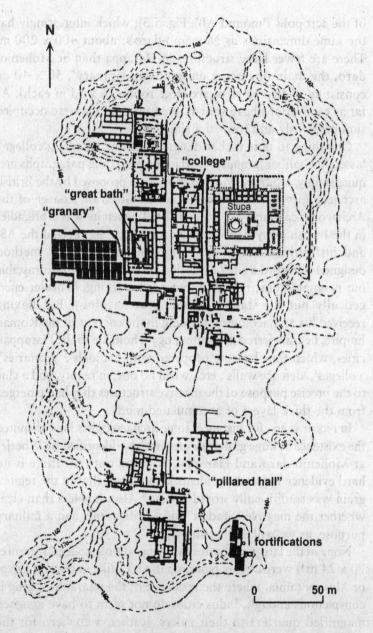

Fig. 5.1. Mohenjo-daro's acropolis, with the main structures. (© ASI)

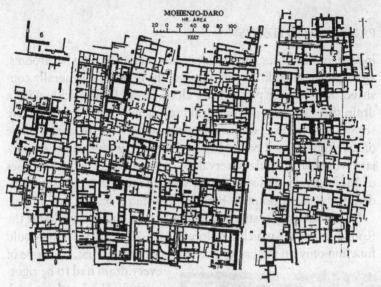

Fig. 5.2. An area of Mohenjo-daro's lower town. (© ASI)

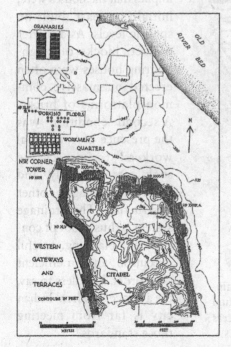

Fig. 5.3. A part of Harappa's 'mound AB' (acropolis) and adjoining structures, with the 'granary' at the northern end. (© ASI)

PAMPERED CITIZENS

Indeed, most houses, even modest ones, had their own bathrooms, an unprecedented luxury in that age; the bathroom generally consisted of a sloping platform of close-fitting fired bricks, with a drain through the outer wall taking waste waters to a collective sewer; this, in turn, was connected to a network of drains made of carefully aligned baked bricks (Fig. 5.4), with cesspits or soak jars provided at regular intervals to collect sullage. In a few houses of Mohenjo-daro's lower town, vertical terracotta pipes embedded in the walls point to bathrooms located on the first floor!

Such a sanitary system, unrivalled in the ancient world till the Roman Empire—which developed some 2000 years later—could function only on the basis of certain conditions. First, the slope of every drain had to be rigorously calculated, which implies that the houses were, initially at least, built on specific levels. As a matter of fact, blocks of neighbouring houses were often erected on massive common platforms of bricks. A second condition was the presence of 'municipal workers' to inspect the soak pits regularly and remove the sullage or other obstruction. The drainage system is thus proof of considerable planning, careful execution, and an efficient civic order. Needless to say, the average 'modern' Indian city is far from meeting those standards!

Fig. 5.4. A part of Lothal's drainage system; from the individual bathing platforms, used waters flowed out of the town. (© ASI)

A third essential condition was the availability of plentiful water supply. The solutions for ensuring this varied from city to city: Mohenjo-daro had an estimated 600 to 700 wells, a huge number by today's standards, and Michael Jansen[2] calculated that an inhabitant of that city could get water at an average distance of 35 m, again something that his or her counterpart in the less privileged parts of our cities can only dream of. The cylindrical wells, 15 to 20 m deep, were carefully constructed with special trapezoid (that is, wedge-shaped) bricks (Fig. 5.5); owing to their shape, the bricks would lock together if water or loose soil pressed on the well's outer sides—a remarkably ingenious solution to the problem of inward collapse that plagues stone wells. 'Two thousand years later,' Jansen remarks, 'even the Romans usually used rectangular linings (mostly made of wood) which often collapsed due to the enormous pressure of the soil.'[3] Harappa had fewer wells and probably used a large reservoir, while Dholavira diverted water from two neighbouring streams through a series of dams, and preserved it in a complex system of reservoirs. Clearly, Harappans valued both water and cleanliness.

In addition, there is evidence of privies in many houses, and garbage bins in the streets where citizens would come and dump their household refuse. Again, neither could have remained in working order without efficient civic authorities.

Houses were generally built with bricks, sun-dried or kiln-fired

Fig. 5.5. A typical Harappan cylindrical well with trapezoid bricks (Mohenjo-daro). (© ASI)

(mostly the latter at Mohenjo-daro). I have already mentioned the usual ratios of their dimensions, 1:2:4, found in many brick sizes: 7x14x28 cm most commonly for houses, and 10x20x40 cm or a little more for city walls. Such bricks are very close in size and proportion to our modern bricks, in contrast to the bricks of the historical era, which were generally larger and more squarish. Amusingly, this misled some of the early explorers (and brick robbers) of Indus cities into believing that the ruins lying below their feet must have been fairly recent[4]—a small error of judgement of some four millennia!

The walls of houses were usually 70 cm thick, which points to one, sometimes possibly two, upper storeys. Larger houses—with as many as seven rooms on the ground floor—probably belonged to rich traders or officials, but are often found next to much more modest dwellings.

Writing in 1926, as he was beginning his own large-scale excavation at Mohenjo-daro, Marshall's imagination was fired by the realization that the city testified to 'a social condition of the people far in advance of what was then prevailing in Mesopotamia and Egypt'.[5] Five years later, he summed up his impression of the care lavished on the average Indus citizen:

> There is nothing that we know of in pre-historic Egypt or Mesopotamia or anywhere else in Western Asia to compare with the well-built baths and commodious houses of the citizens of Mohenjo-daro. In those countries, much money and thought were lavished on the building of magnificent temples for the gods and on the palaces and tombs of kings, but the rest of the people seemingly had to content themselves with insignificant dwellings of mud. In the Indus Valley, the picture is reversed and the finest structures are those erected for the convenience of the citizens.[6]

A PROSPEROUS CIVILIZATION

During its Mature phase, the Indus civilization had, from all available evidence, a flourishing and varied industry. Towns, both big and small, had manufacturing units: smithies for the production of copper and bronze tools, weapons and other objects; kilns for the firing of bricks and pots; workshops for the cutting of stone tools and the manufacture of beads and other ornaments; and also units for potters, carpenters, weavers or seal makers. Many of those activities depended on materials that were not available locally and, therefore, on a brisk internal trade: copper and tin, gold and silver, semi-precious stones, timber and cotton must have been among the most valued commodities. Such exchanges necessarily involved diverse communities, some specialized in the extraction of metal ore or semi-precious stones, others in agriculture or in transport along the waterways; in fact, for centuries or more, today's fishing community of the Mohanas (or Muhannas) has been engaged in this last activity along the Indus. It is even likely that nomadic groups took part in the movements of resources and helped establish trade routes between distant regions.

Indeed, a striking trait of the Harappan character is an eagerness to reach out (Fig. 5.6): we have already noted a few outposts along the Makran coast as well as in Afghanistan, but merchant colonies were most likely established in Oman (called Magan in ancient times), Bahrain (ancient Dilmun), and Failakah (an island of Kuwait, also part of Dilmun). In all those places, evidences of Mature Harappan pottery, seals, beads, weights and other objects (such as combs of ivory) have surfaced in recent decades, some of them going back to 2500 BCE or, possibly, a few centuries earlier.[7]

Further up, Ur, Kish and other Mesopotamian sites, as well as Elam's Susa, have together yielded some forty Indus seals. Besides other Harappan articles, characteristic long carnelian beads as well as shorter beads with designs of white lines bleached onto the surface (or 'etched beads') were found in Ur's royal cemetery. It appears that Mesopotamian rulers were particularly fond of Harappan jewellery. But not just that: Mesopotamian tablets mention wood, copper, tin, carnelian, shell, ivory, as well as peacocks and monkeys, as coming from a region called 'Meluhha'. The listed items fit perfectly with goods from the Indus civilization, which is why most scholars have identified 'Meluhha' with it. The illustrious founder of the Akkadian dynasty, Sargon, who ruled in the twenty-third century BCE, proudly recorded in tablets how ships from Dilmun, Magan and Meluhha, richly loaded with exotic goods, would lay anchor at the harbour of his capital Akkad, which was, at least, 300 km upstream from Ur on the Euphrates. Ur being the usual port for disembarkation, this additional journey points to the special importance or prestige attached to the merchandise brought from these distant regions.[8]

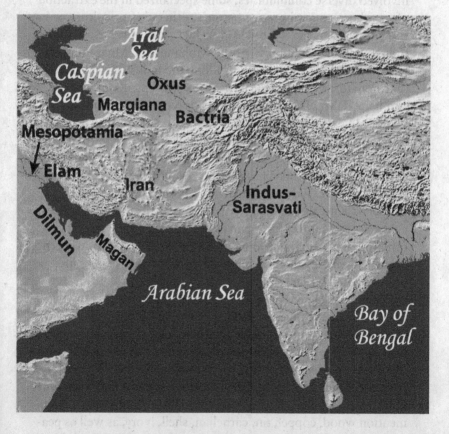

Fig. 5.6. Sphere of interaction among several Bronze Age civilizations of the third millennium BCE. (See timeline in Table 4.1.)

The evidence, however, is strangely one-sided: hardly any object of Mesopotamian origin has emerged from the Indus cities. Various hypotheses have been advanced about the raw materials or finished goods, perishable or not, that Harappan traders might have brought back home, with guesses ranging from silver and copper to wool, incense and dates; but without firm evidence, they remain guesses. Let us hope that some Harappan shipwreck will, one day, emerge from the Persian Gulf.

Archaeologists also disagree on how far this external trade might have contributed to the overall prosperity of Harappan society, but it does seem likely that workshops or small industrial settlements were set up particularly for the export of goods, especially along the coast. This seems to have been the chief function of Balakot, a small site west of the Indus delta which specialized in shell bangles, or of the town of Lothal (near Ahmedabad), and it might be the reason why Dholavira, a major production centre of beads and other crafts, was located in the Rann of Kachchh. Some scholars have also argued that small colonies for the manufacture of trade goods must have been located right in Dilmun, or even in Mesopotamia.

Although no directly Mesopotamian artefact has been found in the Indus civilization, a few objects (such as cylinder seals from Mohenjo-daro or Kalibangan) and art motifs (notably a deity controlling two standing tigers) reflect some Mesopotamian influence and confirm long-standing contacts. In the opinion of the archaeologist Dilip Chakrabarti, 'this contact lasted from c. 2600 BC—1300 BC';[9] the first date, which emerged from the Royal Cemetery of Ur, neatly coincides with the beginning of the Mature Harappan phase. Recent finds of remains of seafaring boats in Kuwait, dated to the six millennium BCE,[10] suggest that contacts with the region may have started much earlier, but precise evidence is lacking.

Traders are thought to have followed a sea route that hugged the Makran coast and, with likely halts in Oman and Bahrain, continued all the way to the top of the Persian Gulf—a 2500-km voyage that implies no mean ship-making and sailing skills. While flat-bottomed river boats have been depicted on a few seals and tablets, nothing is known of the Harappan seafaring boats or ships.

Sea voyages always tickle the imagination, but we can also visualize picturesque multi-ethnic caravans plodding rugged overland routes through today's Afghanistan and Iran. Starting from Mohenjo-daro and climbing the Bolan Pass, merchants, perhaps guided by nomads, would have crossed into the basin of the Helmand river and reached, among other cities, Mundigak, not far from today's Kandahar. Excavated in the 1950s by the French archaeologist Jean-Marie Casal, Mundigak revealed evidence of Harappan contact, such as humped bulls and pipal leaves painted on pottery.[11] It would have been one of the several starting points towards the Iranian plateau, and Harappan artefacts have indeed come up at many Iranian sites,[12] such as Tepe Yahya, Shahdad, Hissar, Shah Tepe—or at the fascinating site recently discovered near the southeastern city of Jiroft, where impressions of Indus seals and carnelian beads have been recovered in substantial numbers.[13]

Strangely, however, as with Mesopotamia, almost no artefacts of clearly Iranian origin made their way to the Indus region. 'Nearly all the evidence of Harappan relations with the West has been brought to light in foreign territories (the Persian Gulf, Mesopotamia, Iran) and *not* in the Indus territories,'[14] as another French archaeologist, Henri-Paul Francfort, put it. There is no consensus among experts to explain this one-sidedness.

The Harappans adventured not just westward, but also northward. Their presence is visible in the ancient region of Bactria, on the northwestern flank of the Hindu Kush mountain range (Fig. 5.6). We mentioned Shortughai earlier, on the Amu Darya, explored under Francfort's direction; apart from the likely exploitation of lapis lazuli mines, its location far removed from the Harappan heartland suggests that it may also have been a stage in a westward outreach. Indeed, there are signs of Harappan presence as far as Altyn Tepe, Gonur or Namazga Tepe in Margiana (in today's Turkmenistan, to the east of the Caspian Sea), and as early as the end of the fourth millennium BCE—in other words, four or five centuries *before* the start of the urban phase.[15] This is an important confirmation of long-standing contacts between faraway regions. Those cities bordering Turkmenistan's Karakum Desert belong to a different civilization altogether, called the 'Oxus civilization' or the 'Bactria–Margiana Archaeological Complex' (BMAC), which the Harappans were clearly interacting with, as they were with Dilmun, Magan, Mesopotamia and the Iranian plateau. All those civilizations were, in turn, in contact with each other: globalization is not exactly a new concept!

But here again, while Bactria's presence is visible along the borderlands of the Indus civilization (especially towards the end of the Mature phase), artefacts from Margiana are non-existent. This broad unidirectionality—from the Indus outward—may be interpreted in different ways, but it does suggest that the Harappans were the ones who took the initiative to reach out.

ARTS AND CRAFTS

The trademark Harappan long and slender beads of carnelian, so prized in Mesopotamia, actually involved a technological feat: the length-wise drilling of a small hole for the string, which was done over several days of hard work with drill bits of a specially hardened synthetic stone. Other beads were made of agate, amethyst, turquoise or lapis lazuli; combined with disks and fillets in gold or silver, they permitted the creation of a great variety of ornaments. Bangles constituted another category of highly prized ornaments, whether made of gold, bronze, conch shell, glazed faience or humble terracotta. Many statuettes of women wearing bangles have been unearthed, giving us a fair idea of the various ways in which they were worn. Some of the small sites were wholly dedicated to the bangle industry, perhaps even created for it—for instance, in the coastal areas of Gujarat where shell was easily available.

Harappans produced pottery in large quantities (Fig. 5.7), something archaeologists are grateful for, since almost all objects of a perishable nature (wood, cloth, reed, etc.) have disappeared without a trace in the climate of the Northwest—and, along with

Fig. 5.7. A Harappan painted pot with motifs of intersecting circles, pipal leaves, birds and hatching (Harappa, cemetery R 37). (© ASI)

them, a whole chunk of Harappan life. Wheel-made and kiln-fired pottery is generally distinguished by designs painted in black on a red background, although numerous variations exist; among the most typical designs are geometric ones such as intersecting circles, fish scales, wavy lines, etc., and realistic ones like pipal leaves, fishes, peacocks, deer or bulls.

This brief survey by no means exhausts the list of crafts: weavers used wheel-spun thread and, besides cotton, evidence of silk came to light recently at two sites;[16] other craftsmen excelled at stone and ivory carving, carpet-making, inlaid woodwork and decorative architecture.

Bronze has been mentioned a few times as one of the pillars of urban development, and Harappans procured its main ingredient—copper —from mines in Baluchistan and Rajasthan, perhaps through nomads or non-Harappan communities specializing in its extraction. Ingots of smelted copper ore were transported to the smithies located in the towns and cities, where they were purified. Many objects were made directly from pure copper, but a variety of alloys were created through the natural or deliberate addition of tin (for bronze), lead, nickel or zinc; arsenic was another additive, used mostly to make tools with sharper edges. Although a precise understanding of the processes involved remains to be worked out, Harappan coppersmiths must have experimented for centuries before they found the right techniques and proportions to forge bronze chisels that were hard enough to dress stones (on a massive scale at Dholavira), or saws that could neatly cut hard conch shells. They made many other bronze objects, from axes to vessels, razors to mirrors, spears to arrowheads. Some less utilitarian applications included bronze statuettes cast with the 'lost wax' technique, such as the famous 'dancing girl' (Fig. 5.8).[17]

Agriculture was another pillar of the urban order, and was perfected not over centuries, but over millennia, as we saw at Mehrgarh. At some point, though probably not everywhere at the same time, ploughing and intensive techniques such as intercropping came into play. At Kalibangan, for instance (Fig. 5.9), excavators found a field of the pre-urban period (around 2800 BCE) with an ingenious double network of perpendicular furrows: the

Fig. 5.8. The 'dancing girl', a bronze figurine from Mohenjo-daro. (© ASI)

Fig. 5.9. Kalibangan's 4800-year-old ploughed field. (© ASI)

long ones were spaced out in a north–south direction and sown with taller crops (such as mustard); that way their longer shadows, cast mid-day during the winter season, did not fall on the shorter plants (such as gram) that were grown in the east–west furrows.[18] The major crops were barley and wheat (grown in winter), along with various millets (grown during the summer monsoon), vegetables and grapevine—whether for the grapes themselves or for some sort of wine is unclear. Rice has been found at a few sites in Gujarat, and also at Harappa and in Cholistan,[19] but was probably not a frequent or regular crop. Hunting and fishing supplemented agriculture; in fact, Harappans were so fond of fish that they had dried saltwater fish transported all the way from settlements by the Arabian Sea to Harappa! Domestication of cattle, sheep, goats and fowls began millennia before the Mature phase, at least in the Mehrgarh region. All in all, Harappans seemed to have had a diverse diet. Cotton was an important crop throughout the region, and fed the textile cottage industry.

Naturally enough, Harappan life had room for dancing, painting, sculpture and music; there is, for instance, some evidence of drums and stringed instruments, and several statuettes are frozen in dance postures—not the 'dancing girl', ironically, whose jaunty stance is actually static. Drama is suggested by a number of expressive masks, and puppet shows were probably a treat for the young and not-so-young. The Harappans indulged in a possible ancestor of the game of chess, as evidenced by one terracotta set of chessmen found at Lothal (Fig. 5.10). Other kinds of gaming

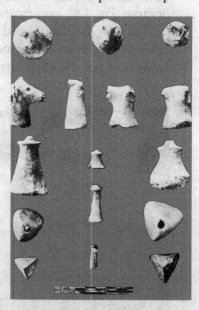

Fig. 5.10. A possible ancestor of the game of chess, found at Lothal. (© ASI)

boards and pieces have come up at several sites, as well as cubical dice almost identical to those used today. Children were not neglected, judging from the exquisite care with which craftsmen fashioned toy oxcarts and figurines, spinning tops, marbles, rattles and whistles. And they could also amuse themselves with pet dogs and monkeys, possibly pet squirrels and birds too, many of which have been depicted in figurines.

Harappan women appear to have enjoyed a status of some importance, as the terracotta figurines depicting them are far more numerous than those depicting men. Some figurines portray women in daily occupations, kneading dough or suckling a baby, sometimes also in comical postures that archaeologists are not quite sure how to interpret. But another category evokes a religious context, and we will turn to it when we probe Harappan religion.

One of the persisting riddles of this civilization is its writing system, which appears fully developed at the start of the Mature period, although on earlier pottery some signs were written singly or in groups of two or three. Indus signs, as they are called, have been found carefully engraved not only on some 3500 steatite seals of the same type as those Marshall and his colleagues had marvelled at, but also on hundreds of terracotta tablets, a few of copper and silver, pottery and ornaments, among other media. Unfortunately, none of the numerous proposed decipherments has received wide acceptance: an entire aspect of Harappan life remains closed to us.

Even the purpose of the seals is debated: a few impressions on soft clay have shown that they were sometimes used to seal and identify bales of goods being shipped; but with little or no sign of wear and tear, most seem to have been kinds of 'identity cards'. Their occasional use as amulets is also not ruled out. Did they represent a clan (symbolized by the animal depicted on many seals), a city or region, a community, a ruler, a trader, a type of goods, a deity, or a combination of these? We have only question marks here. At least we know that the seals were fired for several days in special kilns that reached a temperature of 1000°C, making them hard enough to give repeated impressions on soft clay; such an expense of time and labour shows the importance attached to those mysterious objects.

In all the daily activities of the craftsman, the brick-maker or the humble drain cleaner, what stands out is care and a sense of organization. This is not a 'spectacular' civilization; as a matter of fact, early archaeologists, especially European ones, complained at times of its 'monotony': no great pyramid, no glorious tomb, no awe-inspiring palace or temple, no breathtaking fresco or monumental sculpture. But there is certainly an all-pervading sense of order: weights, seals or bricks were standardized, wells and drains were maintained for centuries, streets and public spaces were kept free from encroachments (something, again, almost unthinkable in today's India!).

A HARAPPAN EMPIRE?

If the Indus civilization did not build pyramids, it left behind a few sphinx-like riddles for us to ponder on, besides the script. Perhaps the most puzzling of them is: Who determined or imposed this order? Who controlled and coordinated urban structures, access to raw materials, industries, trade and agriculture? Who made sure that weights from the banks of the Yamunā to Gujarat and Baluchistan had the same values, or that bricks respected the same proportions? Everyone agrees that civic authorities were unusually efficient—but also unusually discreet, to the point that they left no direct evidence of themselves.

Influenced by the formation of great empires in Egypt, Mesopotamia, Persia and Rome, many early archaeologists spoke of an 'Indus Empire', with Mohenjo-daro as its capital. That broadly remains the view of Raymond and Bridget Allchin: they visualize a 'forgotten Indian leader' who, around 2600 BCE, unified the Indus heartland in order to control the trade with Mesopotamia.[20] But the hypothetical 'Indian leader' apart, this theory of a 'centralized state power'[21] runs into serious difficulties.

The first is the enormous distances involved, over 2000 km from east to west or north to south if we look at the remotest sites. Even if rivers, when navigable, permitted fairly quick communication between important sites, many of the outlying settlements had to be reached by bullock cart: it would have taken many days to carry an order from Mohenjo-daro to remote settlements in Haryana or Punjab. Such a far-flung 'empire' would have been fragile and unmanageable without a strong military control, for which no evidence exists.

A second problem is the surprising absence of any obvious depiction of a ruler, emperor or king or chieftain, or again of any structure recognizable as a palace or a royal tomb. The Allchins themselves acknowledge that 'the relative invisibility of royalty, with all its claptrap and accoutrements, in the Harappan state, stands in marked contrast to the prominence of these features in Egypt or Mesopotamia.'[22] For some reason, here the ruling class did not seek to deify or glorify itself, and J.-F. Jarrige suggests that 'the absence of a truly royal iconography in the Indus world is already an Indian trait'.[23] Indeed, as pointed out by D.K. Chakrabarti, there is no contemporary depiction of the Mauryan emperor Ashoka, and were it not for his edicts inscribed on stone, archaeology would have had very little to show for his existence. Chakrabarti thus makes the point that the 'value system' of Indian kings 'was different and the royal power was also tempered by an ideal of duty'.[24] Third, to suggest that the Harappan state rose in response to the Mesopotamian trade appears artificial. Most of the basic ingredients of Harappan urbanism—fortifications, standardized brick ratios, drains, metal and bead industries, internal and external trade, seals, even writing—can be found in earlier phases, albeit embryonic, scattered or fragmented and were, in any case, converging. And, again, the benefits the Harappans derived from their external trade remain unidentified.

Alternative models have therefore been put forward. At the other end of the spectrum, Jim Shaffer and Diane Lichtenstein proposed that the Harappans 'do not appear to have developed a centralized structure based on hereditary elites'. Their society was rather 'a complex cultural mosaic of related but distinct ethnic groups',[25] and amounted to a delicate assemblage of neighbouring chiefdoms, which does not quite meet the standard of a 'state'. Gregory Possehl agrees with this model and proposes up to nine 'domains' centred around five major cities: Mohenjo-daro, Harappa, Ganweriwala (in Cholistan), Rakhigarhi (in Haryana) and Dholavira (in the Rann of Kachchh); the political structure, in his view, was a corporate one consisting of 'a series of "councils" or gathering of leaders, rather than a king'.[26]

B.B. Lal, the doyen of Indian archaeologists, excavator at Kalibangan and author of one of the most complete studies of the civilization,[27] also proposes distinct Harappan regions, counting eight of them, but sees in them a parallel with the *Mahājanapadas*, the sixteen 'proto-republics' of early historical times, some two millennia later; in this perspective, the Harappan regions would turn into many states.[28] We would have, in effect, a confederacy of regional powers sharing a common culture and common trade interests, but each with its own regional stamp, which would explain variations that have come to light in terms of the pottery styles or religious practices. Chakrabarti favours a similar picture of 'multiple kingdoms centred around the major settlements of the region'.[29]

J.M. Kenoyer, who spent many years excavating at Harappa, develops a parallel model of city-states.[30] In his view,

> the Indus state was composed of several competing classes of elites who maintained different levels of control over the vast regions of the Indus and Ghaggar–Hakra Valley. Instead of one social group with absolute control, the rulers or dominant members in the various cities would have included merchants, ritual specialists, and individuals who controlled resources such as land, livestock, and raw materials. These groups may have had different means of control, but they shared a common ideology and economic system as repre-sented by seals, ornaments, ceramics, and other artifacts.[31]

Even if the said elites, which probably occupied Mohenjo-daro's and Kalibangan's 'citadels' or Dholavira's massive 'castle', were indeed 'competing', it was clearly in a context of cooperation for mutual benefit. Thus, in Kenoyer's view, trade and religion, rather than military might, were the real instruments of authority; indeed, no piece of Harappan art glorifies rulers, conquest or warfare.[32]

Another US archaeologist, Rita Wright, emphasizes 'a growing awareness that [the Harappan civilization] does not fit into the social, political and economic categories developed for the study of other states', such as Mesopotamia or Egypt, which had centralized administrative structures. 'Among the Harappans, on the other hand, a pattern of decentralization appears to have persisted.' In the formative era, Wright also notes 'an absence of factionalism' and 'a unified material culture', which, to her, point to 'production and distribution systems based upon kinship or community-related organization'.[33] She suggests, in effect, that such a system could have persisted in the urban period.

Whether it was an empire or a confederacy of chiefdoms or city-states, this civilization thus displays an individuality of its own based on decentralization and a community-based distribution of power—two traits that any rural Indian of today will instantly relate to. It also permitted regional variations while integrating them in an overarching cultural framework. Though not spectacular at first glance, this 'unity in diversity', a third typical Indian trait, was to have profound repercussions on the history of the subcontinent. The archaeologist D.P. Agrawal puts it this way:

> In a third millennium context, when communication and transport must have been difficult, the credit for unifying the north and west of the subcontinent goes to the Harappans. They were the first to achieve this unification of a society with so much diversity.[34]

A PEACEFUL REALM?

Kenoyer's reference above to the invisibility of 'military might' brings us to a second riddle. Archaeologists who first dug at Harappa or Mohenjo-daro were used to glorious depictions of warfare and conquest found all over ancient Sumer, Egypt, China or Greece. To their great puzzlement, nothing of the sort emerged from Mohenjo-daro's dust: no sign of military structure; not a single helmet or shield; not a trace of armed conflict at any point of time; no seal or jar depicting a battle, a captive or a victor. This apparently unnatural pattern repeated itself in site after site. The British archaeologist Jane McIntosh, who recently authored a book on the Indus civilization entitled *A Peaceful Realm*, explains her chosen title thus:

> One of the most surprising aspects of the Indus Civilization is that it seems to have been a land without conflict. There are no signs of violence and no depictions of soldiers or warfare in the Indus art. When we look at the other civilizations we can see how unusual and unexpected this is.[35]

As unusual as the rulers' invisibility, this double riddle will long remain unsolved, but it is doubtless intimately linked to the values central to Harappan culture.

True, a few bronze weapons, mostly spearheads and arrowheads, have been found, but we know that the Harappans practised hunting. Archaeologists have also pointed out that without a central ridge for reinforcement, the spearheads would have made for rather ineffectual weapons—perhaps they were largely ceremonial, or intended for sentries who controlled the flow of goods at the city gates.

Also, as I explained earlier, terms like 'citadel' or 'defence walls' give a warlike slant to those structures. But apart from the absence of evidence of warfare, the massive fortifications that define many of the cities and towns would actually have made poor defences.[36] Of course, outer fortifications would have guarded against local tribes or marauders. But in all likelihood, their real purpose was three-fold: to provide protection against floods to which some sites (such as Mohenjo-daro or Lothal) were certainly prone; to control the movement of goods coming into or leaving the city; and to define the urban space in tune with certain sacred concepts (which we will return to in Chapter 10).

Lest this picture of a prosperous, orderly, industrious and peaceful civilization appear too rosy, we must remember that it remains very incomplete: less than 10 per cent of the 1140 known Mature Harappan sites have been substantially excavated,[37] and the figure drops below 5 per cent if we include all the phases. This leaves most of them buried with their secrets, including a few giant ones such as Ganweriwala in Cholistan or Pathani Damb in Baluchistan. Despite eight decades of hard work, our understanding of this civilization is still in its 'early phase'.

Regrettably, in today's India and Pakistan (let us forget Afghanistan), archaeology, afflicted by bureaucratic red tape, limited resources and obsolete methods, is not viewed as a priority. What made the Indus civilization tick, in close interaction with neighbouring civilizations yet so different from them, will long remain as inscrutable as the Sphinx of Giza.

6

From the Indus
to the Sarasvatī

Textbooks often state that Mohenjo-daro and Harappa were the first sites of the Indus civilization to have been 'discovered'. That is not quite correct: they are, to be precise, the cities where the epoch and nature of this civilization were first identified. Before them, another site had been substantially explored: Kalibangan, in northern Rajasthan. About halfway between Hanumangarh and Suratgarh, the site lies on the left or southern bank of the Ghaggar river. We first discussed it in Chapter 3 in relation to geological studies of the Ghaggar's now dry bed, and it is time to return to the region and to the river, which though defunct, holds crucial information in store for us.

TESSITORI AT KALIBANGAN

In April 1917, four years before Sahni began excavating Harappa, Luigi Pio Tessitori, a young Italian Indologist who had come to India in 1914, started digging at Kalibangan. The story of his tragically short life has been vividly captured by Nayanjot Lahiri.[1] Well-versed in Sanskrit, Pali, Prakrit, Bengali and Hindi, apart from a few dialects of Rajasthani, Tessitori developed a sort of love affair with the rich bardic lore of Rajasthan. He started documenting oral and written chronicles of the states of Jodhpur and Bikaner, convinced that their critical study would help reconstruct a good deal of the history of the region. After Marshall took him into the Archaeological Survey, Tessitori, moving briskly across the sands of Bikaner, added to his documentation of bardic traditions the study of inscriptions and a survey of ancient mounds in the region—a heavy double assignment in view of the environment in which he worked: 'Distances between one village and another are often enormous, and the camel is the only means of conveyance available.'[2]

On camelback, therefore, Tessitori explored Bikaner:

> On February 16, 1918 I went to Suratagadha* [Suratgarh] again, to make from there a tour to the west and explore the ancient *theris*,[†] which my travellers had referred us being found in large numbers all along the dry bed of the Ghagghar. This river, locally known under the name of Hakaro or Sotara, but commonly referred to as the *nali* 'canal,' or *dariyava* 'sea,' irrigated in ancient times all the northern part of what now forms the territory of the Bikaner State, from Bhatanera [Bhatnir]—the modern Hanumanagadha [Hanumangarh] to Vijnora [Bijnor, close to the international border], and thence running across the territory of Bahawalpur, went to join the Indus.[3]

Except for the junction with the Indus (which Tessitori, of course, did not observe himself), his description agrees with those of his predecessors. And like some of them (notably Tod, Colvin and Mackeson), Tessitori did not use the name 'Sarasvatī': Bikaner's bardic lore did evoke a bygone age when the Ghaggar was flowing and bringing prosperity to the region, but it does not appear to have associated the river with the lost Sarasvatī (the same is true of the Hakra in Cholistan). That association was only found upstream, in today's Haryana, more precisely between Ad Badri and Pehowa.

His official duties apart, Tessitori must have felt especially attracted to those 'ancient *theris*':

---

* Tessitori made it a habit to Sanskritize the spellings of the places he visited; Kalibangan, for instance, would become 'Kala Vangu'.

† *Theri* or *ther* is the local word for 'mound'.

From the vestiges of antiquity which are still abundantly scattered along its bed, it is clear that the Ghagghar once bathed with its waters a florid and prosperous region. Now the bed is dry, and like an immense road of glaring whiteness, crosses a scene of desolation, which is only broken here and there by a small village built of mud, or a field of rape-seed. Otherwise the river bed is barren, a clean sheet of argil, slippery and impracticable to the camel in the rains, hard and intersected by cracks during the rest of the year, and on both its banks and sometimes even in the middle the ancient *theris* raise their heads all red with fragments of bricks and pottery.[4]

Two of those *theris* or mounds, near the village of Kalibangan, arrested Tessitori's attention (Fig. 6.1), and he wrote in his report that they contained 'vestiges of a very remote, if not prehistorical antiquity'[5]—a highly perceptive observation, when so little was known of India's prehistory. He also noted that the mounds had suffered from a massive plunder of bricks for the laying of a section of the Jodhpur–Bikaner railway—the same cynical brick-robbing that Cunningham had noted at Harappa a few decades earlier.

Tessitori's limited excavations at Kalibangan in 1917 and 1918 brought to light a few brick structures, pottery unrelated to known types, a cylindrical well of trapezoid bricks, stone flakes and three mysterious seals, two of them with unknown signs. Oddly, he chose to omit the seals from his report to Marshall; had he mentioned them, Marshall would very likely have made a connection with the black stone seal from Harappa published by Cunningham. We can indulge in the speculation that he might then have ordered further excavations at Kalibangan; had this happened, Tessitori would have been immortalized as the discoverer of a civilization called the 'Ghaggar civilization' or, perhaps, the 'Kalibangan civilization'!

Fate, however, decided otherwise. With his mother taken seriously ill, Tessitori had to leave for Italy abruptly; he reached home too late to see her alive. After a few months, he returned to India, but fell ill on the ship. Once in India, his condition worsened rapidly; he breathed his last in Bikaner in November 1919, and was buried there. He was barely thirty-two.

While in Italy, Tessitori had vainly tried to identify the signs on the Kalibangan seals, and Lahiri suggests that he must have finally made up his mind to show them to Marshall after his return to India. Death denied him that chance. With Tessitori leaving the most telling clues out of his report, Marshall never associated Kalibangan with the civilization unearthed at Harappa and Mohenjo-daro. For decades, the 'Indus Valley' remained the core area, actively investigated, while Kalibangan and other sites of the Ghaggar Valley slumbered on under the sands.

Fig. 6.1. A view of Kalibangan's mounds from the Ghaggar's bed (photo taken during A. Ghosh's expedition of 1950). (© ASI)

AUREL STEIN AND THE SARASVATĪ

The region saw its next explorer of importance in the person of one of the most colourful and intrepid archaeologists of the twentieth century: Marc Aurel Stein. Born in Budapest in 1862, this Jewish Hungarian studied in Austria, Germany and finally at Oxford, where he majored in archaeology, mastering many European languages in the process, besides Persian and Sanskrit.

Drawn very early to Asia, he travelled to India when he was twenty-five, and became the principal of Lahore's Oriental College. He occupied his leisure time by editing and translating Kalhana's *Rājatarangini*, Kashmir's well-known historical chronicle.

But Stein thirsted for wider horizons, and after a brief stint in Calcutta, embarked on an expedition to Central Asia in 1900. Three more expeditions followed till 1930, and their outcome ensured Stein's lasting fame. Over seven years, Stein covered some 40,000 km on horseback and on foot, during which he explored, surveyed and, occasionally, excavated China's western region of Xinjiang,* especially the Tarim basin and its forbidding Takla Makan Desert. Tracing ancient caravan routes into China, including the legendary Silk Road, he brought to light much long-lost Buddhist art. His most spectacular discovery, in 1907, was the Cave of the Thousand Buddhas, which had been sealed eight centuries earlier; he managed to acquire many of its treasures, including paintings and thousands of rare scrolls, and bring them to Britain, along with manuscripts

Fig. 6.2. Marc Aurel Stein. (© ASI)

---

* Formerly spelt 'Sinkiang' and earlier known as 'Chinese Turkestan'.

from other sites. Those achievements earned him a knighthood in 1912 (he had acquired British citizenship in 1904).

When he was not roaming Central Asia or living in a tent in Gulmarg with his dog, Sir Aurel Stein worked for the ASI; but he remained bitten by wanderlust, probing in Iran the connection between the Mesopotamian and the Indus civilizations, or exploring Roman frontier defences in Iraq. His work on the subcontinent was extensive nonetheless, even if it often gives an impression of having been done on the run. In the Swat Valley (the northernmost part of today's Pakistan), he traced some of the cities visited or besieged by Alexander the Great; while in Waziristan, Baluchistan and the Makran coast, he identified many prehistoric sites, including quite a few that later proved to be Harappan.

The least known part of Aurel Stein's work happens to be the one that concerns our story: his exploration of the states of Bikaner and Bahawalpur (Fig. 6.3), which he undertook in the winter of 1940–41—at the ripe young age of seventy-eight. Stein seems to have been fascinated by inhospitable regions, and we may imagine that he heard the call of the Great Indian Desert's desolate landscape of endless sand dunes. But as a Sanskritist, he was also intrigued by the legend—or the mystery—of the lost Sarasvatī and the traditions echoing the legend. The title of a paper he published in 1942 makes that clear: 'A Survey of Ancient Sites along the "Lost" Sarasvatī River'.[6] (He wrote a more detailed report the next year, which remained unpublished until 1989.[7]) However, that was not his first contribution to the search for India's bygone rivers: in 1917, he had authored a paper 'On Some River Names in the Rigveda', in which he discussed the identities of the rivers listed in the Rig Veda's *Nadīstuti sūkta*, observing that 'the identity of the first four rivers here enumerated . . . is subject to no doubt. They correspond to the present Ganges, Jumna, Sarsuti, Sutlej . . . The order in which the first four are mentioned exactly agrees with their geographical sequence from east to west.'[8]

Twenty-four years later, then, he organized an expedition to the region. Here is, in his own words, how he was drawn to the quest:

> On my return to India ... a survey of any remains of ancient occupations along the dry river-bed of the Ghaggar or Hakra, which passes from the easternmost Panjab through the States of Bikaner and Bahawalpur down to Sind, seemed attractive. Traditional Indian belief recognizes in this well-marked bed the course of the sacred Sarasvatī, once carrying its abundant waters down to the ocean and since antiquity 'lost' in desert sands.[9]

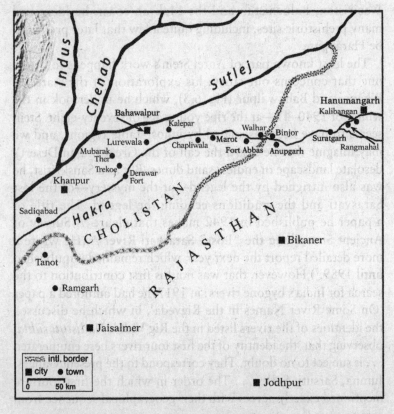

Fig. 6.3. Some of the cities, towns, villages and mounds visited by Aurel Stein in the Ghaggar–Hakra Valley and Rajasthan.

Let us mark, once again, the recognition of the Ghaggar–Hakra bed as the Sarasvatī in 'traditional Indian belief'. Stein added that the easternmost tributary of the Ghaggar was 'still known as the Sarsuti (the Hindi derivative of Sarasvatī) [which] passes the sacred sites of Kurukshetra near Thanesar, a place of Hindu pilgrimage'.[10]

Like the nineteenth-century explorers of the region, he was struck by 'the width of its dry bed within Bikaner territory [that is, downstream of Hanumangarh]; over more than 100 miles [160 km], it is nowhere less than 2 miles [3.2 km] and in places 4 miles [6.4 km] or more'. He also noted the presence of numerous mounds along the bed of the Ghaggar–Hakra: 'The large number of these ancient sites contrasts strikingly with the very few small villages still on the same ground.'[11] The region had clearly supported a much larger population in the past. He also observed that 'the bed shows a firm loamy soil, easily distinguished from the light sand on either side',[12] which is precisely the contrast captured by satellite photography.

Amused, Stein recorded, at Jandewala on the Ghaggar (in Bikaner), a 'popular tradition [that] recognizes the place where a ferry service is supposed to have crossed the river to Mathula on the opposite bank, a distance of more than 3 miles'—or 5 km, but of course without a drop of water between the two banks! 'Still more striking, perhaps,' he continued, 'is the name of Pattan-munara, the "Minar of the ferry", borne by an old site in Bahawalpur territory which is similarly believed to mark a ferrying place across the Hakra, the bed of which is here, if anything, still wider.'[13]

Fascinating as these local traditions may be, they need to be correlated, if possible, with literary and archaeological evidence. Stein's first landmark was therefore the Veda:

> In at least three passages of the Rigveda mentioning the
> Sarasvatī, a river corresponding to the present Sarsuti and
> Ghaggar is meant. For this we have conclusive evidence in
> the famous hymn, the 'Praise of the rivers'* (Nadīstuti)

---

* See extracts from the Nadīstuti Sūkta in Chapter 2, pp. 37–38.

which, with a precision unfortunately quite exceptional in Vedic texts, enumerates the *Sarasvati* correctly between the *Yamuna* (Jumna) in the east and the *Sutudri* or Sutlej in the west.[14]

This is in perfect agreement with what we saw in this book's first part: putting together the Rig Vedic descriptions of the Sarasvatī and 'traditional Indian belief', Stein had no doubt as to the identity of this broad, dry bed running through a scorched expanse of sand. And he hoped that the study of the bed's topography and 'of old sites on its banks' would 'be helpful to the student of early Indian history, still so much obscured by the want of reliable records and the inadequacy of archaeological evidence.'[15] His hope would be more than fulfilled, as his work was going to set off astonishing discoveries in the following decades.

Meanwhile, with 'very generous arrangements for the survey from Maharaja Ganga Singhji, that remarkable ruler of the Bikaner State',[16] Stein set off from Bikaner to Suratgarh in December 1940. The 'generous arrangements' included 'the use of a motor car', which allowed him and his small team to visit an impressive number of sites in the region. The team included the late Krishna Deva, then a young archaeologist, and now well known to students of temple architecture, among other fields.

Villagers must have goggled at this rare car raising a cloud of sand as it hurtled around Suratgarh, Hanumangarh and Anupgarh, stopping mostly to inquire about mounds known in the area. They must have stared more at this spry elderly white man scrutinizing potsherds dotting their surface. A few trial trenches dug between Hanumangarh and Anupgarh convinced Stein that most sites in that area belonged to the historical era, such as the impressive ruins of Rangmahal, near Suratgarh, which date from the Kushan age (first to third centuries CE).

Some 22 km northeast of Rangmahal, Stein stopped at 'two large mounds' near the hamlet of Kalibangan—the same mounds probed by Tessitori. (Stein was unaware at the time of Tessitori's explorations: only after the completion of his own did he come across Tessitori's report, 'comprising 228 closely written foolscap pages'.[17]) Strangely, Stein failed to relate Kalibangan to the Indus civilization, noting merely that it was 'an extensive site used mainly for burning bricks and for pottery'.[18] It was nothing of the sort. As B.K. Thapar, one of Kalibangan's excavators, put it decades later, Stein 'failed to recognize that the painted pottery found on the site in fact belonged to the Indus civilization and the two mounds represented occupational deposit thereof and not the accumulation of kiln remains'.[19] Perhaps he was in a tearing hurry to move on to Cholistan while the temperature was tolerable. Tessitori, studying Kalibangan *before* anything of the Indus civilization was known, had displayed more intuition when he sensed a 'prehistorical antiquity' at the site.

Stein, similarly, let pass a number of Harappan sites on his way to Anupgarh, convinced that most of them, like Rangmahal, belonged to historical times.

Instead of crossing into the Bahawalpur state from Anupgarh (Fig. 6.4), he returned to Bikaner on 23 January 1941, and after

Fig. 6.4. A view of the Ghaggar's wide bed at Anupgarh, as Aurel Stein must have seen it (photo taken in 1950 during A. Ghosh's expedition). Note the bank on the right. (© ASI)

a few days' halt proceeded to Jodhpur and Jaisalmer. From there, he travelled by lorry to Ramgarh, making a note of 'a number of wells of no great depth in a wide sandy drainage bed'.[20] At Ramgarh, our party had to switch to camels and horses; riding through Tanot, a former stronghold of the Bhati Rajputs, they crossed into Bahawalpur on 10 February.

Stein's account of his month-long exploration of Cholistan is enlivened by interesting forays into the region's history and a warm eye for details, ranging from ingenious agricultural practices in a very arid environment to traces of the old caravan route between Multan and Delhi. Moving 'upstream' a dry Hakra, he rode up to Marot and Fort Abbas (less than 50 km west of Anupgarh), then turned back towards Derawar, finally reaching the town of Bahawalpur when the rapidly rising heat put a stop to the expedition, though not before he had conducted a trial excavation at one of the mounds on the way.

Unlike in Bikaner, from Fort Abbas 'right down the Hakra as far as my survey extended west of Derawar', Stein related 'prehistoric mounds with pottery of the chalcolithic period'. At many sites, besides 'flint blades' and 'cakes of clay', he found 'painted pottery [which] closely resembled that of numerous chalcolithic sites explored by me in British Baluchistan and Makran, and also that of the now well-known great Indus Valley sites'. Clinchingly, at one place, Stein found 'sherds with incised characters which appear on many inscribed seals from Mohenjo-daro and Harappa'. Altogether, there were 'very numerous prehistoric mounds' in the Hakra Valley with 'close similarity in the shapes of vessels, terracotta, and shell ornaments'.[21]

That was the high point of Stein's expedition: despite its limitations, it established for the first time the existence, in the Hakra Valley, of sites related to the Harappan culture. Moreover, taking all periods together, he identified some eighty new sites, which in itself was a rich harvest.

Archaeology apart, some of Stein's remarks on hydrographic changes in the Ghaggar–Hakra basin are worth noting. He observed that the Hakra's bed became wider near Walhar (close to today's Indo-Pak border, on the Pakistani side), north of which he found 'levels between the sand ridges of the Cholistan which unmistakably represent an ancient winding bed of the Sutlej, that once joined the Hakra between Walar and Binjor'.[22] That is precisely one of the Sutlej's palaeochannels, which we noted earlier (p. 61). As regards the Ghaggar upstream, Stein produced testimonies of a water flow sometime during historical times. In his view, the two evidences put together proved that a large river had once existed in the valley, which explained 'how the Sarasvatī has come in hymns of the Rigveda to be praised as a great river'. Clearly, therefore, 'a great change has affected the Sarasvatī river or Ghaggar since reference to it was made in Vedic texts . . . Lower down on the Hakra the main change was due to the Sutlej having in late prehistoric times abandoned the bed which before had joined the Ghaggar'.[23]

Marc Aurel Stein completed his report in 1943, noting how his work in Bikaner would 'rank among the happiest memories of all my years in the plains of India'.[24] Indefatigable, he prepared for a fresh expedition, this time to Afghanistan: he had long asked for permission to explore that country, and it had finally come. But his rich and eventful life came to an end soon after he reached Kabul; he was buried there just a month short of his eighty-first birthday.

Krishna Deva's summary of Stein's work on the subcontinent is an apt assessment:

> Stein was essentially a geographer and an explorer and is to be admired for his indomitable courage and spirit of adventure in undertaking hazardous journeys through difficult terrain. He discovered a large number of Chalcolithic and related sites in the Great Indian Desert and the entire reach of the Indo-Iranian borderlands, covering Northern and Southern Baluchistan and a good part of Iran. He was a pioneer and a pathfinder and was to Indian protohistoric archaeology what Alexander Cunningham was to Indian historical archaeology.[25]

Stein's survey of the Sarasvatī sites was too rapid to explore in depth the connection between those 'prehistoric mounds' and the brilliant cities of the Indus Valley, yet the evidence he unearthed in Cholistan was enough to send colleagues on the trail a few years later. Also, it goes to his credit that he was the first to attempt a synthesis between three different streams of evidence: the Rig Veda's testimony, local traditions and archaeology. That synthesis rested on the identification of the Sarasvatī with the bed of the Ghaggar–Hakra, an identification which left no doubt in Stein's mind.

A HARVEST OF SITES

With the 1947 Partition, all forty-odd known Harappan sites went over to Pakistan, except two (a minor one near Rupar in Punjab, and a larger one in Saurashtra, viz. Rangpur). Indian archaeologists must have felt almost bereaved (or was it orphaned?): they had been given a splendid ancient civilization, and within hardly a quarter of a century it was snatched away from them. There was only one thing to be done: probe whether that civilization may have extended to this side of the newly created border, and if so, how deep inside.

According to a recent article by Nayanjot Lahiri, one man convinced Jawaharlal Nehru in 1948 to push through a project of 'explorations in Jaisalmer and Bikaner': the well-known historian and administrator 'Sardar' K.M. Panikkar, who was then the Dewan of Bikaner. Panikkar had, in fact, met Aurel Stein when the latter visited Bikaner eight years earlier to prepare for his survey of the Ghaggar, and in his autobiography, Panikkar notes how Stein mentioned to him that if his work were carried forward, it would show that the Indus civilization originated in this tract. Whether these were Stein's very words or were coloured by Panikkar's own conviction we cannot say, but his note to Nehru, evidently referring to Stein's explorations, shows great foresight:

> With the separation of the Pakistan Provinces, the main sites
> of what was known as the Indus Valley Civilisation have

gone to Pakistan. It is clearly of the utmost importance that archaeological work in connection with this early period of Indian history must be continued in India. A preliminary examination has shown that the centre of the early civilisation was not Sind or the Indus Valley but the desert area in Bikaner and Jaisalmer through which the ancient Saraswati flowed into the Gulf of Kutch at one time.[26]

Nehru endorsed Panikkar's note and got a special grant of 10,000 rupees released to the Archaeological Survey of India for the purpose.

Amalananda Ghosh was the first to test the waters. Before he was nominated director general of the ASI in 1953 (a post he held for fifteen years), he spent two winters exploring the valleys of the Sarasvatī and the Drishadvatī, as he called the Ghaggar and the Chautang respectively (Figs 6.5 and 6.6). Besides surface

Fig. 6.5. The expedition team in the Sarasvatī Valley in 1950. From left to right: Debala Mitra, Amalananda Ghosh, Ballabh Saran and Shruti Prakash.[27] (© ASI)

explorations, he conducted a few limited excavations. By Ghosh's reckoning, the 'sand-banks' of the lower section of the Ghaggar were 5 to 10 km apart. His initial observation marks a watershed, figuratively as well as literally:

> In view of Stein's statement which had led us to believe that nothing very ancient would be found in the region, it was a great thrill for us when even on the first and second days of our exploration we found sites with unmistakable affinities with the culture of Harappa and Mohenjo-daro. And a few subsequent days' work convinced us that the Sarasvatī valley had been really a commingling of many rivers, not only geographically, but culturally.[28]

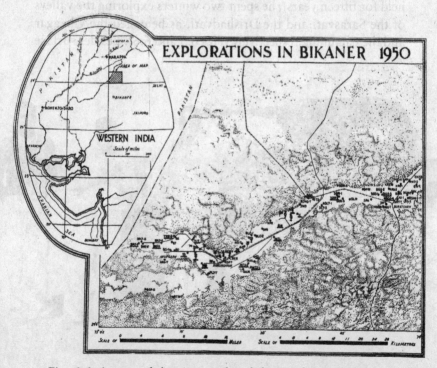

Fig. 6.6. A map of the sites explored during the 1950 survey. All the sites plotted are located on the edges of the Sarasvatī's bed, or in it. (© ASI)

Ghosh's thrill is understandable: the Indus civilization did extend into the new Indian nation. But how far? In all, he identified no less than 100 sites, of which 25 displayed a true Harappan culture, the easternmost being Kalibangan (Fig. 6.1). He suspected, rightly, that more sites were bound to come to light further east, and concluded in the meantime that 'the valleys of the Sarasvatī and the Drishadvatī must be regarded as very rich indeed in archaeological remains'.[29] The other 75-odd sites belonged to later cultures, mostly the Painted Grey Ware and the Rangmahal. We have met the second, which belongs to the first centuries CE; as regards the first, abbreviated as PGW in archaeological literature, it was a village-based culture extending from Punjab to Uttar Pradesh and dating from the late second millennium BCE, at the start of the Iron Age.

Ghosh ended his report with an important reflection on the flow of the bygone river: the Harappan sites 'on the bank of the Sarasvatī' could not have been established there 'had the river been dead during the lifetime of the culture'.[30] He was the first archaeologist to identify Harappan sites on the Indian side of the 'Sarasvatī Valley', as he called it, and also the first to assert that the river must have been in flow while those sites were thriving.

At this point, further discoveries became inevitable. In 1960, Suraj Bhan began a survey of Haryana—that is, further upstream in the valleys of the Sarasvatī and the Drishadvatī, as he himself called those two dry beds.[31] Apart from working out a chronology of the phases involved, Bhan discovered many new sites, including Rakhigarhi, Siswal, Mitathal and Balu (he was joined by Jim Shaffer for a season in 1977). In addition, between the present Yamuna and the Chautang's bed, he identified three palaeochannels—as many clues to the eastward migration of the Yamunā.[32] Further explorations in Punjab and Haryana were conducted by K.N. Dikshit in 1963 and, from 1975 to 1980, by Jagat Pati Joshi, Madhu Bala and Jassu Ram, who added considerably to the list of new sites.[33] Other explorers of the region include Katy F. Dalal, R.S. Bisht and V.S. Wakankar.

Moving downstream, let us return to the Cholistan Desert,

where Aurel Stein had spotted the first Harappan settlements along the Sarasvatī's dry bed. Following in his footsteps, the Pakistani archaeologist Mohammad Rafique Mughal undertook a systematic exploration of this unrelenting expanse of sand dunes and scrub vegetation in 1974.[34] Over four gruelling seasons, Mughal covered almost 500 km in Cholistan and came upon numerous spots strewn with potsherds and terracotta cakes, which testified to intense life and activity where, today, even goats and cattle find it hard to survive under the scorching sun. His discovery of 363 pre-urban, urban and post-urban sites of the Harappan tradition, combined with those on the Indian side, transformed the conventional picture of the Indus civilization forever.

Of those 363 sites, ninety-nine belong to the 'Hakra Ware' phase, which is roughly dated 3800–3000 BCE and is regarded as preceding the Early Harappan phase (which is why these sites are not included in the tables below). In addition, Mughal identified fourteen sites of the post-Harappan PGW culture, the same that Ghosh had first spotted on the Indian site of the valley.

A similar windfall awaited explorers in Gujarat. In 1954, the Indian archaeologist S.R. Rao identified a few Harappan settlements, including the well-known port town of Lothal, some 60 kilometres southwest of Ahmedabad, which he proceeded to excavate the next year. J.P. Joshi surveyed Kachchh and Saurashtra for a few years from 1964, discovering numerous settlements, including Dholavira (in 1966) and Surkotada. More sites came to light in the region through surveys by P.P. Pandya, Gregory Possehl and Kuldeep Bhan, among others.

The sum total of the explorations was simply prodigious and could be ranked among the most important archaeological discoveries of the twentieth century, even though we rarely hear about it—especially in India, where most school textbooks describe the 'Indus Valley' civilization as it was known in the 1930s!

If we take the Sarasvatī basin to mean the Ghaggar–Hakra and its tributaries, as did Stein and Ghosh and many of their followers, almost 2400 settlements related to the Indus civilization have come to light there: 640 Early, 360 Mature, and almost 1400 Late Harappan (Table 6.1), according to figures recently compiled by the late Indian archaeologist S.P. Gupta and his team.[35] No one could have foreseen such a density of settlements 1000 km away from Mohenjo-daro.

Table 6.1. Distribution of Harappan sites in the Sarasvatī basin (adapted from a list compiled by S.P. Gupta, with inputs from G. Possehl and M. Rafique Mughal).[36]

Sarasvatī basin (east to west)	Early Harappan	Mature Harappan	Late Harappan	Total
Haryana	558	114	1168	1840
Indian Punjab	24	41	160	225
Rajasthan	18	31	0	49
Cholistan (Pakistan)	40	174	50	264
Total	640	360	1378	2378

But that was not all. Further east, over forty sites, three-fourths of them of the Mature phase, have come to light in the *doab* ('two rivers') or the interfluvial region between the Yamuna and the Ganges, which is today the western part of Uttar Pradesh. No Harappan site has so far been spotted east of the Ganges. In other words, the Ganges is the eastern boundary of the Indus civilization, just as the Tapti marks its southern boundary. (There are a few Late Harappan sites in Maharashtra's Godavari basin, such as Daimabad, but none of the Mature phase sites has been identified so far south.)

Gujarat also turned out to be dotted with Harappan sites— over 500 of them (mostly in Kachchh and Saurashtra), with more than 300 of the Mature phase, and very few of the Early phase.

Put together, the explorations outside the Indus Valley proper have vastly expanded our Harappan horizons. The overall picture is summarized in Table 6.2, with a grand total of over 3700 sites—a long way from the forty-odd at the time of Partition.

Table 6.2. Overall distribution of Harappan sites.[37]

Regions of the Subcontinent	Early Harappan	Mature Harappan	Late Harappan	Total
Sarasvatī basin (Table 6.1)	640	360	1378	2378
Uttar Pradesh	2	32	10	44
Himachal, Jammu and Delhi	1	–	4	5
Gujarat	11	310	198	519
Pakistan's Indus basin and western regions*	385	438	12	835
Total	1039	1140	1602	3781

A few caveats are in order at this point. Tables 6.1 and 6.2 do not give us a count of *separate geographical* sites: because a given site appears twice if it has two phases (say, Early and Mature), and three times if it has all three phases, the actual count of geographical sites is much less, somewhere between 2000 and 2500. There may also be errors: possible duplications apart, most sites have been identified through the method of surface collection, or at best a trial pit; as a result, some of the sites detected as 'Late' may conceal earlier phases. In addition, a small proportion of the settlements in densely populated areas are temporary or 'camp sites', to use Mughal's term in the case of Cholistan,[38] which may or may not qualify as genuine settlements. Lastly, while I have tried to include recent finds from India and Pakistan, some may have been left out, and new sites keep coming to light all the time.[39] The tables should therefore be viewed as broadly indicative; the distribution patterns they point to are unlikely to be altered much, and those are more important than the numbers themselves.

So what conclusions can we draw from this 'mushrooming' of Harappan sites?

---

* Those western parts include, from north to south, the Swat Valley, the North-West Frontier Province (NWFP), Waziristan, Zhob, Baluchistan and the Makran coast.

From the Indus to the Sarasvatī   141

THE 'INDUS–SARASVATĪ CIVILIZATION'

The first is a touchy question of terminology: unquestionably, the Indus civilization is no longer restricted to the 'Indus Valley'. If we limit ourselves to the Mature phase, Baluchistan alone has 129 sites against 108 in Sind, where Mohenjo-daro is located;[40] Gujarat has 310, while the Sarasvatī basin has 360—four times as many as Sind. Table 6.3 shows the relative concentration of Mature sites in these four regions:

Table and Chart 6.3. Region-wise distribution of Mature Harappan sites.

Region	No. of Mature Sites	Percentage
Sarasvatī basin (Haryana, Indian Punjab, north Rajasthan, Cholistan)	360	32%
Gujarat	310	28%
Baluchistan	129	11%
Sind	108	9%
Pakistan's Punjab[41]	60	5%
Others	173	15%
Total	1140	100%

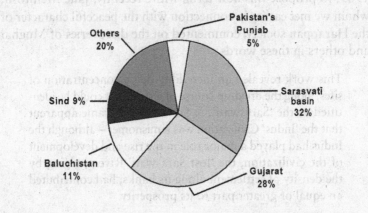

The last column of Table 6.3 is eloquent: almost one-third of all Mature Harappan sites are located in the Sarasvatī basin, and over one-fourth in Gujarat alone: together, these two regions hold 60 per cent of all Mature sites. Clearly, the designation of 'Indus civilization' is no longer quite apt—much less is that of 'Indus *Valley* civilization'. An easy way out is to opt for 'Harappan civilization', after the first identified site (or 'type site'), and indeed the term, though a bit dated, is still used by many archaeologists; but it hardly helps us to grasp the civilization's geographical extent, which happens to be one of its specificities.

In 1998, Kenoyer gave a lucid synthesis of what we have explored so far; he noted that apart from the Indus,

> another ancient river, the Saraswati or Ghaggar–Hakra had taken its course along the eastern edge of the plain. Numerous surveys in the deserts of Cholistan and Rajasthan made it clear that large numbers of settlements dating from the fourth to the first millennium B.C. were situated along the banks of this other major river system . . . Now that we know of the presence of the ancient Saraswati river (also known as the Ghaggar–Hakra along its central stretches), some scholars refer to this culture as the Indus–Sarasvatī civilization.[42]

Among the scholars in question, S.P. Gupta was the first, in 1989, to propose this new term. More recently, Jane McIntosh, whom we met earlier in connection with the peaceful character of the Harappan society, commented on the discoveries of Mughal and others in these words:

> This work revealed an incredibly dense concentration of sites, along the dried-up course of a river that could be identified as the 'Saraswati'. . . Suddenly it became apparent that the 'Indus' Civilization was a misnomer—although the Indus had played a major role in the rise and development of the civilization, the 'lost Saraswati' River, judging by the density of settlement along its banks, had contributed an equal or greater part to its prosperity.

This led McIntosh to the following conclusion on the issue of terminology:

> Many people today refer to this Early state as the 'Indus–Saraswati Civilization' and continuing references [in her book] to the 'Indus Civilization' should be seen as an abbreviation in which the 'Saraswatī' is implied.[43]

Despite such plain assessments of the share of the Sarasvatī region in the Harappan world, the designation 'Indus–Sarasvatī civilization' has not caught on. There are several reasons for this, apart from a predictable reluctance to alter a time-honoured terminology.

The first is that the new term still does not include Baluchistan's or Gujarat's numerous sites (nor also, to be precise, those east of the Yamuna). Even with this restriction, 'Indus–Sarasvatī' is certainly more comprehensive and closer to the mark than 'Indus' alone.

A second reason is an objection raised by some archaeologists that the high concentration of sites along the Sarasvatī and the small number along the Indus might be something of an optical illusion. As an example, Shereen Ratnagar, a professor of archaeology who has particularly researched and written on the Indus civilization, asserts that 'fewer Harappan sites lie along the banks of the Ghaggar–Hakra than is made out . . . Where the Sarasvati *Valley* sites are concerned, we find that many of them are sites of a local culture . . . some of them showing Harappan contact, and comparatively few are full-fledged Mature Harappan sites'.[44] But such a statement is questionable, since the said 'local cultures' can just as well be viewed as regional variations of the Harappan culture: in Baluchistan or Gujarat, archaeologists have long noted such distinctive regional stamps, yet never sought to exclude sites of these two regions from the Harappan sphere.

In reality, there is little scope for disputing the identification of Harappan sites in the Sarasvatī basin by Ghosh, Joshi, Mughal or Bhan, unless we are prepared to question their professional competence, which none of their colleagues, to my knowledge, has ever done. If anything, their judgement has been confirmed wherever their surveys have been followed by actual excavations: Rakhigarhi, Banawali, Kalibangan, Lothal, Surkotada and Dhola-vira are shining examples of their surveying skills. Moreover, even if we assumed that dozens of the sites surveyed were erroneously labelled as Harappan (which is very unlikely), it would hardly make a difference to the overall numbers.

Ratnagar further tries to tip the scales by proposing that 'many sites near the Indus may have been washed away when the river flooded or changed its course'.[45] That is a better point, and we have already noted the whims of the Indus; indeed, it is also fairly certain that the ruins of some sites must have been buried under the river's sediments. But in the absence of evidence, their number must remain conjectural, and even if tens or hundreds of them were destroyed by the Indus, that would in no way obliterate the Sarasvatī sites: the term 'Indus–Sarasvatī', proposed by Gupta, noted by Kenoyer and accepted by McIntosh, by no means excludes 'Indus'.

Kenoyer's remark on the 'large numbers of settlements' in the Sarasvatī region figured in his 1998 *Ancient Cities of the Indus Valley Civilization*, one of the best introductions to the field and a fine synthesis of Harappan society, technology and crafts. More recently, we see him cast doubt on those 'large numbers'; writing in 2006, he suggests that 'most sites along the dry river channel are relatively small, and even the few large ones are not as large as the major cities on the Indus or its tributaries'.[46] Coming from such a seasoned archaeologist, this statement is surprising: according to Possehl's recent figures,[47] the average size of Mature Harappan sites in the Sarasvatī region is 13.5 ha, while that of the sites in Sind is 8 ha. If anything, it is the Indus sites that are 'relatively small'. Rakhigarhi in Haryana, in the Sarasvatī basin, for example, has seven mounds spreading together over 105 ha.

Even prior to the Mature phase, the presence in the Sarasvatī basin of 640 Early Harappan sites (nearly 63 per cent of all known sites of that phase, see Table 6.2), with at least four of them in the range of 20 ha,[48] shows that the region was not 'colonized' at the start of the urban phase, but was part of the vast process of convergence that culminated in the rise of Harappan urbanism over much of northwest India.

So why not use the term 'Indus–Sarasvatī civilization'? The real reason is that, much like Gaṅgā losing her way in Shiva's hair, the Sarasvatī found herself entangled in the Aryan controversy. We will have to wait till the last part of this book to see whether the legendary river manages to flow out of it.

Until then, let us not miss the central point of the momentous findings of the post-Partition era: although 'Indus–Sarasvatī civilization' suits the archaeological record better than 'Indus civilization', the issue of terminology is secondary and will, in time, settle on its own. What matters is that this civilization had not one, but several heartlands: Baluchistan, the Indus basin, the Sarasvatī basin and Gujarat.

THE VERDICT OF ARCHAEOLOGY

In the 1820s, we saw Tod record a tradition that blamed the Ghaggar's disappearance for the region's 'depopulation', a word also used by Colvin; the two Oldhams made similar observations. Tessitori sensed that 'the Ghaggar once bathed with its waters a florid and prosperous region'. Those early explorers would have been delighted to see the findings of archaeology endorse their view. According to M. Rafique Mughal:

> Archaeological evidence demonstrates that the Hakra flood plain was densely populated between the fourth and the second millennia B.C.[49]

And such a population density, in what is today a perfectly arid region barring a few wells along the Hakra's bed, could not have been sustained 'had the river been dead during the lifetime of the culture', as we saw A. Ghosh put it. V.N. Misra, a distinguished archaeologist and prehistorian with a life-long experience of Rajasthan, summed up the verdict of archaeology in these words:

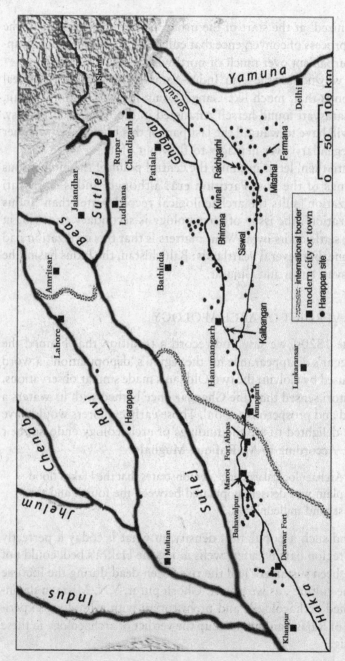

Fig. 6.7. Early Harappan sites in the Sarasvatī basin.[50]

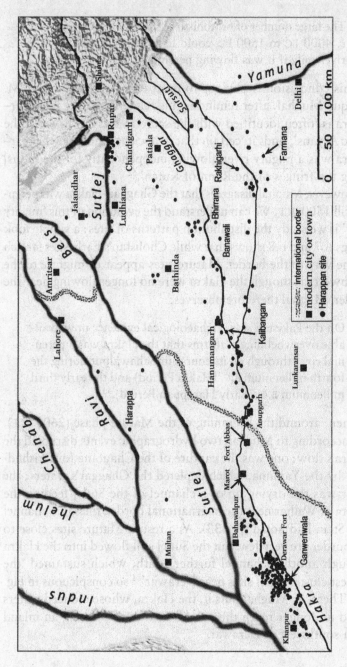

Fig. 6.8. Mature Harappan sites in the Cholistan Desert.

The large number of protohistoric settlements, dating from
c. 4000 BC to 1500 BC, could have flourished along this
river only if it was flowing perennially.[51]

This conclusion is obvious to most other archaeologists. M.
Rafique Mughal, after reminding his readers that the Ghaggar–
Hakra is 'often identified with the sacred Sarasvatī River of the
Vedic Aryans', finds it 'certain that in ancient times the Ghaggar–
Hakra was a mighty river, flowing independently [of the Indus]
along the fringes of the Rann of Kutch'.[52]

However, Mughal disagrees that the Ghaggar–Hakra was perennial till 1500 BCE. We can understand the evolution of this 'mighty
river' if we study the distribution patterns of sites: a simple look
at Figs 6.7 and 6.8 shows that while Cholistan's Early sites stretch
all the way to the border, Mature sites appear to migrate to the
southwest, as though the Hakra were no longer flowing near the
border. Mughal therefore observes:

> On the Pakistan side, archaeological evidence now avail-
> able overwhelmingly affirms that the Hakra was a peren-
> nial river through all its course in Bahawalpur during the
> fourth millennium B.C. (Hakra Period) and the early third
> millennium B.C. (Early Harappan Period).[53]

Then, around the beginning of the Mature phase (2600 BCE),
still according to Mughal, two hydrographic events disrupted the
Hakra's flow: one was the capture of the Chautang (or Drishadvatī) by the Yamunā, which depleted the Ghaggar's waters; the
other was the drying up of a channel of the Sutlej feeding the
Hakra at Walhar near the international border, the same channel
that Stein had noted (p. 133). As a result, Mature sites close to
the border are very few. But the Sutlej still flowed into the Hakra
through another channel further south, which sustained 'the
highest clustering of sites near Derawar'[54] so conspicuous in Fig.
6.8. There, as Mughal puts it, the Hakra, whose reduced waters
could no longer reach the sea, 'fanned out', forming an inland
delta southwest of Derawar.

Mughal's inferences are quite consistent with the picture of the Sarasvatī that we have built so far, but he adds a degree of confidence in dating the start of the Hakra's depletion. And his chronology happens to be in excellent agreement with the iso-topic study by Geyh and Ploethner cited earlier (p. 76), which dated the Hakra's palaeo-waters between 10900 and 2700 BCE: the last date suggests that the Hakra stopped flowing just before the start of the Mature phase in the area tested, between Fort Abbas and Fort Mojgarh—both the date and the area match Mughal's. So does Clift's conclusion (p. 76) that 'between 2000 and 3000 BCE, flow along . . . the Ghaggur-Hakkra River ceased'.

Mughal's thesis that the river broke up before the start of the Mature phase has been further strengthened by a recent survey of the Indian side of the Ghaggar basin. The Indian archaeologist Vasant Shinde and his Indian and Japanese colleagues, revisiting a number of sites of the region, first remind their readers that 'the Ghaggar–Hakra River has been identified as the ancient Saraswati and Chautang as Drishadvati very often referred to in the Rg Vedic period.'[55] They sum up their findings in these terms:

> The archaeological survey carried out by the present authors in 2007 in parts of Hanumangarh and Ganganagar Dis-tricts of Rajasthan and Bhiwani and Rohtak Districts of Haryana have recorded some of the sites with the help of the GPS [Global Positioning System]. Surprisingly all the sites near Anupgarh area are actually located in the Ghaggar River course. This is very interesting and suggests that the Ghaggar (Saraswati) River had dried much before the emergence of the pre-Harappan culture in this area.[56]

We thus have four streams of evidence converging on a major disruption of the Sarasvatī in the third millennium BCE, and probably before the start of the Mature phase.

Gregory Possehl's analysis also starts from the observation that 'settlement patterns in the area indicate a strong flow from the Sarasvati and Sutlej into the Cholistan area, as far as Fort Derawar'.[57] He adds:

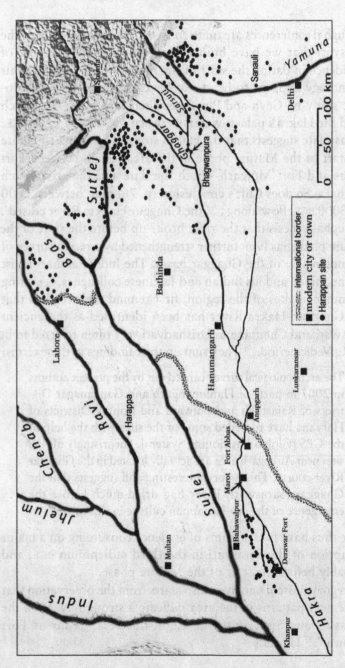

Fig. 6.9. Late Harappan sites in the Cholistan Desert.[58]

It seems that during the Indus Age the Sarasvati was a large
river and that water that now flows in the Yamuna and/or
Sutlej Rivers made it so. Over time these waters were with-
drawn and the Sarasvati became smaller, eventually dry.
The agency for these changes was the tectonic reshaping
of the doab [interfluve] separating the Yamuna from the
rivers of the Punjab.[59]

The agency for the changes was 'tectonic' because, as Valdiya
and others suggested earlier (p. 66), all it would have taken to
divert the Yamunā and the Sutlej away from the Sarasvatī is a
slight uplift of the doab. Such an uplift could occur progressively
as a result of the continued northward movement of the Indian
tectonic plate, or more suddenly in the event of a powerful earthquake in this seismically active region. Irrespective of the precise
cause of the Sarasvatī's depletion, Possehl proposes a synthesis
of archaeological and geographical studies (mainly Wilhelmy's
for the latter) in three stages—a chronology 'actually founded
in archaeological data and the study of settlement patterns of the
Indus Age'.[60] His maps[61] present the following scenario:

1. Till about 3000 BCE, the Sarasvatī, whose tributaries include
   the Yamunā and the Sutlej, is in full flow (more or less as
   in Wilhelmy's map, Fig. 3.8). This corresponds broadly with
   the Early phase.
2. At some point during the Mature phase, the Yamunā gets
   captured by the Gangetic system, resulting in the drying up
   of the Drishadvatī and of middle sections of the Sarasvatī.
   The Sutlej shifts westward and its braided channels meet the
   Ghaggar–Hakra at several points between Hanumangarh
   and Fort Abbas.
3. In the post-urban phase (2000–1500 BCE), the Sutlej
   pursues its migration and meets the Hakra downstream of
   Fort Abbas. The Sarasvatī and its tributaries are reduced to
   seasonal rain-fed rivers in their upper reaches.

Although the actual sequence of events may have been more
complex, this scenario is compatible with the distribution of

Harappan sites of various phases in the region, and with all the other evidence that we have surveyed so far: from topography, local traditions and textual descriptions.

But archaeology has more to say. On the Indian side of the border, not only are the Early and Mature Harappan sites crowding the banks of the Ghaggar, the Chautang and their tributaries (Figs 6.7 and 6.8), they are also *completely absent* along the present courses of the Sutlej (except in its upper reaches during the Mature phase) and the Yamuna,[62] a splendid confirmation that these two rivers did not occupy their present beds while the Indus–Sarasvatī civilization flourished.

And when we come to the Late phase (Fig. 6.9), we see an extraordinary proliferation of settlements (160 in India's Punjab and almost 1200 in Haryana alone) hugging the piedmonts of the Shivaliks, visibly clinging to the last rain-fed streams flowing down the hills, while not a single site can be spotted in the central part of the Sarasvatī's basin: the river's wide bed further downstream must have been almost bereft of water.

A LIFELINE

We have travelled a long way. Before we set off on fresh explorations, let us take stock, first with Jane McIntosh, who in her latest book on the Indus civilization restates in clear terms the contribution of the Sarasvatī:

> In the Indus period the Saraswati river system may have been even more productive than that of the Indus, judging by the density of settlement along its course. In the Bahawalpur region, in the western portion of the river, settlement density far exceeded that elsewhere in the Indus civilization . . . While there are some fifty sites known along the Indus, the Saraswati has almost a thousand . . .
>
> [The Yamuna] shifted its course eastward early in the second millennium, eventually reaching its current bed by the first millennium, while the Drishadvati bed retained only a small seasonal flow; this seriously decreased the volume

of water carried by the Saraswati. The Sutlej gradually
shifted its channel northward, eventually being captured by
the Indus drainage ... The loss of the Sutlej waters caused
the Saraswati to be reduced to the series of small seasonal
rivers familiar today. Surveys show a major reduction in
the number and size of settlements in the Saraswati region
during the second millennium.[63]

We then turn to the *Encyclopædia Britannica*:

Several hundred sites [of the Indus civilization] have been
identified, the great majority of which are on the plains of
the Indus or its tributaries or on the now dry course of the
ancient Sarasvatī River, which flowed south of the Sutlej
and then southward to the Indian Ocean, east of the main
course of the Indus itself.[64]

Those lines were written by Raymond Allchin, who thus
acknowledged the identification of the Ghaggar–Hakra with the
Sarasvatī. Indeed, in a recent book co-authored with Bridget
Allchin, he reminisced how it was for them 'a most moving experience to stand on the mound at Kalibangan, and to see still
preserved in the modern cropping the area of the flood plain of
the Sarasvatī still clearly visible'.[65] They also accepted their
colleagues' view that 'the major reduction of sites [along the
Sarasvatī] in the Early Post-urban* period (c. 2000–1700 BC)
... strongly suggests that a major part of the river's water supply
was lost around that time'.[66]

Finally, in a wide-ranging survey entitled 'Indus Civilization
and the Rgvedic Sarasvatī', V.N. Misra supports the view that
the river was depleted by the loss of the Yamunā and the Sutlej.
His conclusion leaves no room for ambiguity:

The description of the location, size and desiccation of the
Sarasvatī River in the Vedic, epic and classical literature

---

* 'Early Post-urban' is the beginning of what most archaeologists have called
the Late Harappan phase.

perfectly matches the features and history of the Ghaggar–
Hakra River. Therefore it can be stated with certainty that
the present Ghaggar–Hakra is nothing but a remnant of the
Rgvedic Sarasvatī which was the lifeline of the Indus
Civilization.[67]

One major lifeline, that is, with the other being the Indus. Just
like Mesopotamia, this urban civilization emerged around these
two major river systems; but here, one of them was already on
its way to extinction.

7

New Horizons

A brief visit to four important sites on the Indian side of the border will complement our acquaintance with Indus–Sarasvatī urbanism: they all bear the Harappan stamp, but because they sharply differ from each other, they open new horizons on what was already a rich and complex civilization.

Let us start from the Sarasvatī's upper reaches and go with the current.

BANAWALI

This Harappan city of about 10 ha was found in the Fatehabad district of Haryana, on the bank of an old bed of the Ghaggar. According to R.S. Bisht, who directed the excavations in the 1970s, 'Banawali was an important administrative headquarters or provincial capital and a prosperous trading centre along the Sarasvatī during the Indus times.'[1]

The site was already occupied in the pre-urban phase, with some evidence of fortifications and bricks following the typical Early Harappan proportions of 1:2:3. At the start of the urban phase, 'all the pre-existing residential houses were razed to the ground and fresh ones were raised with the newly introduced bricks and with thicker walls of better workmanship'.[2] Those 'newly introduced bricks' followed the standardized proportions of 1:2:4, and this 'razing to the ground' is one more illustration of the 'clean-slate strategy' we saw in the Indus region.

The site of the Mature phase has a layout not found anywhere

155

else so far (Fig. 7.1), with an overall trapezoidal shape and a semi-elliptical acropolis. Another unique feature of Banawali is the presence of a six-metre-wide, V-shaped moat outside the town's fortifications, which was most likely a protection from floods when the river was in spate.

While the streets of the acropolis are mostly at 90° angles, those of the lower town follow a more complex radial pattern; but several of them are precisely oriented along the north–south axis,

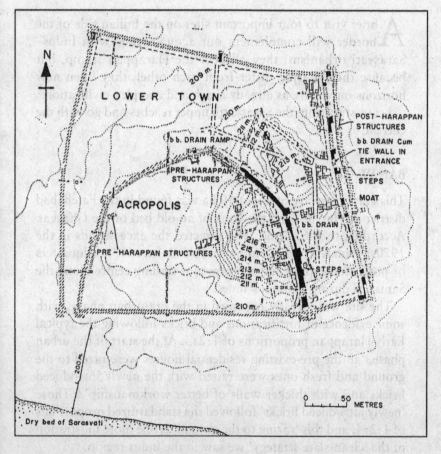

Fig. 7.1. The Harappan town of Banawali, in Haryana. (© ASI)

and the larger ones are a comfortable 5.4 m wide. Some rich traders lived there, judging from the presence of seals, hoards of jewellery and stone weights in some of the bigger houses. One of them boasted a paved living room and a bathroom complete with a raised washbasin!

Perhaps the most remarkable structure unearthed at Banawali's acropolis (Fig. 7.2) is a small building shaped as a semi-ellipse—precisely the shape of the acropolis. As if to make it amply clear that this was a conscious choice and not an accident, the building harbours an altar that once again conforms to a semi-elliptical (or apsidal) shape. There can be little doubt that this building was a small temple dedicated to fire worship (we will return to it in Chapter 10).

Fig. 7.2. Banawali's fire temple, with the apsidal altar in the centre. (© ASI)

KALIBANGAN

Some 200 km downstream from Banawali, we come to Kalibangan, on the left bank of the Ghaggar. Indeed, just a few kilometres further downstream is the confluence with the Chautang,
still so conspicuous on satellite photographs (Fig. 3.3). Gregory
Possehl puts it this way, 'Kalibangan . . . is strategically located
at the confluence of the Sarasvatī and Drishadvatī Rivers and
must have played a major role as a way station and monitor of
the overland communications of the Harappan peoples.'[3]

Kalibangan, like Banawali, saw an Early phase, complete with
fortifications, rectangular houses, streets and even drains. In its
Mature phase, however, this town embodied a very different
concept of town planning from Banawali's, even though it was
of about the same size: 11.5 ha for the area within fortifications,

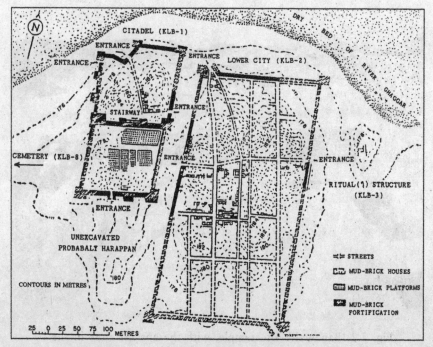

Fig. 7.3. Plan of Kalibangan, on the Sarasvatī. (© ASI)

and probably a few more hectares outside. Here, the acropolis
and the lower town were twin enclosures, in the form of two
oblique parallelograms whose longer sides were oriented north–
south (Fig. 7.3). In this, Kalibangan followed the general scheme
of Mohenjo-daro (Fig. 5.1), whose acropolis occupied a separate
mound to the west of the lower town. Mohenjo-daro's acropolis
is thought to have measured some 200 x 400 m, while Kalibangan's
was precisely 120 x 240 m—in both cases, the ratio of length to
breadth is 2:1. A massive east–west wall further divides the acropolis into two rhombs of nearly 120 x 120 m each. But Kalibangan
is luckier than Mohenjo-daro in that the lower town's fortifications are largely traceable, measuring at least 360 x 240 m.

The lower town's streets formed a well-planned and carefully
maintained grid; their widths, starting from the narrowest, were
1.8 m, 3.6 m, 5.4 m and 7.2 m, in a perfect geometric progression of 1:2:3:4. (This pattern is partly visible at other sites: we
just saw, for instance, street widths of 5.4 m at Banawali.) As with
the overall town plan, we must note the Harappan engineers' and
planners' fondness for precise proportions: they did not believe
in leaving things to chance, as our 'modern' municipal authorities
seemingly do. No urban jungle in those protohistoric times!

The only structures permitted on the streets were small brick
platforms jutting out near house entrances, where people evidently
sat together in the evening to chat and exchange the day's news:
perhaps the arrival of a caravan of traders from Harappa, less
than 200 km away, or the latest gossip from Rakhigarhi and
other large urban centres upstream—unless it was simply the
recent harvest in the fields around the town. Houses were, as elsewhere, organized around a central courtyard, and surplus of
wealth (what we call 'luxury') is visible in some of them in the
form of tiled floors decorated with the typical Harappan motif
of 'intersecting circles' (Fig. 7.4).

At Harappa (Fig. 5.3) the acropolis (on mound AB) is also in
the shape of a parallelogram, measuring roughly 200 x 400 m
(the same size as at Mohenjo-daro), while a recessed entrance on
its northern side faces a now dry riverbed of the Ravi. We find a

Fig. 7.4. A tiled floor in a house at Kalibangan. (© ASI)

similar device at the northern end of Kalibangan's acropolis, facing the Sarasvatī's dry bed and wide enough to allow carts in and out. Such a layout makes eminent sense with rivers acting as important links between towns and regions; the recess must have been designed to afford a measure of control on the movement of people and goods.

While the northern portion of the acropolis was residential in nature, the southern brought to light a series of massive brick platforms oriented along cardinal directions. According to B.B. Lal, who conducted the excavations with B.K. Thapar and J.P. Joshi, the area must have been reserved for ritual purposes.[4] There are several clues to this effect. First, as far as can be judged, it had no regular houses or other buildings. Second, both accesses to it, through the partitioning wall in the north and an entrance in the southern fortification wall, were stairways, therefore disallowing the movement of carts: there must have been a specific reason to compel inhabitants to reach the area on foot. Third and more explicit, on one of the platforms, a row of seven oval-shaped structures, five of them fairly intact, were found next to each other, sunk in the ground, with a slender stele of clay standing in the middle of each of them. They contained ash and charcoal, which prompted the excavators to identify them as fire altars. Their location alongside a wall made the officiants sit facing east, the direction still

favoured today in rituals; behind them was a half-buried terracotta jar containing more ash and charcoal; nearby, a few bathing pavements and a well suggest ablutions. In every detail, the
complex is evocative of religious rituals, and we will return to it
when we discuss Harappan religion. Interestingly, the same kind
of altar with a central stele was found in many individual houses,
and Lal attributes a religious purpose to them, since cooking was
done in the open courtyards.

On another of the brick platforms, a carefully built rectangular
pit of burnt bricks measuring 1.5 x 1 m contained antlers and
bones of bovids, evidently sacrificed as part of a ritual.

LOTHAL

This important site of Gujarat is located some 70 km southwest
of Ahmedabad, near the Bhogavo, a tributary of the Sabarmati
river; the Sabarmati flows into the northern end of the Gulf of
Khambat (or Cambay) some 23 km downstream.[5] At 7 ha, Lothal
is modest in size, though, as often, there is evidence of habitations extending outside the fortified area (Fig. 7.5). The town's
peripheral wall is massive, from 12 to 21 m thick, and was clearly
intended to offer a measure of protection against floods, whose
repeated onslaughts left tell-tale marks of ravage on the town
and probably brought about its end.

Lothal's town planning follows the pattern of Banawali in one
respect: the acropolis is within the town, not separate from it like
Kalibangan's; tucked in the southeast corner, it is demarcated not
by internal fortifications, but by a separate platform of mud
bricks almost four metres high. It has wide streets, well-designed
drains, and a row of twelve bathing platforms in a perfectly
straight line (Fig. 5.4 shows a few of them)—a layout that hints
at more than a purely utilitarian purpose. The acropolis also
boasts a large building identified as a warehouse, with square
platforms where we can visualize the goods being packed, tied,
sealed, lifted on the shoulders of coolies and finally taken away.
The building seems to have suffered a fire, as some of the mud

bricks are partly burned; but we should be grateful for that, as otherwise the sixty-five sealings (impressions of seals on clay) found there might not have been preserved; some of those sealings still bore the impression of the ropes tied around the bundles of goods waiting to be shipped.

The lower town reveals considerable industrial activity dealing with beads of various semi-precious stones, shells and metal working among other crafts, all of them using techniques that have been well-documented at other Harappan sites. The presence of sacrificial and fire altars recalls the structures found at Kalibangan, but here they are found in individual houses or in streets. We will study one of them in Chapter 10.

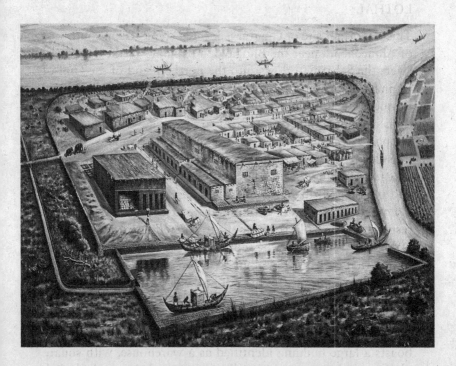

Fig. 7.5. An artist's impression of Lothal (Gujarat). Note the dockyard in the foreground and the warehouse on the left. The lower town is in the background. (Not to scale.) (© ASI)

The most remarkable structure, alongside the town's eastern side, is a 217-m-long, 36-m-wide basin (Fig. 7.6). (Its proportions, incidentally, are almost exactly in the ratio of 6:1.) If we consider that its 1.5 to 1.8 m-thick walls were made of millions of carefully adjusted baked bricks, we will have an idea of the energy and resources deployed on its construction. No other Harappan site has so far come up with such a huge water structure (as long as two-and-a-half football fields!). In view of stone anchors and marine shells found in it, S.R. Rao, the excavator, identified it as a tidal dockyard: at high tide, boats sailing up the Gulf of Cambay would have easily pushed on upstream the Bhogavo before berthing at Lothal's basin. There are other considerations, too: its vertical walls are ideal for such a purpose, and the flat top of the town's eastern fortification would have acted as a wharf; the proximity of the warehouse with its numerous sealings is another clue to the export of goods; a seal evocative of contact with the Persian Gulf was found elsewhere at Lothal; and an inlet channel was identified at the basin's northern end, while a spillway for overflowing waters was spotted at the southern end.

Here again, not everyone agreed that it was a dockyard, especially in view of the two sharp bends in the defunct stream leading to the dockyard. But the alternate theory of a water reservoir has

Fig. 7.6. Lothal's huge baked-brick basin, almost 220 m long, thought to have been a dockyard. (© ASI)

been rather less convincing: the basin would have been unconscionably large for the purpose; a normal reservoir would be expected to have slanted walls with steps leading down into it (as we can see at Dholavira); and what is more, sullage from one of the town's major drains emptied right into the basin.[6] A recent study, by three Indian scientists, of multi-spectral satellite imagery combined with an analysis of sediments around Lothal has lent considerable support to the concept of a tidal dock: the evidence of former estuaries inland demonstrate that the sea level was higher during Lothal's heyday, while an analysis of the satellite photographs reveal that 'a meandering, tidally influenced river flowed from the north past Lothal. Tidal waters would thus have been used to approach up to and slightly beyond the town of Lothal',[7] which is just what S.R. Rao had proposed some four decades earlier.

It may, however, be that Lothal was not a point of direct export, and that small river boats rather than larger seafaring ships took the goods away to a point of trans-shipment on Saurashtra's coast. But Lothal's association with the sea seems clear enough. Even today, at high tide, sea water enters the lower reaches of the old riverbed. And when the excavators first explored the site, they found that at that spot villagers were worshipping a sea-goddess named Venuvatimātā. But soon, an incident occurred which aroused the goddess's displeasure. Let us hear the story from Rao himself:

> Before extending the operations to this sector [of the warehouse] the stones in worship representing the sea-goddess had to be removed against the wishes of the labourers. A few days later there was an accident resulting in injury to some labourers and the death of one of them. Immediately the labourers attributed the accident to the sacrilege committed by us in removing the goddess from her original place of worship, and refused to work on the site. They were later satisfied when the goddess was re-installed elsewhere with some ceremony. This incident is particularly mentioned here to show how strong is the tradition of worshipping the sea-goddess at Lothal.[8]

DHOLAVIRA[9]

Discovered by J.P. Joshi in 1966 on the Khadir island of the Rann of Kachchh, and excavated two decades later under the direction of R.S. Bisht, this site had quite a few surprises in store for the archaeological world, not the least of which was its very location, in the middle of what is today a harsh and arid landscape. But we saw how the sea reached higher in the Gulf of Khambat, and in a study of changes in the sea level around Gujarat, U.B. Mathur recently argued that this was also the case in the Rann: in Mature Harappan times, it was a 'shallow arm of the sea',[10] and therefore navigable. (Indeed we know from Greek records that it was still partly so in the first century BCE.[11]) It is likely, then, that Dholavira had easy access to the sea.

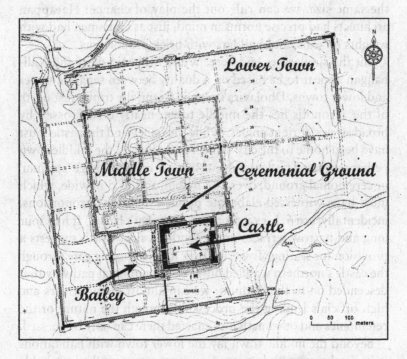

Fig. 7.7. Plan of Dholavira, in the Rann of Kachchh. (© ASI)

In the opinion of the Allchins, 'Dholavira appears to be one of the most exciting discoveries of the past half century!'[12] Exciting for the following three reasons at least.

The first is its unique town planning (Fig. 7.7): though it followed some of the classical Harappan norms, its overall concept departed from everything we have seen so far. At 47 ha, Dholavira's fortified area is four times that of Kalibangan. The city is bracketed between two small seasonal streams. As at Lothal, its acropolis is inside the city, but as at Kalibangan, it consists of two adjoining fortified enclosures of similar size, named 'Bailey' and 'Castle' by the excavator, the latter no doubt because of its massive walls of mud bricks flanked by dressed stones. Remarkably, the bailey's dimensions, 120 x 120 m, are exactly those of the two portions of Kalibangan's acropolis. Since Lothal's acropolis (119 x 118 m on an average) is also of almost the same size, we can rule out the play of chance: Harappan architects had precise norms in mind, just as craftsmen had with weights or seals, and builders with brick proportions.

But the similarities end here. While Mohenjo-daro and Kalibangan appear to be based on a duality between separate upper and lower towns, Dholavira's plan is essentially triple: just north of the acropolis lies the middle town, neatly criss-crossed by broad streets at right angles. While the bailey and the castle must have been home to the city's rulers and officials, the middle town perhaps sheltered traders and craftsmen. It boasted a huge 'stadium' or ceremonial ground, over 283 m long and 47.5 m wide, which must have witnessed elaborate public events. (Its proportions, incidentally, are 6:1, exactly those of Lothal's basin.) It had four long and narrow terraces on its southern side, which suggests a provision for seating. Towering over it, an imposing gate through the castle's northern wall led down to a ceremonial pathway that descended on to the stadium: we can almost picture rulers and high officials leading the procession, though the nature of the ceremonies and other activities enacted there can only be guessed.

Beyond the middle town lay the lower town with habitations in its northeastern and eastern sectors; common workers probably lived there. With architectural hierarchy being a reflection of social stratification, it would be tempting to interpret the three successive enclosures and the presence of more habitations outside the city's fortifications as the signs of a functional caste system; yet we must resist the temptation until much more is known about Harappan society and its internal workings. (Let us keep in mind, too, that a Kshatriya or warrior class is conspicuously absent from Harappan society.)

Dholavira is the only known Harappan site where stone was used on such a scale. Stone dressing was done with chisels of hardened bronze, and we will have some inkling of the task involved if we remember that the castle's fortifications, up to 18.5 m wide in places, were made of mud bricks flanked by high stone walls; within its width a few rooms were built with dressed stones, and in some of them highly polished segments of pillars, both square and circular, were found in their original places (Fig. 7.8). Such

Fig. 7.8. A room in the eastern gate of the castle's fortifications at Dholavira. Note the two square bases of stone pillars and one circular segment. (© ASI)

segments, with a central hole, were piled up on top of one another, and when the desired height was reached, a wooden pole was inserted through the whole column to keep it together—an ingenious alternative to monolithic pillars.

There is an unexpected feature in Dholavira's town planning, which has to do with the specific proportions followed by its enclosures, and we will have a peep at it in Chapter 9.

Water conservation is Dholavira's second hallmark, inseparable from the first. The city had a few wells, with the most imposing of them (Fig. 7.9) being in the castle, but great care was taken to store every possible amount of rainwater: a series of huge reservoirs hugged the castle's eastern and southern fortifications; the largest two measured about 73 x 29 m and 33 x 9 m respectively, with the latter carved out of massive rock, making it, in Bisht's opinion, 'the earliest ever rock-cut example'[13] of water structure (Fig. 7.10). They were partly fed by rainwater harvested from the

Fig. 7.9. A stone well in Dholavira's castle. (The woman at the bottom gives the scale.) Note the grooves on the stone slab, made by sliding ropes. (© ASI)

castle, where complex stone structures were built to that effect. Elsewhere, huge stone drains, high enough for a man to walk through, directed storm water to the western and northwestern sections of the lower town separated by broad bunds, creating in effect as many reservoirs. Their main supply, however, came from the two seasonal streams to the north and south of the city, whose waters were slowed down by a series of dams and partly deflected to the lower town. Altogether, as much as a third of Dholavira's area was intended to conserve water: in effect, the monsoon must have turned it into a kind of lake city.

Two important conclusions flow from Dholavira's skills in water management—which, once again, will long remain the envy of our modern Indian cities. First, the size of the storm-water drains points to the sudden inrush of water during heavy rains, while the dams, the rainwater harvesting structures and the sheer hugeness of the reservoirs reflect a desire to save every drop of the precious liquid: rains must have been rare overall. In other words, the pattern of rainfall was more or less what it is today

Fig. 7.10. Dholavira: a huge rock-cut reservoir ('SR3'), south of the castle.

in Kachchh. Second, we find at Dholavira the same obsession with water as at Mohenjo-daro: there, most archaeologists have seen in it a religious trait, keeping in mind the Great Bath, the vast number of wells, and the luxury of the bathrooms.

Its town planning apart, Dholavira shot into prominence because of a unique find: an inscription almost three metres long, found lying on the floor of one of the chambers of the castle's northern gate. It was not inscribed there; its ten signs, each over 35 cm high, were made of a crystalline material which must have been embedded in a wooden plank, and the whole 'signboard' was probably hung above the northern gate, where it would have been visible to much of the middle town. In terms of size, there is no remotely comparable inscription from any other Harappan site. (Of course, boards with signs simply carved or painted on a plank would have vanished without a trace; it is the crystalline material alone that was preserved in this case.)

Although the Dholavira signboard has not helped crack the script, it does show that a substantial number of people—at least those assembled on the ceremonial ground just below, in this case—were expected to read it. This gives the lie to earlier theories that knowledge of the script was reserved for a small 'elite'.

After a few centuries, Dholavira's admirable urban order suffered an eclipse. The civic maintenance came to be neglected; the city shrank to a small settlement, which was eventually abandoned. After an interval, new people came and occupied the site for a while, but their rough circular dwellings had no connection with the previous planned houses, nor were any of the classical Harappan features visible. Gone was the splendour of the city with its massive acropolis towering over wide streets and huge water reservoirs.

The new dwellers could not stay very long. The last standing buildings crumbled, and sand and mud slowly buried the ruins, sending them to sleep for some four millennia.

8

When Rivers Go Haywire

Why this brilliant civilization disintegrated after seven or eight centuries is perhaps the greatest enigma of its enigmatic evolution. In fact, a few archaeologists question the very concept of an 'end'. There is no doubt that towards the end of the third millennium, the striking cohesion of the urban order, which had taken shape over long ages, crumbled over a century or two. Most cities were abandoned; the few that still harboured inhabitants saw the complete loss of a civic order: no more standardized bricks or neat streets or drains or garbage bins—in a word, settlements that began to resemble suburbs of our Indian cities of the twenty-first century!

What might have triggered this collapse? The only safe answer is, we do not know for sure; there are several possible explanations, all of them plausible.

A MAN-MADE END?

There are, broadly speaking, three schools of thought on the issue: the first attributes the end of the Indus cities to a destruction wrought by invaders; the second rests its case on political or economic turmoil; the third lays emphasis on environmental upheavals of various kinds.

By man-made destruction a bloody invasion is generally meant, possibly by Aryans carried across the Khyber Pass by their conquering impulse: the militarily superior, horse-riding Aryans swooped down on unsuspecting Harappans and sacked their orderly cities. But on the basis of hard evidence marshalled during the last few decades, the archaeological community has long discarded such a blood-and-thunder end for the Indus–Sarasvatī cities. Not only has the evidence initially proposed (such as skeletons found in a street of Mohenjo-daro) been categorically rejected, but archaeologists have also agreed that there are no traces of the arrival of a new culture from Central Asia, such as we should expect in the case of an Aryan invasion or migration.[1]

There are a few advocates of violence caused by marauders or some internal social turmoil; for example, some scholars have tried to make much of 'vandalized' statues found at the end of the Mature phase.[2] However, as Kenoyer pointed out, some of those statues 'may have been damaged in the collapse of a building or through natural weathering'.[3] In his opinion, 'there is no evidence for violent conflict in the Indus cities during the late phase of occupation, though there may have been increased banditry along trade routes and outside of the cities.'[4]

In the last analysis, human aggression and violent social upheavals remain wholly conjectural in the Harappan context: no doubt the social order must have vastly changed with the great urban breakdown, but more likely as a consequence than as a cause of it.

The same uncertainty surrounds the thesis that a drastic reduction in external trade, evidenced in Mesopotamia around 1900 BCE, might have triggered a chain reaction in Harappan society, depriving it of a source of wealth and rendering many craftsmen jobless. While the reduction in trade is a fact, whether it was a prime cause or a concomitant circumstance cannot be determined at this stage.

There are subtler propositions in the category of a systemic collapse. One, expressed by Possehl, envisages that the 'Indus ideology', which we see at work in the high civic order, was perhaps 'too perfect'[5]—in other words, too set in its ways and unable to adapt to 'changing conditions'. There may well be some truth in this ingenious hypothesis, but it is hard to put it to test and it does not explain what the changing circumstances might have been; moreover, by spreading to very diverse regions and exploiting a wide array of natural resources, the Harappans did demonstrate a degree of adaptability.

More convincing, to my mind, is the view put forth by Dilip Chakrabarti: 'The Harappans eventually came to be rather thinly stretched on the ground, and the weakening of their political fabric became almost inevitable . . . The Harappans overstretched themselves.'[6] There may be merit in this perspective, as we know that the Harappan state was not held together by a strong centripetal force such as military coercion; the complex internal relationships between the different classes and communities may have become increasingly difficult to maintain or coordinate across the vast Harappan world. Kenoyer proposes, for instance, that 'the widely extended trade and political networks would have been seriously impacted by minor changes in economic productivity . . .'[7]

Both Chakrabarti and Kenoyer, however, also acknowledge the play of environmental factors, which are of two kinds: humanly induced and natural. Before we turn to them, we need to explore a crucial question: In what kind of environment did the Harappan cities develop?

DID HARAPPAN URBANISM RISE IN AN ARID PHASE?

The answer to this question depends largely on whether the Indian monsoon was more copious or less than it is now. If it was the former, were today's parched regions of northwest India and Pakistan covered with lush forests babbling with streams? Many climatic and environmental studies have come up with elements of an answer—unfortunately with divergent results. It is well established, for instance, that as the planet warmed at the end of the last Glacial Age, the southwest monsoon intensified on the subcontinent around 8000 BCE. But what happened afterwards?

Among the first major studies, Gurdip Singh's, in 1971, remains a reference. It was based on palynological evidence from three lakes of Rajasthan, and envisaged a wet climate during the Mature

phase followed by a sharp decline in rainfall around 2000 BCE.[8]*
In 1984, V.N. Misra refuted Singh's chronology on the basis of
archaeological and other evidence, which in his view showed that
'the semi-arid and arid environments' of the region were already
established in Harappan times.[9] Moreover, Singh's radiocarbon
dates, once recalibrated by Shaffer and Lichtenstein,[10] pushed the
wet phase into Early Harappan times and, therefore, placed the
Mature phase in an already marked trend to aridity.

A decade after Gurdip Singh's study, R.A. Bryson and A.M.
Swain also examined ancient pollen from the lakes of Rajasthan,
and opted for a similar high rainfall model (especially high winter rainfall), with aridity setting in sometime before 1800 BCE.[11]
This study, which confirmed Singh's initial interpretation, remains
often quoted too, but here also, it was pointed out that after
recalibration, this phase of higher rainfall should be 're-dated to
a pre-Mature Harappan period'.[12]

In other words, if the recalibration exercises are accepted, these
two studies support the view that 'the climate of [the Greater Indus
Valley] was not markedly different in the third millennium BC
from the one we have today', as Possehl puts it.[13] Indeed, this is
the dominant opinion among archaeologists today, and in support
of it, several new studies can be cited besides the above two. We
have already seen three of them. One, Marie-Agnès Courty (p. 62)
deduced from her study of soils and archaeological deposits in
the Ghaggar–Chautang region that 'climatic conditions have
actually fluctuated very little since the Protohistoric period and
have therefore remained semi-arid'.[14] Two, Geyh's and Ploethner's
work (p. 76) showed that the Hakra had stopped flowing before
2700 BCE in a section close to the Indian border. Three, Rao's
and Kulkarni's isotope study (p. 74) of palaeo-waters in western
Rajasthan found no recharge after about 3000 BCE.

Besides, in 1983, M.B. McKean studied pollen and sediments
in the region of Balakot (northwest of Karachi) and concluded:

---

* Palynology is the study of pollen, often (as here) of fossilized pollen, a good
marker of ancient climate and environment.

'There is nothing in the Balakot pollen data, which might suggest that the climate during the protohistoric period in Las Bela was decidedly wetter than at present.'[15] And in 1999, Y. Enzel and eight colleagues analysed sediments of the now mostly dry lake of Lunkaransar and found that it held water in 8000 BCE, began to decline around 4000 BCE, and dried up by 3500 BCE.[16]

Fig. 8.1 graphically captures the above seven studies, all of which conclude that the Mature Harappan phase developed in an arid environment.

OR, WAS IT IN A WETTER PHASE?

That is not the end of the matter, however. Against the above seven studies, we can array seven others (Fig. 8.2), delineated below, that tend towards an apparently opposite view:

♦ In 1983, R.J. Wasson and six Indian colleagues probed sediments in the Didwana lake of Rajasthan, which still holds some salty water (Fig. 8.3). They found that 'freshwater, high lake level conditions prevailed' between 4000 and 2000 BCE.[17] This precisely includes the Mature Harappan phase.

♦ In 1996, P.D. Naidu, studying planktonic foraminifers from the Arabian Sea, found that the upwelling, and therefore the southwest monsoon, was at its lowest from about 1500 BCE to 800 CE. The preceding period, therefore, appears to have had greater monsoon intensity.[18]

♦ In 1999, Ulrich von Rad and five colleagues studied sediments in the Arabian Sea off Karachi and concluded that 'precipitation decreased in southern Pakistan after 4000–3500 yr BP',[19] that is, after 2000 BCE, which agrees with the preceding study.

♦ A year later, palynologist Netajirao Phadtare examined pollen and peat in the Garhwal Himalayas (west of the Gangotri glacier) and found evidence of 'a warm, humid climate, with highest monsoon intensity' from about 4000 to 2500 BCE; after 2000 BCE, there was 'a sharp decrease in temperature and rainfall', reaching a minimum about 1500 BCE. Phadtare

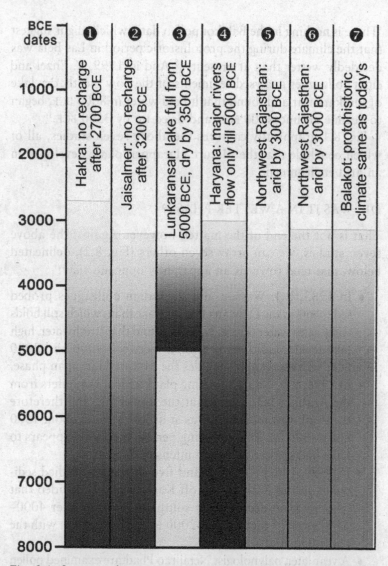

Fig. 8.1. Seven studies pointing to an arid environment during the Mature Harappan phase: (1) Geyh and Ploethner on the Hakra; (2) Rao and Kulkarni in the Jaisalmer region; (3) Enzel, et al. at Lunkaransar; (4) M.A. Courty in Haryana and north Rajasthan; (5) Gurdip Singh on Rajasthan lakes; (6) Bryson and Swain on Rajasthan lakes; (7) McKean at Balakot. Compare with Fig. 8.2.

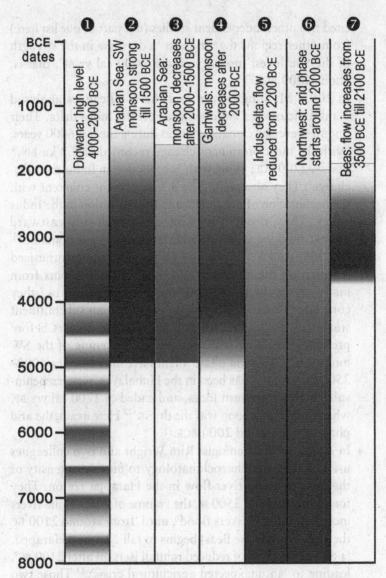

Fig. 8.2. Seven studies pointing to a wetter environment during the Mature Harappan phase: (1) Wasson, et al. at Didwana; (2) Naidu in the Arabian Sea; (3) von Rad, et al. off Karachi; (4) Phadtare in the Garhwals; (5) Staubwasser, et al. in the Indus delta; (6) Gupta, et al. in the Northwest; (7) Wright around Harappa. Compare with Fig. 8.1.

cited five other independent studies (not part of our list here) from other regions that support 'a decrease in the strength of the Southwest monsoon about 4000 cal yr BP', that is, about 2000 BCE.[20]

♦ In 2003, M. Staubwasser and three colleagues analysed planktonic oxygen isotope ratios off the Indus delta. Their findings revealed climatic changes during the last 6000 years, 'with the most prominent change recorded at 4.2 ka BP',* that is, 2200 BCE, along with 'a reduction in Indus river discharge'. They observed, 'The 4.2 ka event is coherent with the termination of urban Harappan civilization in the Indus valley. Thus, drought may have initiated southeastward habitat tracking within the Harappan cultural domain.'[21]

♦ In 2006, Anil K. Gupta and three colleagues synthesized research on the monsoon and other climatic inputs from many sources including their own. 'It appears to us,' they concluded, 'that the arid phase in the Indian subcontinent started ca 5000–4000 cal yrs BP [calibrated years before present] coinciding with a stepwise weakening of the SW monsoon ... The arid phase might have intensified ca 4000–3500 cal yrs BP as has been in the Himalayas, western peninsula and northwestern India, and ended ca 1700 cal yrs BP, when the SW monsoon was the driest.'[22] Here again, the arid phase starts around 2000 BCE.

♦ In 2008, the archaeologist Rita Wright and two colleagues used models of archaeoclimatology to plot the intensity of the monsoon and river flow in the Harappa region. They found that 'around 3500 BC the volume of water in the rivers increases, and the rivers flood', until 'from around 2100 BC the river flow [in the Beas] begins to fall'. Around Harappa, 'a 600-year period of reduced rainfall [sets in] after 2100 BC', leading to 'an unexpected agricultural crisis'.[23] Those two dates roughly bracket the Early and much of the Mature phases.

---

* Ka = kilo-annum, or 1000 years.

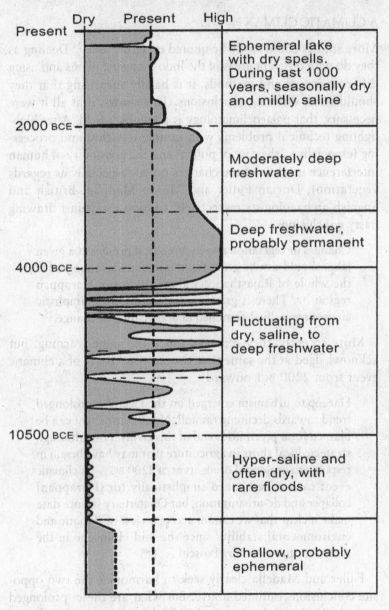

Fig. 8.3. A curve of the water level of Didwana Lake, Rajasthan (adapted from R.J. Wasson, et al.).

A CLIMATIC CLIMAX?

More studies could easily be quoted on either side.[24] Dealing as they do with different areas of the Indo-Gangetic plains and using different inputs and methods, it is hardly surprising that they should reach differing conclusions. This shows, if at all it were necessary, that palaeoclimatology is a complex field. After highlighting technical problems with sample selection and processing (especially in the case of pollen) and the possibility of human interference in some of the changes noted (especially as regards vegetation), Dorian Fuller and Marco Madella, British and Spanish archaeologists respectively, caution us against drawing hasty conclusions:

> Changes in vegetation and hydrology, if present at a given lake, should not be generalized into climatic changes for the whole of Rajasthan, let alone the entire Harappan region . . . There is growing discomfort with simplistic environmentally determined understanding of change.[25]

More recently, they repeated much the same warning, but acknowledged at the same time the indirect effects of a climatic event from 2200 BCE onward:

> Harappan urbanism emerged on the face of a prolonged trend towards declining rainfall. No climatic event can be blamed for a precipitous end of this civilisation, although strategic local shifts in agriculture that may have begun in response to prolonged droughts at ca 2200 BC . . . A climatic event cannot be blamed simplistically for [Harappan] collapse and de-urbanisation, but Quaternary science data make it clear that we cannot accept a view of climatic and environmental stability since the mid-Holocene in the region (as promoted by Possehl . . .).[26]

Fuller and Madella clearly seek to harmonize the two opposite conclusions outlined above. But what are these 'prolonged droughts' taking place around 2200 BCE? They are, in fact, a very widespread phenomenon that affected Egypt and Turkey,[27]

Mesopotamia (bringing about the end of the Akkadian empire[28]), large parts of Africa,[29] China[30] and, even, North America.[31] If attributing the end of the Indus civilization to this single event would indeed be 'simplistic', to ignore its impact altogether is certainly unreasonable. There may be a grain of truth in the Mahābhārata's mention of 'a great drought of twelve years' or the disappearance of thousands of lakes.

ENVIRONMENTAL ISSUES

Climatic and environmental conditions are two distinct things. Even if we accept that the Harappan climate was moving towards aridity, it does not follow that the ecosystem was as degraded as it is today.

Early archaeologists such as John Marshall had argued that the widespread use of baked bricks and the depiction on Indus seals of animals such as the elephant, the rhinoceros, the water buffalo and the gaur (often misnamed as the 'Indian bison') pointed to a moister and greener environment. In reply, it has been observed that those animals were still to be seen in parts of the Indus Valley till recent decades or centuries, and therefore, except for denser gallery forests along the rivers, the environment need not have been markedly different in Harappan times.

Nevertheless, if that were the case, it would be hard to explain the presence at Kalibangan of bone remains of the elephant, the one-horned rhinoceros, the water buffalo, several deer species and the river turtle. For archaeozoologist Bhola Nath, 'the remains of these animals show that the climate at that time was more humid than the arid climate of present day'.[32] To his colleagues S. Banerjee and S. Chakraborty, the occurrence at Kalibangan of the rhinoceros in particular 'strengthens the geological evidence that the desert conditions of this area are of recent origin'.[33] Moving to Gujarat, P.K. Thomas observes that the same animal 'is identified from a large number of Harappan and Chalcolithic sites ... [and] inhabited a major part of the Gujarat plains in the protohistoric period ... The identification of large herbivores like rhinoceros, wild buffalo and probably wild cattle at many of the Gujarat Harappan sites suggests that the ecological conditions were more congenial for animal life during the protohistoric period in Gujarat'.[34]

Taking all viewpoints into consideration, I propose to strike a middle path and accept Thomas's more 'congenial', lusher conditions in Harappan times together with a wetter climate, gradually moving towards aridity, and culminating in a prolonged drought around 2200 BCE.[35]

This takes us to the question of human interference: did the Harappans contribute to an ecological degradation of their environment? Initially proposed by Wheeler, this theory is known as the 'wearing out of the landscape' and argues that the Harappans' industrial activities must have accelerated deforestation: baking bricks or pots, working copper and a host of other activities from the making of faience to plain cooking demand fuel—that is, wood. Mohenjo-daro alone consumed many millions of baked bricks and thousands of tons of timber; construction apart, its population of at least 40,000 souls must have put a considerable strain on the local environment in terms of firewood collection and agriculture.

Nowadays, archaeologists generally disagree that this could have hastened the city's demise,[36] arguing that the rich Indus alluvium would have soon regenerated the forests on its banks: in 1961, R.L. Raikes and R.H.J. Dyson[37] calculated that '400 acres of gallery forest would have been sufficient for the building of Mohenjo-daro at intervals of about 140 years'.[38] But such calculations do not take into account the daily consumption of fuel wood for bronze and pottery industries and for cooking. Also, Walter Fairservis, while endorsing the calculations of Raikes and Dyson, added his own concerning the amount of fodder consumed by the cattle used in Mohenjo-daro, both as a source of food (dairy products and meat) and for ploughing. His conclusion was that

three-quarters [of Mohenjo-daro's fodder needs] had to be obtained by foraging in the surrounding forests and grasslands. This formidable assault on the indigenous flora most certainly affected the ecology and had an adverse effect on the land and aided the spread of the active floodplain.[39]

Grazing, and possibly overgrazing, should be added to this picture. Man-made damage could also have been compounded by natural factors: in Mohenjo-daro's case, deforestation and land degradation would have made annual floods more violent and the Indus more prone to shifts. Indeed, there is evidence that 'within at least 500 years of existence of the city, the river must have changed its course several times'.[40]

Also, in a general trend towards aridity, even small shifts in land or water use can tip the scales towards desertification; recent and tragic examples of this have been witnessed in regions as different as the Sahel and Inner Mongolia. Ecological damage inflicted by the intense industrial activity and population concentration of Indus cities could have set off such a vicious circle, or rather a spiral. With all their ingenuity, the Harappans might have taken the land's bounty for granted—just as we do today.

MOHENJO-DARO AND THE INDUS

Environmental changes apart, rivers have their own whims and fancies.

A thesis first propounded by M.R. Sahni in the 1950s, and expanded a decade later by Robert Raikes and George Dales, proposed evidence of a tectonic uplift that might have dammed the course of the lower Indus, provoking destructive floods that would have engulfed Mohenjo-daro. It rested its case on one such event observed as recently as in 1819, when an earthquake raised a huge embankment called 'Allah's bund' in the northern part of the Rann of Kachchh: it was 3 to 8 m high, over 100 km long and 25 to 30 km wide! This natural dam impounded eastern courses of the Indus, submerging an area of some 5000 km² and swallowing numerous villages, until it was breached a few years later by the sheer pressure of the waters. Something of the sort could have happened at Mohenjo-daro, they reasoned. And several excavators have reported 'the presence of massive disruptive floods throughout the history of the city',[41] in the words of George Dales.

But that thesis was challenged in the 1960s, notably by the archaeologist H.T. Lambrick, who found the evidence unconvincing. He proposed that, quite on the contrary, the Indus shifted *away* from Mohenjo-daro (in a process known as 'avulsion'*): 'The surrounding country, starved of water, immediately began to deteriorate.'[42] The deterioration would have stemmed not just from the loss of the river, but also from that of its yearly floods that watered the soil in time for the winter crop and fertilized it with rich alluvium. Worse, the river-based communication network that Mohenjo-daro vitally depended on, in Michael Jansen's opinion,[43] would have been completely disrupted. Louis Flam, a US archaeologist who has done considerable research in Sind, recently elaborated that 'a major change ... in the main river channel would have brought widespread abandonment of many sites and a movement of population out of the Lower Indus basin into adjacent and more "stable" areas'.[44]

These, then, are the two contending theories on Mohenjo-daro and Sind, both unproven, although the second one is now more favoured. But unless we go by the obsolete view of an emperor sitting enthroned at Mohenjo-daro, its abandonment alone need not have brought about the end of the whole civilization; the Sarasvatī basin and Gujarat could have absorbed at least some of the distant impact.

THE DEATH OF A RIVER

If the evidence is inconclusive in the case of the Indus, in the Sarasvatī's it is far more convincing, and of two kinds.

First, the abandonment of Kalibangan has been dated to around 1900 BCE, although with some imprecision in the radiocarbon

---

* Avulsion occurs when a meandering river cuts through the base of a loop, resulting in a straighter course and leaving behind a lake in the place of the old meander.

samples.[45] This town was clearly of importance, and must have depended on the Sarasvatī for water as well as communication; the river's disappearance would have understandably brought about its end.

At this point, it is sometimes objected that sites away from the Sarasvatī were also abandoned more or less during the same epoch, and therefore some other cause must have been at play. Our second type of evidence disposes of the objection: the radical changes in site distribution occurring between the Mature and the Late phases cannot but be a reflection of hydrological changes. We saw in Figs 6.8 and 6.9 how the section of the Hakra bed close to today's international border between India and Pakistan was deserted: Cholistan has 174 Mature sites, but just 50 Late ones (a drop of 71 per cent), all of them clustered around faraway Derawar Fort; on the Indian side of the border, northern Rajasthan, with 31 Mature Harappan sites, has none at all of the Late phase, while further upstream in Haryana, over a thousand Late sites mushroom (Table 6.1). The only possible conclusion from the complete absence of Late Harappan sites on either side of the border is that the central portion of the Sarasvatī had stopped flowing.

Not only would this have greatly affected the hundreds of Harappan sites in the region, it would also have had repercussions in Sind: let us recall that the loss of the Sarasvatī was caused partly by the eastward capture of the Yamunā, and partly by the progressive desertion by the Sutlej, which ended up joining the Beas. The latter desertion, envisaged by many scholars since the nineteenth century, is confirmed by archaeological evidence as argued in Chapter 7. But the Beas is a tributary of the Indus, which suddenly found itself swollen by the very waters that the Sarasvatī had lost! 'As a result,' write the Allchins, 'the Indus floods would have become greater in volume and more erratic.'[46] Kenoyer makes the same point, linking the Indus's eastward 'swing' to the capture of part of the Sarasvatī's waters by the Indus system.[47] Flam is more specific: 'The Sutlej River has the highest average annual discharge of all the main Indus tributaries of the Punjab as they exit their mountain catchments and enter the plains', and therefore 'an increase in water and sediment discharge of that magnitude [provoked by the westward shift of the Sutlej] would have had dramatic effects downstream in the Lower Indus Basin.'[48]

This domino effect provides a coherent explanation covering both core regions: the Sutlej's shift causes the Sarasvatī's final desiccation and aggravates the Indus floods, which wash away some sites and cut others off or bury them under sediment. This would also explain why so few Late Harappan sites have been found in Sind: only six of them have been identified.[49]

Whether things happened exactly in that way we will only know after a great deal more exploration. In the meantime, let us stress the consensus among archaeologists on the radical consequences of the Sarasvatī's disappearance. To those quoted above—Mughal, Possehl, the Allchins, Kenoyer and Flam—we can add many more, among them the following:

♦ B.B. Lal: 'The obvious result [of the diversion of the Saras-vatī's waters into the Yamunā system] was the migration of the [Harappan] people towards the north-east where some water was still available in the uppermost reaches of the Sarasvatī and Ghaggar and further east in the upper plains of the Gangā–Yamunā *Doāb*.'[50]

♦ Dilip Chakrabarti: 'The Sutlej which was the main supplier of water volume through the Ghaggar–Sarasvatī–Hakra channel, shifted and joined the Indus River drainage. The Yamuna was likely to have played a [similar] role in the fate of the Drishadvati system[51] … To a considerable extent the process [of weakening of the political fabric of the Indus civilization] must have been linked to the hydrographic changes in the Sarasvati–Drishadvati system.'[52]

♦ Jane McIntosh: '[The desertion of the Drishadvati and the Sutlej] is typical of the instability of the river courses in the Indus plains—but in the case of the Saraswati, the effect was not localized but devastating on a major scale. Cities, towns, and villages were abandoned, their inhabitants drifting to other regions of the Indus realms and eastward towards the

Ganges, pushing back the centuries-old eastern boundaries of Indus culture and venturing into uncharted territory.'[53]

♦ D.P Agrawal: 'It is obvious that in north and west Rajasthan tectonically changed paleochannel configurations were a major factor which affected the human settlements, perhaps from the pre-Harappan times onwards. Major diversions cut off the vital tributaries and growing desiccation ... dried up the once mighty Saraswati and Drishadvati rivers.'[54]

♦ V.N. Misra: 'Late Harappan sites are concentrated on the tributaries of the [Sarasvatī] river, originating in the Siwalik Hills. They appear to be a consequence of the desiccation of the river and mass migration of the population to less dry regions near the Siwalik Hills and across the Yamunā.'[55]

♦ Marco Madella and Dorian Fuller: 'Archaeological research in Cholistan has led to the discovery of a large number of sites along the dry channels of the Ghaggar–Hakra river (often identified with the lost Sarasvati and Drishadvati rivers of Sanskrit traditions) ... The final desiccation of some of these channels may have had major repercussions for the Harappan Civilisation and is considered a major factor in the de-centralisation and de-urbanisation of the Late Harappan period.'[56]

However, the Sarasvatī's disappearance does not rule out other factors in the decline of the Indus–Sarasvatī civilization. Possehl, for instance, acknowledging that 'over the course of the third and second millennia, the Sarasvati dried up',[57] still prefers a socio-cultural cause for the end of the urban phase. In this perspective, the natural cataclysm could have been a sort of *coup de grâce* delivered to an already weakened socio-political fabric. Exactly in what order each contributory factor played its part, we may never know.

LESSON FROM THE PAST

Over a few centuries—this much we know—the great river died. The word is apt, for we forget too easily that a river, just like a living organism, is born, thrives, declines and disappears. In fact, the phenomenon is happening once more before our eyes: all glacier-fed Himalayan rivers—including the Ganges, the Yamuna, the Brahmaputra and the Indus—are threatened by the rapid melting of the glaciers that constitute their perennial sources. Current studies estimate that within thirty to fifty years, all of them will be reduced to the status of rain-fed, seasonal rivers.[58] The chain of repercussions this will have on the whole of South Asia is beyond comprehension—at least beyond that of our statesmen, who are too busy with 'global' matters to even begin to grasp this disaster in the making under their very noses.

There is a difference, however, between the Sarasvatī's disappearance and that of the Ganges or the Brahmaputra. The first was a 'natural calamity', as we might call it (though deforestation in Haryana and Punjab could conceivably have accelerated the desertion of the Sutlej and the Yamunā). But the second will be wholly man-made, as our hyperactivity overheats the planet and global warming causes glaciers and ice sheets to melt away. The most optimistic among environmentalists believe that we still have a few years to reverse the trend; but that will require a bold, united effort across regional and world powers, and there optimism collides with a big question mark.

The twenty-first century may well mark the end of the 3000-year-old Ganges civilization. Somewhere along the way, we have forgotten that it was essentially riverine. Even if numerous seasonal streams persist, they will not sustain the current density of population. While the scattered Late Harappans were able to adapt themselves to the new situation, fall back on rural settlements or create new ones, relocating themselves when necessary, where will the multitude of their Gangetic successors migrate?

Part 3

FROM SARASVATĪ TO GANGĀ

'From the Neolithic time till almost today there has never been, in spite of spectacular changes in the course of time, a definite gap or break in the history of the subcontinent.'

Jean-François Jarrige

'A continuous series of cultural developments links the so-called two major phases of urbanization in South Asia ... The essential of Harappan identity persisted.'

Jim Shaffer

9

The Tangible Heritage

Did the Indus–Sarasvatī civilization, then, vanish without a trace? Very nearly so, if we are to believe many histories of India.

In a recent work, Romila Thapar, a noted historian of ancient India, writes that after the collapse of the Indus cities, 'the material culture shows no continuities'.[1] In this perspective, though minor cases of survival might be spotted here and there, the Harappan world completely disintegrated: 'The civilization did indeed come to an end,'[2] as Shereen Ratnagar puts it, stressing 'the end of the traditions of sculpture, writing, architecture and, presumably, also seafaring'.[3] Most of the second millennium BCE would then be a long 'dark age', as it has often been called, until urbanism was finally reborn in the Ganges Valley in the first millennium BCE—but urbanism of a kind wholly unrelated to its Harappan antecedent.

Some archaeologists have shared this view: A. Ghosh, for instance, wrote in 1973, 'All the scanty data at present available taken into consideration, the possibility of Harappan urbanism surviving or resuscitating in the upper Ganga basin through the Late Harappan and ochre-coloured ware* sites in the middle of the first millennium BC may be forthwith rejected . . .'[4] But Ghosh rested his case mostly on the study of pottery, and data from other fields are no longer so 'scanty' as they were in his time.

In fact, evidence that has been growing by leaps and bounds

---

* This ochre-coloured pottery (OCW or OCP) is now often regarded as a degenerate form of Late Harappan pottery.

during the last few decades has been painting a very different picture. Some archaeologists, such as Possehl, now speak of 'transformation'[5] rather than 'end' of the Indus–Sarasvatī civilization; in the terminology proposed by Jim Shaffer, the Late Harappan phase (roughly 1900–1300 BCE) is called the 'Localization Era', to reflect the splintering of the Harappan tradition into localized forms no longer cohesively held together. In that view, there is no 'end', but a series of transitions that reflect both 'continuity and change',[6] in Kenoyer's words. Shaffer goes so far as to suggest that the end of Harappan urbanism might itself be something of an illusion:

> The often stated disappearance of urban centers noted for the Late Harappan [phase] is an assumption[7] ... There is no conclusive archaeological evidence to indicate that large 'urban' settlements disappear.[8]

Far more extensive excavations will alone put this challenging statement to test. What concerns us here is the quantum of continuity: did the Harappan culture fizzle out, or were some of its elements transmitted to the historical developments in the Gangetic region, where India's classical civilization grew? If it was the latter, were those transmissions of a fragmented, incidental sort ('disconnected'[9] as Ratnagar calls them), or did they form a more substantial body, a significant bridge between the two cultures?

This debate has been growing in intensity in recent decades for a reason extraneous to archaeology: scholars who hold that hypothetical Aryans invaded or migrated into the subcontinent towards the middle of the second millennium BCE divide India's protohistory into the 'pre-Aryan' and 'Aryan' eras, with the Harappan world falling into the former and the Gangetic into the latter. In this view, these two civilizations, being the creations of different peoples speaking different tongues, using different technologies, and having very different religions and cultures, are perforce separated by a gulf: a 'Vedic Night', as it was often called or, in Wheeler's phrase, a 'Vedic Dark Age'.[10]

The Indus civilization is thus seen as brilliant, no doubt, but ephemeral and solitary—an island in space and time: 'That civilization is not the direct origin of the Indian civilization',[11] writes the French scholar Bernard Sergent, the 'direct origin' being the Ganges civilization supposedly created by the recently arrived Vedic Aryans. Between the two is an 'immense "gap". . . the historical discontinuity between Harappan India and historical India'.[12]

'Discontinuity' is indeed the keyword of the invasionist perspective, which has been the dominant one since the days of Marshall, who was perhaps the first to label the Harappan culture as 'pre-Aryan'. In 1961, the noted British prehistorian and archaeologist Stuart Piggot, another proponent of the 'Dark Age'[13] concept, affirmed that 'the long-established [Harappan] cultural traditions of northwestern India were *rudely and ruthlessly interrupted* by the arrival of new people from the west'.[14] A.L. Basham concurred, finding the culture of the incoming Aryans '*diametrically opposed* to its [Harappan] predecessor'.[15] The contrast is total, the gap unbridgeable. More recently, the US Sanskritist Michael Witzel, an ardent proponent of the Aryan invasion theory, wrote, 'The Indo-Aryans, as described in the Rig-Veda, represent something definitely new in the subcontinent. Both their spiritual and much of their material culture are new.'[16]

Therefore the question before us is: Was the Ganges civilization built upon a legacy from its predecessor (and if so, how much of a legacy), or was it completely unrelated to it as the above scholars assert? Let us begin with the 'material' aspect before we move to the 'spiritual' in the next chapter.

URBANISM AND ARCHITECTURE

Excavations of historical urban centres in the Gangetic region have been disappointingly few and limited in extent, with many of them lying buried under modern cities and therefore being largely inaccessible. Even with such limited data, Jim Shaffer[17] and the British archaeologist Robin Coningham,[18] among other scholars, have highlighted parallels between the Harappan city and its counterpart of later historical times. For instance, both generally had an internal planning based on a grid plan; both had monumental public architecture; both had enclosing fortifications.

In a recent study,[19] Piotr A. Eltsov went further and proposed that in both cities, fortifications had a symbolic rather than a utilitarian role, standing for authority and segregation; in other words, they played the same part as grandiose palaces, temples or royal burials did in other civilizations (such as the Egyptian). Eltsov also noted the absence of palaces in the early Gangetic cities[20] (to the limited extent of the excavations), which echoes the same absence in the Indus–Sarasvatī cities. A careful, site-by-site analysis of such features led him to squarely place the Harappan and the Gangetic city within the same framework, the origins of which, he suggested, went back to pre-Harappan times: 'The ethos of the ancient Indian Civilization is shaped during the Neolithic and Chalcolithic Periods.'[21]

Fig. 9.1. Kaushambi's fortifications, with a revetment of baked bricks. (© ASI)

Let us be a little more specific. We have seen fortifications at a number of Harappan sites, from Kalibangan to Dholavira; Mohenjo-daro's and Harappa's mounds are also thought to have been fortified. Walled enclosures were of vital importance to the Harappan mind, although a practical usefulness did not seem to be their primary purpose. We find the same situation in historical cities such as Mathura, Kaushambi (both on the Yamuna), Rajghat (near Varanasi), Rajgir, Vaishali (both in Bihar), Shishupalgarh (near Bhubaneswar) and Ujjain (near Indore). The last city's mud fortifications, for instance, were as wide as 75 m, 14 m high, and ran for some 5 km; it would have taken no less than 4200 labourers toiling for a whole year to erect them! Kaushambi's 6 km-long rampart of compact clay was about 20 m wide at the base and rose to 9 m; it was strengthened in places by massive revetments of large baked bricks (Fig. 9.1). Shishupalgarh's rampart was 33 m wide, over 7 m high and formed a perfect square with a perimeter of 4.8 km.[22] The fact that so much labour and energy were spent to erect these colossal fortifications in both the Harappan and Gangetic cities strengthens Eltsov's thesis of a common tradition.

Moats often girdle fortifications: we saw one around Banawali, and other Harappan sites are also thought to have had protective moats; they become the norm with most historical cities (for instance, Kaushambi, Rajgir, Shishupalgarh and Ujjain), and are reflected in the meticulous instructions spelt out by Kautilya in his famous treatise on governance, the *Arthashāstra*, which is usually dated to the age of Chandragupta Maurya in the fourth century BCE.

Parallels can also be found in the layout of streets. Kalibangan had street widths standardized in an arithmetic progression: 1.8 m, 3.6 m, 5.4 m and 7.2 m; we find traces of such a system at Kaushambi as well,[23] where a road 2.44 m wide is broadened to the exact double of 4.88 m; more significantly, the *Arthashāstra*[24] prescribes streets in widths of two, four or eight *dandas*, with the *danda* being a unit of length generally taken to be about six feet or 1.8 m. More than the actual values, this concern for standardization appears to have Harappan roots (we saw it in the brick ratios, too, and will soon see it in the system of weights).

We marvelled at the garbage bins along the streets of Indus cities, and find them again at Taxila's Bhir Mound, for instance.[25] As regards the splendid Harappan drainage system, it is true that nothing so systematic or extensive has so far been unearthed from historical cities, but that could be partly due to the limited nature of the excavations; even then, drains of baked bricks, sometimes as part of sewerage systems, did emerge at Taxila,[26] Hastinapura, Kaushambi, Mathura and other sites.

Town planning apart, the structures also exhibit continuity. Pillared halls are a case in point: at Mohenjo-daro, a hall with four rows of five pillars each finds an echo in distant Pataliputra (today's Patna), where a large hall with eight rows of ten pillars overlooks an ancient canal.[27] The common ratio (5:4 and 10:8) is intriguing to say the least, and hard to ascribe to mere coincidence.

We noted (Fig. 7.2) the unique shape of Banawali's apsidal temple; it finds a parallel in Atranjikhera[28] (some 90 km northeast of Agra), where an apsidal temple is dated around 200 BCE (Fig. 9.2). Roughly 8 x 6.5 m in size, it is about one and a half times larger than Banawali's structure, but of similar proportions, with the only difference being the square platform at its centre, where the worshipped deity probably stood.

Coming to the Harappan house, it has often been shown how

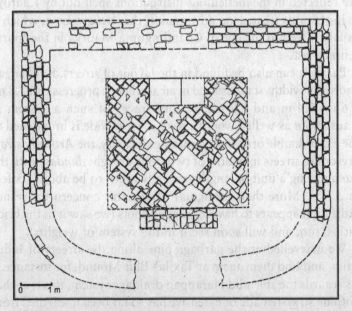

Fig. 9.2. An apsidal temple at Atranjikhera (c. 200 BCE). Compare this with Banawali's apsidal temple, Fig. 7.2. (© ASI)

it follows a few specific plans, generally based on a central yard with rooms on three sides and a wide entrance on the fourth—a general layout which persisted in historical sites (such as Bhita near Allahabad) and is still found in many parts of today's rural India. In fact, in a detailed study, Anna Sarcina demonstrated in 1979 the similarity of house plans at Mohenjo-daro with those in modern Gujarat.[29]

Construction techniques also survived. B.B. Lal documented a few:[30] for instance, a peculiar mixture of terracotta nodules and charcoal was found not only in the flooring of Kalibangan houses, but also in those of neighbouring villages 4500 years later; its ability to keep insects and dampness away is doubtless the reason for the persistence of this tradition. At Pirak, Jarrige (whom we met as the excavator of Mehrgarh) and his colleagues were 'very struck' by a pattern of 'four levels of niches symmetrically arranged all along the walls', and even more struck when they found an identical pattern of niches in the houses of nearby Hindu quarters that had been abandoned at the time of Partition—3000 years after their Harappan predecessors.[31]

The trademark Harappan well, built with trapezoid bricks (see Fig. 5.5), did not disappear either; it has come to light at quite a few historical sites, even in the south.[32] Huge soak jars of terracotta also remained in use in post-Harappan times.[33]

Taken together, the above traits establish that despite significant differences, urban developments in the Indus–Sarasvatī and Ganges regions do belong to 'a single Indo-Gangetic cultural tradition which can be traced for millennia'; in the words of Jim Shaffer, 'a continuous series of cultural developments links the so-called two major phases of urbanization in South Asia', the Harappan and the historical. His conclusion is plain: 'the essential of Harappan identity persisted'.[34]

I must, therefore, disagree with Shereen Ratnagar's assertion, quoted at the beginning of this chapter, that the Harappan architectural tradition disappeared; the above examples demonstrate that quite a few of its aspects survived, even if new styles and structures did appear in the Gangetic plains.

THE CODE BEHIND DHOLAVIRA

An unexpected case of continuity in the urban field emerges from
Dholavira in the Rann of Kachchh. As we noticed when we
visited the extraordinary site (Fig. 7.8), this city presents us with
a unique town plan. Looking at it, US astrophysicist J. McKim
Malville was impressed by 'the apparent intent . . . to interweave,
by means of geometry, the microcosm and the macrocosm'.[35] But
how did this 'interweaving' actually work?

When the excavator, R.S. Bisht, measured the city's fortifications[36] (Table 9.1), something odd alerted him: he found that
the various enclosures respected specific proportions rather than
random ones (we have noted often enough the Harappans' love
for precise ratios). The overall city's proportions (771 x 617 m)
are very precisely in the ratio 5:4 (that is, the length is five-fourths
of the width, or 1.25 times the width, or again 25 per cent longer
than the width). As if to make it clear that this is not the mere
play of chance, Dholavira's planners applied the same ratio to
the castle's dimensions, both inner and outer. In fact, just before
the Mature phase, the castle, which was the earliest part of the
city, had slightly different proportions: it was subjected to
alterations so as to bring its dimensions in line with the desired
proportions—one more clue that they were consciously chosen.

Table 9.1. Dholavira's principal dimensions (rounded off to the
nearest metre).

Dimension	Measurement (in metres)	
	Length	Width
Lower town (entire city)	771	617
Middle town	341	290
Ceremonial ground	283	47
Castle (inner)	114	92
Castle (outer)	151	118
Bailey	120	120

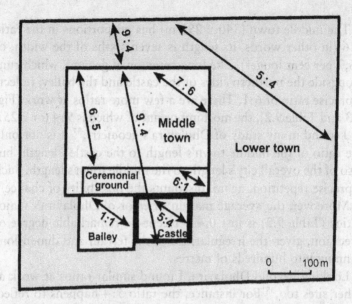

Fig. 9.3. Dholavira's plan with the principal ratios at work.

Table 9.2. Main ratios at work at Dholavira, with margins of error.

Dimensions	Ratio	Margin of Error (%)
Castle, inner*	5 : 4	0.9
Castle, outer*	5 : 4	2.4
Bailey*	1 : 1	0.0
Middle town*	7 : 6	0.5
Ceremonial ground*	6 : 1	0.7
Lower town (entire city)*	5 : 4	0.0
Castle's outer to inner lengths†	4 : 3	0.7
Middle town's length to castle's inner length†	3 : 1	0.4
Middle town's length to castle's outer length†	9 : 4	0.2
City's length to middle town's length†	9 : 4	0.6
Middle town's length to ceremonial ground's length†	6 : 5	0.3

* proposed by R.S. Bisht   † proposed by Michel Danino

The middle town (340 x 290 m) has proportions in the ratio 7:6 (in other words, its length is seven-sixths of the width, or 16.7 per cent longer). The long ceremonial ground, which runs alongside the northern sides of the castle and the bailey, reflects a precise ratio of 6:1. There are a few more ratios at work (Fig. 9.3 and Table 9.2), the most important of which is 9:4 (or 2.25): as I found in my study of Dholavira's geometry,[37] it is not only the ratio of the middle town's length to the castle's length, but also of the overall city's length to the middle town's length. Such a precise repetition, again, discounts the possibility of chance.

Moreover, the average margin of error of Dholavira's major ratios (Table 9.2) is just 0.6 per cent—a remarkable degree of precision, given the irregularities of the terrain and dimensions running into hundreds of metres.

Looking beyond Dholavira, I found similar ratios at work at other sites too.[38] For instance, the ratio 5:4 happens to reflect the proportions of Lothal (whose overall dimensions are 280 x 225 m), of Harappa's 'granary', a huge building measuring 50 x 40 m, and of a major building in Mohenjo-daro's 'HR' area measuring 18.9 x 15.2 m. I could not help noting that the 'assembly hall', also called 'pillared hall', located on the southern part of the acropolis, had four rows of five pillars each (5 x 4), while its dimensions (about 23 x 27 m) were in the ratio 7:6, thus reflecting Dholavira's main two ratios! Or, if we look at the ratio 9:4, we find it at Mohenjo-daro again in a long building located just north of the Great Bath, which measures 56.4 x 25 m. (Other ratios clearly identifiable at Mohenjo-daro's acropolis include 3:1, 3:2, 7:4 and 7:5.)

The emerging pattern is that when it came to fortifications and major buildings, rather than leave it to chance or circumstance, Harappans preferred to follow specific ratios, which they must have regarded as particularly auspicious. Their motives may have been aesthetical or religious, or both—perhaps also cosmological, as Mckim Malville proposed. Whatever they were, we find the same love for ratios in much of Sanskrit literature, and sometimes the very same ratios.

Take the case of Dholavira's main ratio, 5:4. The Shatapatha Brāhmana describes the trapezoidal sacrificial ground,[39] the *mahāvedi* (No. 1 in Fig. 9.4), where the fire altars are placed: its

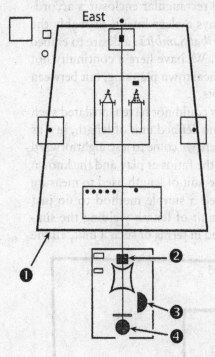

western side is thirty steps long while the shorter eastern side is twenty-four steps—a proportion of 1.25 or 5:4. A few centuries later, India's most ancient texts of geometry, the *Shulba-sūtra*s, giving minute instructions on the construction of multi-layered altars, repeat the same proportions for the *mahāvedi* but in terms of precise linear units rather than steps.[40]

Fig. 9.4. Overall plan of the *mahāvedi*.

We find the ratio 5:4 again a millennium later, prescribed in various traditions of *Vāstu-shāstra*, the Indian science of architecture. Thus, in his encyclopaedic *Brihat Samhitā*, Varāhamihira states that for a 'king's palace . . . [the] length is greater than the breadth by a quarter'.[41] In other words, the length is equal to the width plus one-fourth of the width—that is, five-fourths of the width, or 5:4, as with Dholavira's city and castle enclosures. Should we be tempted to dismiss this as a coincidence, Varāhamihira states in the very next verse that in the case of the house of a commander-in-chief '[the] length exceeds the width by a sixth',[42] that is to say, seven-sixths or 7:6—the same proportion as Dholavira's middle town!

It was in fact this double identity between Dholavira's two main ratios and those of Varāhamihira three millennia later that drew my attention to Dholavira's geometry: it would have been more 'practical' for the Dholavirian engineers to plan the city's enclosures as perfect squares; that they chose to depart from this more utilitarian shape and build rectangular enclosures according to specific proportions betrays a clear intent, probably the same as Varāhamihira's in the *Brihat Samhitā*: a desire to embed auspiciousness in the town plan. We have here a continuity not just between Harappan and classical town planning, but between the Harappan and Vedic concepts.

But then, Dholavira's planners could not have translated such ratios onto the land without some defined unit of length, just as we would today use the metre. Here we come to a straightforward mathematical problem: given all the ratios at play and the known dimensions, can we work out the unit of length used to measure the city's enclosures? I proposed a simple method to do just that,[43] and calculated that the unit of length yielding the simplest results was 1.9 m. Expressed in terms of such a unit, all the

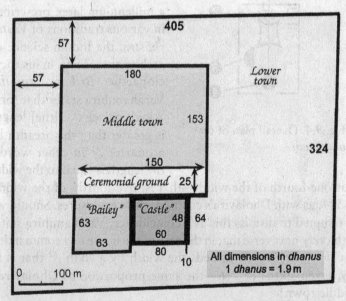

Fig. 9.5. Dholavira's dimensions expressed in terms of a unit equal to 1.9 m.

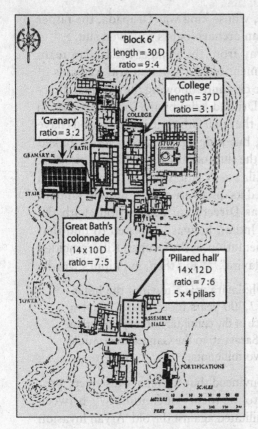

Fig. 9.6. Proportions and units of major buildings of Mohenjo-daro's acropolis (D = 1.9 m).

city's dimensions took on unexpectedly felicitous expressions (Fig. 9.5); the average margin of error with respect to the actual dimensions was a negligible 0.6 per cent.

Applying the same unit to structures at other Harappan sites gave striking results.[44] Fig. 9.6 summarizes the ratios and measurements found in the major buildings of Mohenjo-daro's acropolis, but such whole multiples of Dholavira's unit appeared elsewhere too, for instance at Harappa, Kalibangan and Lothal.

There is more to say about the unit of 1.9 m, but we must first take a leap into historical times and pay a brief visit to Dholavira's 'twin city'.

FROM DHOLAVIRA TO KĀMPILYA

In the 1990s, while Dholavira was being excavated in the Rann of Kachchh by R.S. Bisht and his team, an Italian team led by the Indologist Gian Giuseppe Filippi visited the sleepy village of Kampil in the Farrukhabad district of Uttar Pradesh in the mid-Ganges Valley. A. Cunningham had probably been the first to propose, in 1878, that this was the Mahābhārata's Kāmpilya, the capital of South Pāñchāla, whose king was Drupada, the father of Draupadī; several Indian archaeologists followed suit.

But five kilometres away from the village, the Italian team found a rectangular settlement of 780 x 660 m with remains of fortifications enclosing the city and following the cardinal directions; the place is called 'Drupad Kila' by the local villagers, in one more association with the epic. Substantial excavations have not yet been carried out, but judging from potsherds, baked bricks and other artefacts, the site goes back several centuries BCE.

Irrespective of Drupad Kila's association with the Mahābhārata, when G.G. Filippi presented its discovery to R.S. Bisht in January 1998 (when the latter was Director of Excavations with the Archaeological Survey of India), he was 'surprised to find that the dimensions and the orientation of the Drupad Kila coincided exactly with those of Dholavira'.[45]* But then, in Filippi's words:

> The problem is that Dholavira was a town of the Indus–Sarasvatī civilization, 2,000 years older than Kāmpilya. This fact offered evidence of the continuity of only one urban model from the Indus–Sarasvatī to the Ganges civilizations in the time frame of two millennia.[46]

Filippi was therefore convinced that his team's discovery provided 'important support to the theory of continuity'[47] between the two civilizations and militated against the old 'Aryan Invasion Theory'.[48]

Pending excavations, Drupad Kila provides one more link between India's two urban phases. Let us turn to a few others.

WEIGHTS AND MEASURES

The standardized Harappan system of weights greatly impressed the early excavators: it was 'unique in the ancient world'.[49] Shaped as cubes or truncated spheres, made of chert or semi-precious stone, the weights start below a gram and stop over 10 kg, with

---

* Dholavira's dimensions are 771 x 617 m, while Kampilya's are 780 x 660 m (respectively 1 per cent and 7 per cent greater).

some 14 stages in between. Taking the smallest weight (about 0.86 g) as a unit, a first series grows geometrically, with the next weight being twice that unit, the next twice again, etc.; to be precise, the series runs 1, 2, 4, 8, 16, 32, 64. The fifth weight in the series, 13.6 g, is the most common in the archaeological record. Then, instead of going on doubling the weights (which would give 128, 256 and so on), the series switches to multiples of the lower weights: we thus have 160 units, followed by 200, 320, 640, 1600, 3200, 6400, 8000 and, finally, 12,800.

Such a double series is also at the root of the weight system described in the *Arthashāstra*, as Indian metrologist V.B. Mainkar highlighted, who in addition showed that the actual weights described there in terms of a tiny seed called *gunja* precisely match their Harappan counterparts.[50]

The match is not just textual but historical too: towards the middle of the first millennium BCE, coins made of silver began to be issued in the Indo-Gangetic region, each bearing several punch marks depicting various motifs. Carefully weighing thousands of these punch-marked coins, from Taxila in particular, the historian-cum-mathematician D.D. Kosambi noted in 1941 how there was 'every likelihood of the earlier Taxila hoard being weighed on much the same kind of balances and by much the same sort of weights, as at Mohenjo-daro some two thousand years earlier'.[51]

The British Indologist John E. Mitchiner[52] went a step further and established correlations between the traditional system of weights used in India till recent decades and Harappan weights (Table 9.3), with a difference smaller than 1.8 per cent. Such a close match between the two systems is beyond the realm of coincidence.

Indeed, the survival of the Harappan weight system in different forms is one of the clearest cases of continuity with classical India. Although some scholars, such as R.S. Sharma, chose to see in it nothing but 'accidental similarities',[53] most archaeologists have accepted it. 'The Indus weight system is identical to that used in the first kingdoms of the Gangetic plains . . . and is still in use today in traditional markets throughout Pakistan and India,' writes Kenoyer.[54] (Of course, this is no longer quite true for India because of the widespread adoption of the metric standard, but elderly Indians will understand what he had in mind.)

Table 9.3. Mitchiner's comparison between Harappan and traditional weights: the match is almost perfect.

Harappan Weights						
Unity	1	2	4	8	16	32	64
Value in grams	0.8525	1.705	3.41	6.82	13.64	27.28	54.56
Traditional Indian Weights						
'Rattis'	8	16	32	64	128	256	512
'Karshas'	1	2	4	8	16		
Value in grams	0.8375	1.675	3.35	6.70	13.40	26.80	53.60

Do we find such a survival in the field of linear measures? The answer is admittedly less straightforward. The clearest connection, proposed by Mainkar again, rested on a piece of ivory found by S.R. Rao at Lothal, which bore twenty-seven slightly irregular graduation lines spanning 46 mm. This points to an average unit of 1.77 mm, and Mainkar proposed that this unit was precisely one-tenth of the traditional *angula* described in Kautilya's *Arthashāstra*.[55] Defined as the maximum width of the middle finger, or as eight grains of barley placed width-wise next to each other, the *angula* (literally 'finger') is the Indian equivalent of the digit found in civilizations as far apart as Egypt, Mesopotamia, China, Greece, Japan or the Roman Empire, where it varied from 1.6 to 1.9 cm. Early scholars attributed the last value to the Indian *angula*, but that was mainly because it amounted to a convenient 3/4 inch; more precise estimations by Mainkar and his colleague L. Raju[56] led them to a value of 1.78 cm. Naturally enough, Mainkar suggested that this was very close to ten divisions of the Lothal scale (1.77 cm), a view tentatively accepted by the historian of Indian science Debiprasad Chattopadhyaya.[57]

Three other scale-like objects have come to light in the Harappan cities so far. The first, discovered by Ernest Mackay in his

1930–31 season at Mohenjo-daro, was a broken piece of shell bearing eight divisions of precisely 6.7056 mm each, with a dot and a circle five graduations apart, which suggests a decimal system. However, attempts by Mackay, its discoverer, to relate such a unit to dimensions in Mohenjo-daro were, by his own admission, not very successful, and he suspected the existence 'of a second system of measurement'.[58] The second scale, found at Harappa, was a piece of bronze rod with four graduation lines at an interval of 9.34 mm; nothing much could be made out of it. Finally in the 1960s, a rough 9 cm-long piece of terracotta with what seemed to be graduation lines came to light at Kalibangan; it remained half-forgotten until R. Balasubramaniam, an expert in metallurgy, noted for his work on the Delhi Iron Pillar, recently examined it: he found a unit of 1.75 cm to make perfect sense of the graduations.[59] This establishes not only a close connection with the Lothal unit of 1.77 mm, but also a direct link with the *Arthashāstra*'s *angula*. The latter link is a powerful one, as Balasubramaniam showed in addition that most divisions on the terracotta scale were one-eighth of 1.75 cm, and we have just seen that one of the two definitions given for the *angula* in the *Arthashāstra* is based on eight grains of barley—each grain being therefore one-eighth of an *angula*.

The Kalibangan scale, rough though it may be, provides a direct connection with linear measures of the historical era. Can we get an independent confirmation of this important claim? I propose that we can.

I referred earlier to a unit of 1.9 m which, according to my calculations, is at the root of Dholavira's town planning; if we take an average *angula* of 1.76 cm between the Lothal and the Kalibangan scales, we find that Dholavira's unit is precisely 108 times that measurement: 190 ≈ 108 x 1.76 (the margin of error is a microscopic 0.04 per cent). Now, it so happens that the *Arthashāstra* lists several units of length besides the *angula*; one of them is the *dhanus* (or 'bow'), which is defined thus: '108 *angulas* make a *dhanus*, a measure [used] for roads and city-walls . . .'[60] The parallel between the *Arthashāstra*'s *dhanus* of 108 *angula*s and Dholavira's unit of 108 times the Lothal–Kalibangan *angula* seems too striking to be a mere coincidence, especially when the *Arthashāstra* specifies that the *dhanus* is to be used 'for roads and city-walls'. This naturally suggests that the *angula–dhanus* system is of Harappan origin. Moreover, from the humble baked brick to doorways, many dimensions can be expressed neatly in terms of an *angula* of 1.76 cm, as I showed recently.[61]

There is nothing surprising about a Harappan *angula* of 1.76 cm, since, as I mentioned earlier, it falls within the range of the traditional digit in other cultures (1.6–1.9 cm). But why create a unit of 108 rather than 100 *angula*s when the Harappans, as their system of weight demonstrates, commonly used multiples of ten? Varāhamihira gives us a clue in his *Brihat Samhitā*[62] when he states that the height of a tall man is 108 *angula*s, that of a medium man ninety-six *angula*s, and that of a short man eighty-four *angula*s (the same heights apply to statues of various deities[63]); using our Harappan *angula* of 1.76 cm, we get 1.90, 1.69 and 1.48 m respectively, quite consistent with 'tall', 'medium' and 'short'. This pragmatic definition based on the human body makes sense: the Harappan *dhanus* is the height of a tall man.

Astronomical considerations may also have however played a part: 108 happens to be the distance between the sun and the earth in terms of the sun's diameter, as the Indologist and scientist

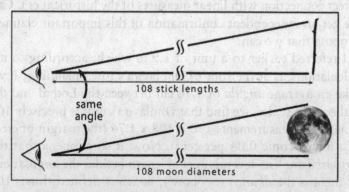

Fig. 9.7. Verifying that the distance between the sun (or moon) and the earth is 108 sun (or moon) diameters.

Subhash Kak pointed out.[64] Although this statement may sound too sophisticated for the protohistoric age, in reality it takes no more than a stick to verify it (Fig. 9.7): view the standing stick at a distance equal to 108 times its length and you will see it exactly as large as the sun or the moon (in mathematical language: its apparent height will be the exact apparent diameter of the sun or the moon).

Such an observation would have been well within the Harappans' competence: the Finnish scholar Erkka Maula, studying small drilled holes on ring stones found at Mohenjo-daro,[65] demonstrated that, like their contemporaries in Egypt and Mesopotamia, the Harappans devoted considerable attention to tracking the sun's path through the year—the only way to plan the next sowing or, perhaps, prepare for a festival coinciding with the spring equinox.

Whatever the exact origin of number 108 may be (and it is sacred in many traditions from Japan to ancient Greece to northern Europe), its long tradition in classical Hinduism (108 Upanishads, dance postures, rosary beads ...) does seem to have Harappan roots.

As regards the *dhanus* of 1.9 m, which I calculated at Dholavira, R. Balasubramaniam showed in a recent study[66] that in combination with an *angula* of 1.76 cm, it expressed all the dimensions of the Delhi Iron Pillar with unexpected harmony (Fig. 9.8): the pillar's total length of 7.67 m, for instance, is precisely four *dhanus*; the pillar's diameter, thirty-six

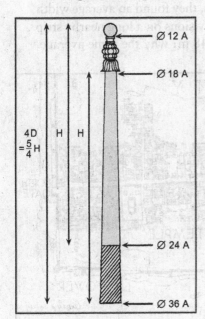

Fig. 9.8. Dimensions of the Delhi Iron Pillar expressed in terms of D = Dholavira's *dhanus* (1.9 m), A = Dholavira's *angula* (1.76 cm).

angulas at the bottom, shrinks to twenty-four *angulas* at ground level, finally to taper off at twelve *angulas* at the very top. If this were not enough, the ratio between the pillar's entire length (7.67 m) and the portion above the ground (6.12 m) is 5 : 4, verified to 0.2 per cent—again, Dholavira's master ratio! This bears out what we have already concluded from the texts: Harappan ratios and linear units survived the collapse of the Indus cities and passed on to those of the Ganges Valley.

This survival found one more compelling confirmation in recent original research conducted by two architects, Indian Mohan Pant and Japanese Shuji Funo.[67] Their starting point was Thimi, a town east of Kathmandu that has existed for some fifteen centuries or more. Measuring blocks defined by a succession of regularly spaced east–west streets, they found an average width of 38.42 m; besides, a pattern of divisions on a long nearby strip of fields yielded an average of 38.48 m: why the same average,

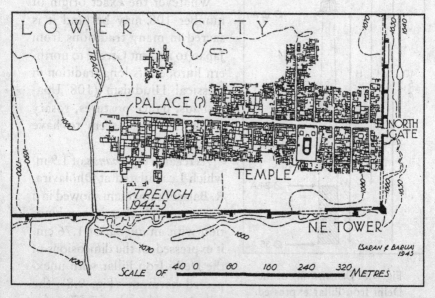

Fig. 9.9. Plan of a part of Sirkap, Taxila, excavated by Marshall. Note the regular spacing of the side streets perpendicular to the main north–south street. (© ASI)

and what did this number mean? Pant and Funo then jumped a millennium back into the past and turned their attention to the highly regular street pattern at Sirkap, one of Taxila's three mounds, excavated by Marshall over many years (Fig. 9.9). A detailed study of Marshall's plan established that the average distance between parallel streets was—38.4 m! Moreover, on the nearby Bhir mound, also excavated by Marshall, they found 'a number of blocks [of houses] in contiguity with a width of 19.2 m',[68] which is, of course, just half of 38.4 m.

Pant and Funo, trying to make sense of such regular patterns, were led to correlate these dimensions with the *Arthashāstra* system of linear measures: they adopted a *danda* ('stick' or 'rod', a synonym for the *dhanus*[69]) of 108 *angula*s, and, as prescribed by the text, a *rajju* (or 'rope') of ten *danda*s and a *paridesha* of two *rajju*s. Their *danda* had a value of 1.92 m, so that the block dimensions of 19.2 m were equivalent to 1 *rajju*, and those of 38.4 m became a neat one *paridesha*. At the other end of the scale, the value of the *angula* was 1.78 cm (1.92 m divided by 108).

These results, which I was unaware of when I researched Dholavira's system of units, are very nearly identical to the values I calculated there (1.9 m, 1.76 cm). It is extraordinary that Pant and Funo's work, proceeding from completely independent methods, led them to adopt exactly the same system as the one I worked out at Dholavira, and with almost exactly the same values for the basic units.

Pant and Funo did not stop at historical cities: they travelled back in time once more and studied Mohenjo-daro's plan.[70] In three different parts of the city, they found that the dimension which frequently occurs in major cluster blocks is 19.20 m—in other words, one *rajju* again—and also smaller grids of 9.6 m (5 *danda*s or *dhanus*). Their conclusion was straightforward:

> There is continuity in the survey and planning tradition from Mohenjodaro to Sirkap and Thimi . . . The planning modules employed in the Indus city of Mohenjodaro, Sirkap of Gandhara, and Thimi of Kathmandu Valley are the same.[71]

This continuity is the most eloquent example of the Harappan legacy in the field of town planning and linear measures.

TECHNOLOGY AND CRAFTS

Let us briefly turn to other fields. Almost every Harappan technology and craft speaks of continuity. Thus the ingenious bronze casting method known as 'lost wax casting', used to cast the figurine of the 'dancing girl', for instance, continued to be used later and spread throughout the subcontinent;[72] traditional communities of bronze casters using just the same technique can still be found, as at Swamimalai in Tamil Nadu. As regards craft techniques, Dales, Kenoyer, Rao, Lal and several other archaeologists have documented how, from bangle-making to bead-making, from the working of shell to that of ivory, today's traditional craftsmen often perpetuate Harappan techniques, even if they integrate new materials or new styles. In order to produce blue glazed ceramics, some of them use the same copper oxide pigments as did the Harappans; they drill, bleach and colour long semi-precious beads in the same manner. In fact, when archaeologists want to understand Harappan techniques, they often look around and consult today's traditional craftsmen—a case in point being today's bead industry of Khambat, at the top of the gulf of the same name, some 30 km away from Lothal.[73]

Techniques apart, many objects of daily use have survived with hardly any change, as B.B. Lal illustrated recently[74]—be it toiletry articles, the frying pan, the humble *kamandalu* (a small water pot with a handle), or the wooden writing tablet, the *takhti*.[75] Games too: much like their Harappan predecessors, children of north India still play (or used to play till recently) with rattles, whistles, spinning tops and flat pottery disks; toy carts, crafted by Harappans to keep their children amused, were frequently unearthed in the Ganges cities. As regards the Indus dice (Fig. 9.10), they could easily be confused for the modern ones (except for a different arrangement of the dots). Harappans apparently loved board games, and the set of terracotta pieces found at

Fig. 9.10. Sketch of a few Harappan dice.

Lothal (Fig. 5.10) does evoke the modern game of chess, as S.R. Rao pointed out, or at least an ancestor of it.

Ornaments provide us with arresting cases of survival: the omnipresent bangle to start with, which Indian women have remained as fond of as their Harappan forerunners; even the manner of wearing it—fully over the left arm, for instance, as with the 'dancing girl'—can still be seen in the rural and tribal parts of Rajasthan and Gujarat. Anklets[76] (Fig. 9.11) and nose or ear studs,[77] documented at Mohenjo-daro and other sites, of course constitute an integral part of the finery of today's Indian woman. Even the married Hindu woman's custom of applying vermilion at the parting of the hair has Harappan origins: figurines found at Nausharo and elsewhere show traces of red pigment at the same spot.[78] Some

Fig. 9.11. An anklet on a broken bronze figurine from Mohenjo-daro. (© ASI)

orthodox Hindu men continue to wear an amulet tied to the upper right arm, exactly where the so-called 'priest–king', whom we shall meet presently (Fig. 10.18), displays one; or sometimes they apply sacred ashes or sandalwood paste at the same spot.

Harappan agriculture was heavily dependent on the ox cart, whose shape remained virtually unchanged till recent times, judging from the many small-scale toy models; even its wheelbase, measured from cart tracks found at Harappa, is the same as that of today's cart.[79] Fields were ploughed, and a terracotta model of ploughshare found at Banawali would arouse little surprise in the peasant of today. We noted earlier that (Fig. 5.9) Kalibangan's fields were ploughed with a double network of perpendicular furrows; when the excavators tried to understand the reason behind this peculiar arrangement, they turned to the nearby village of Kalibangan and saw peasants ploughing their fields in exactly the same manner—almost 5000 years later!

As regards navigation, three representations of boats have survived, but none of those of seafaring ships. The depictions (Fig. 9.12) at least show that the boats plying on the Indus in Harappan times had the same shape as today's traditional Sindhi boat: raised sides and a high central cabin.[80]

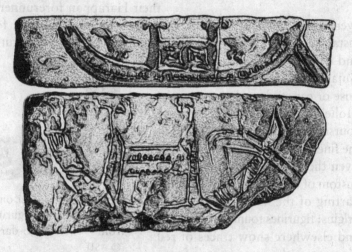

Fig. 9.12. Sketches of two tablets depicting Harappan river boats.

From the very beginning of their explorations, archaeologists have frequently stressed more such revealing cases of material survival of the Harappan civilization, though they may have sought to explain them in different ways. We may sum up with Kenoyer:

> There appear to be many continuities [between the Indus and later historical cultures]. Agricultural and pastoral sub-sistence strategies continue, pottery manufacture does not

change radically, many ornaments and luxury items continue to be produced using the same technology and styles
. . . There is really no Dark Age isolating the protohistoric
period from the historic period.[81]

Such is the positive verdict of archaeology. It does not mean that
there was no change in the post-Harappan age—that would be
impossible, given the upheaval that the collapse of the urban order
must have caused. The civic administration certainly disintegrated,
the standardized brick sizes were gradually abandoned or altered,
and long-distance trade and the Indus seals disappeared.

But one oft-quoted disappearance—that of the Harappan
writing system—may have been exaggerated, and it is worth
probing the case of the vanishing script.

THE INDUS SCRIPT

This writing system remains the most exasperating riddle of this
civilization: over 4200 inscriptions, most of them on seals, tablets
or pottery, made up of about 400 signs, only 200 of which are
used more than five times. Some of these signs appear on pottery
a few centuries before the urban phase,[82] but generally in isola-
tion. In the present state of our knowledge, the full-fledged script
appears to be born with the cities, and fades away with them.

Well over a hundred candidates—from the most serious experts
to a colourful crowd of self-styled decipherers—have offered their
key at the feet of this sphinx, which has, however, remained
stubbornly mute. Why so many worshippers? Because of the cruel
absence, so far, of any bilingual inscription, such as the famous
Rosetta stone that enabled Champollion to decipher Egyptian
hieroglyphics. Also because the inscriptions are so short: five to
six signs on an average (twenty-six for the longest, with many
seals having just a sign or two)—such brevity appears to exclude
full sentences and makes verification virtually impossible.

Basing themselves on similarities in the shapes of signs, scholars
have compared the Indus script with the Sumerian, proto-Elamite,

Fig. 9.13. A few examples of Indus writing on seals. (© ASI)

Old Semitic and Etruscan scripts—even with the Rongo-Rongo signs of Easter Island! Some have read names of godheads, names of kings, cities or regions, while others have opted for administrative titles, communities or clans, goods, metals, agricultural produce, or just numbers. Most would-be decipherers have tried to read a recon-structed 'proto-Dravidian' into the script, although serious attempts based on Sanskritic readings have not been lacking. In the end, the only safe statement is that the seals played an important part in trade, and permitted the identifi-cation of either traders or their goods.

Once the Indus script disappears, around 1800 BCE, we have to wait until the fifth century BCE for the first historical script—Brāhmī—to appear in a developed form.[83] Brāhmī is the mother of all Indian scripts (and several Southeast Asian ones), but since the nineteenth century, the majority of scholars have regarded it as deriving from, or inspired by, a Semitic script (with Aramaic being the one most often suggested of late). This view, which ultimately remains speculative, may have prevented a serious study of candidates for a possible transmission of the Indus writing tradition to historical times, a few examples of which are intriguing, at the very least (Fig. 9.14).

The first comes to us from Bet-Dwarka, an island near the northwestern tip of Saurashtra; named after the nearby mainland

town of Dwarka, it is traditionally associated with Krishna. At
Bet-Dwarka, Late Harappan antiquities have been identified and
dated between the nineteenth and fourteenth centuries BCE.[84]
Two potsherds bearing inscriptions have come to light, one of
which is in a script evidently akin to the Indus script but evolving
towards simplified shapes.[85] It drew the attention of Indian
epigraphists, but whether or not it constitutes a 'missing link' must
remain in suspense until more similar finds come to light. In the
same category, the mysterious inscription in the Vikramkhol cave
(in Orissa), some 10 m long and 2 m high, was studied by the
eminent epigraphist K.P. Jayaswal, who concluded in 1933: 'The

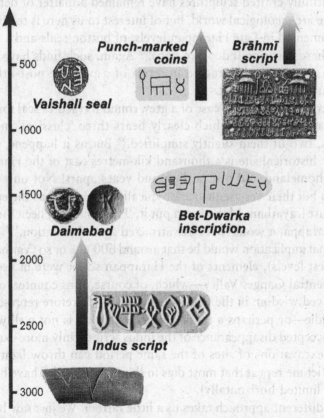

Fig. 9.14. From the Indus to the Brāhmī scripts (in BCE dates).

Vikramkhol inscription supplies a link [in] the passage of letter-forms from the Mohenjodaro script to Brāhmī.'[86] This inscription does not appear to have received the attention it deserves, although several epigraphists have used it to argue in favour of an indigenous origin for the Brāhmī script.

Daimabad, a Late Harappan site of the Godavari Valley in Maharashtra, shot into prominence in 1974 with the chance discovery of an unparalleled hoard of massive bronze sculptures weighing 65 kg altogether and consisting of an elephant, a rhinoceros, a buffalo and a standing man driving a light chariot pulled by a pair of bulls. The exact date and provenance of these beautifully crafted sculptures have remained a matter of debate in the archaeological world, but of interest to us here is the find, documented in Late Harappan levels, of button seals and a few potsherds bearing Indus-like signs.[87] Again, such finds have not been systematically studied in terms of a possible post-urban evolution of the script.

Very different is the case of a grey, round terracotta seal found at Vaishali (Bihar), which clearly bears three 'classical' Indus signs, two of them slightly simplified.[88] But as it happens, this early historical site is a thousand kilometres east of the Harappan homeland and over a thousand years apart! Not only the signs but their very sequence is typically Harappan; as the epigraphist Iravatham Mahadevan put it, 'Had [the seal] been found at Harappa, it would not have attracted special attention.'[89] The normal implication would be that around 600 BCE or so (Vaishali's earliest levels), elements of the Harappan script were in use in the central Ganges Valley—which, of course, runs counter to all received wisdom in the field. Vaishali's seal therefore represents a riddle—or perhaps a tantalizing clue that all is not well with the accepted disappearance of the Indus script. Only more extensive excavations of sites of the same period can throw light on this (let me repeat that most digs in the Ganges Valley have been very limited horizontally).

A different approach takes us a little farther. We just saw how the punch-marked coins of the early historical era reflected the

Harappan standards of weight. But the connection between the two systems appears to run deeper.* In 1935, the archaeologist C.L. Fabri pointed to odd parallels between depictions of animal motifs on the coins and on Indus seals (Fig. 9.15):

> While going through the signs [on the punch-marked coins], I was immediately struck by certain animal representations. The most frequent ones are those of the humped Indian bull, the elephant, the tiger, the crocodile, and the hare. Now all these animals occur also on the seals of Mohenjo-daro and Harappa. Not only are the subjects similar, but there are similarities in such small details that one must necessarily

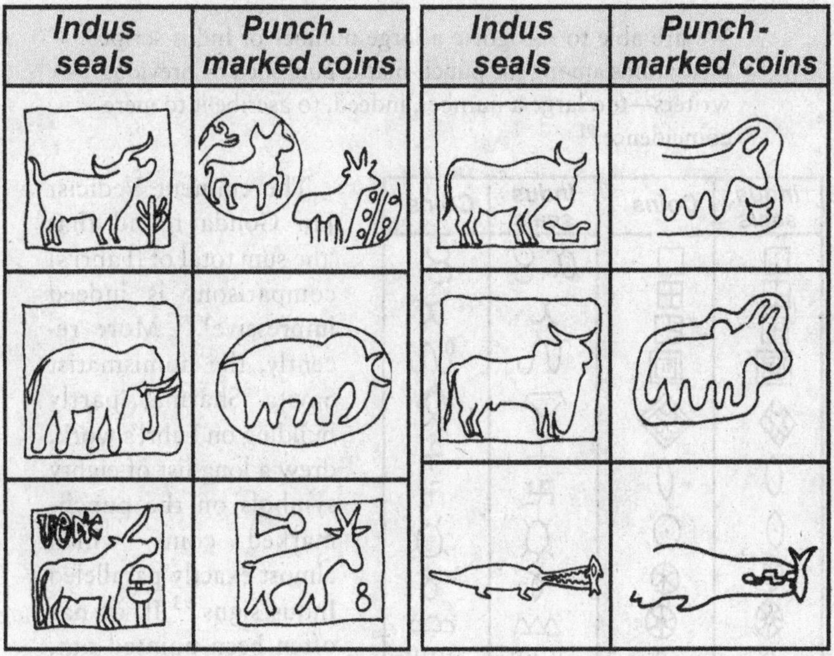

Fig. 9.15. A few of the similarities between animal symbols on Indus signs and punch-marked coins pointed out by C.L. Fabri.

---

* The symbols on punch-marked coins do not constitute a writing system based on a language; I am only looking here at the survival of Indus symbols in themselves, irrespective of whether or not something of their meaning was preserved.

suppose that they are not due to mere chance or to 'similar working of the human mind.'[90]

Fabri went on to describe those 'small details': for instance, in both cases the crocodile holds a fish that seems to hang in front of its jaws; the bull has a manger in front of it; a typical Harappan motif of a single-horned bull (or unicorn) facing a ritual stand (Fig. 10.14) appears generally preserved (except that the bull now has two horns); and in both cases, all animals face right.

Fabri added a comparison of Indus signs with symbols on the punch-marked coins, bringing out striking parallels between the two, some of which are reproduced in Fig. 9.16.

Overall, Fabri's conclusion was:

> We are able to recognize a large number of Indus script pictograms among the punch-marks published by previous writers—too large a number, indeed, to ascribe it to mere coincidence.[91]

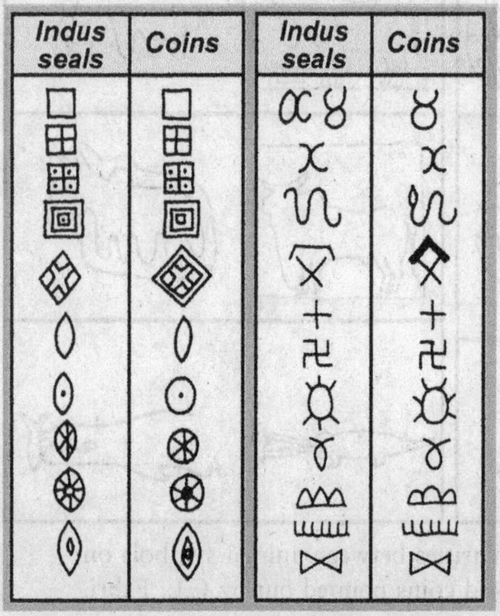

Fig. 9.16. A few symbols common to the Indus script and punch-marked coins, adapted from Fabri.

The eminent Vedicist Jan Gonda found that 'the sum total of [Fabri's] comparisons is indeed impressive'.[92] More recently, the numismatist Savita Sharma, partly building on Fabri's work, drew a long list of eighty symbols on the punch-marked coins which almost exactly paralleled Indus signs.[93] If, as has often been pointed out, simple geometric designs can be expected to be common to many scripts, parallels between more complex shapes, such as the ones illustrated in Fig. 9.17, appear, once again, well beyond the play of chance.

A third and more ambitious approach seeks to directly bridge the gap between the two scripts. Among the very first scholars who dared to grasp the nettle, Stephen Langdon[94] and G.R. Hunter[95] independently proposed in the early 1930s, parallels between the signs of these two systems (interestingly, Hunter called the Indus script 'Proto-Indian'). Quite a few attempts followed suit, but none could make any real progress towards a decipherment: clearly, a few similarities,

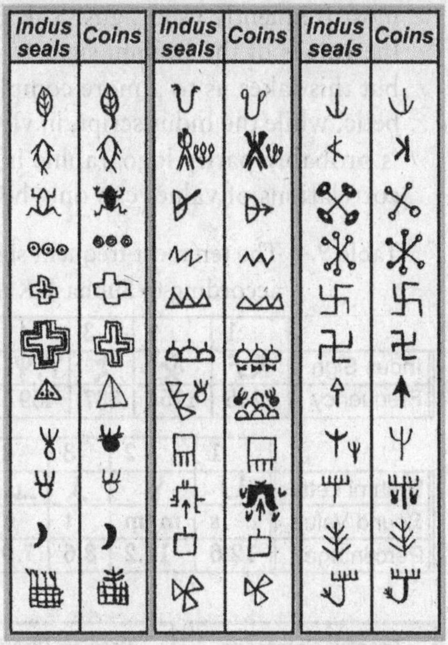

Fig. 9.17. A few symbols common to the Indus script and punch-marked coins, adapted from Savita Sharma.

however intriguing, are not enough. Recently, Subhash Kak, whom we met a little earlier, proceeded differently: without prejudging the nature of the Harappan language, he statistically analysed the ten signs most frequently used in each script (using the text of Ashoka's famous edicts for Brāhmī).[96]

Table 9.4 summarizes Kak's results: the first three pairs are almost identical (if we turn the second, the 'fish', upside down, an inversion frequent enough in historical scripts); three other pairs are also excellent candidates. (Kak proposes two more, but they are less compelling in my view.) As it is, we have six strongly correlated pairs, a high proportion that militates in favour of an organic relationship between the two scripts—if they were wholly unrelated, we should find no particular likeness between their most frequently used signs. Kak goes further and tries to apply the values of the Brāhmī signs to their Harappan counterparts, but this takes us to a more complex question: Brāhmī is alphabetic, while the Indus script, in view of its large number of signs, is probably partly logographic in nature; this means that such correlations of values can only be speculative at this stage.

Table 9.4. The ten most frequent signs in Indus and Brāhmī scripts, according to Subhash Kak.

	1	2	3	4	5	6	7	8	9	10
Indus Sign										
Frequency	2245	1254	837	459	411	406	343	256	243	292

	1	2	3	4	5	6	7	8	9	10
Brāhmī Letter										
Sound Value	s	m/ṃ	t	n	p	y	v	r	d	c
Percentage	12.6	11.2	8.6	7.9	6.9	6.5	5.1	4.6	4.2	4.0

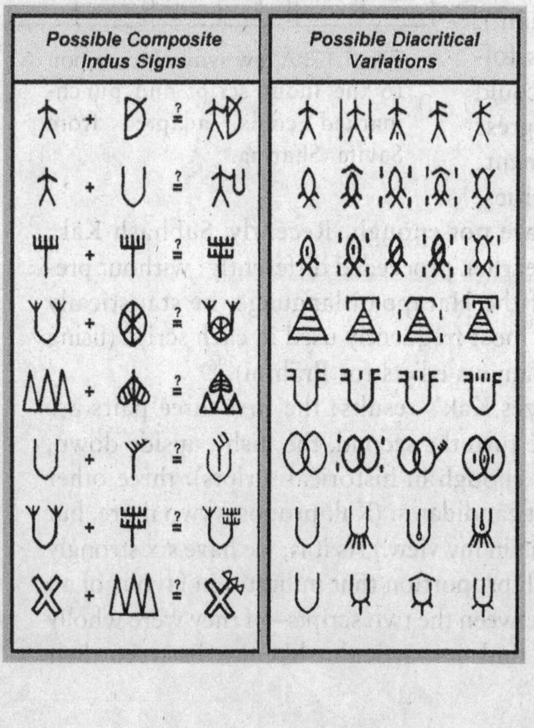

Fig. 9.18. Examples of possible composite signs (left column) and diacritical marks (right column) in the Indus script.

Finally, experts have long pointed to two important structural features of the Indus script: its use of composite signs and modifiers (Fig. 9.18), which respectively call to mind the use of composite letters and diacritical marks in Brāhmī to denote vowels (just as in later Indian scripts). If the Indus script is unrelated to the Brāhmī, we will once again have to invoke a rather remarkable double coincidence. While preferring the dominant view on the Semitic origin of Brāhmī, the epigraphist Richard Salomon was prudent enough to point out that 'some historical connection between the Indus Valley script and Brāhmī cannot decisively be ruled out'.[97]

Dilip Chakrabarti is more positive:

> It may not be illogical to think that the Indus writing tradition lingered on in perishable medium till the dictates of the new socio-economic contexts of early historic India led to its resurgence in a changed form.[98]

This was also the opinion of India's greatest epigraphist of the twentieth century, D.C. Sircar, who wrote in 1953: 'The ancient [Indus] writing . . . may have ultimately developed into the Brāhmī alphabet several centuries before the rise of the Mauryas in the latter half of the four century BC.'[99]

True, the survival of elements of the Indus script and their evolution towards Brāhmī can only be proved once the script is deciphered, or if more missing links between the two come to light; until then, however, there is no reason to accept as final a verdict of complete disappearance of the former and sudden appearance of the latter.

CHANGE IN CONTINUITY

What we have seen so far constitutes only a small part of the material aspects of the Harappan legacy. Of course, the historical age threw up its own innovations, from iron technology to new architectural concepts and an efflorescence of art forms. But given the disintegration of Harappan urbanism and the ensuing

millennium-long reorganization, it is no one's case that Harappan
culture lived on unchanged: what has been gaining acceptance
in recent decades is rather the overarching concept of 'change in
continuity', which does justice to the situation. As J.-F. Jarrige
puts it, 'from the Neolithic time till almost today there has never
been, in spite of spectacular changes in the course of time, a
definite gap or break in the history of the subcontinent.'[100]

D.P. Agrawal sums up the situation with these words:

> It is strange but true that the type and style of bangles that
> women wear in Rajasthan today, or the vermilion that they
> apply on the parting of the hair on the head, the practice of
> Yoga, the binary system of weights and measures, the basic
> architecture of the houses etc. can all be traced back to the
> Indus Civilisation. The cultural and religious traditions of
> the Harappans provide the substratum for the latter-day
> Indian Civilisation.[101]

Let us now turn to these 'cultural and religious traditions' and
see how much of a 'substratum' we find in them.

10

The Intangible Heritage

Beginning with Marshall, many archaeologists and scholars have drawn parallels between traits of Harappan religion and culture and those of later, classical India. At times, subtle considerations make one feel that a certain 'Indianness' is at play. We saw, for example, how Jarrige noted the absence of a royal iconography in the Indus world to be 'already an Indian trait', or how Wright detected in Harappan society a 'community-related organization', which is in tune with the later common Indian pattern. When we combine such traits with the parallels noted earlier in the fields of architecture (fortifications, the absence of palaces, etc.) and governance (multiple kingdoms or city-states), the sense of a thread running through these two ages becomes inescapable.

Suggestive as this approach may be, there is much more to be said on the intangible aspect of the archaeological record. In the following pages, I will supplement the work of many scholars with my own research in the field.

SYMBOLS

Symbols and motifs conveniently bridge the gap between the tangible and the intangible: their survival is easy to document, but the concepts they illustrate are often debatable.

The most obvious example is perhaps the symbol known as the 'swastika' (Fig. 10.1), incised on hundreds of Harappan tablets, generally single but occasionally double (and with no preferred direction, let it be added to answer a frequent question).

Fig. 10.1. The swastika on a Harappan tablet (left), and on pottery of the early historical era (top right: Rupar; bottom right: Ahichchhatra). (© ASI)

The swastika continues to be depicted on pottery at several early historical sites,[1] on punch-marked coins, on some of Ashoka's edicts and other early inscriptions,[2] where it symbolizes auspiciousness, harmony and growth. We cannot be sure whether it had the same significance for the Harappans, though that is not unlikely. At any rate, its graphic survival is beyond question.

Another typical Harappan symbol is the 'endless knot' (Fig. 10.2): it reappears unchanged in Gujarat in several inscriptions of the ninth century CE, and can still be seen today in some of the *rangoli*s (or *kolams* in South India) drawn by Hindu women

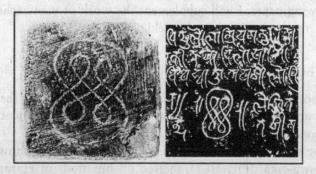

Fig. 10.2. The Harappan 'endless knot' (left), and the same symbol on an historical inscription[3] (right).

in front of their houses, where it often represents the child Krishna's footprint.

The motif of 'intersecting circles' is a frequent one on Harappan pottery, also found on floor tiles at Balakot and Kalibangan (Fig. 7.4), some 800 km apart. Dilip Chakrabarti points out that 'an identical design occurs on top of the Boddhi throne'[4] at Bodh Gaya, which dates from the third century BCE, some two millennia later.

About three-quarters of all Indus seals depict a single-horned bull-like creature generally called a 'unicorn'. Almost invariably, this majestic animal faces a 'ritual stand' (Fig. 10.14) whose enigmatic significance has been much debated: Marshall saw in it an incense burner while, more recently, I. Mahadevan closely argued in favour of a sacred filter for Soma, the Vedic elixir.[5] Regardless of the symbol's actual significance, Mahadevan showed that the stand itself, or an object resembling it, was portrayed on historical coins, with a bull or an elephant facing it,[6] and this important case of continuity has been generally accepted. Fabri, as we saw in the preceding chapter, had also pointed to one such instance (Fig. 9.15). I must add that some of the cups used in Vedic rituals for the offering of libations have a curiously similar shape.[7]

A host of other symbols are common to Indus seals or pottery and punch-marked coins or other historical artefacts: concentric circles, the hollow cross, the tree on a raised platform or enclosure ('tree in railing', Fig. 10.3), the fish, the peacock, the antelope . . .

Harappan tablet	Tree motif on punch-marked coins

Fig. 10.3. The Harappan tree (left), and its historical counterpart (right).

Also the pipal leaf, and the tree itself, regarded as sacred in the Vedas, where it is called *ashvattha*;[8] it continues to be revered as the Bodhi Tree under which the Buddha attained illumination, and remains among the most sacred trees in India today.

ART AND ICONOGRAPHY

Harappan art is disappointingly frugal if we compare it with that
of ancient Egypt, Mesopotamia or ancient China; at times one
wonders if the motto of the Harappan artists was 'Small is beautiful'! Their artistic ability is beyond question, as the exquisite
jewellery or the carefully incised seals demonstrate; but the small
scale of most artefacts and their limited output does contrast
rather glaringly with the artistic exuberance of classical India. (Of
course, wood carving, painting on cloth and other art forms
dependent on perishable material disappeared forever, leaving us
with a truncated view of Harappan art.)

Despite these limitations, we have unmistakable examples of
transmission of artistic concepts to the historical period: classical
art motifs frequently evoke Harappan ones.

Such is the case with the most famous Indus seal (Fig. 10.4):

Fig. 10.4. The famous 'Pashupati' seal. Inset: A *nandipada*
symbol from Mathura.[9] (© ASI)

the 'Pashupati' seal found at Mohenjo-daro, so called by Marshall because he saw in it the 'Lord of the Beasts' (*pashupati*) of Vedic literature. Let us momentarily leave aside that interpretation and concentrate on the iconography. At the centre is an impressive figure seated in a yogic posture on a low platform; it strikes any Indian eye as being familiar: it is a common motif in Buddhist* and Jain iconography, and Shiva is also often represented in the same posture. The god—he must be one, since he is reproduced on many seals and tablets—has three faces, heralding the depiction of three-headed Hindu gods (such as the *trimūrti*). His tricorn headdress is also not unfamiliar: it evokes classical symbols such as the *nandipada* or the *triratna* common in Buddhist art (at Bharhut and Sanchi for instance), and is depicted on punch-marked coins, as T.G. Aravamuthan pointed out in 1942.[10]

Next to the mythical unicorn, a majestic bull, generally humped, is among the animals frequently depicted on Indus seals (Fig. 10.5), and must have been an object of special reverence. Many scholars have seen in it a precursor of Nandi, Shiva's mount.

In the Harappan statuary, a category of figurines represents what archaeologists have identified as a mother goddess, basing themselves on the heavy ornamentation of most figurines (Fig. 10.6, left), and also on a pair of pannier-like cups on both sides of the head, which were used as oil lamps (as proved by stains of soot). Curiously, statuettes of the mother

Fig. 10.5. A humped bull on an Indus seal. (© ASI)

---

* I was intrigued by the frequent depiction of two antelopes under the throne of the Buddha (at Ajanta, for instance), just as in the 'Pashupati' seal (often two lions take the place of the antelopes). But the art historians I consulted were sceptical of a possible Harappan connection.

goddess made two millennia later, in Mauryan times (Fig. 10.6, right), often bear similar traits: both have the same extravagant wreath of large flowers around the face, the same double necklace (the lower one with a pendant), a similar girdle, often a short skirt, sometimes also similar huge earrings.[11] Stylistic considerations apart, the chief difference between the two is the loss of the side cups (although it appears that they are preserved in some

Fig. 10.6. Sketch of two mother goddesses: from the third millennium BCE (left) to the second century BCE (Mathura style, right).

Fig. 10.7. A Harappan female 'centaur' (cylinder seal from Kalibangan); she watches two warriors who appear to be competing for a woman. (© ASI)

traditional Gujarati art); the fan-shaped headdress is also gone, but other historical figurines still display it.[12]

Another Harappan deity is a kind of female 'centaur' (Fig. 10.7); it is striking that the same concept reappears in classical Hindu art in the form of the *kinnarī* or *gandharvī*.

Finally, a standing Harappan god often appears between two open branches of a pipal tree; on some of the tablets the branches close up at the top and we have a full arch, plainly a device intended to exalt the god (Fig. 10.8). The same device is used in classical art, where an arch surrounds a seated Buddha[13] or a standing Shiva, enhancing their glory.

Fig. 10.8. A Harappan god (left) under an arch of pipal leaves; Shiva (right) under an arch of fire. (© ASI)

It could be objected that in none of the above cases do we have an unbroken chain of transmission from Harappan times—we rather have a chain of missing links!—and that these parallels may, in reality, be nothing more than independent artistic creations occasionally coming up with similar concepts. The objection is theoretically valid, but in practice, there is little likelihood that such a variety of highly specific iconographic devices could have had wholly independent origins. And it is precisely the totality of these devices of Harappan art that gives it an intangible yet unmistakable air of 'Indianness': thus Stella Kramrish, one of the most distinguished experts on Indian art, felt that 'in certain respects some of the Mohenjo-daro figurines can be compared with the work by village potters and women made to this day in Bengal'.[14] At a more formal level, she was convinced that 'the beautiful

Maurya sculpture presupposes continuity in the artistic traditions since the Harappa period'.[15] The French Vedic scholar Jean Varenne also noted how 'several of these [Harappan] themes (figures seated in the "lotus posture", mythical animals, celebration of dance) appear as constants in Indian art'.[16]

Harappan art holds occasional surprises. At Lothal, S.R. Rao[17] found two pottery sherds which appear to narrate folk tales well known to many Indian grandmothers: in one of them (Fig. 10.9), two crows perched high on a tree hold fishes in their beaks while a fox-like animal below seems to be craftily concocting some way to get at that succulent food. La Fontaine, who attributed the origin of his *Fables* to India, would have been surprised to learn that 'the Crow and the Fox' was a 4500-year-old tale—with the fish turning into cheese somewhere between the protohistoric Gulf of Khambat and the elegant salons of seventeenth-century French literary circles . . .

Fig. 10.9. A potsherd from Lothal: two crows and an envious fox. (© ASI)

RELIGIOUS LIFE

The religious life of the Harappans has often been the object of comparisons with later Indian religions, at both the external level of customs and traditions and the conceptual level reflected in Vedic and post-Vedic literature. Here also, archaeologists and scholars of religion have broadly concurred that a Harappan 'substratum' remains perceptible, but there is much disagreement regarding the mechanism of transmission. Before we discuss this, let us survey objectively the salient parallels in the field.

An easy method would be to transport a Hindu villager of today to a Harappan city. He would perhaps first note the importance of cleanliness in daily life and observe, in accordance with archaeologists, that beyond mere hygiene, ritual purification through water was a trait of Harappan religion as it is of later Indian religions;[18] he would marvel at such ceremonies as the Great Bath and would not miss the structure's obvious likeness to the ritual bathing tanks of later Hindu temples.[19] He might mingle with a religious procession through the streets of Mohenjodaro (a few tablets depict such events[20]), and watch as oil lamps are lit and libations poured with conch shells (whose mouths were sawn open), or as priests blow through their conches (whose tips were sawn off) to announce a holy moment or invoke a god.[21] He would feel at home with sacred symbols like the swastika, the pipal leaf or an occasional trident (*trishūla*), and would find that some *linga*s have much the same shape as those in his village temple (Fig. 10.10). The worship of the pipal tree or of a mother goddess would surprise him in no way.

Our villager's experience might be best summarized by John Marshall's stimulating observation made in 1931:

> Taken as a whole, [the Indus Valley people's] religion is so characteristically Indian as hardly to be distinguished from still living Hinduism.[22]

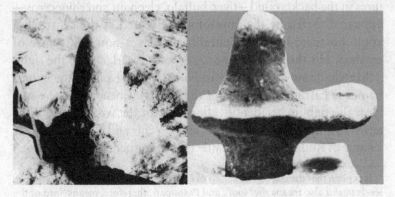

Fig. 10.10. *Lingas* found at Harappa (left) and Kalibangan. (© ASI)

But commonalities do not stop with the folk aspect of religion; they run deeper, and despite the general opinion (including Marshall's) that Indus culture is 'pre-Aryan' and therefore non-Vedic, it is tempting to probe the Vedic texts for echoes of themes evoked on Harappan seals and tablets.

Harappan gods and goddesses have been the objects of numerous studies, most of them partly speculative in nature: since the script remains mute, their pictorial representations alone guide us. The bull (Fig. 10.5), for instance, is omnipresent on Harappan seals and pottery, and it is also the animal that the Rig Veda exalts above all others: great gods such as Indra or Agni are frequently lauded as 'the Bull' in an obvious symbol of might. Harappan figurines depict a mother goddess often enough, and again the Vedic hymns implore various aspects of the Mother: Sarasvatī, Ushas, Ilā, Aditi, Prithivī, Bhāratī . . . But such parallels, though interesting, are inconclusive, since both the bull and the mother goddess were worshipped in many other ancient cultures. In central India, for instance, the cult of a mother goddess is attested as early as 8000 or 9000 BCE![23] The issue is, therefore, whether we can establish stronger connections resting on a group of specific traits.

PROTO-SHIVA AND THE BUFFALO

Let us return to the 'Pashupati' seal (Fig. 10.4). Four wild creatures in the background—tiger, buffalo, elephant and rhinoceros—appear dwarfed by the imposing god seated at the centre in a yogic posture, who indisputably exudes a powerful sense of mastery. His three faces gaze to the left, ahead, and to the right.

Marshall saw in him a 'proto-Shiva' because one of the latter's names is Pashupati or 'lord of the beasts'. I believe that he was basically right in his identification, but for the wrong reason: the term 'Pashupati', which appears in the Yajur and Atharva Veda as a name of Rudra, applies to cattle (*pashu*) rather than wild beasts.*

---

* It is plain that the concept of a 'lord of cattle' is to be understood at a symbolic level: *pashu* also means the 'soul', and Pashupati, therefore, means 'lord of the souls'. This is the same symbolism as the later image of Krishna with the cows.

But in a series of praises of Soma, the divine nectar, the Rig Veda presents the striking image of a 'Buffalo of wild beasts'[24] (*mahisho mrigānām*), a designation that seems to suit this godhead wearing buffalo horns and surrounded by wild beasts. Moreover, in the Veda, Soma is often associated with Rudra,[25] sometimes even fused with him,[26] and Rudra is Shiva's terrible form. If we remember that Shiva is also Yogīshvar, Yoganāth, that is, the 'lord of yoga', as well as Mahākāleshwar, the lord of Time—represented on the seal, I suggest, by the three faces for past, present and future—this impressive seal from Mohenjo-daro presents us with a series of concepts and attributes consonant with those classically associated with Shiva.

This identification finds further support in the symbol of the *trishūla,* which the head-dress, as a whole, evokes; the trident is independently depicted on a few seals, and is one of the signs of the Indus writing system. Finally, we have just seen the presence of *linga*-shaped objects of worship. Altogether, the evidence of the cult of a Shiva-like ('proto' or not) deity in the Indus–Sarasvatī civilization does build up into a consistent whole.

Fig. 10.11. A seal depicting the same deity as in Fig. 10.4. (© ASI)

As an aside, I must disagree with Marshall and other scholars who labelled Shiva a 'Dravidian' god, since Shiva first appears in the Rig Veda as Rudra and in the Yajur Veda under his own name.[27] Also, in an attempt to connect the seal's deity with some hypothetical 'pre-Aryan' phallus worship, several scholars have described him as ithyphallic, but that is doubtful: what appears to be an erect phallus is more likely the folds of a loin cloth; other seals of the same god in the same posture (Fig. 10.11) confirm this.

A few other scenes evoke familiar themes.

A motif encountered on several tablets is that of the slaying of a buffalo. In a two-sided moulded tablet found at Harappa a

few years ago (Fig. 10.12),[28] one side depicts a figure pinning the buffalo down with his leg and spearing him, while another figure seated in a yogic posture looks on, wearing a tricorn head-dress—clearly our 'proto-Shiva' again, and a presence that lends a ritual

Fig. 10.12. Sketch of a tablet from Harappa.

dimension to the slaying (as does the fact that this is one of the very rare 'violent' scenes depicted on the Indus seals). The Veda alludes to the sacrifice of a buffalo,[29] but as many scholars have remarked, this Harappan motif rather calls to mind that of goddess Durga slaying the buffalo–demon Mahishāsura. This theme likely has Harappan origins, although a more diffused origin cannot be ruled out (the Todas of the Nilgiris, for instance, practise the ritual sacrifice of the buffalo, though not through spearing).

Another seal, often called the 'Divine Adoration' seal (Fig. 10.13), narrates a ritual that has been the object of many differing interpretations. The figure standing between two branches of a pipal tree and the kneeling figure wear an identical tricorn head-dress and plait of hair: could they be one and the same? Are the seven

Fig. 10.13. Sketch of the 'Divine Adoration' seal.

figures at the bottom female (the seven mothers) or male (the seven rishis)? Is the noble-looking, human-faced ram being led to sacrifice, or does it stand for another deity? Could the object on the stool, which appears to have two hair buns on the side, be a human head? Or does its arched handle point to a *kamandalu*? There are no easy answers to these questions, but we do find the worshipper's physical attitude precisely described in the Rig Veda: thus the poet prays 'with uplifted hands'[30] or with 'bended knees';[31] Agni is to be approached 'kneeling with adoration',[32] and so are Indra[33] and Sarasvatī.[34]

On a seal from Chanhu-daro, we witness an unusual scene: a gaur (the Indian 'bison') with a human-like face mates with a woman lying supine, from whose head a plant emerges.[35] As Raymond and Bridget Allchin point out, this motif 'may be compared with the Vedic theme of the union of heaven and earth (*dyavaprithivi*), the latter represented as the Earth Mother (*mata bhumi*) and the former by the bull of heaven (*dyaur me pita*)'.[36] Indeed, throughout the Rig Veda, heaven and earth constitute a constant couple, representing our 'father and mother',[37] as it were, sometimes fused into a single deity;[38] and an important hymn[39] entreats God Parjanya as the Bull to 'deposit his seed in the plants', in an almost perfect evocation of the seal's motif (including the *gaur*'s human face).

THE UNICORN

No attempt to make sense of themes depicted on Indus seals can afford to ignore the unicorn motif (Fig. 10.14). What could be its significance? And if it bears some relation with Vedic symbolism, why is the unicorn absent from classical iconography? The bull, elephant and buffalo perdure, but not this graceful one-horned creature.

Nevertheless, the notion of a 'unicorn' does not end with Harappan culture: in later Hindu mythology, Vishnu's first avatar, the fish who saves Manu when the Great Flood engulfs the earth, wears a single horn on his head, to which Manu ties his boat.

Fig. 10.14. An Indus seal depicting a unicorn facing a ritual stand. (© ASI)

Also, as the historian A.D. Pusalker[40] noted long ago, another *avatar* of Vishnu, Varāha or the Boar, is sometimes called *ekashringa* or 'one-horned'. In the Mahābhārata, Krishna himself expounds to Arjuna a long list of his incarnations and names; coming to the same avatar, he says, 'Assuming, in days of old, the form of a boar with a single tusk . . . I raised the submerged Earth from the bottom of the ocean. From this reason am I called by the name of *Ekasringa*.'[41] The motif of a one-horned deity is therefore not foreign to Hindu mythology.

But to my mind, it is again the Rig Veda that helps us most here. Harappans depicted horned tigers, horned serpents and horned composite animals, and many Vedic deities have one, two, three, four horns (or more!). In the Veda, the horn is more than a mere glorifying device: thus Agni or Indra destroys the enemy's den 'like a bull with sharpened horn';[42] Soma, also likened to a bull, 'brandishes his horns on high and whets them'.[43] The horn (*shringa*) is not always mentioned explicitly: thus Indra is 'like a bull who sharpens [his horns]'[44] or tears his enemies apart 'like a sharp bull'.[45] Moreover, Indra's weapon is the *vajra* or thunderbolt, which he 'whets for sharpness, as a bull [whets his horns]';[46] it is a 'sharpened' weapon.[47] Thunderbolt or horn, therefore, has the same function—that of the aggressive, pointed divine power concentrated on a hostile point. Obligingly, as often, the Rig Veda gives us the key to its own symbolism: it describes Savitar, the sun god, as 'spreading his horn of truth'[48]—*ritasya shringa*, with '*ritam*' signifying 'truth' or the 'cosmic order', the Rig Vedic antecedent of *dharma*.

If one were to create an iconography for this whole symbolism, it would be hard to think of a better one than the unicorn. Moreover, the Rig Veda compares the Maruts (a family of violent gods) to bulls whose horn is 'uplifted unto the highest',[49] just as we see on the seals.* Even the invariably double or S-shaped curve of the unicorn's horn, executed so carefully that it must have a precise meaning (the bulls' horns, by contrast, have a single curve), could be explained within the same Vedic imagery, as a means to represent in a compact space the 'hundred joints' of Indra's thunderbolt.[50]

That the unicorn actually stood for Indra in the eyes of Harappans cannot be proved, but its affinity with the Vedic concepts of a mighty bull with a sharpened horn certainly calls for attention.

FIRE WORSHIP

Two more elements of Harappan culture throw important bridges across the 'Vedic Night'. The first is fire worship, evidenced by a few altars that have come to light in Harappan cities.

We have already seen (Fig. 7.2) the peculiar apsidal altar on Banawali's acropolis, itself enclosed within an apsidal structure. When it was uncovered towards the end of the partial excavations at this site, R.S. Bisht noted that the altar 'was full of fine loose ash';[51] a large jar was found in the structure. Seven years ago, Banawali's altar came on the screen as I showed slides of the Indus–Sarasvatī civilization to venerable Vedic scholars assembled in a field at Pañjal, in Kerala.[52] Some of them, masters of one or several of the Vedas, interrupted me to point out that the semi-circular shape is one of the three basic shapes of fire altars (called dakshināgni), with the other two being the square (āhavanīya) and the circle (gārhapatya); the three could be seen on the grounds of the conference, and are still in use in various ceremonies.[53] (They are visible inside the enclosure to the west of

_____
* Here, as in a few of the above cases, the Sanskrit word shringa appears in the singular.

the *mahāvedi*, see Fig. 9.4, Nos 2, 3 and 4). While those Vedic scholars of Kerala recognized in the Banawali structure a fire altar, Bisht reached a similar conviction independently: to him, this clearly non-utilitarian structure enclosing an altar with layers of ashes could only be a temple dedicated to fire rituals.

Further down the Sarasvatī, at Kalibangan, we already visited a series of seven altars located atop a brick platform on the southern side of the acropolis (p. 160). Sceptics suggested that this could be a community kitchen, with the central steles acting as base for the pots,[54] but this is unlikely for several reasons. One, generally kitchen ovens or hearths used for cooking had a lateral opening for the insertion of firewood, but that is not the case for Kalibangan's seven altars. Two, the central steles, with diameters of 10 to 15 cm, are too slender to support pots. Three, here again the altars contained ashes (with some charcoal), but no bone remains[55] as one would expect from domestic hearths, since we know that Harappans were non-vegetarian. The scales are thus clearly tipped in favour of some fire ritual.

Fig. 10.15. A square fire altar at Lothal, with a painted jar in front. This altar was located on Street 9, suggesting a public function. (© ASI)

Such altars were also found in some individual houses of Kalibangan's lower city; further east, outside the fortified lower city,
a small but badly eroded mound produced a unique complex of
altars—neither apsidal nor rectangular, but more or less circular
this time: a large altar, over 2.5 m in diameter, was irregularly
surrounded by five small ones, all of them containing ash and
terracotta cakes. Noting the presence of altars on Kalibangan's
three mounds, Raymond Allchin remarked, 'These three contexts
suggest that fire rituals formed a part of the religious life of the
town, at a civic, domestic and popular level.'[56]

Moving to Saurashtra, Lothal yielded similar structures not
only of an oval shape, but also a few square ones too. Here also,
the excavator S.R. Rao concluded that the latter could not have
been kitchen hearths: among other reasons, they are much too
large (about 2.7 m square) and some were located right on the
street.[57] One of them (Fig. 10.15) showed depressions in the top
row of bricks, probably designed to hold vessels in place, and a
post hole in a corner. But it also offered three strong clues to the
Vedic fire ritual. A fine painted jar of terracotta with a broad
mouth was placed against the altar; a few steps away, a terracotta
ladle[58] was found, with blackened edges and bottom pointing
to contact with fire. It would have been the right instrument for
making offerings to the fire of oil, milk and clarified butter drawn
from the jar. (Incidentally, both sacrificial jar and ladle figure in
the Vedas in association with the constant theme of libation.)

The third clue emerges from a comparison with the *Shulbasūtra*s, ancient technical texts that I briefly invoked in relation to
the proportions of the *mahāvedi*; they give elaborate geometrical
instructions on the construction of altars of various shapes—
falcon, tortoise, wheel, or a simple square. The last has, on one
side, a small platform jutting out, called the 'handle' of the altar
(Fig. 10.16). Lothal's structure is about half the size of the
*Shulbasūtra*s' square altar, but surprisingly, on one side, it has a
small platform which looks very much like the 'handle'. Moreover,
the length of the platform is one-fourth of the altar's side—
exactly as with the *Shulbasūtra*s' square altar.[59] The 'coincidence'

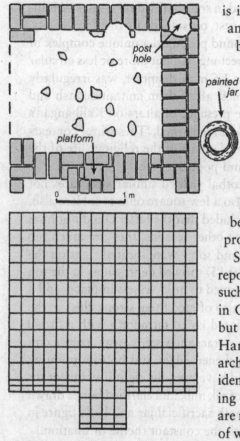

is intriguing, to say the least, and while the *Shulbasūtras* belong to a later age, some of the concepts they articulate appear to have originated in the Harappan tradition. At any rate, if Lothal's structure, located on one of the town's main streets, with its platform, jar and ladle, was not a fire altar, no better explanation has been proposed so far.

Such fire structures have been reported from other Indian sites, such as Nageshwar, Vagad (both in Gujarat) and Rakhigarhi,[60] but not from Mohenjo-daro or Harappa. (At Mohenjo-daro, archaeologists have occasionally identified one or another building with a temple,[61] but there are no clues as to the exact type of worship conducted in them.)

Fig. 10.16. Comparison between Lothal's altar (top) and the square altar of the *Shulbasūtras* (bottom). (The scale applies to Lothal's altar alone.)

It may be that fire worship was only practised in the Sarasvatī Valley (Banawali, Rakhigarhi, Kalibangan) and in Gujarat. Conversely, mother-goddess figurines are common in Mohenjo-daro and Harappa but rare in the Sarasvatī region. Pending more extensive excavations, it is legitimate to assume a certain regionalization of the Harappan religion: it was not uniform but allowed for 'diversity of practice',[62] as Possehl puts it.

The presence of fire worship in the Sarasvatī region and in

Gujarat has generated a good deal of interest as well as disbelief: not all scholars have accepted it as readily as Allchin, Lal, Rao or Joshi. The reason for such scepticism is plain enough: in the Indian context, fire worship conjures up Vedic culture.

YOGA

So does another Harappan practice, which has caused a lot of scholarly ink to flow. The impressive 'proto-Shiva' is seated in such a way that he rests on his toes with the two heels in contact; several more seals and tablets represent a figure—very likely the same 'proto-Shiva'—seated in the same manner on a low platform or pedestal. This posture has sometimes been wrongly identified as *padmāsana*, for in the lotus posture, the legs are crossed, which is not the case here. At least two scholars—T. McEvilley[63] and Yan Y. Dhyansky[64]—went into minute detail to establish that this posture is the classical *mūlabandhāsana*, a difficult *āsana* whose function is to help awaken the *kundalinī*.

Besides, at Mohenjo-daro, Harappa and Lothal, excavators found figurines in different postures recalling other *āsanas*.[65] A striking example from Harappa (Fig. 10.17) shows a man seated cross-legged with his hands joined in the traditional Indian *namaste*: an average Indian would be hard put to decide whether it was made 4500 years ago or yesterday!

Even more arresting is the famous 'priest–king' (Fig. 10.18). At the time of its discovery at Mohenjo-daro, it was often speculated that, as in Mesopotamia, the city must have been governed by a class of 'priest–kings'; with no

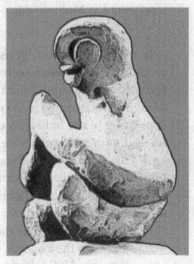

Fig. 10.17. Sketch of a terracotta figurine from Harappa.

Fig. 10.18. Sketch of the 'priest–king' found at Mohenjo-daro.

evidence in support of this hypothesis, it was gradually abandoned, but the label stuck to the statuette. This impressive personage has also been compared to figurines from Bactria on stylistic grounds,[66] but even if one admits some likeness, there is a fundamental difference: as early as in 1929, the Indian archaeologist Ramaprasad Chanda pointed out that the figure's 'half-shut eyes looking fixedly at the tip of the nose'[67] signified a distinctly Indian trait not to be found anywhere else, which suggested specific techniques of meditation.

In other words, our 'priest–king' is deep in contemplation—an attitude not known to be attached to kings or priests, especially of the Mesopotamian sort: as Wheeler noted, 'the fixed Mesopotamian stare is very different from the contemplative expression of the Indus faces'.[68] Though quite unlike the powerful god with a tricorn head-dress, our personage is part of the same cultural complex of yoga, if we take the word in its central sense of inner exploration and mastery. Dilip Chakrabarti refers to him as a 'Shramana' (ascetic) or a 'sacred person',[69] certainly a better description than that of a priest or a king.

It is often claimed that there is no notion of yoga in the Rig Veda, and that the concept of a 'Harappan yoga', if admitted, can still be pre-Vedic. But while the Rig Veda does not use the term 'yoga', it asks for our thoughts to be harnessed or yoked to a higher consciousness:

The illumined yoke their mind and they yoke their thoughts
to the illumined godhead, to the vast, to the luminous in
consciousness.[70]

In many hymns (as, later, in the Bhagavad Gītā), the metaphor
of the well-yoked chariot transparently stands for mastery over
the instrument: horses are 'yoked by thought'[71] or 'yoked by
prayer'[72] to the chariot.* Central to the Rig Veda's quest for
immortality is the effort to release Agni, the divine fire 'who
dwells in creatures, in whom all creatures dwell, [but who] is
hidden within mortals by hostile powers'.[73] There would be
much more to say on the spiritual pursuit of the Rig Vedic rishis,
but while it is couched in a language very different from that of
the Upanishads, its goal and methods are the same.[74]

If 'Yoga was present in India five thousand years ago',[75] as
Dhyansky concludes in his paper entitled 'The Indus Valley Origin
of a Yoga Practice', there is no need to invoke some unknown
and unverifiable 'pre-Vedic' tradition.

LIFE AND DEATH

Harappan funerary practices were of several types. Some of the
dead were buried in earthen graves often lined with bricks, their
heads generally to the north, the direction used today during
cremation (since the feet should point southward, towards Yama's
realm). Some were buried in wooden coffins, but that seems to
be the exception rather than the rule; whether they were rulers,
high officials or high priests we may never know, although the
last is not unlikely in the case of a few skeletons wearing neck-
laces of beads and various amulets. Some burials were symbolic
ones containing grave offerings with no bones. Other modes of
burial, in big urns devoid of bones, may have involved cremation, and since the overall number of graves only accounts for a

---

* Such passages use words like *yuga*, *yukta* and *yoga*, derived from the Sanskrit
root *yuj*, which expresses the idea of joining or uniting (it is cognate with the
English 'yoke' or the French '*joug*').

fraction of the population, cremation is often believed to have been practised by the lower strata of the society at least.

Even if the graves were reserved for an elite, they were quite plain in comparison with the sumptuous royal tombs of ancient Egypt: nothing marked them out in the landscape, and an assortment of pots of various sizes and shapes was all that accompanied the dead, along with a few personal objects (beads, rings, bangles or copper mirrors)—there was no gold, no frescoes, no decorated sarcophagus, nothing to cause awe in the grave's discoverer. Several archaeologists have pointed out that this restraint may hold a message: Harappans did respect their dead, but did not believe in glorifying them. To ancient Egyptians, there was eternal life after death; pharaohs and members of the social elite therefore had to be suitably 'equipped' with every possible luxury. In contrast, if Harappans did believe in some afterlife, as the grave offerings show, they preferred to keep their wealth in circulation,

Fig. 10.19. A peacock painted on a Cemetery H urn at Harappa: a recumbent human can be seen inside the bird.

favouring life over death—that is, indeed, a characteristic Indian attitude.

Another approach comes from D.D. Kosambi, who drew attention to a funerary urn at Harappa (the Cemetery H phase): on it is painted a peacock with a circular body, inside which can be seen a recumbent human figure (Fig. 10.19). Kosambi found here a parallel to the Mahābhārata's reference to the dead 'having been eaten by birds and insects of various sorts, but specifically by peacocks'.[76] I may add that a Rig Vedic hymn, which speaks of 'a glory beyond this realm' to which we pass through old age, mentions 'man-consuming birds'[77] in the very next verse.

A bird was also sculpted on the lid of a terracotta pot in one of the graves at the recently discovered Harappan site of Sanauli, a few kilometres east of the Yamuna. This unique site turned out to be an extensive burial ground: 116 graves have so far been excavated, and the full extent of the cemetery is thought to be some four hectares, prompting the excavators to call it a 'necropolis'.[78] They felt tempted to correlate some of the unique artefacts and burial modes that came to light in Vedic literature, but more research is needed to put this on a sound footing. Meanwhile, we should note the discovery of an oblong trough of clay: its vitrified inner walls and the presence of ash and charred human bones point to cremation, perhaps the first direct evidence of the practice.

VEDIC VS HARAPPAN

There are other, subtler threads connecting the two civilizations of early India, or bridging the Harappan and Vedic cultures. We noted earlier the community-based distribution of power (and, probably, functions) in Harappan society, a culture of 'unity in diversity', and the absence of glorified rulers—traits equally visible in the early stages of the Ganges civilization. On an ethical level, the four classical goals of life—*dharma* (the cosmic and individual order), *artha* (wealth), *kāma* (pleasures) and *moksha* (liberation)—constituted the cultural foundation of historical

India; referring to this four-fold order, Kenoyer judiciously observes that the Indus rulers appear to have observed the first three concepts by promoting trade and wealth 'without the extensive use of military coercion'.[79] Indeed, with the just noted Harappan tradition of yoga and meditation, we are entitled to make out the presence of the fourth concept too—*moksha*!

If we return to Dholavira's town planning (p. 198), we can discern two important Vedic concepts at play. The first is the *addition of unity*, visible in the ratios (5:4 is nothing but ¼ plus one unit; 9:4 is the same plus another unit), and crucial to the calculations of fire altars in the *Shulbasūtra*s, for instance.[80] This addition to the unit of a fraction of itself represents, at a deeper level, a process of expansion, of auspicious increase symbolizing or inviting prosperity, and it becomes a standard method of generating auspicious proportions in classical Hindu architecture.[81] The second Vedic concept is that of *recursion* or repetition of a motif, also visible in classical architecture as a way of repeating the initial unity and of growing from it.[82] (In temples, *shikharas* of increasing height build up towards the towering last one.) At Dholavira, the ratio 5:4 found in the castle's proportions is repeated in those of the lower town; again, the ratio 9:4, between the lengths of the 'castle' and the middle town, is repeated between the lengths of the middle and the lower towns. In view of the very low margins of error, such a double repetition can only have been deliberately designed.

Many more meeting points between Harappan and Vedic cultures have been proposed right from the 1920s onwards.[83] But scholars have proposed widely divergent explanations to account for them.

At one end of the spectrum, Asko Parpola, a Finnish Sanskritist, has been a strong advocate of the theory that Harappans were Dravidian speakers (a theory first propounded by Marshall). His well-known work on the Indus script is essentially based on Dravidian readings; if it has not gained acceptance, it is mostly because it could make no headway beyond a few seals. But it is fascinating to note how, in order to explain Harappan motifs,

Parpola takes constant recourse to Vedic and classical Hindu, Buddhist and Jain concepts and themes. For example, he parallels Kalibangan's row of seven fire altars with the seven altars within the *mahāvedi* of the Vedic Soma sacrifice (Fig. 9.4).[84] He gives a fairly central place to the 'Dravidian' god Murugan, but correlates him with Harappan symbols through the Vedic god Rudra and other elements of Sanskrit literature. His reading of the iconography of the 'Divine Adoration' seal (Fig. 10.13) draws on the Brāhmanas, Purānas, the two epics and a traditional sacrifice to Durga; it weaves an entire symbolism around the constellation of Rohini (which holds an important place in early Vedic literature) and sees in the seven standing figures at the bottom of the seals the 'seven mothers' or else the seven wives of the rishis and, therefore, the Pleiades (*Krittikā*). None of this is remotely 'Dravidian'!

We saw earlier how I. Mahadevan, who has also proposed Dravidian readings of a few seals, interpreted the ritual stand placed in front of the unicorn as a sacred filter for Soma—the extraction, filtering and consumption of which form a core theme of the Rig Veda.

How do such scholars reconcile the apparent contradiction between a supposedly Dravidian-speaking population and important Vedic cultural themes? They do so simply by assuming that all these components of Harappan religion and mythology were somehow 'borrowed' from the Late Harappans by the freshly arrived Aryans, who then integrated them in their Vedic literature.

At the other end of the spectrum, we meet archaeologists who see no need for such a device, finding no trace of the Aryans' arrival on the ground, and who therefore prefer to equate the Harappan with the Vedic. Dholavira's excavator R.S. Bisht, for instance, finds that the city's upper, middle and lower towns 'temptingly sound analogous to three interesting terms in the *Rig-Veda*, viz., "*parama*" [upper], "*madhyama*" [middle] and "*avama*" [lower] . . .'[85] 'In the tripartite divisions of the Harappan city of Dholavira,' he claims, 'we find what the Vedic seers were trying to conceive of in supernatural and divine world'.[86] Bisht also extracts from hundreds of passages of the Rig Veda numerous terms for villages and towns, fortifications, houses of various types, rooms, even doorways—a rich material vocabulary that belies the conventional view of early Vedic people as 'pastoral' or 'nomadic', and ignorant of anything remotely resembling city life.

A few years ago, the scholar Bhagwan Singh went further and listed hundreds of Rig Vedic words related to trade, industry, etc.[87] Even if one may often hesitate to accept his interpretations, as I do, once again the sheer diversity of the vocabulary is puzzling. In the field of governance, for instance, B.B. Lal asks, 'What do we do with terms like *rājan, samrāt, janarāj, rāstra, Samiti, sabhā, adhyaksa*, etc. occurring in the Vedic texts, which clearly refer to categories of rulers, assemblies, etc.?'[88] The spacious assembly halls at Mohenjo-daro and Harappa come to mind.

Opposing such a perspective is the dominant view that the Rig Veda, apart from reflecting a non-urban environment, knows the horse (which is absent from Harappan iconography), but not writing (known to Harappans), and that linguistic considerations prevent us from dating the Rig Veda beyond the middle of the second millennium BCE. The debate—which is inextricably linked with the Aryan invasion or migration theory—has been raging for eight decades, and is not likely to end soon. It has generated a copious literature, including a few wide-ranging studies highlighting the complexity of the issue, and bringing in new disciplines such as anthropology, genetics and astronomy.[89] A growing number of participants in the debate (myself included) have argued that the stark contrast between the Harappan and the Vedic, proposed by linguists, historians and other scholars, remains rooted in colonial misconceptions and misreadings of the Vedic texts. At the same time, it is fair to stress that there are complexities and potential pitfalls in trying to equate a popular culture, such as the Harappan, with a textual one, such as the Vedic.

But my purpose in this chapter and the preceding one was not to enter into that labyrinthine debate; it was limited to offering a glimpse of the overall legacy of the Indus–Sarasvatī civilization: in whatever way we may wish to explain it, a manifold *cultural*

continuum emerges between the Indus and the Ganges civilizations. As Lal puts it:

> Even today there is no walk of life in which we cannot discern
> the grass-roots features of this ancient [Harappan] civili-
> zation: be it agriculture, cooking habits, arts, crafts, games,
> ornaments, toiletry, religious practices or social stratifica-
> tion.[90]

In no way does archaeology or literature justify the picture of
a tradition 'rudely and ruthlessly interrupted by the arrival of
new people from the west', as Piggot asserted, with the fabled
Aryans in mind. Nor is the Gangetic culture 'diametrically
opposed' to the Harappan culture, as Basham would have it.

As a result, the old concept of a 'Vedic night' throwing open a
gaping chasm between the two civilizations now stands rejected.
According to Kenoyer, 'It is clear that this period of more than
700 years was not a chaotic Dark Age, but rather a time of reorganization and expansion.'[91] To be precise, 'current studies of the
transition between the two early urban civilizations claim that
there was no significant break or hiatus.'[92] Jarrige agrees: 'This
famous vacuum that was sometimes called Vedic night ... has
been filling up more and more thanks to numerous findings.'[93]
In his opinion, the considerable changes that followed the end
of the Indus cities are to be understood 'within the framework
of a continuity with the preceding millennia, without any radical
break of the sort too often proposed earlier'.[94] Shaffer is equally
categorical: 'The previous concept of a Dark Age in South Asian
archaeology is no longer valid.'[95]

There is, however, a crucial element of the debate that is missing
here: the Sarasvatī. The lost river has been summoned as a witness,
and since in between she became the goddess of *vāch*, or speech,
she deserves a fair hearing.

11

The Sarasvatī's Testimony

The rediscovery of the 1500 km-long bed of the Sarasvatī in the nineteenth century has far-reaching repercussions on our understanding of the origins of Indian civilization.

Let us briefly survey the ground we have covered. The most ancient Indian text in our possession, the Rig Veda, reveals a keen awareness of the geography of the Northwest, an awareness expressed mostly through river names. Among them is the Sarasvatī, a mighty, impetuous river flowing 'from the mountain to the sea' and located between the Yamunā and the Shutudrī (Sutlej). Subsequent Vedic literature—the Mahābhārata, several Brāhmanas and Purānas among other texts—paint a consistent picture of the location, break-up and recession of the river. As a matter of fact, when nineteenth-century British officials explored the region, they found quite a few seasonal streams rising in the Shivalik Hills, but no major river flowing between the Yamuna and the Sutlej.

They did record three things, however: a tradition that there was once a river flowing westward through the region (the 'Lost River of the Indian Desert'); a broad, dry bed called the Ghaggar or Hakra, partly filled during strong monsoons; and, at the foot of the Shivaliks, a small stream called 'Sarsuti', flowing down from a *tīrtha* which tradition claims to be the source of the ancient Sarasvatī.

In the same nineteenth century, these findings, correlated with the testimony of Sanskrit texts, convinced most Indologists that the bed of the Ghaggar–Hakra was the relic of the Sarasvatī.

By the turn of the century, maps and gazetteers reflected that identification. The 'lost river' had been found again—the only question marks left had to do with the exact process of its decline, and whether it had reached the sea on its own or was a tributary of the Indus.

To Max Müller and other Indologists of his time, the Sarasvati's disappearance was a milestone in the timeline of ancient India: because 'the loss of the Sarasvati is later than the Vedic age', it provided in effect 'a new indication of the distance which separates the Vedic age from that of the later Sanskrit literature.'[1]

In the next century, the twentieth, archaeology added a dramatic new piece to the puzzle by unearthing, along the dry beds of the Ghaggar–Hakra and its tributaries, numerous sites small and large, many of them belonging to a civilization named after the Indus. Changes in the distribution patterns of these sites both in India and Pakistan suggested that the Ghaggar–Hakra had started breaking up sometime in the third millennium, and that by 1900 BCE, much of its central basin had gone dry. A further confirmation of this was that some of the post-urban sites were found right on the dry bed of the Ghaggar.[2]

The jigsaw puzzle might now be said to be complete, and we would be justified in affixing, with a satisfied flourish, a final curlicue at the end of the saga.

But wait—there is a catch. Sarasvati, standing in the witness box, looks as if she is about to make some awful confession.

Let us contemplate the picture painted by J.M. Kenoyer in 1998:

> In the east, the ancient Saraswati (or Ghaggar–Hakra) river ran parallel to the Indus . . . Towards the end of the Indus Valley civilization, the ancient Saraswati had totally dried up and its original tributaries were captured by two other mighty rivers . . . The gradual drying up of the Saraswati river is an event documented both geologically as well as in the sacred Vedic and Brahmanical literature of ancient India . . . Many episodes of the Rig-Veda take place along the sacred Saraswati.[3]

This is a fine summary of much that we have explored so far (and Kenoyer goes on to refer to Oldham and Wilhelmy). But then, if 'the ancient Saraswati had totally dried up' towards the end of the Indus civilization, that is, around 1900 BCE, and if 'many episodes of the Rig-Veda take place along the sacred Saraswati', does it not follow that the said episodes took place *before the end of the Indus civilization*, while the river was flowing? There seems to be no escape from this conclusion.

Yet, following Max Müller, all conventional history books and encyclopædias tell us that the Rig Veda's hymns were composed by 'Aryans' who entered the subcontinent around 1500 BCE and pushed on towards the Yamuna–Ganges region, crossing it sometime between 1200 and 1000 BCE. Whatever the exact dates proposed (there are countless variations of this scenario), the said Aryans could only have settled in the Sarasvatī region after 1400 or 1300 BCE—centuries after the river had 'totally dried up', in any case. We are, therefore, asked to believe that the Aryans crossed at least five large rivers—the Indus and its four tributaries (see Fig. 2.2)—to settle down on the banks of a long, dry river, which they went on to extol as 'mighty', 'impetuous', 'best of rivers', etc. The proposition is incongruous in the extreme.

Of the two scenarios, the first alone is plausible: the hymns that praise the Sarasvatī—and some of them are found in the oldest books of the Rig Veda[4]—must have been composed while the river was still flowing, which can be no later than the third millennium BCE.

The contradiction between the two scenarios is vividly illustrated in a fine book on the Indus civilization, authored in 1997 by Raymond and Bridget Allchin. We have already quoted from it their 'most moving experience' at Kalibangan, where they gazed at 'the flood plain of the Sarasvatī still clearly visible' north of the settlement. Like Kenoyer, the Allchins acknowledge that the Sarasvatī

continued to flow down to c. 2000 BC. The major reduction of sites in the Early Post-urban period (c. 2000–1700

BC) . . . strongly suggests that a major part of the river's
water supply was lost around that time; while the final
settlement pattern of the Late Post-urban period indicates
that the river was by then dry (i.e. by c. 1300–1000 BC).[5]

Yet earlier in the same book, the Allchins state that the Sarasvatī
is 'recorded in the Rig Veda as a major river between c. 1500 and
c. 1000 BC'.[6] But how is that possible when archaeological evidence, in their own words, shows the river to have lost 'a major
part of its water supply' between 2000 and 1700 BCE? This
chronological impossibility is the result of the above phrase
'between c. 1500 and c. 1000 BC'—artificial dates that rest purely
on the old Aryan invasion theory, not on any physical evidence.

Gregory Possehl notes the same contradiction and attempts to
resolve it. We referred earlier (p. 149) to his long and useful
discussion on the Sarasvatī's evolution and the river's chronology
'actually founded in archaeological data'. In agreement with his
colleagues, Possehl explains that 'at the end of the third millennium the strong flow from the Sarasvatī dried up'.[7] Aware of the
Rig Veda's eulogies of the river, he proposes that they may be
merely 'recollections' of the time when the Sarasvatī was 'a river
of great magnitude'.[8] Why 'recollections' is unclear: the text's
vivid descriptions of the river evoke anything but that. Possehl
does not however press his own explanation, and comes to the
crux of the whole issue:

> This [the drying up of the Sarasvatī towards the end of the
> third millennium] carries with it an interesting chronologi-
> cal implication: the composers of the Rgveda were in the
> Sarasvatī region prior to the drying up of the river and this
> would be closer to 2000 BC than it is to 1000 BC, some-
> what earlier than most of the conventional chronologies for
> the presence of the Vedic Aryans in the Punjab.[9]

But 'somewhat earlier' is quite a euphemism for a whole
millennium or more. If the Vedic Aryans 'were in the Sarasvatī
region' earlier than 2000 BCE, they must have entered the subcontinent between 2400 and 2200 BCE at the very latest, bringing

us to a date that no proponent of the Aryan migration into India would be prepared to accept.

In a word, the Aryan theory collides head on with a Sarasvatī drying up in the late third millennium.

THE SARASVATĪ AND THE ARYAN PROBLEM

While Kenoyer, the Allchins and Possehl cautiously refrain from concluding, Indian archaeologists such as B.B. Lal, S.P. Gupta, V.N. Misra, Dilip Chakrabarti,[10] apart from other scholars, have proposed to put two and two together: the poets who sang the praise of the Sarasvatī lived on its banks while it flowed, therefore before 'the end of the third millennium', as Possehl just told us.

Moreover, the Vedic rishis state that the river flowed 'from the mountain to the sea', which takes us back to an even earlier date: as we saw (p. 151), Possehl's maps point to a break-up of the river during the Mature Harappan phase,[11] in agreement with Mughal's analysis of the pattern of sites in Cholistan (p. 149) and with two independent isotope studies; Fig. 6.8 reflects this clearly. That hymn from the seventh *mandala* of the Rig Veda must, therefore, have been composed before 2500 BCE—a whole millennium earlier than the conventional dates.

Yet, not all early Sanskritists would have objected to such a date. Moritz Winternitz, a noted German Indologist, for example, chose to disagree with the dominant chronology:

> We cannot explain the development of the whole of this great [Vedic] literature if we assume as late a date as round about 1200 BC or 1500 BC as its starting point. We shall probably have to date the beginning of this development to about 2000 or 2500 BC . . .[12]

This period is precisely the Mature phase of the Indus–Sarasvatī civilization—although Winternitz could not have known that, for he wrote the lines in 1907, long before the discovery of Harappa and Mohenjo-daro. In 1923, just a year before Marshall announced this discovery to the world, Winternitz was invited by Rabindranath Tagore to Vishwa Bharati; in the course of a lecture given in Calcutta, alluding to Max Müller and his followers, Winternitz made this extraordinary statement:

> I, for my part, do not understand why some Western scholars are so anxious to make the hymns of the Rgveda and the civilisation which is reflected in them so very much later than the Babylonian and Egyptian culture.[13]

There is a key word here: 'civilization'. Ever since Max Müller made it a dogma that the Rig Veda reflected a 'primitive', 'nomadic' and 'pastoral' culture, those labels have stuck, despite much contrary evidence provided by the text itself. In 1958, for instance, Sanskritist and linguist B.K. Ghosh, who accepted the mainstream invasionist view, nevertheless felt compelled to observe that 'the Rgveda clearly reflects the picture of a highly complex society in the full blaze of civilisation.'[14]

This leads us to a weighty question: we are told that the Harappan culture is pre-Vedic and therefore 'non-Aryan', and that the Aryans entered the Indus plains in the mid-second millennium BCE. We know where the latter lived and composed their hymns: apart from terms like *saptasindhava*, the hymn in praise of rivers (Fig. 2.2) shows that the whole of the Northwest was the Rig Vedic arena. But that also happened to be precisely the core Harappan territory—and only one civilization has been found there, not two: on the ground, no material culture has been found that might be identified with any 'Aryan' settlements. J.-M. Casal's statement made forty years ago still holds good:

> Until now, Aryans have eluded all archaeological definition. So far, no type of artefact, no class of pottery has been discovered that would enable us to say: 'Aryans came this way; here is a typically Aryan sword or goblet!'[15]

Many scholars have, nevertheless, attempted to identify the elusive Aryans with this or that regional culture of Late Harappan times (Gandhara Grave of the Swat Valley, Pirak, Cemetery H, Painted Grey Ware, etc.), but besides their mutual incompatibility, all these hypotheses rest on arbitrary choices of what might constitute, on the material level, an 'Aryan culture'. Besides, none of them covers the entire conjectured migratory path of the Aryans from Central Asia to the Ganges.

In fact, two points have been broadly accepted by the archaeological world: the absence of any intrusive material culture in the Northwest during the second millennium BCE,[16] and the biological continuity evidenced by the skeletal record of the region during the same period, a continuity confirmed by over a dozen recent genetic studies.[17] In other words, the arrival of the Aryans—an event which, we are told, would radically change the face of the subcontinent's cultural and linguistic landscape—is completely invisible on the ground.

If we add to this the cultural continuity discussed in the previous two chapters and the testimony of the Sarasvatī, the simplest and most natural conclusion is that Vedic culture was present in the region in the third millennium.

At this stage, it would be tempting to lay down the equation 'Harappan = Vedic' as the next logical step. To quote B.B. Lal:

> The geographical area covered by the Rigvedic people, as given in *Rig-Veda* 10.75 [the hymn to the rivers, see Fig. 2.2], lay from the Gaṅgā–Yamunā on the east to the Indus on the west. A simple question may now be posed: Which archaeological culture occupied the above-mentioned region during the period prior to 2000 BC [when the Sarasvatī dried up]? The inescapable answer is: it was the Harappan Civilization.[18]

Lal, however, pleads for patience till the Indus script has been conclusively deciphered. Moreover, we cannot cut the 'Aryan knot' without studying its tentacular ramifications into linguistics, archaeoastronomy, anthropology and genetics, comparative mythology and religion, besides a few other fields. Any proposed solution to the Aryan problem must satisfy, or at least answer, all those disciplines and their legitimate demands. We must leave that attempt to another study.[19]

The purpose of our journey through the mists of the Bronze

Age is to follow the evolution of the Sarasvatī river and delineate its twin role: it was not only 'the true lifeline of Vedic geography', in Renou's words, but also, in those of V.N. Misra, 'the lifeline of the Indus Civilization' (along with the Indus).

But not everyone agrees. As the implications of the Sarasvatī's chronology have grown clearer in the last two decades, voices have been heard questioning the identification of the Vedic Sarasvatī with the dry Ghaggar–Hakra bed—sometimes voices of the same scholars who had earlier endorsed that identification.

Romila Thapar, for example, in 1974 mentioned 'the change in the course of the Sarasvatī river with a consequent encroaching of the desert'[20] as one among the likely causes for the decline of the Harappan cities. Again, in a textbook on *Ancient India* in 1987 (reprinted till 2000 at least), she wrote:

> The Aryans at first settled in the Punjab. Gradually they moved south-eastwards into the region just north of Delhi. There used to be a river flowing nearby called Saraswati but the water of this river has now dried up. Here they remained for many years, and here they prepared the collection of hymns known as the *Rig-Veda*.[21]

The first half of this statement reflects the common theory of an Aryan migration into India, while the second half evidently endorses the Sarasvatī's location and relationship with the composers of the Rig Vedic hymns. Yet in 2002, Thapar states, 'The identification of the Ghaggar with the Sarasvatī, mentioned in the Rig-Veda, is controversial.'[22]

The 'controversy', if there is one, must then be recent: there was none in the days of Aurel Stein or A. Ghosh. But rather than dwell on it, we will benefit from a discussion of current objections to the identification of the Vedic river.

AN AFGHAN SARASVATĪ?

One line of argument has resuscitated a theory first put forth over a century ago. One of its early proponents was Edward

Thomas,[23] an Indologist, who in 1883 argued that the original Sarasvatī did not belong to the plains of the Punjab, but was the Helmand of southern Afghanistan. (Alfred Hillebrandt, a German Sanskritist, propounded a similar thesis a few years later.) That river, the largest of the region, flows westward from the southern flank of the Hindu Kush massif and ends in a depression close to the Iranian border. In the ancient Avestan language,* its name (rather that of its chief tributary, the Arghandab) was 'Harahvaitī', linguistically akin to 'Sarasvatī'. (The letter 's' becomes 'h' in Avestan, as for instance in 'Hapta Hindu', which corresponds to the Rig Veda's 'Sapta Sindhu'.)

In Thomas's thesis, the Aryans, in their southward movement from Central Asia, stayed in the Helmand basin for a while; then, entering the Indian subcontinent and fighting their way eastward, they crossed the Indus and its tributaries, till they came upon today's Sarsuti: though it was always, in Thomas's opinion, a small stream, which gave the intruding Aryans 'so shadowy an impression', he suggested that they transferred to it the name of the Sarasvatī in memory of the 'grand waters'[24] they had loved in Afghanistan.

This moving scenario—we can almost picture the brave Aryans fatigued by their Long March and longing to rest in the maternal arms of the mighty river goddess—has been dusted off, deromanticized and recycled by some of today's critics of the Sarasvatī–Ghaggar identity.

Among them, Rajesh Kochhar, an Indian astrophysicist, presented in 2000 what is probably the most closely argued thesis. Although he accepts that 'the Ghaggar had a far more dignified existence in the past than it has today' and must have 'flowed into the Nara and further into the Rann of Kutch without joining the Indus',[25] he is nonetheless convinced that the Ghaggar–Hakra cannot have been the Rig Vedic Sarasvatī, and presents twelve points to that effect. Let us hear the salient ones.

---

* Avestan is the ancient Iranian language of the *Avesta*, the sacred book of Zoroastrianism.

The first is that even if the Sutlej and the Yamunā flowed into the Ghaggar, 'the confluence would affect the Hakra part [in Cholistan] of the Ghaggar–Hakra channel, not the Ghaggar part [in today's India]'. That is to say, above the confluence with the Sutlej and the Yamunā, 'the basic character of the Ghaggar would not change. It would still be a rainwater stream in low hills . . . The Rgvedic description of Sarasvatī as a mighty, swift river that cuts the ridges of the hills does not fit the Ghaggar of today. It would have neither fitted the Ghaggar of the past.'[26] But the first part of the argument is based on wrong data. While it is true that some or most of the Yamunā's waters would have joined the Ghaggar's (through the Chautang) near Suratgarh, nothing rules out a partial flow of the Yamunā into the Markanda Valley, as proposed by geologists Puri and Verma (p. 64). Even leaving aside the Yamunā's case, the Sutlej undeniably joined the Ghaggar far above the international border; it did so through several palaeo-channels, one of which is still visible from Rupar and has been confirmed (p. 69) by satellite imagery: earlier we heard many researchers emphasize the Ghaggar's considerable widening not far from Shatrana (Fig. 3.1). It is therefore not just the 'Hakra part' (in Cholistan) that would have been swollen by the Sutlej's waters, but much of the Ghaggar too. As regards the Sarasvatī 'cutting the ridges of the hills', even allowing for some poetic licence, it is, again, entirely possible within the scenario proposed by Puri and Verma; even without it, it is clear that the Markanda, at least, once carried much more water than it does today, and during the monsoon at least, it would have been impressive enough to justify such a language.

Kochhar's second point, also stressed by Michael Witzel,[27] carries more weight. In the Rig Veda's third book, which counts among the earliest, rishi Vishvāmitra addresses the rivers Vipāsh (the Beas) and Shutudrī (the Sutlej). The two rivers have joined and flow together 'to the sea' (samudra), but Vishvāmitra, after duly praising them, wishes them to reduce their flow below the axle of his chariot so that he and his Bharata followers may cross over. The rivers, perhaps flattered, oblige and promise to bend 'like a nursing mother' and yield to the sage 'like a girl to her lover'.[28] Kochhar and Witzel argue that since the Sutlej was joining the Beas, this early hymn was composed when it had already deserted the Ghaggar—which, in that case, must have been reduced to a small stream, and could not have been the 'mighty Sarasvatī'. Both of them therefore conclude that the Ghaggar was in Vedic times more or less what it is today.

But there are alternative explanations. Although Kochhar speaks of the 'event'[29] of Vishvāmitra's crossing, this particular hymn can scarcely be historical: two large rivers accepting to drastically reduce their combined flow and let chariots through their beds may not sound quite as grandiose a miracle as the parting of the Red Sea, but it is a miracle nonetheless: in actual fact, at no point of time would the confluence of the Beas and the Sutlej have been fordable. Either we accept that the Rig Veda's 'style is generally quite hyperbolic',[30] as Witzel himself argues in another context, or the hymn is an allegory with some concealed meaning.

Even if we concede a confluence of the Sutlej with the Beas, there is no reason to take it as a permanent state of affairs. As noted earlier, the region's flat alluvial terrain makes the Sutlej a capricious river. We saw (p. 33) how the *Imperial Gazetteer* of 1908 recorded the Sutlej's flow into the Hakra in 1000 CE; the same gazetteer observed that the Sutlej 'has changed its course more than once in historical times':

> By 1245 the Sutlej had taken a more northerly course, the Hakra had dried up . . . Then [after the sixteenth century] the Sutlej once more returned to its old course and rejoined the Ghaggar. It was only in 1796 that the Sutlej again left the Ghaggar and finally joined the Beas.[31]

Wilhelmy, whose work on the Sarasvatī figured in Chapter 3, also conducted a meticulous study of the history of the Indus system, in which he endorses this view: 'This early confluence of the Sutlej and Beas was by no means the end of the matter. Both rivers have separated and rejoined several times in the last 2000 years.'[32]

But in fact, we are misled—both in the Rig Vedic hymn and in the above gazetteer—into regarding the Sutlej as a single-bed river flowing *either* into the Ghaggar *or* into the Beas. Rather, the number of its palaeobeds between those two rivers (which include, among others, the Patialewali, the Wah and the three Naiwals) suggests that it had various stages of 'braidedness'—also hinted at by the legend of Vasishtha's attempted suicide conveyed in the Mahābhārata (p. 62). Whether the Sutlej's complex history will ever be fully known is doubtful, but at no past stage can we rule out multiple branchings into both the Ghaggar and the Beas. Moreover, the Beas itself is known to have 'changed its course considerably since ancient times', as Macdonell and Keith record in their *Vedic Index*,[33] and we cannot be sure of its location in the early Vedic age. In other words, this Rig Vedic hymn is of little help in reconstituting the riverine landscape of the time.

Kochhar's other arguments, all of them minor as compared to the above, appear artificial or forced.[34] He writes for instance, 'It is strange that a river system containing such majestic rivers as the Satluj and Yamuna should be known by the name of a puny rainwater stream such as Ghaggar.'[35] But the whole point, as he himself concedes, is that the Ghaggar had a 'far more dignified existence in the past', and that happens to fit the Rig Vedic descriptions.

Or he argues, rightly, that 'the Sarasvatī hymns in the Rgveda are older than or contemporaneous with the Indus hymns', and concludes—wrongly—that 'If this Sarasvatī were identical with the Ghaggar, then the archaeological sites on the Ghaggar should have been at least as old as the Punjab–Sind sites. What is observed is otherwise.'[36] Leaving aside the solitary case of Mehrgarh, this is by no means certain: Mohenjo-daro seems to have had no pre-urban phase (as cogently argued by Michael Jansen[37]); Harappa's earliest occupation, according to recent findings,[38] goes back to the Hakra Ware phase (starting about 3800 BCE), named after a type of pottery identified by Mughal along the Hakra. The same Hakra phase is in evidence further upstream at Kalibangan[39] and Kunal,[40] and at several recently explored sites in Haryana, such

as Kheri Meham, Girawad and Farmana.[41] The first occupation
at nearby Bhirrana appears to have begun even earlier, during or
before the fifth millennium BCE.[42] Until many more radiocarbon
dates are available from both regions—the Indus and the Ghaggar–
Hakra basins—we cannot say which one has the 'older' sites. Nor
is the issue as important as Kochhar makes it out to be: there is
no valid reason why the antiquity of the hymns should exactly
match the antiquity of the sites.

At any rate, having decided that the Ghaggar–Hakra could not
have been the Vedic Sarasvatī, he looks for the latter in Afghanistan, and opts for the Helmand (Thomas's old theory, although
Kochhar does not name him). The evidence supplied for this identification is limited to malleable descriptions of the Sarasvatī in
the Rig Veda, and a similarity between one of them and a por-
trayal of the Helmand in the *Avesta*. Kochhar is, however, aware
that the Rig Veda associates the Gaṅgā and Yamunā to the Sarasvatī and, therefore, proposes to transfer those two rivers too
to Afghanistan: they were originally, in his view, tributaries of
the Helmand,[43] and that is where we must look for the stage
of the Rāmāyaṇa's events: 'Rāma himself must have lived in
Afghanistan.'[44]

The thesis is bold, but it runs into many difficulties when we
recall the plot of the epic. However, here I will confine myself to
spelling out the chief weaknesses in the identification of the Vedic
Sarasvatī with the Afghan Helmand:

1. It implies (and Kochhar says as much[45]) that the Rig Vedic
   people would have transferred the name of a medium-sized
   river (today's Helmand) to a petty stream on the road to
   complete desiccation, which would be a bizarre way of
   glorifying the former's memory. In 1886, R.D. Oldham, the
   geologist whose survey of the Ghaggar we quoted earlier,
   ridiculed the Afghan Sarasvatī thesis (then propounded by
   Thomas) precisely on this ground, protesting that it 'implies
   an almost incredible degree of childishness in the ancient
   Aryans'.[46] The objection stands.

2. Then, if the migrating Aryans were so attached to a Sarasvatī left behind in Afghanistan, it is unclear what prevented
   them from transferring its name to the Indus—the first river
   they encountered after descending into its vast plains—or
   to any one of its respectable tributaries from the Jhelum to
   the Sutlej, which they would have crossed before reaching
   the largely defunct Ghaggar. It stretches the imagination to
   picture them having a sudden afterthought some 200 or
   300 years after they left Afghanistan, and lauding the
   bygone Sarasvatī by transferring its hallowed name to a
   petty seasonal stream.
3. None of the other rivers named in the Rig Veda, from the
   Gangā to the Sindhu, flows outside northwest India. There
   is no ground to transfer the Gangā and Yamunā to Afghanistan, and certainly no tradition there or in the *Avesta* to
   that effect.
4. Other aspects of the Rig Veda that are incompatible with
   an Afghan setting have long been noticed, such as mentions
   of the elephant, the *gaur*, peacocks, and a typically Indian
   flora.[47] And this Indian flora and fauna appear not just in
   the last books of the Rig Veda, but right from the older ones.

'SAMUDRA' IN THE RIG VEDA

A fifth objection demands our attention. In the Rig Veda, the
Sarasvatī flows 'from the mountain to the sea' (*giribhya ā
samudrāt*)—but the Helmand ends in a swampy depression, not
in the sea: it is a land-locked river. Although Kochhar is silent on
this point, other defenders of the Afghan thesis have argued that
the word *samudra* should not be taken to mean the sea or ocean,
but just any 'large body of water'.[48] This argument is not new: a
few early Indologists, convinced that the Aryans, who had freshly
arrived from Central Asia, could not have known about the sea,
decided that *samudra* in the Rig Veda does not mean what it does
in classical Sanskrit.

However, it is now over seven decades since M.L. Bhargava

rejected this contention in the first chapter of his unrivalled *Geography of Rgvedic India*, quoting numerous references from the hymns.[49] More recently, historian and Sanskritist P.L. Bhargava covered the same ground again, and concluded that 'the evidence for the Vedic Indians' familiarity with sea and maritime navigation is so varied and so overwhelming that it is really impossible to dismiss it as a mere figment of imagination'.[50] Other Vedic scholars, such as David Frawley[51] and Nicholas Kazanas,[52] have argued along similar lines.

While the word *samudra* (literally meaning 'gathering of the waters') does carry a metaphorical meaning at times, most of its 160 occurrences are plain enough. Thus Indra is 'as extensive as the sea';[53] elsewhere, he carries two chieftains or kings safely over the sea.[54] Rishi Vasishtha is so eminent that he is compared to 'the sea's unfathomed greatness'.[55] The 'eastern and western seas'[56] are mentioned, as well as islands.[57] Several hymns[58] sing the legend of Bhujyu, who was treacherously abandoned in the middle of the 'billowy ocean', but rescued by the Ashvins, the heavenly horsemen twins, who fly to his help in the form of two birds and bear him swiftly for three days and three nights 'to the sea's farther shore',[59] finally bringing him back safely 'in a ship with hundred oars',[60] one of the many mentions of vessels. (The Ashvins themselves, interestingly, are the 'sons of the Sea'.[61])

In none of these occurrences can the word *samudra* stand for a swampy Afghan lake: the picture of the ocean imposes itself. As a matter of course, and in spite of their adherence to the Aryan invasion theory, early translators of the Rig Veda into English used the words 'sea' or 'ocean' in all such passages.

And, as is their wont, the hymns build on the physical reality to create a powerful symbolism for the inner reality: thus, in a striking image of the spiritual quest, 'the seven mighty rivers seek the ocean';[62] two seas, one above and one below,[63] clearly stand for the superconscious and subconscious realms; or again, we find a 'sea of milk'[64] and, quite transparently, the 'ocean of the heart'[65] (*hrdyāt samudra*). Even in such passages, substituting a lake for the sea will hardly do. As regards the boat or the ship, it is often the symbol of the crossing to a safer or truer shore: 'The ships of truth (*satyasya nāvah*) have borne the pious man across'.[66]

Returning to the Sarasvatī, there is simply no good reason not to accept at its face value the phrase 'flowing from the mountains to the ocean' (so rendered by both Wilson and Griffith, the two nineteenth-century translators of the Rig Veda into English). We can now read with profit Max Müller's comment on the same hymn, partly quoted earlier and written in 1869:

> Here we see *samudra* used clearly in the sense of sea, the Indian sea, and we have at the same time a new indication of the distance which separates the Vedic age from that of the later Sanskrit literature. Though it may not be possible to determine by geological evidence the time of the changes which modified the southern area of the Penjāb and caused the Sarasvatī to disappear in the desert, still the fact remains that the loss of the Sarasvatī is later than the Vedic age, and that at that time the waters of the Sarasvatī reached the sea.[67]

Such is the natural conclusion flowing from the hymns: the 'Vedic age' precedes the Sarasvatī's disappearance. And Max Müller, for all his straitjacket chronology, accepted, as we saw earlier (p. 51), that the Vedic river coincided in location with the Sarsuti.

ALL IMAGINATION?

Within a year of the publication of Kochhar's book, the Sarasvatī was unceremoniously hauled from the witness box to the dock: the well-known Indian mediaevalist historian Irfan Habib[68] authored a paper whose title is its conclusion: 'Imagining River Sarasvatī'. His thesis, subtitled 'A Defence of Commonsense', is radical: to him, the Sarasvatī as a river never existed, except in the rishis' and our imagination.

Let us hear the prosecution. The first charge is easy to deal with: 'The Sarsuti running past Thanesar is too petty a stream to fit the picture of a great river that the Rigveda's verses cited above suggest.' True, but this does not help us, for the Rig Veda nowhere says or implies that the Sarasvatī was limited to today's Sarsuti; the scholarly consensus has been that the latter is no more than a relic or memory of the former.

Habib then argues a case of mistaken identity: a better candidate than the Ghaggar would be the Sirsa river,* which runs from Kalka in a northwesterly direction to meet the Sutlej above Rupar (marked in Fig. 3.4). But while the Sirsa does derive its name from 'Sarasvatī' (one more clue to local memories of the river), its modest stature as a minor tributary of the Sutlej—which, because of its well-defined valley, it would have held in ancient times too—cannot match the textual descriptions. Moreover, the Sirsa was never 'lost' and would render meaningless the whole subsequent tradition of *Vinashana*, the place where the Sarasvatī disappears in the sands of the desert. Finally, the Sirsa does not flow 'from the mountain to the sea'.

Habib's next point is a curious one: 'The Ghaghar and Sarasvati were separate rivers and did not join each other at all before Firoz Tughluq forced such a junction' in the fourteenth century by digging a canal 'from the Ghaggar . . . to the fort of Sarsati'. Sarsati (one more relic of the ancient river's name) is today's city of Sirsa (see Fig. 3.1), in Haryana's westernmost district. If the Sarsuti did not meet the Ghaggar, where then did it flow? Habib proposes that 'the Haryana Sarasvatī [was] a small isolated river, probably drying up near Sirsa . . . It had no natural connection with any other river, and so could not have been at the heart of any system.' The point is untenable: the Sarsuti (rather the combined Sarsuti–Markanda, since, as I pointed out earlier, the Sarsuti is technically a tributary of the Markanda) did flow into the Ghaggar, and the point of confluence was not around Sirsa, but some 120 km upstream! This was, as pointed out as early as 1893 by C.F. Oldham,[69] near Shatrana, and all subsequent surveys have endorsed the location: it is well marked on several maps

---

* Not to be confused with the city of Sirsa cited earlier (and again in later paragraphs).

reproduced in this book (Figs 2.3, 3.1, 3.4 and 3.8). What flowed through Sirsa, therefore, was the combined Ghaggar–Markanda–Sarsuti: the Sarsuti was never an 'isolated' or 'separate' river. Tughluq's canal might have been intended to stabilize the flow of the Ghaggar or divert some of its waters; either way, it is irrelevant to the issue of the lost river.

The argument that follows is more challenging; it can be summarized thus: in the *Nadīstuti* hymn we are familiar with the fact that 'the Yamuna, Sarasvati and Sutudri [Sutlej] are recognised as three distinct rivers' (see p. 38). Experts who have argued that the Yamunā flowed into the Sarasvatī (Figs 3.4 and 3.8) have proposed several channels for the purpose, some close to the Shivaliks, and others further south that are part of the Chautang system identified with the Vedic Drishadvatī. In the first case, 'the Yamuna should have surely retained its own name; and the Vedic Sarasvati, then, could not have existed at all'. In the second, not only would the Drishadvatī have had no existence of its own, but also the Ghaggar north of it would still be carrying very little water and therefore could hardly be called a 'mighty river'. Similarly, if the Sutlej flowed from Rupar into the Ghaggar, 'it would then be the Sutudri that the Ghaghar would be called, and not Sarasvati, an insignificant rain-fed seasonal stream on its own'. Although the paradox is well turned, it rests on at least three unstated assumptions: that all those rivers had well-defined single beds; that they alone were present in the area and no other; and that the Vedic Sarasvatī was today's Sarsuti. In the synthesis that I will propose in the next chapter, none of these assumptions is accepted.

Habib then lists four canals dug to divert waters from the Yamuna into the Chautang between the fourteenth and seventeenth centuries, and regards the Yamuna's failure to change its course westward by enlarging those canals as proof that the river always flowed eastward. However, this ignores the possibility of a tectonic uplift of the Sarasvatī basin or subsidence of the Yamunā's, which, as we saw earlier, was proposed by several experts as a likely explanation for the Yamunā's desertion of the

Sarasvatī basin; in such an event, it follows that the river could not have 'climbed back' into the now raised watershed.

In the end, if, as Habib concludes, 'All claims built upon the greatness of River Sarasvati are, accordingly, nothing but castles in the air, however much froth may be blown over them,' how do we explain the primeval froth whipped up in the Rig Veda? Should we assume that the rishis, having perhaps consumed an overdose of Soma, hallucinated on the banks of a skimpy Sarsuti? Habib offers a more generous explanation: 'Sarasvati in most of the references to it in the Rigveda is not a particular river, as in a few undoubted cases it is, but the river in the abstract, the River Goddess. When the poet priest here sings of Sarasvati, he sings not of a particular river he sees, not a particular river named Sarasvati, nor any of the *Sapta Sindhavah* (Avestan, Hapta Hindu), but a mighty sister of these rivers, or, alternatively, one containing all of them . . .'

In other words, the Sarasvatī is a generic river, not a specific one—a pure mythological creation, somewhat like an inverse image of the Styx in ancient Greece. Certainly, the Sarasvatī is mythologized and deified in the Rig and Yajur Vedas, and more so in later literature, but this cannot be the whole explanation. If Sarasvatī were 'the river in the abstract', why place it specifically after the Gangā and the Yamunā and before the Sutlej, or in company with the Drishadvatī and the Āpayā?[70] Surely, all those other rivers cannot be 'abstract' ones, too? Also, some of the Sarasvatī's descriptions in the Rig Veda (such as 'breaking through the ridges of the mountains', 'flowing from the mountain to the sea', the river's 'two grassy banks') evoke physical rather than abstract traits. And what can one say of specific instructions found in the Shatapatha Brāhmana,[71] for instance, where one is asked to collect Sarasvatī water first among several others and sprinkle the combined waters on a king for his consecration? Are these abstract waters, too?

There is no need to dwell on Habib's criticism of the rare scholars who assert, probably in a flush of overenthusiasm at the river's rediscovery, that the Sarasvatī was 'mightier than the Indus', for

I agree with him that such a statement receives justification neither in the Rig Veda nor in archaeology. But it is also not legitimate to suggest that the proponents of the Ghaggar–Sarasvatī identity are guilty of 'false patriotism', as he does at the conclusion of his paper. Were we to accept the charge, we should equally lay it at the door of C.F. Oldham, Pargiter, Aurel Stein, Mortimer Wheeler,[72] Jean-Marie Casal,[73] Asko Parpola,[74] the Allchins, Gregory Possehl, Jane McIntosh and the late Pakistani archaeologist Ahmad Hasan Dani[75]—all of whom supported the same identity.

Indeed, in his conclusion, Habib himself can be seen injecting ideology into the issue: to him, claims about the 'once "mighty" Sarasvati' amount to the 'taking away of the Indus ("Sarasvati") culture from the Dravidians and non-Aryans'—a throwback to nineteenth-century notions of such racial entities, notions that have thankfully been abandoned by today's anthropologists and geneticists.

To locate the Sarasvatī in the Ghaggar system is not a matter of patriotism true or false, but rather, to borrow from Habib's subtitle, a matter of commonsense: centuries after the Rig Veda's hymns, why should a few Brāhmanas state that the same river now 'vanishes' at a particular point? Could the Mahābhārata indulge in long descriptions of the Sarasvatī's course, including ashrams and *tīrtha*s on its banks, if there was no river at all? 'Commonsense', it seems to me, dictates that rather than ascribe an overactive imagination to our early poets, we should acknowledge that the numerous references to the Sarasvatī across the literary corpus build a remarkably consistent picture—and one that happens to match the regression of the Ghaggar–Hakra system.

DID THE SARASVATĪ FLOW TO THE SEA?

I have saved two points presented by Irfan Habib for separate treatment. In the first, he argues that the Ghaggar–Hakra could not have flowed to the sea and must have ended in Cholistan. Curiously, after denying both the Yamunā and the Sutlej to the

Ghaggar–Hakra, Habib now explains that the Hakra must have had enough water to sustain 'the Harappan (as well as pre-Harappan and post-Harappan) sites [that] seem to run in a large belt along the Hakra river, and are especially numerous around Derawar'—so where did the Hakra get its waters from? He proposes that 'given the earlier natural conditions, the Desert River could come down to the Bahawalpur Cholistan, fed by its own rain-fed Siwalik and Terai tributaries.' Habib does not seem to realize that this nullifies his whole line of argument so far: if, as he now admits, there *was* in the end a river, rain-fed or otherwise, flowing from the Shivalik to Cholistan, and sustaining some 170 settlements there, it cannot have been a puny stream, for the distance involved is no less than 1000 km! In that case, what exactly is the objection to naming this 'Desert River' the Sarasvatī?

Let us, however, proceed with the point at issue. Habib offers the absence of Harappan sites beyond Cholistan as proof that the 'Desert River', however it may have been named at the time, vanished in the sands of Cholistan. In fact, in recent years, at least

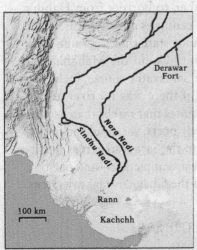

Fig. 11.1. Louis Flam's proposed continuity between the Hakra (flowing through Derawar Fort) and the Nara.[81]

five Harappan sites appear to have been spotted in the Hakra Valley beyond Cholistan,[76] but even if their existence is confirmed, we will admittedly be very far from the concentration found in Cholistan. Following Aurel Stein, who had already described the Derawar region as 'deltaic',[77] Possehl also proposes that the Sarasvatī (as he calls the river) ended in an 'inland delta'.[78] But other archaeologists take the contrary view of nineteenth-century surveyors such as Oldham (p. 32), Raverty (p. 26) and Sivewright (p. 27) that the river did flow on to the sea through the valley of the Nara: Louis Flam, for instance, sees a continuity between the Hakra and the Eastern Nara, whose valley ends at the northern fringe of the Rann of Kachchh:

> There is little doubt and little disagreement that the Hakra–Nara Nadi was a seasonal river with perennial character-istics during the fourth and third millennia B.C. . . . Southwest of Fort Derawar . . . the Hakra Course becomes increasingly unclear and intermittently becomes 'lost' beneath the sand dunes which have encroached upon the area. Remnants of the Hakra's course re-emerge where dunes are less numer-ous. From Fort Derawar to the south, the Hakra can be aligned with the Raini and Wahinda remnants, which sub-sequently connect with and blend into the Nara channel.[79]

Flam painstakingly builds a synthetic picture that includes a lower course of the Indus, east of where it flows today: the river joined the Nara at the latter's estuary in the Rann of Kachchh (Fig. 11.1). As regards the Nara's upstream course,

> The Nara Nadi* originated in the Hakra River of Choli-stan . . . During at least part of the third millennium B.C. the Sutlej River was a tributary of the Hakra River in Cho-listan . . . not a tributary of the Indus as it is today . . . There is clear archaeological and geomorphological evidence that sometime near the end of the third millennium B.C. the Hakra River was captured by the Gangetic system and the Sutlej River discharge was diverted to the Indus system.[80]

M. Rafique Mughal agrees with Flam. I quoted earlier his con-viction that 'in ancient times the Ghaggar–Hakra was a mighty river, flowing independently [of the Indus] along the fringes of the Rann of Kutch'. Another clue is the fact that the lower course, the Nara, is also known as 'Hakro', according to Mughal.[82] Wilhelmy, too, is quite explicit on this point:

---

* Nadī = 'river' in Sanskrit.

> In the local usage, the lower course [i.e. the Nara] is also
> given the name Hakra. The local people were probably
> aware of the continuity of the entire line of valleys and that
> a single river flowed here once upon a time.[83]

And more recently, Bridget Allchin drew a map of the lower
Indus in which the Nara's lower course down to the sea is labelled
'Hakra'.[84] Clearly, then, the Hakra's continuity with the Nara
cannot be rejected out of hand; scientific surveys and archaeological explorations of the short stretch between the Hakra and
the Nara can alone provide a definitive answer.

NO SARASVATĪ IN HARAPPAN TIMES?

Irfan Habib quotes a geological study of the region by a joint
Indo-French team. I cited earlier (p. 62) Marie-Agnès Courty's
study of sediments in the Ghaggar–Chautang region: she pointed
out the difference between 'true grey sands' of clearly Himalayan
origin and some 7 or 8 m of alluvium covering them—the latter
consisted mainly of alternating layers of loamy sand and silty clay,
and could only have originated from weaker streams flowing
from the Shivaliks, and not from the inner Himalayas. Consid-
ering that it would have taken several millennia for this 8-m layer
to accumulate, Courty naturally concluded that 'Yamuna-like
rivers, rising from the Himalayas, stopped flowing in the study
area well before the Protohistoric [i.e., Harappan] period'.

In other words, no Sarasvatī of Himalayan origin could have
flowed in Harappan times, if such a river ever existed at all. 'This
should be definitive,' comments Habib, and we can understand
his sense of triumph. Indeed Henri-Paul Francfort, director of the
French side of the team, cautioned against 'the illusory existence
of protohistoric settlements concentrated along the banks of an
immense perennial river, the ancient Sarasvatī', and added, 'We
know now, thanks to the fieldwork of the Indo-French expedition,
that when the protohistoric peoples [i.e., the Harappans] settled
in this area no large perennial river had flowed there for a long
time.'[85]

What an anticlimax to our long journey! The mythical river was just that in the end: a myth. With a view to mislead us, sacred texts made up a non-existent mighty river and narrated its disappearance; local traditions of a 'lost river' signified a wishful concoction; early explorers, geologists, geographers such as Wilhelmy, and countless archaeologists including Aurel Stein and A. Ghosh fell victims to a mirage created by the treacherous desert. Before we turn the page on what, it now appears, was no more than a lovely legend, let us take a closer look at the implications of the radical French thesis.

Francfort is well aware of the numerous settlements in the Ghaggar–Chautang region. Where did they find water for agriculture if there was no 'large perennial river' and if, moreover, the region's climate, according to Courty's analysis, was already well into an arid phase? Francfort proposes that those settlements would have used 'vast irrigation systems',[86] and his colleague Pierre Gentelle envisages 'the existence of long canals for irrigation',[87] bringing water from the Yamunā to the Chautang region. What that involved on the part of the Harappans was, in Francfort's words, 'the construction, maintenance and management of canals more than 200 km long, and therefore quite a remarkable stage of social development for the civilization'.[88] In reality, if water was to be diverted from the Yamunā all the way to Kalibangan, the canal would have to be not 200 km in length but twice as long; and if we include ramifications needed to reach all major sites, the total length of the irrigation network would be well over 1000 km. Yet, despite suggestions by Francfort's team, such protohistoric canals have not come to light so far.

Instead, what their digital processing of satellite photographs did bring out is a network of 'hydrographic fossil systems' some 300–500 m wide. Francfort calls them 'canals', but explains in the next sentence that they 'mark the courses of ancient natural waterways which were used and perhaps, in some places, rerouted by man. These traces of small river channels, which were completely unknown until now, appear to have reached all of the archaeological sites'.[89] 'River channels' and 'natural waterways' are not exactly 'canals', and even admitting that the Harappans used a few of these waterways for agriculture, it is hardly credible that they could have diverted enough water from the Yamunā to fill this vast network—and prevented its regular siltation.

Also, if there were no rivers flowing west of the Yamunā, why did they take so much trouble routing and maintaining those canals when they could have quite simply gone and settled closer to the Yamunā and its fertile banks? And there's the rub: as the maps show eloquently, there were no Early Harappan sites close to the Yamunā (Fig. 6.7) and very few sites of the Mature phase (Fig. 6.8).

There must be a less artificial explanation for these networks of 'natural waterways' in the Ghaggar–Chautang region. I suggest that it partly lies in the high rainfall that the Shivaliks were experiencing at the time. We saw in Chapter 8 some studies contradicting the thesis that the Harappan milieu had entered a phase of aridity. In particular, Netajirao Phadtare (p. 177) found evidence of 'a warm, humid climate, with highest monsoon intensity' in the Garhwal Himalayas from about 4000 to 2500 BCE (which takes us to the Mature Harappan phase), with a 'sharp decrease' after 2000 BCE. Along the same lines, Rita Wright and her colleagues (p. 179) found waters in the Beas to increase around 3500 BCE until around 2100 BCE, when 'the river flow begins to fall'; the last date also marked the start of 'a 600-year period of reduced rainfall' around Harappa.

This may not be the last word on the question, but let us note that the regions researched by Phadtare and Wright are on either side of the upper catchment area of the Sarasvatī basin. If their results are confirmed, precipitation must have been high there also (though not necessarily in the plains below), from which two consequences follow. The first is that we can do away with 'canals' bringing water all the way from the Yamunā: Francfort's 'natural waterways' would simply have carried waters streaming down from the Shivaliks. Conceding that a small part might have been diverted to irrigation, their excess flow would ultimately collect in the main trunk of the Ghaggar. That it did hold water in

Mature Harappan times is proved by the location of important settlements close to, or on, the main channels, as a look at Fig. 6.8 makes clear. Why should the Harappans have built Kalibangan on the very edge of the Ghaggar if the river was dry? Banawali and Rakhigarhi are also located along important channels of the Ghaggar and the Chautang respectively: here as in Punjab and Sind, river communication was vital for the larger settlements.

The second consequence of a more intense monsoon in the catchments is that the sedimentation rate for the accumulation of the 8-m layer of alluvium above the grey sand of Himalayan origin would have been much faster than was estimated by Courty, who assumed an arid regime for the region. Even if the plains were arid or gradually becoming so, a high annual precipitation in the Shivaliks and above would alter the picture, as it would create many perennial streams in the foothills—which would inevitably collect in the Ghaggar.

A few more points militate against the scenario proposed by Courty and Francfort. Primarily, the concentration of sites farther downstream, in Cholistan, which, in Mughal's opinion, could only have been sustained by a 'mighty' Ghaggar–Hakra; such a cluster is impossible in the absence of perennial rivers or streams (as Habib himself admitted). Let us recall an isotopic study (p. 76) of the Hakra waters, which found them in flow till about 2700 BCE. Equally revealing is the obvious scattering of sites already noted at the end of the urban phase (Figs 6.8 and 6.9): the drastic change in the settlement pattern, with the total abandonment of the Ghaggar's middle basin, cannot be explained without some equally drastic change in the hydrographic landscape. Yet the French team will admit of none: rejecting the existence of a river flowing in the Ghaggar's bed, they cannot very well discuss its desiccation.

For those reasons, their findings have not found favour with archaeologists: Mughal, Possehl, Misra and others do mention them, but continue to refer to a perennial Ghaggar partly fed by the Sutlej and the Yamunā.

Nor would their thesis satisfy impartial readers of the Rig Veda and subsequent texts. Francfort is, of course, aware of this last point, and offers two ways out of the contradiction. In the first, he asks whether 'the mythical Sarasvatī could be a memory of real and very ancient large rivers that watered the region after the melting of Himalayan glaciers'.[90] But nothing in the texts sounds or feels like a 'memory'. The Rig Veda reminds the great river that the Purus, a Vedic clan, 'dwells on your two grassy banks'.[91] The Mahābhārata depicts not only Balarāma's pilgrimage along those banks, but how the final dreadful battle between Bhīma and Duryodhana took place 'on the southern side of the Sarasvatī', on a spot selected because 'the ground there was not sandy'.[92] Such specific details (there are many others) cannot be 'memories' of bygone ages. Moreover, even Indologists who accept the Aryan invasion or migration framework will shudder at the suggestion that the Vedic Aryans, reaching a dry Ghaggar around 1200 BCE, would have adopted the local (and therefore alien, if not hostile) tradition of a great river that had flowed there long, long ago— at least four or five millennia, according to Francfort's chronology —a tradition that could have meant nothing to them.

Francfort, apparently not too convinced himself, adds, 'Or if the Sarasvatī was not a purely spiritual river, would it be too poetical to imagine that the vast networks of canals that irrigated the region are what come under the designation of "Sarasvati"?' A 'purely spiritual river' is somewhat like Irfan Habib's 'river in the abstract', and I need not repeat the many objections to such a concept. As regards the vast networks of canals, whose physical existence remains unproved in the first place, it would be unkind to belabour the point, since nothing in the Rig Veda, least of all the descriptions of the Sarasvatī, refers to anything resembling a canal.

MORE OBJECTIONS

Courty's work on the Ghaggar's sediments can be fruitfully contrasted with a study published in 2004 by geologist Jayant K. Tripathi and three of his colleagues (one Indian and two German), who also sought to establish the 'absence of a glacial-fed, perennial Himalayan river in the Harappan domain'.[93] Since this study has often been quoted in Internet circles as the ultimate proof that the Sarasvatī never existed, we need to give it due attention.

The method adopted is a standard one: the analysis of specific isotopes found in sediments (here, isotopes of strontium and neodymium, two metallic elements occurring only in compounds). The authors' chief conclusion, in summary, is that 'Yamuna, Ganga and Satluj . . . derive their sediments from the Higher Himalayas unlike the Ghaggar, which originates and derives its sediments from the Sub-Himalayas [i.e. the Shivaliks] only'. This conclusion is at variance with that of Puri and Verma (p. 64), who found evidence of Higher Himalayan sediments as far as the Markanda Valley.

But there are major problems with this study. The authors do not provide the number of samples taken nor their precise locations. Judging from a very imprecise map,[94] no sample was actually taken from the Ghaggar's bed, and certainly none from any of the palaeochannels of the Sutlej and the Chautang; this restricts the value of the study. Also, samples were taken between the Sutlej (near Rupar) and the Ganges, at a depth of 1 to 9 m, but none of the results is given in terms of depth, as if it made no difference. If there are really no Higher Himalayan sediments down to a depth of 9 m, it clashes with Courty's observation (p. 62) of 'true grey sands at a depth of over 8 m [in the Ghaggar], identical to those of the Yamuna and the Sutlej' (elsewhere,[95] Courty speaks of 7 m).

Tripathi and his colleagues differ from Courty on two more grounds. The first is one of chronology: they arbitrarily attribute to the studied sediments a date bracket of 'between 2 to 20 Ka [kilo-annum]', curiously basing themselves on the 'personal communication' of other experts rather than on their own isotopic analysis. But the lower date of 20,000 years appears invalid: in Courty's analysis, the same sediments accumulated after the last Ice Age, that is, in the last 10,000 years or so. Second, while she finds evidence of semi-arid conditions in the Ghaggar basin, they opt for Phadtare's model of 'abundant monsoon precipitation in the Sub-Himalayan region', as a result of which 'the Palaeo-Ghaggar must have been a mighty river with broad channels'.

So here again, if there was in the end a 'mighty' Ghaggar which ultimately dried up, why could it not be the Sarasvatī? The authors do not answer this question, but appear to think that a Vedic Sarasvatī could only have originated in the higher Himalayas: 'the River Ghaggar is not the Saraswati as far as its origin in the glaciated Himalayas is concerned'. However, that is a *non sequitur*, since nothing in the Vedic texts expressly demands a glacial origin. If we have a 'mighty Ghaggar' in Harappan times, whatever the origin of its waters, it seems to me that the authors have proved the case of the Sarasvatī rather than disproved it.

Finally, there is a serious problem with Courty's and Tripathi's approaches: both fail to notice the Sutlej's contribution to the Ghaggar, since they do not find in the latter the Higher Himalayan sediments that the former would have carried. Yet we saw earlier (p. 262) Wilhelmy's assertion that 'both rivers have separated and rejoined several times in the last 2000 years', and, as examples, the *Tarikh-i-Mubarak Shahi*'s testimony (p. 46) that the Sarasvatī joined the Sutlej in the fifteenth century, or the *Imperial Gazetteer*'s mention of the Sutlej finally leaving the Ghaggar in 1796. Either the geological data is inadequate or wrongly interpreted, or the Sutlej somehow deposited its Higher Himalayan sediments before joining the Ghaggar. Raikes's finding (p. 60) of 'shallow beds of a fine silty sand' at more or less regular intervals in the upper layers of sediments of the Ghaggar was perhaps closer to the truth.

Deep contradictions of the above sort between several scientific studies are to be expected in geophysical disciplines; they simply mean that more precise research is required before final conclusions can be securely reached. They also emphasize the need for studies of the Sarasvatī basin that will integrate data from inter-related fields—geology, palaeoclimatology, isotope analysis and archaeology in particular. As of now, such multi-disciplinary studies are non-existent.

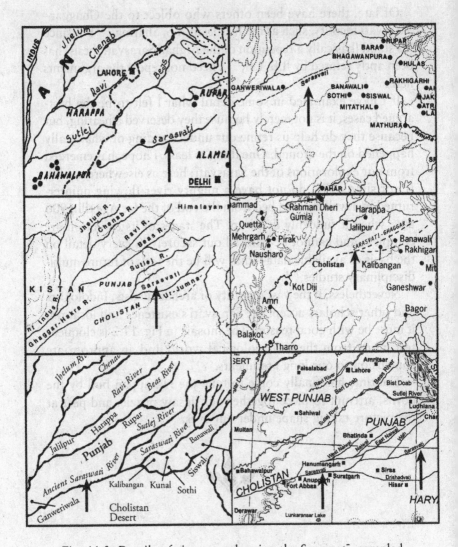

Fig. 11.2. Details of six maps showing the Sarasvatī, sampled from the works of a few archaeologists. Clockwise from top left corner: J.-M. Casal,[96] G. Erdosy,[97] R. and B. Allchin,[98] G.L. Possehl,[99] J. McIntosh[100] and J.M. Kenoyer.[101] (Arrows pointing to the Sarasvatī are my additions.)

Of late, there have been others who object to the Ghaggar–Sarasvatī identity, such as the historian R.S. Sharma,[102] but since his stand (basically a repetition of the Afghan Sarasvatī thesis) has been aptly refuted by B.B. Lal,[103] I need not repeat the arguments here.

If I have examined in some detail what I felt to be the best-argued cases, it is not merely because they deserved a hearing, but because they do help us refine our understanding of what really happened on the ground. One thing at least, I hope, has emerged from our explorations of the Sarasvatī: here as elsewhere, reality is not simple. We do not have a mighty river flowing uninterrupted in a well-defined bed from the end of the Ice Age till 1900 BCE, when it suddenly dried up. The stages of its evolution are complex, and cannot be worked out securely in every detail on the basis of available data—that will be the task of future multidisciplinary studies.[104]

Nevertheless, if the vast majority of archaeologists, Indologists and other scholars accept the Sarasvatī's existence and location, it must be with good reason. The mosaic in Fig. 11.2 is eloquent testimony from the archaeological world and an appropriate conclusion to our long arguments.

The time has finally come to take the Harappan bull by the horns, attempt to piece together our jigsaw puzzle, and peer at the picture taking shape under our eyes.

Epilogue:
Sarasvatī Turns Invisible

The web of our story has been woven with strands of various fabrics and colours: literature, tradition, geology, archaeology, climatology and a few more.

The literary strand was our starting point, and I hope to have shown that the testimony of ancient texts cannot be brushed aside, especially when it tells a consistent tale. No doubt, there will be 'hyperbole' and, more to the point, a good deal of mythologizing: literalist readings will only land us into complete confusion. When, for instance, the Rig Vedic poet exclaims that the Sarasvatī 'surpasses in might all other waters', it need not mean that he went out to measure the flow of all Sapta Sindhus in cubic metres per second and found the Sarasvatī sitting at the top of the chart. But when he tells us that the river rose in the mountain and flowed between two others, we have no ground to disbelieve him, especially when later texts confirm this with a wealth of details.

Nor can local traditions be scorned if they recollect a time when a river filled what is now a broad, dry bed in an arid landscape of sand dunes. Again, we may quibble over dates or whether the bygone river really 'filled' the bed, but not over the fact of the river's existence—which is why scholars from Tod to Stein accepted the testimony of the folklore on the 'Lost River of the Indian Desert'—a testimony strengthened by the presence of five rivers named after the Sarasvatī in the Yamuna–Sutlej divide: the four mentioned earlier (pp. 46–50) and the Sirsa discussed in the last chapter (to which we may add the city of Sirsa itself).

THE SARASVATĪ AND THE YAMUNĀ

To reconstruct the main stages in the river's life—in a manner which, I believe, respects all the strands of our web—I will begin with a useful clue in the Mahābhārata. In two places at least, the epic tells us that the Sarasvatī's course in the mountain was close to the Yamunā's. In the more precise passage of the two, Balarāma climbs to a *tīrtha* on the Sarasvatī called 'Plakshaprāsravana' (the name of the river's source as we saw earlier) and, from there, soon reaches the Yamunā. To reach Plakshaprāsravana, he has 'not proceeded far in his ascent'[1] of the mountain: the area is not far above the plains. Indeed, while Balarāma is enjoying himself bathing in *tīrtha* after *tīrtha*, Nārada, the ever-meddlesome emissary of the gods, happens along and apprises him of the terrible slaughter that has taken place on the battlefield of Kurukshetra; today, he adds, the final battle between Bhīma and Duryodhana is due to take place. Balarāma promptly dismisses his entourage and, regretfully tearing himself away from the river—'repeatedly casting his eyes with joy on the Sarasvatī'[2]—descends from the mountain to reach the spot in time on the river's southern bank, not far from Kurukshetra. There is nothing 'hyperbolic' about the passage: Balarāma's ascent as well as descent are brief affairs, so that the *tīrthas* he visits must have been in the Shivaliks,[3] probably in the Markanda or the Bata Valley, as scholars have often proposed.

Proximity apart, the Sarasvatī's relationship with the Yamunā is indeed a key issue. We saw in Chapter 3 how some geologists envisage that the Yamunā and the Tons once flowed together westward into the Bata–Markanda corridor. In such a scenario, however, there would be a single Sarasvatī–Yamunā in the plains: the Yamunā would have no separate existence (except above its confluence with the Tons). Also, while the Markanda Valley is indeed 'anomalously wide',[4] suggesting a greater flow than this rain-fed river could have had on its own, it seems to me that the combined Yamunā–Tons–Markanda should have left a deeper signature on the plains than can be detected today (through satellite imagery, for instance).

THE SARASVATĪ IN FULL FLOW

I will, therefore, take a middle path and propose that the Shivalik landscape was such that only a portion of the Yamunā–Tons ran westward into the Markanda Valley, with the rest flowing southward through a smaller and higher opening than today's 'Yamuna tear'. The westward branch was the Sarasvatī (which would explain why the Markanda does not appear in the Rig Veda), while the southward was the Yamunā.

When it touched the plains, the Yamunā divided once more, as Cunningham (see his map in Fig. 2.3) and R.D. Oldham (p. 24) proposed, and others after them: because its terraces occupied a higher level than today, part of the river flowed southwest, joining minor streams to form the Drishadvatī of old. In the plains, the Yamunā was thus a double river—which would conveniently explain the root meaning of the word *yamunā*: 'twin'. At the western end of the divide, the Sutlej—or, more likely, only a branch of it—joined the Ghaggar around Shatrana. Fig. 12.1 summarizes the proposed hydrography of the region.

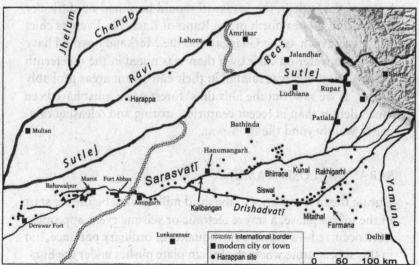

Fig. 12.1. Proposed reconstruction of the hydrography of the Sarasvatī basin in its first stage, during the Early Harappan phase.

This state of things fits well with the pre-urban stage of the Indus–Sarasvatī civilization (Fig. 6.7): many sites are found along or near the Drishadvatī's course and the Ghaggar's after its confluence with the Sarasvatī, in a virtually unbroken chain all the way to Cholistan. The almost complete absence of sites away from the major watercourses or their tributaries appears to confirm a general trend towards aridity.

This stage of a Sarasvatī in full flow also suits the Rig Vedic descriptions of the river, including its designation as 'seven-sistered'. Let us recall Vivien de Saint-Martin's sagacious remark: 'The ancient designation of Sarasvatī very much appears to have embraced, apart from the chief watercourse flowing far to the west, the totality of the streams flowing down from the mountain close to each other before they unite in a single bed.' Again, 'seven' need not be taken literally, but the number does suggest that the Sarasvatī of that age comprised all the tributaries together, from today's Sarsuti in the east to the three Naiwals in the west (Fig. 3.1).

Fed with a portion of the Yamunā's waters and a portion, at least, of the Sutlej's, the Sarasvatī would have had no difficulty in reaching the sea north of the Rann of Kachchh. Even its chief tributaries, such as the Ghaggar and the Markanda, would have held more water on their own than was noted in the nineteenth century: not only was rainfall in their catchment areas probably higher, as we saw, but the Shivaliks' forest cover must have been much denser than in recent centuries, storing and releasing rainwater well beyond the monsoon.

SARASVATĪ LOSES YAMUNĀ

During the first centuries of the third millennium, before the start of the urban phase, a severe tectonic or seismic event appears to have occurred—a massive earthquake, in ordinary parlance, but in this special zone where the Indian plate pushes under the Eurasian, faulting, upthrust or subsidence can be important side effects of seismic episodes. K.S. Valdiya details such phenomena and gives an example of a geologically attested earthquake some-time after 3000 BCE farther downstream the Yamunā;[5] I also quoted the case of the archaeologically attested earthquake that damaged Kalibangan's Early settlement, farther to the west, around 2700 BCE, and another during the same epoch at Dholavira.

This is about the time when our hypothetical event (or, more likely, chain of events) struck the upper Sarasvatī basin, broadening the Yamunā's passage through the Shivaliks and forcing her southward, while in the plain below, its bed subsided: the 'East Yamunā' captured most of the waters of the 'West Yamunā', and both the Markanda–Sarasvatī and the Drishadvatī found their flow severely depleted (though the pattern of settlement suggests a westward branching off of the Yamunā further south). But such a capture may not have happened overnight; as Louis Flam puts it, 'It should be noted that river capture and the drying of the captured stream are *not* single event phenomena occurring over a short period of time'.[6]

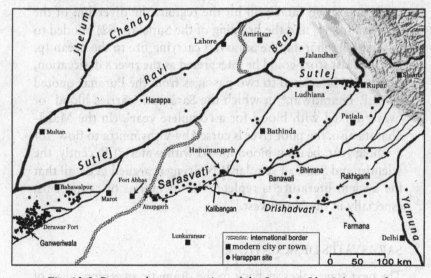

Fig. 12.2. Proposed reconstruction of the Sarasvatī basin's second stage, during the Mature Harappan phase: the Sarasvatī loses the Yamunā, but is still fed by a branch of the Sutlej.

Two key archaeological data confirm this second stage (Fig. 12.2): the number of sites along the Drishadvatī gets considerably reduced from the Early to the Mature phases and, as pointed out by Mughal, a segment in the Hakra's upper stretch is now devoid of sites. On the other hand, a number of Mature sites rather neatly aligned along the Wah (or Sirhind) unequivocally testify to a branch of the Sutlej flowing there. At the same time, Mature sites west of Rupar and all the way to Ludhiana show that the Sutlej flowed there, too—it was bifurcated, at the least.

The texts also give us two major clues for this stage: the earliest mentions, in the Brāhmanas, of 'Vinashana' or the place where the Sarasvatī disappears—if we can trust the site distribution pattern (Fig. 12.2), that spot would be very close to today's international border. And intriguingly, the Pañchavimsha Brāhmana makes it clear that Vinashana is located below the Sarasvatī–Drishadvatī confluence[7]—precisely what the Mature sites tell us.

We saw in the literature a few more hints, albeit more diffuse ones, that some cataclysm hit the region: the diversion of the Yamunā (p. 61) and the braiding of the Sutlej (p. 62) alluded to in the Mahābhārata, the Sarasvatī carrying fire to the ocean (p. 44). The last story could be interpreted as the river's desiccation, or it could be related to two passages from the Purānas quoted by O.P. Bharadwaj,[8] in which the Sarasvatī 'carries blood' or 'water mixed with blood for a complete year'. (In the Mahābhārata also, the poor river is cursed by Vishvāmitra to flow 'for a whole year, bearing blood mixed with water'.[9]) Recently, the scientist and Sanskrit scholar R.N. Iyengar argued in detail that the ancient literature is replete with memories of cataclysms, especially in the Northwest.[10]

SARASVATĪ'S DESICCATION

The next stage takes us back to the dramatic sweeping away of the Mature Harappan sites from the Sarasvatī's heartland: a big void (Fig. 12.3) suddenly stares at us in the region between

Shatrana and Cholistan. Sites like Kalibangan and Banawali are abandoned, with no Late occupation as at Harappa or Dhola-vira, for instance—here, for some reason, most people found it impossible to stay on, even in a de-urbanized context. Instead, the Late sites appear to cling to the Shivalik foothills from the Ravi to the Ganges. A few alignments suggest some flow of water in the Drishadvatī and from the Sutlej, but the main trunk of the Sarasvatī appears to have gone dry. (One of the Sutlej's channels further downstream also fed a few last Cholistan sites.)

If we cannot invoke a complete desertion of the upper Saras-vatī by the Sutlej, then a sharp drop in rainfall in the Shivaliks— detected by a few studies, as we saw—perhaps dealt, in effect, a deathblow to a depleted river system. The monsoon-fed streams flowing down the hills would have been enough to sustain hundreds of small, 'back-to-village-life' settlements, but we must suspect the onset of desertification in the central section.

This scenario—which differs in some details from those cited

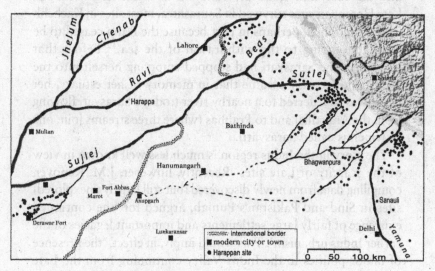

Fig. 12.3. Proposed reconstruction of the Sarasvatī basin's third stage, during the Late Harappan phase: the Sarasvatī's central basin has gone dry.

earlier—is consistent with the archaeological record, several of the recent climatic studies, and major descriptions of the river system in the literature. Yet, I would not presume to regard it as final or complete: a full account of the river's evolution should discuss and evaluate in much greater detail than we can at present the region's tectonic history, phenomena of erosion (resulting in river capture, for instance), changes in land use and agricultural practices, and ecological degradation. Not only would that take us beyond the scope of our story, but much data in these and other fields are still missing. Our scenario will, therefore, doubtless be refined or even corrected, but I am confident it will hold its ground at least in its major lines.

IN SEARCH OF GREENER PASTURES

Various movements can be discerned in the wake of the great urban collapse. From Gujarat, for instance, a southward push into the Tapti and Godavari Valleys is in evidence.[11] Although Late Harappan sites survived in Saurashtra, most sites in Kachchh were abandoned, perhaps in part because the Rann ceased to be navigable owing to the withdrawal of the sea.[12] Before that happened, the Sarasvatī had stopped emptying herself into the Rann, and we may assume that in memory of her estuary, her name was transferred to a nearby river (today's Sarasvati flowing from the Aravallis) and to Prabhas (where three streams join, one of which is called Sarasvati).

The story in the Indus region is much less well known in view of the scarcity of Late sites. Recently, however, J.M. Kenoyer, compiling data from newly discovered (but still largely unexplored) sites in Sind and Pakistan's Punjab, argued for 'the continued existence of fairly large settlements and important legacies of the earlier Indus urbanism'. This would imply, in effect, 'the presence of major polities in the Indus Valley continuing from the Late Harappan right through to the Mauryan periods'.[13] If this approach is confirmed by excavations, one more considerable gap will be filled.

Returning to the central Sarasvatī basin, many Late Harappans stayed close to the Shivaliks, while others perhaps went south towards the northern parts of the Aravallis, where some streams still carried water. But the most conspicuous movement after the urban phase is towards and across the Ganges: as J.P. Joshi observed, 'the increase in frequency of sites while moving from the west to the east . . . [establishes] the eastward movement of the late Harappans in Punjab, Haryana and western U.P.'[14] Or, according to Jim Shaffer:

> *This shift by Harappan . . . groups is the only archaeo-*
> *logically documented west-to-east movement of human*
> *populations in South Asia before the first half of the*
> *first millennium BC.*[15]

The bold italic type is not mine but Shaffer's, and is intended to stress that an eastward migration of invading Aryans is simply nowhere in the picture: the Late Harappans' 'west-to-east movement' is the only one detectable on the ground, and it is the one that would sow the seeds of the future Ganges civilization. Even as the Sarasvatī dwindled, it served as a bridge between the Indus and the Ganges, or between the Harappan and the Gangetic.

Thus is simply explained the considerable cultural continuity detailed in Chapters 9 and 10: despite dramatic new developments in technologies, agriculture and social structures, archaeology reveals no sharp break—instead, in Shaffer's words again, we have a 'cultural continuum stretching from perhaps 7000 BC into the early centuries AD'.[16]

Here too, this archaeological shift finds an echo in literature and tradition. The Shatapatha Brāhmana,[17] for instance, narrates the oft-quoted legend of Videgha Māthava, probably king of Videha (a region generally identified with a part of north Bihar), who was 'on the Sarasvatī'. Māthava, the story goes, carried Agni, the divine Fire, in his mouth; his family priest invoked the Fire so efficiently that Agni 'flashed forth' from the king's mouth and fell on the earth. Agni then 'went burning along this earth towards the east . . . He burned over all these rivers', stopping finally at the Sadānīrā (identified with the Gandak river). Agni instructed Māthava to take up his abode 'to the east of this river'. The text adds that 'in former times', that region was 'very marshy because it had not been tasted by Agni' but 'nowadays, however, it is very cultivated, for the Brāhmans have caused Agni to taste it through sacrifices'. Agni, falling to the ground near the Sarasvatī, appears to be one more image of the river's drying up. The king—followed, we may assume, by his clan—then migrated eastward to the Gangetic region and resettled there.

To my mind, we have here a fine record of the eastward movement of some of the Late Harappans in search of greener pastures. Another literary reference to the desolation of the Sarasvatī Valley is even more explicit (and it dates a few centuries after the Shatapatha Brāhmana). In a 1963 essay on a Sanskrit word (*arma*) for 'ruins', the Sanskritist Thomas Burrow drew attention to this passage from the *Lātyāyana Shrautasūtra*: 'On the Sarasvatī there are ruined sites called Naitandhava; Vyarna is one of these.'[18] These 'ruined sites' do evoke Harappan cities and towns. That is also Burrow's interpretation, although we may safely ignore his view that the Aryans were responsible for the destruction of these cities[19]—a view comprehensively rejected since the 1960s, since neither the texts nor the archaeological evidence warrant it (leave alone the fact that three to five centuries elapsed between the end of the Indus cities and the purported arrival of the Aryans).

So too, the conventional explanation for the Shatapatha Brāhmana's legend of Videgha Māthava is that it corresponds to the Aryan penetration into the Gangetic plains. Perhaps it does, but again, on the ground, only one movement is perceptible—that of the Late Harappans and their successors (such as the people of OCP and PGW cultures). We should also note that the conventional view of the Ganges Valley as a huge virgin forest that the incoming Aryans had to clear with their iron tools has been proved wrong: the archaeologist Rakesh Tewari recently demonstrated that iron was smelted in settlements of the Central Ganges plains as early as 1800 BCE,[20] and the region, though surely more forested than today, had a 'savannah landscape dominated by grassy vegetation along with thicker wooded pockets from about 15,000 yr. B.P.'[21] In fact, hundreds of agricultural settlements had long been established there, some of them for several millennia, and a still poorly documented cultural convergence or fusion between their inhabitants and the newly arrived Late Harappans must have taken place, which eventually led to the urbanization of the region in the first millennium BCE.

FROM DEATH TO REBIRTH

Be that as it may, the Late Harappans were not ungrateful folk: long nurtured by the Sarasvatī, they had worshipped the river and imbued it—or her—with divinity. Those who migrated away from her increasingly arid basin did not, however, forget her. Eventually reaching the confluence of the Yamunā and the Ganges, they found a convenient way to remember her: evoke her presence there, but an invisible one. The lost river could now flow in a subtle form, adding her sanctity to the other two and forming a sacred trinity of river-goddesses, the *triveṇī sangam*, which became one of the locations for the famous *Kumbhamela* festival.

Not only was the Sarasvatī thus made to connect with the Ganges, but in the course of time, Sarasvatī the goddess passed on many of her attributes to Gangā. In a study of this mythological transfer, the Indologist Steven Darian[22] showed with a wealth of examples how Gangā inherited many of Sarasvatī's characteristics: like her elder sister she was born from Brahmā's *kamandalu*, divided into seven streams, became 'mother of the Vedas', 'identical with the Word or Speech', and a giver of boons; like Sarasvatī's, her waters were regarded as healing and salvific. In many ways, Gangā is an avatar of Sarasvatī, just as the Ganges civilization is a new avatar of the Indus–Sarasvatī civilization.

*

We have reached our destination. The Sarasvatī has been pulled down to the earth from the realm of legend. The river was 'lost', but not forgotten. And even as she dried up, she grew in vigour as an incarnation of Speech and Inspiration. Her last waters gurgling to a stop, the goddess took up her dwelling at the source of every true thought and word—a source unlikely to ever run dry. 'Your excellent waters fill this whole universe',[23] rishi Vasishtha tells the river in the Mahābhārata.

There can hardly be a lovelier metaphor for the eternal rebirth.

*

> *May purifying Sarasvati with all the plenitude of her forms of plenty, rich in substance by the thought, desire our sacrifice.*
>
> *She, the inspirer of true intuitions, the awakener in consciousness to right thoughts, Sarasvatī, upholds our sacrifice.*
>
> *Sarasvatī by the perception awakens in consciousness the great flood and illumines entirely all the thoughts.*

Rig Veda[24]

Notes

1. The 'Lost River of the Indian Desert'

1. BBC News, 'India's "Miracle River" ', 29 June 2002. The same day, the BBC broadcast a radio programme on the topic by Madhur Jaffrey.
2. Tod, James, Lt-Col, *Annals and Antiquities of Rajasthan*, London, 1829–32; republ. Lolit Mohun Audhya, Calcutta, 1894, pp. 239 & 242.
3. Ibid., vol. II, p. 187; this reference is to the first edition of 1832 : it is quoted by the French geographer Vivien de Saint-Martin (see note 22 below), p. 22. I could not consult the first edition of Tod's *Annals* nor locate this passage in the 1894 edition (which is perhaps abridged). It is retranslated here from Vivien de Saint-Martin's French translation and may not be in the exact words used by Tod, though certainly a faithful approximation.
4. Ibid., sec. edn, p. 242.
5. Rennel, James, *Memoir of a Map of Hindoostan; or the Moghul Empire*, London, 1788, p. 71.
6. Tod, James, Lt.-Col., *Annals and Antiquities of Rajasthan,* vol. II, Higginbotham, Madras, 1873, p. 189.
7. I am grateful to Prof. R.N. Iyengar for those references. (About the last, see also Bharadwaj, O.P., 'The Rigvedic Sarasvati', ch. 3 in *In Search of Vedic-Harappan Relationship*°, p. 25.)
8. Colvin, Major, 'On the Restoration of the Ancient Canals of the Delhi Territory', *Journal of the Asiatic Society*, vol. II, March 1833, p. 107.
9. Mackeson, F., Major, 'Report on the Route from Seersa to Bahawulpore', in *Journal of Asiatic Society of Bengal*, vol. XIII, January–June 1844, no. 145–50, p. 302.
10. Ibid., p. 298.
11. Ibid., p. 299.
12. Ibid., pp. 299–300.

To quickly locate the desired reference, follow the page range in the header at the top of the page. Works mentioned in Suggested Further Reading figure here under their titles alone, without subtitles or bibliographical details; to make this clear, their titles are followed here by the symbol °. Thus, *The Sarasvati Flows On*° indicates that full details for this title are to be looked up in the Suggested Further Reading section.

13. Ibid., p. 301.
14. Ibid.
15. Ibid., p. 308.
16. Ganguly, D.C., 'Northern India during the Eleventh and Twelfth Centuries', *The Struggle for Empire*, vol. 5, in Majumdar, R.C., (ed.), *The History and Culture of the Indian People*, Bharatiya Vidya Bhavan, Bombay, 1960–90, p. 93.
17. Majumdar, R.C., 'The Invasion of Timur and the End of the Tughlug Dynasty', *The Delhi Sultanate*, vol. 6, in *The History and Culture of the Indian People*, op. cit., pp. 117–18.
18. Wilhelmy, Herbert, 'Le cadre naturel', in Franz, Heinrich Gerhard, (ed.), *L'Inde ancienne: histoire et civilisation*, Bordas, Paris, 1990, p. 28.
19. Quoted by Stein, Marc Aurel, *An Archaeological Tour along the Ghaggar–Hakra River°*, p. 12.
20. Something of their story and excerpts from their testimonies can be found in Deleury, Guy, *Les Indes florissantes: anthologie des voyageurs français (1750–1820)*, Robert Laffont, Paris, 1991.
21. Schwab, Raymond, *La Renaissance orientale*, Payot, Paris, 1950, p. 38.
22. Vivien de Saint-Martin, Louis, *Étude sur la géographie et les populations primitives du nord-ouest de l'Inde, d'après les hymnes védiques*, Imprimerie Impériale, Paris, 1860, p. i.
23. Ibid., p. lvii.
24. Vivien de Saint-Martin, Louis, *Étude sur la géographie grecque et latine de l'Inde* and *Mémoire analytique sur la carte de l'Asie centrale et de l'Inde*, Imprimerie Impériale, Paris, 1858.
25. Vivien de Saint-Martin, Louis, *Étude sur la géographie et les populations primitives du nord-ouest de l'Inde, d'après les hymnes védiques*, op. cit., p. iii.
26. Ibid., p. 15.
27. Ibid., p. 18.
28. Ibid., pp. 19–20.
29. Rennel, James, *Memoir of a Map of Hindoostan; or the Moghul Empire*, op. cit., p. 71.
30. Gupta, A.K., B.K. Bhadra & J.R. Sharma, 'Sarasvati Drainage System of Haryana: Satellite-Based Study', in *Vedic River Sarasvati and Hindu Civilization°*, pp. 47 & 51.
31. Vivien de Saint-Martin, Louis, *Étude sur la géographie et les populations primitives du nord-ouest de l'Inde*, op. cit., p. 20.
32. The map is from Beveridge, Henry, *A Comprehensive History of India, Civil, Military, and Social*, Blackie & Son, London, 1862, vol. 1.
33. Vivien de Saint-Martin, Louis, *Étude sur la géographie et les populations primitives du nord-ouest de l'Inde*, op. cit., p. 22.
34. Ibid., p. 23.
35. Ibid., p. 24.
36. Hunter, W.W., 'Ganjam' to 'India', *Imperial Gazetteer of India*, vol. 5, Trübner & Co., London, sec. edn, 1885, pp. 54–55.

37. 'Ratlam' to 'Sirmur', *Imperial Gazetteer of India*, vol. 12, Trübner & Co., London, sec. edn, 1887, pp. 261–62.

38. Oldham, R.D., 'On Probable Changes in the Geography of the Punjab and Its Rivers: An Historico-Geographical Study', *Journal of Asiatic Society of Bengal*, vol. 55, 1886, pp. 322–43. (Oldham's paper is partly reproduced in *Vedic Sarasvati*°, pp. 81–88.)

39. Ibid., p. 340.

40. Ibid., p. 342.

41. Ibid., p. 341.

42. Strabo, *Geography*, book XV, I.19, tr. John W. McCrindle, *Ancient India as Described in Classical Literature*, 1901; reprinted Oriental Books Reprint Corporation, New Delhi, 1979, p. 25.

43. Ibid.

44. Raverty, H.G., 'The Mihrān of Sind and Its Tributaries: A Geographical and Historical Study', *Journal of the Royal Asiatic Society*, vol. 61, no. 1 & extra number (1892), pp. 155–206 & 297–508.

45. E.g. Wilhelmy, Herbert, 'The Shifting River: Studies in the History of the Indus Valley', *Universitas*, vol. 10, no. 1, 1967, pp. 53–68.

46. Sivewright, Robert, 'Cutch and the Ran', *The Geographical Journal*, vol. 29, no. 5, May 1907, pp. 518–35. I am indebted to Prof. R.N. Iyengar for drawing my attention to Sivewright's paper, and to M.S. Gadhavi for a scan of Sivewright's map. Prof. Iyengar's own research on the Rann and its identification with the Vedic *Irina* fills many blanks in our understanding of the region: Iyengar, R.N. & B.P. Radhakrishna, 'Geographical Location of Vedic *Irina* in Southern Rajasthan', *Journal of Geological Society of India*, vol. 70, November 2007, pp. 699–705, and Iyengar, R.N., B.P. Radhakrishna & S.S. Mishra, 'Vedic *Irina* and the Rann-of-Kutch', *Puratattva*, no. 38, 2008, pp. 170–180.

47. Sivewright, Robert, 'Cutch and the Ran', op. cit., p. 528.

48. Ibid., p. 530.

49. Snead, Rodman E., 'Recent Morphological Changes along the Coast of West Pakistan', *Annals of the Association of American Geographers*, vol. 57, no. 3, September 1967, pp. 550–65. My thanks to Prof. R.N. Iyengar for drawing my attention to this paper.

50. Sivewright, Robert, 'Cutch and the Ran', op. cit., p. 532.

51. Anonymous (Oldham, C.F.), 'Notes on the Lost River in the Indian Desert', *Calcutta Review*, vol. 59, 1874, pp. 1–27.

52. Oldham, R.D., 'On Probable Changes in the Geography of the Punjab and Its Rivers', op. cit., p. 322.

53. Oldham, C.F., 'The Sarasvati and the Lost River of the Indian Desert', *Journal of the Royal Asiatic Society*, vol. 34, 1893, pp. 49–76.

54. Ibid., p. 51.

55. Ibid. Oldham invokes the *Punjab Gazetteer* of Hissar as evidence (which I have not been able to consult).

56. This is not C.F. Oldham's original map, in which names are hardly legible, but an exact reproduction borrowed from Misra, V.N., 'Climate, a Factor in the

Rise and Fall of the Indus Civilization: Evidence from Rajasthan and Beyond',
in Lal, B.B. & S.P. Gupta, (eds), *Frontiers of the Indus Civilization*°, p. 478.
57. Oldham, C.F., 'The Sarasvatī and the Lost River of the Indian Desert', op.
cit., p. 54.
58. Ibid., p. 60.
59. Ibid., p. 61.
60. Ibid., p. 73.
61. As quoted by Oldham, R.D., 'On Probable Changes in the Geography of the
Punjab and Its Rivers', op. cit., pp. 326–27. (The tradition is mentioned by
C.F. Oldham in his earlier, anonymous article, see note 51 above.) It is R.D.
Oldham who takes 'Kak' to refer to Kachchh.
62. Oldham, C.F., 'The Sarasvatī and the Lost River of the Indian Desert', op.
cit., p. 63.
63. Ibid., p. 76.
64. *Imperial Gazetteer of India*, vol. 23, new edn, London, 1908, p. 179. Quoted
by Vishal Agarwal in 'A Reply to Michael Witzel's *"Ein Fremdling im Rigveda"*', August 2003, available online at: www.omilosmeleton.gr/english/
documents/ReplytoWitzelJIES.pdf (accessed 15 September 2009).
65. Oldham, C.F., 'The Sarasvatī and the Lost River of the Indian Desert', op.
cit., p. 76.

2. The Mighty Sarasvatī

1. Several works refer to descriptions of the Sarasvatī in Vedic and post-Vedic
literature; among them, Bhargava, M.L., *Geography of Rgvedic India*, Upper
India Publishing House, Lucknow, 1964 (but written in the 1930s), is a classic,
followed by Law, Bimalachurn, 'Mountains and Rivers of India (from Epic
and Paurānic Sources)', *Journal of the Department of Letters*, vol. XXVIII,
Calcutta University Press, 1935, pp. 1–31. More recent studies include Bhargava, P.L., *India in the Vedic Age*°, ch. 4; Frawley, David, *Gods, Sages and
Kings*°, part I, chs 2 & 3, and his paper 'Geographical References: The Ocean
and Soma', ch. 4, in *In Search of Vedic-Harappan Relationship*°; Singh,
Shivaji, 'Sindhu and Sarasvatī in the Rigveda and their Archaeological Implication', in *Puratattva*, no. 28, 1997–98, pp. 26–36; Chauhan, D.S., 'Mythical
Observations and Scientific Evaluation of the Lost Sarasvatī River', in *Vedic
Sarasvati*°; and Talageri, Shrikant G., *The Rigveda: A Historical Analysis*°,
ch. 4. For O.P. Bharadwaj's important papers, see note 26 below.
2. Rig Veda, 1.3.12. (Unless otherwise specified, renderings from the Rig Veda
are my own arrangements from several available translations, such as the two
integral translations into English by H.H. Wilson and R.T.H. Griffith—see his
Hymns of the Rig Veda°—and partial translations by Max Müller, Sri
Aurobindo, Louis Renou, Jan Gonda, Jean Varenne, among others.)
3. Rig Veda, 6.61.13.
4. Ibid., 7.95.1.
5. Ibid., 6.61.8.
6. Ibid., 7.36.6.

7. Ibid., 7.96.2.

8. Aurobindo, Sri, *The Secret of the Veda*°, p. 88.

9. Rig Veda, 1.3.11–12 (adapted from Sri Aurobindo's translation).

10. Ibid., 2.41.16.

11. Ibid., 6.61.4. See Ludvik, Catherine, 'Sarasvatī-Vāc: The Identification of the River with Speech', *Asiatische Studien / Études Asiatiques*, vol. 54, no. 1, 2000, p. 120.

12. Ludvik, Catherine, *Sarasvatī: Riverine Goddess of Knowledge*°. See also her important paper mentioned in the preceding note.

13. Müller, F. Max, in *India—What Can It Teach Us?*, first edn 1883, sec. edn 1892; republ. Penguin Books, New Delhi, 2000, p. 149.

14. Rig Veda, 6.61.10, 12.

15. Ibid., 7.36.6.

16. Ibid., 3.23.4.

17. Ibid., 6.61.2.

18. Ibid., 7.95.2.

19. *Vājasaneyī Samhitā* (White *Yajur Veda*), 34.11.

20. Pañcavimsha Brāhmana, 25.10.6 and *Jaiminya Upanishad Brāhmana*, 4.26. See Macdonell, A.A. & A.B. Keith, *Vedic Index*°, vol. 2, p. 300.

21. Ibid., p. 55.

22. 'Plaksha' is the name of the waved-leaf fig tree (*ficus infectoria*). See ibid., p. 54.

23. *The Mahabharata of Krishna-Dwaipayana Vyasa*, tr. Kisari Mohan Ganguli, vol. III, Salya Parva, IX.54, first edn in the 1890s; republ. Munshiram Manoharlal, New Delhi, 2000, pp. 149–150. See also, below, Epilogue.

24. Pañchavimsha Brāhmana, 25.10.16.

25. See references in Bharadwaj, O.P., 'Vinashana', *Journal of the Oriental Institute of Baroda*, vol. 33, nos 1–2, 1983, p. 70.

26. Apart from the paper in the preceding note (pp. 69–88), see Bharadwaj, O.P., 'The Vedic Sarasvatī', in *Haryana Sahitya Akademi Journal of Indological Studies*, vol. 2, nos 1–2, 1987, pp. 38–58; 'The Rigvedic Sarasvatī', ch. 3, in *In Search of Vedic-Harappan Relationship*°; and several chapters in his *Ancient Kurukshetra: Studies*, Harman Publishing House, New Delhi, 1991 and *Studies in the Historical Geography of Ancient India*, Sundeep Prakashan, New Delhi, 1986.

27. Bharadwaj, O.P., *Historical Geography of Ancient India*, op. cit., ch. 9: 'Ganga to Ghaggar with Valmiki'.

28. *The Mahabharata of Krishna-Dwaipayana Vyasa*, op. cit., vol. I, Vana Parva, III.5, p. 15. (I have modernized spelling in this and the following quotations; Ganguli's numbering of the verses do not always coincide with that of the critical edition, which was prepared years later.)

29. Ibid., vol. III, Salya Parva, IX.42, p. 116.

30. Ibid., IX.38, p. 108.

31. Ibid., pp. 108–09.

32. Ibid., vol. I, Vana Parva, III.83, p. 173.

33. Ibid., vol. IV, Anusasana Parva, XIII.146, p. 315.

34. Ibid., vol. I, Vana Parva, III.82, pp. 170 & 173.
35. Ibid., vol. II, Bhisma Parva, VI.6, p. 16.
36. Ibid., vol. I, Vana Parva, III.130, p. 270; see also III.82, p. 172.
37. Ibid., vol. III, Salya Parva, IX.37, p. 104.
38. Ibid., vol. IV, Anusasana Parva, XIII.154, p. 361.
39. Barmer district (western part only): Balasar, Alamsar, Punjasar, Rabbasar, Rattasar, Ramsar, Ranasar, Lilsar, Gangasar, Bakhasar. Jaisalmer district: Ajasar, Dhaisar, Bhadasar, Baramsar. Bikaner district: Lunkaransar, Hathusar, Jaswantsar, Kapurisar, Kamisar, Napasar, Mundsar, Jasrasar, Desilsar, Somalsar, Barsisar, Udramsar, Gersar, Naurangdesar. Hanumangarh district: Rawatsar, Lakhasar, Baramsar, Kansar, Pandusar, Dhannasar, Malsisar. Churu district: Hardesar, Rattusar, Patamdesar, Binjasar, Jodhasar, Bhadasar, Mummasar, Lachharsar, Malasar, Rajaldesar, Gundusar, Kanwarpalsar, Tahindesar, Jaitasar. Jodhpur district (northern part only): Kanasar, Bhojasar, Narsar . . .
40. *The Mahabharata of Krishna-Dwaipayana Vyasa*, op. cit., vol. III, Salya Parva, IX.37, p. 105.
41. Ibid., IX.54, p. 150.
42. Ibid., IX.37, p. 106.
43. Ibid., IX.35, p. 101.
44. Ibid., vol. III, Salya Parva, IX.48 & 51.
45. *Baudhāyana Dharmasūtra*, 1.2.9; *Vasishtha Dharmasūtra*, 1.8; Patañjali's *Mahābhāshya*, 2.4.10 & 6.3.109. For a translation of the first two, see Olivelle, Patrick, *Dharmasūtras: The Law Codes of Āpastamba, Gautama, Baudhāyana, and Vasistha*, Motilal Banarsidass, Delhi, 2000, pp. 199 & 351.
46. Macdonell, A.A. & A.B. Keith, *Vedic Index*°, vol. 2, pp. 125–26.
47. *Manusmriti*, II.17, tr. George Bühler, *The Laws of Manu*, Sacred Books of the East, Oxford, 1886, vol. 25.
48. *Mārkandeya Purāna*, tr. F.E. Pargiter, vol. LVII, The Asiatic Society, Calcutta, 1904; republ. Indological Book House, Varanasi, 1969, pp. 290–306.
49. Kālidāsa, *The Loom of Time: A Selection of His Plays and Poems*, tr. Chandra Rajan, Penguin Books, New Delhi, 1989, p. 149.
50. Ibid., p. 261.
51. *Brihat Samhitā*, XIV.2, *The Brhat Samhitā of Varāha Mihira*, tr. N.C. Iyer, Sri Satguru Publications, Delhi, 1987, p. 81.
52. Bāna, *Harsa-Carita*, tr. E.B. Cowell, F.W. Thomas, London, 1929, pp. 158 & 160, quoted by Darian, Steven, 'Gangā and Sarasvatī: An Incidence of Mythological Projection', *East and West*, vol. 26, nos 1–2, 1976, p. 155.
53. *The Mahabharata of Krishna-Dwaipayana Vyasa*, op. cit., vol. I, Vana Parva, III.83, p. 180.
54. See Bharadwaj, O.P., 'The Vedic Sarasvatī', op. cit., p. 41.
55. Pehowa Inscription of Imperial Pratihāra Dynasty, *Epigraphia Indica*, I.187, pp. 1114–15, quoted by Raychaudhuri, H.C., 'The Sarasvati', *Science and Culture*, vol. VIII, no. 12, June 1943, p. 469, and in *Studies in Indian Antiquities*, University of Calcutta, Calcutta, 1958, p. 129; the inscription is discussed by Bharadwaj, O.P., in 'The Vedic Sarasvatī', op. cit., p. 40.

56. Quoted by Raychaudhuri, H.C., 'The Sarasvati', op. cit., p. 473.

57. Cunningham, Alexander, *The Ancient Geography of India*, sec. revised edn, Calcutta, 1924; reprint Munshiram Manoharlal, New Delhi, 2002, map X, facing p. 375. The map plots Hsüan-tsang's travels in northwest India; for clarity, I have omitted from the detail reproduced here Hsüan-tsang's route reconstituted by Cunningham.

58. Cunningham's story is told in a fine account of the beginnings of archaeology in India: Singh, Upinder, *The Discovery of Ancient India°* (also, more briefly, in Lahiri, Nayanjot, *Finding Forgotten Cities°*).

59. See Bhargava, M.L., *Geography of Rgvedic India*, op. cit., p. 71, with reference to *Archaeological Survey of India Report*, vol. XIV, p. 75.

60. Cunningham, Alexander, *The Ancient Geography of India*, op. cit.

61. Bharadwaj, O.P., 'The Vedic Sarasvatī', op. cit., p. 40.

62. E.g. *A Road Guide to Rajasthan*, TTK Healthcare, Chennai, 2006.

63. *Albêrûnî's India*, tr. Edward C. Sachau, 1888; republ. Rupa & Co., New Delhi, 2002, p. 511.

64. *The Vishnu Purāna: A System of Hindu Mythology and Tradition*, tr. H.H. Wilson, John Murray, London, 1840, pp. lxvi–vii.

65. Rig Veda, 1.32.12, 2.12.3 & 12, 4.28.1, 8.24.27, 8.54.4, 8.69.12.

66. For example, Müller, F. Max, *A History of Ancient Sanskrit Literature°*, p. 7.

67. Müller, F. Max, *Vedic Hymns°*, p. 60.

68. Monier-Williams, M., *Indian Wisdom*,1875; republ. Rupa & Co., New Delhi, 2001, p. xix.

69. Weber, A., *The History of Indian Literature*, Trübner, London, 1878, pp. 4 & 38.

70. Eggeling, Julius, *The Satapatha Brāhmana°*, p. 104.

71. Oldenberg, Hermann, *The Religion of the Veda*, 1894; republ. Motilal Banarsidass, Delhi, 1988, pp. 123 & 171.

72. Fontane, Marius, *Inde védique (de 1800 à 800 av. J.-C.)*, Alphonse Lemerre, Paris, 1881, with the map at the end of the book.

73. Macdonell, A.A. & A.B. Keith, *Vedic Index°*, vol. 2, pp. 435–36.

74. Pargiter, F.E., *Ancient Indian Historical Tradition*, London, 1922; republ. Motilal Banarsidass, Delhi, 1997, p. 313.

75. Gowen, Herbert H., *A History of Indian Literature from Vedic Times to the Present Day*, D. Appleton, New York & London, 1931, p. 96.

76. Ibid., p. 9.

77. The map is found in Pargiter, F.E., 'The Nations of India at the Battle between the Pandavas and Kauravas', *Journal of the Royal Asiatic Society*, 1908, pp. 309–36.

78. Renou, Louis & Jean Filliozat, *L'Inde classique: manuel des études indiennes*, vol. 1, Payot, 1947 ; republ. Librairie d'Amérique et d'Orient, 1985, p. 372.

79. Burrow, T., 'On the Significance of the Term *arma-, armaka-* in Early Sanskrit Literature', *Journal of Indian History*, vol. 41, 1963, p. 162.

80. Basham, A.L., *The Wonder That Was India*, third edn, Rupa & Co., Calcutta, 1981, pp. 31–32.

81. Gonda, Jan, *Vedic Literature (Samhitās and Brāhmanas)°*, pp. 23–24.

82. Bhargava, M.L., *The Geography of Rgvedic India*, op. cit.

83. Law, Bimalachurn, 'Mountains and Rivers of India (from Epic and Paurānic Sources)', op. cit.

84. Raychaudhuri, H.C., 'The Sarasvati', op. cit.

85. Pusalker, A.D., 'Aryan Settlements in India', ch. XIII of *The Vedic Age*, vol. I, in Majumdar, R.C., (ed.), *The History and Culture of the Indian People*, op. cit., pp. 246–48.

86. Sircar, D.C., *Studies in the Geography of Ancient and Medieval India*, first edn 1960, sec. edn Motilal Banarsidass, Delhi, 1971, p. 49.

3. New Light on an Ancient River

1. Ghosh, A., 'The Rajputana Desert: Its Archaeological Aspect', in *Bulletin of the National Institute of Sciences in India*, vol. I, 1952, pp. 37–42, reproduced in S.P. Gupta, (ed.), *An Archaeological Tour along the Ghaggar–Hakra River*, Kusumanjali Prakashan, Meerut, 1988, p. 100.

2. Valdiya, K.S., *Saraswati, the River That Disappeared°*, p. 16, and Raghav, K.S., 'Evolution of Drainage Basins in Parts of Northern and Western Rajasthan, Thar Desert, India', in *Vedic Sarasvatī°*, p. 176.

3. Bakliwal, P.C. & A.K. Grover, 'Signatures and Migration of Sarasvatī River in Thar Desert, Western India', *Records of Geological Survey of India*, vol. 116, parts 3–8, 1988, pp. 77–86, partly reproduced in *Vedic Sarasvatī°*, p. 115.

4. Raikes, Robert L., 'Kalibangan: Death from Natural Causes', *Antiquity*, vol. XLII, 1969, reproduced in *The Decline and Fall of the Indus Civilization*, p. 204.

5. Ibid., p. 208.

6. Ibid., pp. 208–09.

7. Ibid., p. 209.

8. Valdiya, K.S., *Saraswati, the River That Disappeared°*, p. 55.

9. Wilson, H.H., *The Vishnu Purāna*, op. cit., ch. XXV, p. 572.

10. *The Bhāgavata Purāna*, tr. Ganesh Vasudeo Tagare, Motilal Banarsidass, X.65.31, Delhi, 1988, p. 1673.

11. Singh, Gurdev, in *The Geography*, vol. 5, 1952, p. 27, mentioned by Pal, Yash, Baldev Sahai, R.K. Sood & D.P. Agrawal, 'Remote Sensing of the Sarasvati River', first published in *Proceedings of the Indian Academy of Sciences* (Earth and Planetary Sciences), vol. 89, no. 3, November 1980; reprinted in Lal, B.B. & S.P. Gupta, (eds), *Frontiers of the Indus Civilization°*, p. 493.

12. Valdiya, K.S., *Saraswati, the River That Disappeared°*, p. 24.

13. Ibid, p. 60.

14. *The Mahabharata of Krishna-Dwaipayana Vyasa*, op. cit., vol. I, Adi Parva, I.178, pp. 359–60.

15. Courty, Marie-Agnès, 'Le Milieu physique et utilisation du sol', in Henri-Paul Francfort, (ed.), *Prospections archéologiques au nord-ouest de L'Inde: rapport préliminaire 1983–1984*, mémoire 62, Éditions Recherches sur les Civilisations, Paris, 1985, p. 30.

16. Ibid.
17. Courty, Marie-Agnès, 'Integration of Sediment and Soil Information in the Reconstruction of Protohistoric and Historic Landscapes of the Ghaggar Plain (North-West India)', in Frifelt, Karen & Per Sorensen, (eds), *South Asian Archaeology 1985*, Scandinavian Institute of Asian Studies, Occasional Papers no. 4, Curzon Press, London, 1989, p. 259.
18. Puri, V.M.K. & B.C. Verma, 'Glaciological and Geological Source of Vedic Saraswati in the Himalayas', *Itihas Darpan*, vol. 4, 1998, no. 2, pp. 7–36.
19. Ibid., p. 16.
20. Valdiya, K.S., in *Saraswati, the River That Disappeared°*, p. 27.
21. Lal, B.B., et al., *Excavations at Kalibangan*, vol. 1, Archaeological Survey of India, New Delhi, 2003, pp. 99–100.
22. Bisht, R.S., 'Urban Planning at Dholavira: A Harappan City', in Malville, J. McKim & Lalit M. Gujral, (eds), *Ancient Cities, Sacred Skies: Cosmic Geometries and City Planning in Ancient India*, Indira Gandhi National Centre for the Arts & Aryan Books International, New Delhi, 2000, pp. 16–17. Note that Bisht does not propose a precise date for the earthquake but says it occurred 'towards the closing years' of the phase immediately preceding the Mature Harappan phase, which almost everywhere started around 2600 BCE.
23. Valdiya, K.S., *Saraswati, the River That Disappeared°*, pp. 52–54. Valdiya writes that the uplift took place '*after* 3663 ± 215 yr BP', therefore after 3878 BP ('before present') or 1878 BCE.
24. Ibid., p. 53.
25. Pal, Yash, Baldev Sahai, R.K. Sood & D.P. Agrawal, 'Remote Sensing of the Sarasvati River', in Lal, B.B. & S.P. Gupta, (eds), *Frontiers of the Indus Civiliza*Ibid.*tion°*, p. 493.
26. Ibid., p. 494.
27. Ibid., pp. 494–96.
28. Rajawat, A.S., C.V.S. Sastry & A. Narain, 'Application of Pyramidal Processing on High Resolution IRS 1-C Data for Tracing Migration of the Sarasvatī River in Parts of Thar Desert', in *Vedic Sarasvatī°*, pp. 259–72.
29. Sharma, J.R., A.K. Gupta & B.K. Bhadra, 'Course of Vedic River Saraswati as Deciphered from Latest Satellite Data', *Puratattva* (Journal of the Indian Archaeological Society), no. 26, New Delhi, 2005–06, pp. 187–95. I am grateful to Dr A.K. Gupta for his kind collaboration and his permission to reproduce the maps in Figs 3.6 & 3.7.
30. See Ghose, Bimal, Amal Kar & Zahid Husain, 'The Lost Courses of the Saraswati River in the Great Indian Desert: New Evidence from LANDSAT Imagery', *The Geographical Journal*, London, vol. 145, no. 3, 1979, pp. 446–51, which was perhaps the earliest study of satellite imagery. Also Bakliwal, P.C. & A.K. Grover, 'Signatures and Migration of Sarasvatī River in Thar Desert, Western India', op. cit. One such recent view is in Roy, A.B. & S.R. Jakhar, 'Late Quaternary Drainage Disorganization, and Migration and Extinction of the Vedic Saraswati', in *Current Science*, vol. 81, no. 9, 10 November 2001, pp. 1188–95, and the references quoted in that paper.

31. I have enhanced the contrast in Fig. 3.7, changed the watercourses from white to black, and made course numbers clearer in both maps.

32. Rao, S.M. & K.M. Kulkarni, 'Isotope Hydrology Studies on Water Resources in Western Rajasthan', *Current Science*, vol. 72, no. 1, 10 January 1997, pp. 55 & 60.

33. I tentatively offer those corrected dates on the basis of the nearest examples from 'Calibrated Indian 14C Dates', appendix 3 to Agrawal, D.P. & M.G. Yadava, *Dating the Human Past*, Indian Society for Prehistoric and Quaternary Studies, Pune, 1995.

34. The Central Ground Water Board, the Regional Remote Sensing Centre (Jodhpur), the Central Arid Zone Research Institute (Jodhpur), ISRO and the National Physical Laboratory participated in one way or another.

35. Mahapatra, Richard, 'Saraswati Underground', *Down to Earth*, Centre for Science and Environment, New Delhi, vol. 11, no. 12, 15 November 2002.

36. Ibid.

37. Soni, V., D.C. Sharma, K.S. Srivastava & M.S. Sisodia, 'Hydrogeological, Geophysical and Isotope Study to Trace the Course of the Buried "Sarasvati" River in Jaisalmer district, Rajasthan', in Paliwal, B.S., (ed.), *Geological Evolution of Northwestern India*, Scientific Publishers, Jodhpur, 1999, pp. 305–11, quoted by Valdiya, K.S., in *Saraswati, the River That Disappeared°*, p. 29.

38. Srinivasan, K.R., *Paleogeography, Framework of Sedimentation and Groundwater Potential of Rajasthan, India : Central Part of Erstwhile Sarasvati Basin*, a monograph presented at the Geological Society of India in December 1997 at Baroda; also his two project reports of September 1997 submitted to the Ministry of Water Resources by the Sarasvati Sindhu Research Centre, Chennai.

39. Geyh, M.A. & D. Ploethner, 'Origins of a Freshwater Body in Cholistan, Thar Desert, Pakistan', in Dragoni, W. & B.S. Sukhija, (eds), *Climate Change and Groundwater*, Geological Society special publication, vol. 288, London, 2008, pp. 99–109. The two scientists had published an earlier report, 'An Applied Palaeohydrological Study of Cholistan, Thar Desert, Pakistan', in Adar, E.M. & C. Leibundgut, (eds), *Applications of Tracers in Arid Zone Hydrology*, International Association of Hydrological Sciences, publ. no. 232, Vienna, 1995, pp. 119–27.

40. Geyh, M.A. & D. Ploethner, 'Origins of a Freshwater Body in Cholistan', op. cit., p. 102.

41. Ibid., p. 104.

42. Peter Clift, 'Harappan Collapse', *Geoscientist*, vol. 19, no. 9, September 2009, p. 18.

43. Siddiqi, Shamsul Islam, 'River Changes in the Ghaggar Plain', *The Indian Geographical Journal*, vol. 19, no. 4, 1944, pp. 139–46.

44. Ibid., p. 144.

45. Ibid., p. 145.

46. Ibid., p. 146.

47. Ibid.

48. Wilhelmy, Herbert, 'The Ancient River Valley on the Eastern Border of the Indus Plain and the Sarasvatī Problem', in *Vedic Sarasvatī*°, p. 99 (partial English translation of 'Das Urstromtal am Ostrand der Indusebene und das Sarasvatī Problem', in *Zeitschrift für Geomorphologie*, N.F. Supplementband 8, 1969, pp. 76–93).

49. Ibid., p. 108.

50. Ibid., p. 102.

51. Ibid., pp. 107–08.

52. Ibid., p. 97.

4. A Great Leap Backward

1. See Possehl, Gregory L., *Indus Age: The Beginnings*°, pp. 49–51, and Lahiri, Nayanjot, *Finding Forgotten Cities*°, p. 18.

2. Nayanjot Lahiri's *Finding Forgotten Cities*° tells the gripping story of the discovery of the Indus cities and the various pioneers involved. I have drawn mostly from it (also from Possehl, above) for my brief narrative of that discovery.

3. Ibid., p. 24.

4. Upinder Singh's *Discovery of Ancient India*° narrates archaeological explorations in nineteenth-century India, centred on Cunningham, his British assistants and Indian collaborators. Nayanjot Lahiri's *Finding Forgotten Cities*° takes over from that period.

5. See Tewari, Rakesh, 'The Origins of Iron-working in India: New Evidence from the Central Ganga Plain and the Eastern Vindhyas', *Antiquity*, vol. 77, no. 298 (December 2003), pp. 536–544.

6. Sahni, Daya Ram, quoted in Lahiri, Nayanjot, *Finding Forgotten Cities*°, p. 174.

7. Marshall, John, quoted in ibid., p. 177.

8. Ibid., p. 226.

9. Ibid., p. 259.

10. Sayce, Archibald Henry, quoted in ibid., p. 267.

11. Marshall, John, quoted in ibid., p. 272.

12. Jansen, Michael, 'Settlement Patterns in the Harappa culture', in *South Asian Archaeology 1979*, D. Reimer Verlag, Berlin, 1981, pp. 251–269.

13. Misra, V.N., 'Indus Civilization and the Rgvedic Sarasvatī', in Parpola, Asko & Petteri Koskikallio, (eds), *South Asian Archaeology 1993*, Suomalainen Tiedeakatemia, Helsinki, vol. II, 1994, p. 511.

14. Possehl, Gregory L., *Indus Age: The Beginnings*°, p. 26.

15. Some of them are described in Misra, V.N., *Rajasthan: Prehistoric and Early Historic Foundations*°, Agrawal, D.P. & J.S. Kharakwal, *Bronze and Iron Ages in South Asia*°, and Chakrabarti, Dilip K., *The Oxford Companion to Indian Archaeology*° (especially ch. 13).

16. E.g. Lal, B.B., 'Chronological Horizon of the Mature Indus Civilization', in Kenoyer, Jonathan Mark, (ed.), *From Sumer to Meluhha: Contributions to*

the Archaeology of South and West Asia in Memory of George F. Dales, Jr., University of Wisconsin, Wisconsin, 1994, pp. 15–25.

17. Jansen, Michael R.N., 'Mohenjo Daro and the River Indus', in Meadows, Azra & Peter S. Meadows, (eds), *The Indus River: Biodiversity, Resources, Humankind*, Oxford University Press, Karachi, 1999, p. 375.

18. Lal, B.B., *The Earliest Civilization of South Asia°*, pp. 35, 54, 61 & 73.

19. Kenoyer, Jonathan Mark, 'Culture and Societies of the Indus Tradition', in *India: Historical Beginnings and the Concept of the Aryan°*, p. 52.

20. Allchin, Raymond & Bridget, *Origins of a Civilization°*, p. 181.

21. Shaffer, Jim G. & Diane A. Lichtenstein, 'Ethnicity and Change in the Indus Valley Cultural Tradition' in Kenoyer, Jonathan Mark, (ed.), *Old Problems and New Perspectives in the Archaeology of South Asia*, University of Wisconsin, Wisconsin, 1989, p. 123.

22. Jarrige, Jean-François, 'De l'Euphrate à l'Indus', *Dossiers Histoire et Archéologie*, Dijon, 1987, p. 84.

23. Kenoyer, Jonathan Mark, *Ancient Cities of the Indus Valley Civilization°*, p. 39.

24. Rao, L.S., et al., 'New Light on the Excavation of Harappan Settlement at Bhirrana', *Puratattva*, no. 35, 2004–05, pp. 60–68.

25. Chakrabarti, Dilip K., *The Oxford Companion to Indian Archaeology°*, p. 145.

26. Kenoyer, Jonathan Mark, 'Culture and Societies of the Indus Tradition', in *India: Historical Beginnings and the Concept of the Aryan°*, p. 52.

27. Simplified from Possehl, Gregory L., *Indus Age: The Beginnings°*, p. 23.

28. Jarrige, Jean-François, 'Du néolithique à la civilisation de l'Inde ancienne: contribution des recherches archéologiques dans le nord-ouest du sous-continent indo-pakistanais', *Arts Asiatiques*, vol. L–1995, p. 24.

5. The Indus Cities

1. E.g. Kenoyer, Jonathan Mark, *Ancient Cities of the Indus Valley Civilization°*, pp. 64–65.

2. Jansen, Michael R.N., 'Mohenjo Daro and the River Indus', in *The Indus River: Biodiversity, Resources, Humankind*, op. cit., p. 358.

3. Ibid.

4. This is the case of D.R. Bhandarkar, who visited Mohenjo-daro in 1911, ten years before R.D. Banerji, and concluded that the site was just 200 years old on account of its bricks of 'modern type and not of large dimension like the old'! See Gregory Possehl, *Indus Age: The Beginnings°*, pp. 63–64.

5. Marshall, John, 'Mohenjo-daro', *Illustrated London News*, 27 February 1926, quoted by McIntosh, Jane R., *A Peaceful Realm°*, p. 21.

6. Marshall, John, (ed.), *Mohenjo-daro and the Indus Civilization*, Arthur Probsthain, London, 1931, 3 vols, several Indian reprints, vol. I, p. vi.

7. See Cleuziou, Serge, 'The Oman Peninsula and the Indus civilization: A Reassessment', in *Man and Environment*, vol. 17, 1992, no. 2, pp. 93–103.

8. Nissen, Hans J., 'La civilisation de l'Indus vue de la Mésopotamie', in *Les Cités oubliées de l'Indus°*, p. 144.

9. Chakrabarti, Dilip K., *The Oxford Companion to Indian Archaeology°*, p. 175.

10. Lawler, Andrew, 'Report of Oldest Boat Hints at Early Trade Routes', *Science*, vol. 296, 7 June 2002, no. 5574, pp. 1791–92.

11. Casal, Jean-Marie, *La Civilisation de l'Indus et ses énigmes°*, p. 70.

12. See Lal, B.B., *The Earliest Civilization of South Asia°*, pp. 187–88, and Chakrabarti, Dilip K., *The Oxford Companion to Indian Archaeology°*, p. 174.

13. See a summary in Andrew Lawler, 'Middle Asia Takes Center Stage', *Science*, vol. 317, 3 August 2007, pp. 586–90.

14. Francfort, Henri-Paul, 'The Harappan Settlement of Shortughai', in Lal, B.B. & S.P. Gupta, (eds), *Frontiers of the Indus Civilization°*, p. 309 (emphasis in the original).

15. See a summary in Weiner, Sheila, 'Hypotheses Regarding the Development and Chronology of the Art of the Indus Valley Civilization', in Lal, B.B. & S.P. Gupta, (eds), *Frontiers of the Indus Civilization°*, pp. 396 & 413, and in Lal, B.B., *The Earliest Civilization of South Asia°*, pp. 188–190.

16. Good, Irene L., J. Mark Kenoyer & Richard H. Meadow, 'New Evidence for Early Silk in the Indus Civilization', available online at www.harappa.com/har/early-indus-silk.pdf (accessed 31 January 2009).

17. A survey of Harappan metallurgy can be found in Agrawal, D.P., *Indus Civilization°*, chapter 6, section II.

18. Lal, B.B., *India 1947–1997°*, pp. 57 ff.

19. Mughal, M. Rafique, 'Evidence of Rice and *Ragi* at Harappa in the Context of South Asian Prehistory', ch. 5, in Misra, V.N. & M.D. Kajale, (eds), *Introduction of African Crops into South Asia*, Indian Society for Prehistoric and Quaternary Studies, Pune, 2003.

20. Allchin, Raymond & Bridget, *Origins of a Civilization°*, p. 190.

21. Ibid., p. 187.

22. Ibid.

23. Jarrige, Jean-François, 'Du néolithique à la civilisation de l'Inde ancienne', op. cit., p. 14.

24. Chakrabarti, Dilip K., *The Oxford Companion to Indian Archaeology°*, p. 187.

25. Shaffer, Jim G. & Diane A. Lichtenstein, 'Ethnicity and Change in the Indus Valley Cultural Traditions', op. cit., pp. 123–24.

26. Possehl, Gregory L., *The Indus Civilization°*, pp. 6, 57 & 247.

27. Lal, B.B., *The Earliest Civilization of South Asia°*.

28. Ibid., p. 236.

29. Chakrabarti, Dilip K., *The Oxford Companion to Indian Archaeology°*, p. 188.

30. Kenoyer, Jonathan Mark, 'Early City-States in South Asia: Comparing the Harappan Phase and Early Historic Period', in Nichols, D.L. & T.H. Charlton, (eds), *The Archaeology of City-States: Cross-Cultural Approaches*, Smithsonian Institution Press, Washington D.C., 1997, pp. 51–70.

31. Kenoyer, Jonathan Mark, 'Indus Valley Tradition of Pakistan and Western India', *Journal of World Prehistory*, vol. 5, 1995, pp. 369.

32. Kenoyer, Jonathan Mark, *Ancient Cities of the Indus Valley Civilization°*, p. 81.

33. Wright, Rita P., 'The Indus Valley and Mesopotamian Civilizations: A Comparative View of Ceramic Technology', in *Old Problems and New Perspectives in the Archaeology of South Asia*, op. cit., pp. 153–54.
34. Agrawal, D.P., 'The Harappan Legacy: Break and Continuity', in Possehl, Gregory L., (ed.), *Harappan Civilization: A Recent Perspective*, sec. edn, Oxford & IBH, New Delhi, 1993, p. 452.
35. McIntosh, Jane R., *A Peaceful Realm*°, p. 177.
36. See, for instance, Kenoyer, Jonathan Mark, *Ancient Cities of the Indus Valley Civilization*°, pp. 55–56.
37. To be precise, 97 out of 1052 Mature sites have been excavated, according to Possehl, Gregory L., *The Indus Civilization*°, p. 65.

6. From the Indus to the Sarasvatī

1. Lahiri, Nayanjot, *Finding Forgotten Cities*°, chapters 6 & 7.
2. Tessitori, L.P., 'Progress Report on the Work Done during the Year 1917 in Cconnection with the Bardic & Historical Survey of Rajputana', *Journal & Proceedings of the Asiatic Society of Bengal*, New Series, vol. XV, 1919, p. 7.
3. Tessitori, Luigi, 'A Report on Tours in Search of Archaeological Remains Made in Bikaner State during the Years 1916–17 & 1917–18', p. 8. I am indebted to Prof. Nayanjot Lahiri for kindly communicating this extract.
4. Ibid. (This portion is quoted in Lahiri, Nayanjot, *Finding Forgotten Cities*°, pp. 144–45.)
5. Ibid., p. 150.
6. Stein, Sir Aurel, 'A Survey of Ancient Sites along the "Lost" Sarasvatī River', *The Geographical Journal*, vol. 99, 1942, pp. 173–182 ('A Survey' in the following notes).
7. Stein, Marc Aurel, *An Archaeological Tour along the Ghaggar–Hakra River*° (*An Archaeological Tour*° in the following notes).
8. Stein, Sir Aurel, 'On Some River Names in the Rigveda', *Journal of the Royal Asiatic Society*, 1917, pp. 91–99.
9. 'A Survey', p. 173.
10. Ibid., p. 175.
11. 'A Survey', p. 178.
12. Ibid.
13. *An Archaeological Tour*°, p. 96.
14. 'A Survey', p. 176.
15. Ibid., p. 173.
16. Ibid.
17. *An Archaeological Tour*°, p. 11.
18. 'A Survey', p. 179.
19. Thapar, B.K., 'Discovery and Previous Work' in Lal, B.B., et al. *Excavations at Kalibangan*, vol. 1, Archaeological Survey of India, New Delhi, 2003, p. 14.
20. *An Archaeological Tour*°, p. 46.
21. 'A Survey', p. 180.
22. Ibid., p. 179–80.

23. Ibid., p. 182.
24. *An Archaeological Tour°*, p. 3.
25. Deva, Krishna, 'Contributions of Aurel Stein and N.G. Majumdar to Research into the Harappan Civilization with Special Reference to their Methodology', in Possehl, G.L., (ed.), *Harappan Civilization: A contemporary perspective*, Oxford & IBH and the American Institute of Indian Studies, Delhi, 1982, p. 392. (Krishna Deva was so modest that nowhere in this account of Stein's work did he mention his own participation in the Sarasvatī expedition.)
26. Quoted by Lahiri, Nayanjot, 'What Lies Beneath', *Hindustan Times*, New Delhi edn, 16 February 2008.
27. A. Ghosh's assistants were kindly identified by Prof. B.B. Lal on my request.
28. Ghosh, A., 'The Rajputana Desert: Its Archaeological Aspect', in *Bulletin of the National Institute of Sciences in India*, 1952, vol. I, pp. 37–42, reproduced in *An Archaeological Tour°*, p. 101.
29. Ibid.
30. Ibid., p. 105.
31. See Suraj Bhan's entries 'Drsadvati valley', and 'Sarasvati valley' (the latter jointly authored with A. Ghosh), in Ghosh, A., (ed.), *An Encyclopaedia of Indian Archaeology*, Munshiram Manoharlal, New Delhi, 1989, vol. 2, pp. 131 & 394–95. I should add, however, that Bhan appears to have rejected those identifications in recent years.
32. Bhan, Suraj, 'Changes in the Course of the Yamuna and their Bearing on the Protohistoric Cultures of Haryana', in Deo, S.B., (ed.), *Archaeological Congress and Seminar Papers*, Nagpur, 1972, pp. 125–28, noted by Misra, V.N., 'Indus Civilization and the Rgvedic Sarasvatī', op. cit., p. 521.
33. See Joshi, J.P., Madhu Bala & Jassu Ram, 'The Indus Civilization: A Reconsideration on the Basis of Distribution Maps', in Lal, B.B. & S.P. Gupta, (eds), *Frontiers of the Indus Civilization°*, pp. 511–530.
34. Mughal, M.R., *Ancient Cholistan: Archaeology and Architecture°*.
35. Most figures in Tables 6.1 and 6.3 were graciously communicated to me in April 2006 by Dr. S.P. Gupta, who, before his demise in October 2007, was working on a comprehensive *Archaeological Atlas of the Indus–Saraswati Civilization* which takes into account all recent discoveries of Harappan sites. I am however solely responsible for arranging the figures as shown, and have made a few changes in them. See the following note.
36. In Table 6.1, the row titled 'Cholistan (Pakistan)' is drawn from Mughal, M.R., *Ancient Cholistan: Archaeology and Architecture°*, p. 40; as explained in the text, the figure of 40 Early Harappan sites does not include sites of the Hakra Ware phase.
      For the same reason, in Table 6.3, 281 sites of other pre-Harappan phases (Burj Basket, Kili Ghul Mohammad, Kechi Beg, Togau), most of them located in Baluchistan, are not counted. On the other hand, I included 97 Amri-Nal sites in the Early Harappan category of 'Indus basin & western parts of Pakistan', as that culture is now regarded as Early Harappan. In the same Table, I added a row 'Himachal, Jammu & Delhi' borrowed from figures published

earlier by Joshi, J.P., Madhu Bala, and Jassu Ram, 'The Indus Civilization: A Reconsideration on the Basis of Distribution Maps', op. cit. I did not include Maharashtra's Late Harappan sites (said to number over 20), as I could not find reliable figures for them. Finally, S.P. Gupta's numbers for Gujarat's Mature and Late sites were 205 and 182 respectively, but Possehl has 310 and 198 instead (*The Indus Civilization*°, p. 241), which I have adopted.

37. See the above note. I have added 18 Early Harappan and 22 Mature Harappan sites discovered in Sind after 2002 (date of Possehl's tables), see Mallah, Qasid H., 'Recent Archaeological Discoveries in Sindh, Pakistan', in Osada, Toshiki & Akinori Uesugi, (eds), *Linguistics, Archaeology and the Human Past*, Occasional Paper 3, Research Institute for Humanity and Nature, Kyoto, 2008 (see Appendix).

38. Mughal gives the following proportions of 'camp sites': 7.5% for the Early phase, 6% for the Mature phase, and 26% for the Late phase (see Mughal, M.R., *Ancient Cholistan: Archaeology and Architecture*°, p. 53).

39. For instance, recent surveys in Haryana by Surender Singh (in 1989), Manmohan Kumar (in 2006) and Vivek Dangi (in 2006) have brought to light new Harappan sites, but I have been unable to locate phase-wise details.

40. Possehl, Gregory, *The Indus Civilization*°, p. 241.

41. This figure is read from Fig. 2.19 in ibid., p. 49 (phase 'Harappa'); it may not be very accurate.

42. Kenoyer, Jonathan Mark, *Ancient Cities of the Indus Valley Civilization*°, pp. 27 & 29.

43. McIntosh, Jane R., *A Peaceful Realm*°, p. 24.

44. Ratnagar, Shereen, *Understanding Harappa: Civilization in the Greater Indus Valley*°, pp. 7–8. In fact, Ratnagar only acknowledges '83 habitation sites' (p. 21), from Mughal's survey of 174 Mature Harappan sites (Table 6.1), after excluding sites marked as 'industrial' by Mughal (that is, with a special concentration on production of pottery, metallurgical installations, etc.). There is however no logic in such an exclusion: a Harappan 'industrial' site is first and foremost Harappan, and would have necessarily included residential areas; no one has suggested excluding industrial sites from other regions, such as Chanhu-daro or Balakot, from the list of Harappan settlements.

45. Ibid., p. 24.

46. Kenoyer, Jonathan Mark, 'Culture and Societies of the Indus Tradition', in *India: Historical Beginnings and the Concept of the Aryan*°, p. 47.

47. Possehl, Gregory, *The Indus Civilization*°, p. 241.

48. Ibid., p. 45.

49. Mughal, M.R., *Ancient Cholistan: Archaeology and Architecture*°, p. 22.

50. To draw Figs 6.7, 6.8, 6.9, I combined the sites of V.N. Misra's map in 'Indus Civilization and the Rgvedic Sarasvati', op. cit., p. 515, with those of M.R. Mughal's Figs 5 & 6 in *Ancient Cholistan: Archaeology and Architecture*°, pp. 24 & 25. I separated the three phases in Misra's map; I similarly separated the Early and Mature sites in Mughal's Fig. 5 and omitted the PGW sites in his Fig. 6. (I used standard methods of digital photography, such as layering

and superimposition, to place all sites on the maps as precisely as possible.)

51. Misra, V.N., 'Indus Civilization and the Rgvedic Sarasvatī', op. cit., p. 515.
52. Mughal, M.R., *Ancient Cholistan: Archaeology and Architecture*°, pp. 20 & 22–23.
53. Mughal, M. Rafique, 'Recent Archaeological Research in the Cholistan Desert', in Possehl, Gregory L., (ed.), *Harappan Civilization: A Recent Perspective*, op. cit., p. 94.
54. Ibid., p. 26.
55. Shinde, Vasant, et al., 'Exploration in the Ghaggar Basin and Excavations at Girawad, Farmana (Rohtak District) and Mitathal (Bhiwani District), Haryana', in Osada, Toshiki & Akinori Uesugi, (eds), Occasional Paper 3, *Linguistics, Archaeology and the Human Past*, Research Institute for Humanity and Nature, Kyoto, 2008, p. 82.
56. Ibid., p. 84.
57. Possehl, Gregory L., *Indus Age: The Beginnings*°, p. 384.
58. See note 50 above.
59. Ibid., p. 369.
60. Ibid., p. 377.
61. Ibid., pp. 381–83.
62. Misra, V.N., 'Indus Civilization and the Rgvedic Sarasvatī', op. cit., p. 514.
63. McIntosh, Jane R., *The Ancient Indus Valley: New Perspectives*°, pp. 20–21.
64. Allchin, Raymond, 'The Indus Civilization' in *Encyclopædia Britannica*, 2004 (electronic edition).
65. Allchin, Raymond & Bridget, *Origins of a Civilization*°, p. 220.
66. Ibid., p. 213.
67. Misra, V.N., 'Indus Civilization and the Rgvedic Sarasvatī', op. cit., p. 524.

7. New Horizons

1. Bisht, R.S., 'Excavations at Banawali: 1974–77', in Possehl, Gregory L., (ed.), *Harappan Civilization: A Recent Perspective*, op. cit., p. 120.
2. Bisht, R.S., 'Dholavira and Banawali: Two Different Paradigms of the Harappan Urbis Forma', *Puratattva*, no. 29, 1998–99, p. 16.
3. Possehl, Gregory, *The Indus Civilization*°, p. 77.
4. Lal, B.B., *India 1947–1997*°, p. 93 ff.
5. Lothal's data is entirely drawn from the excavation report by Rao, S.R., *Lothal: A Harappan Port Town*, vol. I, Archaeological Survey of India, New Delhi, 1985.
6. For a fuller discussion, see Lal, B.B., *India 1947–1997*°, p. 71.
7. Khadkikar, A.S., C. Rajshekhar & K.P.N. Kumaran, 'Palaeogeography around the Harappan Port of Lothal, Gujarat, Western India', *Antiquity*, vol. 78, 2004, no. 302, p. 901.
8. Rao, S.R., *Lothal: A Harappan Port Town*, op. cit., p. 21.
9. Dholavira's data is mostly from three papers by Bisht, R.S.: 'Dholavira Excavations: 1990–94', in Joshi, J.P., (ed.), *Facets of Indian Civilization: Essays in Honour of Prof. B.B. Lal*, Aryan Books International, New Delhi, 1997,

vol. I, pp. 107–120; 'Dholavira and Banawali: Two Different Paradigms of the Harappan Urbis Forma', op. cit., pp. 14–37; 'Urban Planning at Dholavira: a Harappan City', op. cit., pp. 11–23.

10. Mathur, U.B., 'Chronology of Harappan Port Towns of Gujarat in the Light of Sea Level Changes during the Holocene', *Man and Environment*, vol. XXVII, 2002, no. 2, p. 64. It is doubtful, however, that Dholavira was actually a 'port town' as proposed by Mathur, as, unlike Lothal, it does not seem to have had berthing facilities.

11. *Periplus of the Erythrean Sea*, see quotation and discussion in Iyengar, R.N. & B.P. Radhakrishna, 'Geographical Location of Vedic *Irina* in Southern Rajasthan', *Journal of the Geological Society of India*, vol. 70, November 2007, pp. 699–705. Also Iyengar, R.N., B.P. Radhakrishna & S.S. Mishra, 'Vedic *Irina* and the Rann-of-Kutch', *Puratattva*, no. 38, 2008, pp. 170–180.

12. Allchin, Raymond & Bridget, *Origins of a Civilization°*, p. 165.

13. Bisht, R.S., 'Dholavira and Banawali: Two Different Paradigms of the Harappan Urbis Forma', op. cit., p. 28.

8. When Rivers Go Haywire

1. These issues are discussed in detail in my *Dawn of Indian Civilization and the Elusive Aryans°* and other studies of the Aryan issue: see Suggested Further Reading under that heading.

2. E.g. Ratnagar, Shereen, *Understanding Harappa: Civilization in the Greater Indus Valley°*, pp. 81, 107, 142.

3. Kenoyer, Jonathan Mark, *Ancient Cities of the Indus Valley Civilization°*, p. 100.

4. Kenoyer, Jonathan Mark, 'Culture and Societies of the Indus Tradition' in *India: Historical Beginnings and the Concept of the Aryan°*, p. 68.

5. Possehl, Gregory, *The Indus Civilization°*, p. 244.

6. Chakrabarti, Dilip K., *The Oxford Companion to Indian Archaeology°*, p. 204.

7. Kenoyer, Jonathan Mark, 'Culture and Societies of the Indus Tradition', op. cit., p. 68.

8. Singh, Gurdip, 'The Indus Valley Culture Seen in the Context of Post-glacial Climate and Ecological Studies in North-west India', *Archaeology and Physical Anthropology in Oceania*, vol. 6, 1971, no. 2, pp. 177–189.

9. Misra, V.N., in 'Climate, a Factor in the Rise and Fall of the Indus Civilization: Evidence from Rajasthan and Beyond', Lal, B.B. & S.P. Gupta, (eds), *Frontiers of the Indus Civilization°*, pp. 484.

10. Shaffer, Jim G., and Diane A. Lichtenstein, 'Ethnicity and Change in the Indus Valley Cultural Tradition', in Kenoyer, Jonathan Mark, (ed.), *Old Problems and New Perspectives in the Archaeology of South Asia*, University of Wisconsin, Wisconsin, 1989, pp. 117–126.

11. Bryson, R.A. & A.M. Swain, 'Holocene Variations of Monsoon Rainfall in Rajasthan', *Quaternary Research*, vol. 16, 1981, pp. 135–145.

12. Madella, Marco & Dorian Q. Fuller, 'Palaeoecology and the Harappan

Civilisation of South Asia: A Reconsideration', *Quaternary Science Reviews* 25, 2006, p. 1297.

13. Possehl, Gregory L., *The Indus Civilization°*, p. 15.

14. Courty, Marie-Agnès, 'Integration of Sediment and Soil Information in the Reconstruction of Protohistoric and Historic Landscapes of the Ghaggar Plain (North-West India)', in Frifelt, Karen & Per Sorensen, (eds), *South Asian Archaeology 1985*, Scandinavian Institute of Asian Studies, Occasional Papers no. 4, Curzon Press, London, 1989, p. 259.

15. McKean, M.B., *The Palynology of Balakot, a Pre-Harappan and Harappan Age Site in Las Bela, Pakistan,* PhD thesis, Southern Methodist University, Dallas, 1983, quoted in Madella, Marco & Dorian Q. Fuller, 'Palaeoecology and the Harappan Civilisation of South Asia: A Reconsideration', op. cit., p. 1292.

16. Enzel, Y., et al., 'High-Resolution Holocene Environmental Changes in the Thar Desert, Northwestern India', *Science*, vol. 284, 2 April 1999, pp. 125–128.

17. Wasson, R.J., et al., 'Geomorphology, Late Quaternary Stratigraphy and Palaeoclimatology of the Thar Dune Field', in *Zeitschrift für Geomorphologie*, N.F. Supplementband 45, May 1983, pp. 117–151; partly reproduced in *Vedic Sarasvati°*, p. 222.

18. Naidu, P.D., 'Onset of an Arid Climate at 3.5 ka in the Tropics: Evidence from Monsoon Upwelling Record', *Current Science*, vol. 71, 1996, pp. 715–718.

19. Rad, Ulrich von, et al., 'A 5000-yr Record of Climate Change in Varved Sediments from the Oxygen Minimum Zone off Pakistan, Northeastern Arabian Sea', *Quaternary Research*, vol. 51, 1999, pp. 39–53.

20. Phadtare, Netajirao R., 'Sharp Decrease in Summer Monsoon Strength 4000–3500 cal yr B.P. in the Central Higher Himalaya of India Based on Pollen Evidence from Alpine Peat', *Quaternary Research*, vol. 53, 2000, pp. 122–129.

21. Staubwasser, M., et al., 'Climate Change at the 4.2 ka BP Termination of the Indus Valley Civilization and Holocene South Asian Monsoon Variability', *Geophysical Research Letters*, vol. 30, 2003, no. 8, p. 1425.

22. Gupta, Anil K., et al., 'Adaptation and Human Migration, and Evidence of Agriculture Coincident with Changes in the Indian Summer Monsoon during the Holocene', *Current Science*, vol. 90, 25 April 2006, no. 8, pp. 1082–1090.

23. Wright, Rita P., et al., 'Water Supply and History: Harappa and the Beas Regional Survey', *Antiquity*, 2008, vol. 82, pp. 37–48.

24. For recent reviews see those discussed in Madella, Marco, & Dorian Q. Fuller, 'Palaeoecology and the Harappan Civilisation of South Asia: A Reconsideration', op. cit.; Fuller, Dorian Q. and Marco Madella, 'Issues in Harappan Archaeobotany: Retrospect and Prospect', in Settar, S. & Ravi Korisettar, (eds), *Indian Archaeology in Retrospect*, vol. 2: *Protohistory, Archaeology of the Harappan Civilization,* Manohar & Indian Council of Historical Research, New Delhi, 2000, pp. 317–390; Korisettar, Ravi & R. Ramesh, 'The Indian Monsoon: Roots, Relations and Relevance', in Settar, S. & Ravi Korisettar, (eds), *Indian Archaeology in Retrospect*, vol. 3: *Archaeology and Interactive Disciplines,* Manohar & Indian Council of Historical Research, New Delhi, 2002, pp. 23–59.

25. Fuller, Dorian Q. & Marco Madella, 'Issues in Harappan Archaeobotany: Retrospect and Prospect', op. cit., pp. 363 & 366.
26. Madella, Marco & Dorian Q. Fuller, 'Palaeoecology and the Harappan Civilisation of South Asia: A Reconsideration', op. cit., p. 1283.
27. Gupta, Anil K., et al., 'Adaptation and Human Migration . . .', op. cit., p. 1086.
28. Weiss, H., et al., 'The Genesis and Collapse of Third Millennium North Mesopotamian Civilization', Science, 261–5124, 1993, pp. 995–1004. Also Kerr, R.A., 'Sea-floor Dust Shows Drought Felled Akkadian Empire', Science, vol. 279, 1998, pp. 325–326.
29. Thompson, L.G., et al., 'Kilimanjaro Ice Core Records: Evidence of Holocene Climate Change in Tropical Africa', Science, vol. 298, 2002, pp. 589–593.
30. An, Cheng-Bang, et al., 'Climate Change and Cultural Response around 4000 cal yr B.P. in the Western Part of Chinese Loess Plateau', Quaternary Research, vol. 63, 2005, pp. 347–352.
31. Booth, R.K., et al., 'A Severe Centennial-scale Drought in Midcontinental North America 4200 Years Ago and Apparent Global Linkages', The Holocene, vol. 15, 2005, pp. 321–328.
32. Nath, Bhola, 'The Role of Animal Remains in the Early Prehistoric Cultures of India', Indian Museum Bulletin, Calcutta, 1969, p. 107, quoted by Jagat Pati Joshi, in Lal, B.B., et al., Excavations at Kalibangan, vol. 1, Archaeological Survey of India, New Delhi, 2003, p. 19.
33. Banerjee, S. & S. Chakraborty, 'Remains of the Great One-horned Rhinoceros, Rhinoceros unicornis, Linnacus from Rajasthan', Science and Culture, vol. 39, Calcutta, October 1973, pp. 430–431, quoted by Jagat Pati Joshi in Lal, B.B., et al., Excavations at Kalibangan, op. cit., p. 18.
34. Thomas, P.K., 'Investigations into the Archaeofauna of Harappan Sites in Western India', Indian Archaeology in Retrospect, vol. 2: Protohistory, Archaeology of the Harappan Civilization, op. cit., p. 414 & 417.
35. I developed this point in Danino, Michel, 'Revisiting the Role of Climate in the Collapse of the Indus–Sarasvati Civilization', Puratattva, no. 38, 2008, pp. 159–169.
36. E.g. Possehl, Gregory, The Indus Civilization°, p. 238.
37. Raikes, R.L. & R.H.J. Dyson, 'The Prehistoric Climate of Baluchistan and the Indus Valley', American Anthropologist, vol. 63, 1961, pp. 265–81.
38. In the words of Fairservis, Walter A., 'The Origin, Character and Decline of an Early Civilization', Novitates, no. 2302, 1967, pp. 1–48, partly reproduced in Lahiri, Nayanjot, The Decline and Fall of the Indus Civilization°, p. 261.
39. Ibid.
40. Jansen, Michael R.N., 'Mohenjo Daro and the River Indus', in Meadows, Azra & Peter S. Meadows, (eds), The Indus River: Biodiversity, Resources, Humankind, Oxford University Press, Karachi, 1999, p. 379, note 58, quoting Jorgensen, et al., 'Morphology and Dynamics of the Indus River: Implications for the Mohenjodaro site', in Shroder, J.F.J., (ed.), Himalayas to the Sea: Geology, Geomorphology and the Quaternary, Routledge, London, 1991, p. 324.

41. Dales, George F., 'Mohenjodaro Miscellany', in Possehl, Gregory L., (ed.), *Harappan Civilization: A Recent Perspective*, op. cit., p. 104.
42. Lambrick, H.T., 'The Indus Flood Plain and the "Indus" Civilization', *Geographical Journal*, 1967, 133/4: 483–95, reproduced in Lahiri, Nayanjot, *The Decline and Fall of the Indus Civilization*°, p. 182.
43. Michael Jansen argues that the location of Mohenjo-daro is explicable only through boat transport. See his 'Settlement Networks of the Indus civilization', in *Indian Archaeology in Retrospect, vol. 2: Protohistory, Archaeology of the Harappan Civilization*, op. cit., p. 118.
44. Flam, Louis, 'Ecology and Population Mobility in the Prehistoric Settlement of the Lower Indus Valley, Sindh, Pakistan', in *The Indus River: Biodiversity, Resources, Humankind*, op. cit., p. 317. In the same volume, Michael D. Harvey & Sanley A. Schumm endorse Lambrick's theory of avulsion of the Indus; see their 'Indus River Dynamics and the Abandonment of Mohenjo-daro', pp. 333–348.
45. Lal, B.B., *Earliest Civilization of South Asia*°, p. 245.
46. Allchin, Raymond & Bridget, *Origins of a Civilization*°, p. 211.
47. Kenoyer, Jonathan Mark, *Ancient Cities of the Indus Valley Civilization*°, p. 173.
48. Flam, Louis, 'The Prehistoric Indus River System and the Indus Civilization in Sindh', *Man and Environment*, 24: 2, 1999, p. 55.
49. Possehl, Gregory, *The Indus Civilization*°, p. 241.
50. Lal, B.B., *The Sarasvati Flows On*°, p. 77.
51. Chakrabarti, Dilip K. & Sukhdev Saini, *The Problem of the Sarasvati River*°, pp. 37–38.
52. Chakrabarti, Dilip K., *The Archaeology of Ancient Indian Cities*°, p. 140.
53. McIntosh, Jane R., *A Peaceful Realm*°, p. 190.
54. Agrawal, D.P., *The Indus Civilization*°, p. 304.
55. Misra, V.N., 'Indus Civilization and the Rgvedic Sarasvatī', op. cit., p. 523.
56. Madella, Marco & Dorian Q. Fuller, 'Palaeoecology and the Harappan Civilisation of South Asia: A Reconsideration', *Quaternary Science Reviews*, vol. 25, 2006, pp. 1285–86.
57. Possehl, Gregory L., *The Indus Civilization*°, p. 240.
58. E.g. Wax, Emily, 'A Sacred River Endangered by Global Warming: Glacial Source of Ganges Is Receding', *Washington Post*, 17 June 2007; Chengappa, Raj, 'Apocalypse Now', *India Today International*, 23 April 2007.

9. The Tangible Heritage

1. Thapar, Romila, *The Penguin History of Early India: From the Origins to AD 1300*, Penguin Books, New Delhi, 2003, p. 88.
2. Ibid.
3. Ratnagar, Shereen, *Understanding Harappa: Civilization in the Greater Indus Valley*°, p. 4.
4. Ghosh, A., *The City in Early Historical India*, Indian Institute of Advanced

Study, Shimla, 1973, extracted in Lahiri, Nayanjot, (ed.), *The Decline and Fall of the Indus Civilization°*, p. 302.

5. Possehl, Gregory L., *The Indus Civilization°*, ch. 13.

6. Kenoyer, J. Mark, *Ancient Cities of the Indus Valley Civilization°*, p. 183.

7. Shaffer, Jim, 'Harappan Culture: A Reconsideration', in *Harappan Civilization: A Recent Perspective*, op. cit., p. 49.

8. Jim Shaffer quoted by Possehl, Gregory L., 'The Harappan Civilization: A Contemporary Perspective', in *Harappan Civilization: A Recent Perspective*, op. cit., p. 26.

9. Ratnagar, Shereen, *The End of the Great Harappan Tradition°*, p. 28.

10. Wheeler, R.E.M., 'Archaeological Fieldwork in India: Planning Ahead', *Ancient India*, no. 5, 1949, p. 5.

11. Sergent, Bernard, *Genèse de l'Inde*, Payot, Paris, 1997, p. 105.

12. Ibid., p. 113.

13. Piggot, Stuart, *Prehistoric India*, Middlesex, 1961, partly reproduced in Lahiri, Nayanjot, (ed.), *The Decline and Fall of the Indus Civilization°*, p. 284.

14. Ibid., p. 282. (Italics mine.)

15. Basham, A.L., *The Wonder That Was India*, third edn, Rupa & Co., Calcutta, 1981, p. 29. (Italics mine.)

16. Witzel, Michael, 'Autochthonous Aryans? The Evidence from Old Indian and Iranian Texts', *Electronic Journal of Vedic Studies*, vol. 7, no. 3, 25 May 2001, § 8.

17. Shaffer, Jim G., 'Reurbanization: The Eastern Panjab and Beyond' in Spodek, H. & D.M. Srinivasan, (eds), *Urban Form and Meaning in South Asia: The Shaping of Cities from Prehistoric to Precolonial Times*, National Gallery of Art & University Press of New England, Washington D.C., 1993, pp. 53–67.

18. Coningham, R.A.E., 'Dark Age or Continuum?' in *Archaeology of Early Historic South Asia°*, pp. 54–72.

19. Eltsov, Piotr Andreevich, *From Harappa to Hastinapura°* (based on a 2004 PhD thesis with the same title).

20. Eltsov, Piotr Andreevich, p. 186 of his PhD thesis, 2004 (see note 19).

21. Eltsov, Piotr Andreevich, p. 351 of his PhD thesis, 2004 (see note 19).

22. Coningham, R.A.E., 'Dark Age or Continuum?' in *Archaeology of Early Historic South Asia°*, p. 70.

23. Chakrabarti, D.K., 'Post-Mauryan States of Mainland South Asia (c. BC 185 – AD 320)', in *Archaeology of Early Historic South Asia°*, p. 298.

24. *Arthashastra*, 2.4.3–5. See *The Kautilya Arthasastra*, tr. Kangle, R.P., Motilal Banarsidass, New Delhi, 1986, part II, p. 68.

25. Chakrabarti, Dilip K., *The Archaeology of Ancient Indian Cities*, p. 176.

26. Kenoyer, J. Mark, 'New Perspectives on the Mauryan and Kushana Periods', in Olivelle, Patrick, (ed.), *Between the Empires: Society in India 300 BCE to 400 CE*, Oxford University Press, New York, 2006, p. 39.

27. See Allchin, F.R., 'Mauryan Architecture and Art', in *Archaeology of Early Historic South Asia°*, pp. 236–38.

28. Gaur, R.C., *Excavations at Atranjikhera: Early Civilization of the Upper Ganga Basin*, Motilal Banarsidass, Delhi, 1983, pp. 256-57.

29. Allchin, Bridget, 'South Asia's Living Past', in Allchin, Bridget, (ed.), *Living Traditions: Studies in the Ethnoarchaeology of South Asia*, Oxford & IBH, New Delhi, 1994, p. 5, with reference to Sarcina, Anna, 'The Private House at Mohenjo-daro', in Schotsmans, J. & M. Taddei, (eds), *South Asian Archaeology 1977*, Istituto Universitario Orientale, Naples, 1979, pp. 433-462.

30. Lal, B.B., *The Sarasvatī Flows On*°, pp. 93-95.

31. Jarrige, Jean-François, 'Du néolithique à la civilisation de l'Inde ancienne', in *Arts Asiatiques*, vol. L-1995, École Française d'Extrême-Orient, 1995, p. 24.

32. See Ghosh, A., (ed.), *An Encyclopaedia of Indian Archaeology*, Munshiram Manoharlal, New Delhi, 1989, vol. 1, pp. 304-305. See also Lal, B.B., 'Excavation at Hastinapura and other Explorations in the Upper Ganga and Sutlej Basins 1950-52', *Ancient India*, Archaeological Survey of India, New Delhi, no. 10-11, 1954 & 1955, p. 25, and Mani, B.R., 'Excavations at Siswania (District Basti, U.P.): 1995-97', *Puratattva*, no. 34, 2003-2004, p. 103.

33. E.g. at Tripuri and Vaisali, see *An Encyclopaedia of Indian Archaeology*, op. cit., p. 294; also at Hastinapura, see Lal, B.B., 'Excavation at Hastinapura and Other Explorations in the Upper Ganga and Sutlej Basins 1950-52', op. cit., p. 25 & plates X to XI.

34. Shaffer, Jim G., 'Reurbanization: The Eastern Panjab and Beyond', op. cit., pp. 60, 58 & 63.

35. Malville, J. McKim & Lalit M. Gujral, (eds), *Ancient Cities, Sacred Skies: Cosmic Geometries and City Planning in Ancient India*, Indira Gandhi National Centre for the Arts & Aryan Books International, New Delhi, 2000, p. 3.

36. Bisht, R.S., 'Urban Planning at Dholavira: A Harappan City', in ibid., p. 20.

37. Danino, Michel, (1) 'Dholavira's Geometry: A Preliminary Study' in *Puratattva*, no. 35, 2004-05, pp. 76-84; (2) 'Unravelling Dholavira's Geometry', in Reddy, P. Chenna, (ed.), *Recent Researches in Archaeology, History and Culture (Festschrift to Prof. K.V. Raman)*, Agam Kala Prakashan, Delhi, 2010, pp. 179-193; (3) 'New Insights into Harappan Town-Planning, Proportions and Units, with Special Reference to Dholavira', *Man and Environment*, vol. XXXIII, no. 1, 2008, pp. 66-79.

38. All references in this paragraph can be found in 'New Insights into Harappan Town-Planning, Proportions and Units', op. cit.

39. *Shatapatha Brāhmana*, III.5.1.1-6.

40. The *Baudhāyana Shulbasūtra* 4.3 specifies 30 *prakramas* for the western side and 24 for the eastern, a *prakrama* being defined as 30 *angulas* (or digits), therefore about 53 cm. See Sen, S.N. & A.K. Bag, (eds), *The Sulbasūtras*, Indian National Science Academy, New Delhi, 1983, pp. 81, 171 & 177.

41. Varahamihira, *Brhat Samhita*, 53.4, tr. Bhat, M. Ramakrishna, Motilal Banarsidass, New Delhi, 1981, vol. 1, p. 451.

42. Varahamihira, *Brhat Samhita*, 53.5, ibid., p. 452.

43. In Danino, Michel, 'Unravelling Dholavira's Geometry', op. cit.

44. See Danino, Michel, 'New Insights into Harappan Town-Planning, Proportions and Units, with Special Reference to Dholavira', op. cit.
45. Filippi, Gian Giuseppe & Bruno Marcolongo, (eds), *Kāmpilya: Quest for a Mahābhārata City*, D.K. Printworld, New Delhi, 1999, p. 10.
46. Filippi, Gian Giuseppe, 'The Kampilya Archeological Project', article published online at: http://atimes.com/ind-pak/DC21Df02.html (accessed 15 September 2009).
47. Ibid.
48. Filippi, Gian Giuseppe, & Bruno Marcolongo, (eds), *Kāmpilya: Quest for a Mahābhārata City*, op. cit., p. 11.
49. Kenoyer, Jonathan Mark, *Ancient Cities of the Indus Valley Civilization°*, p. 98.
50. Mainkar, V.B., 'Metrology in the Indus Civilization', in Lal, B.B. & S.P. Gupta, (eds), *Frontiers of the Indus Civilization°*, pp. 144-45.
51. Kosambi, D.D., 'On the Study and Metrology of Silver Punch-marked Coins', *New Indian Antiquary* 4(2), p. 53, quoted by Possehl, Gregory L., in *Indus Age: the Writing System°*, p. 75.
52. Mitchiner, John E., *Studies in the Indus Valley Inscriptions*, Oxford & IBH, Delhi, 1978, p. 14-15, quoted by Possehl, Gregory L., in *Indus Age: the Writing System°*, p. 75.
53. Sharma, Ram Sharan, *Advent of the Aryans in India°*, p. 48.
54. E.g. Kenoyer, Jonathan Mark, *Ancient Cities of the Indus Valley Civilization°*, p. 98.
55. Mainkar, V.B., 'Metrology in the Indus Civilization', op. cit., p. 146. (Mainkar mistakenly divided 46 mm by 27 graduations, which gave him an erroneous value; 46 must be divided by 26 divisions, not by 27 graduations.)
56. Raju, L. & V.B. Mainkar, 'Development of Length and Area Measures in South India–Part 1', *Metric Measures*, Ministry of International Trade, New Delhi, vol. 7, January 1964, pp. 3-12 (see Table, p. 10).
57. Chattopadhyaya, Debiprasad, *History of Science and Technology in Ancient India*, Firma KLM, Calcutta, vol. 1, 1986, pp. 231-33.
58. Mackay, E.J.H., *Further Excavations at Mohenjo-daro*, Government of India, Delhi, 1938; republ. Munshiram Manoharlal, New Delhi, 1998, vol. 1, p. 405.
59. Balasubramaniam, R., 'On the Continuity of Engineering Tradition from the Harappan to Ganga Civilization', *Man and Environment*, vol. 33, 2008, pp. 101-105. Also Balasubramaniam, R. & J.P. Joshi, 'Analysis of Terracotta Scale of Harappan Civilization from Kalibangan', *Current Science*, vol. 95, no. 5, 10 September 2008, pp. 588-89.
60. *Arthashastra* 2.20.19. See *Kautilya Arthasastra*, tr. R.P. Kangle, op. cit., part II, p. 139.
61. Danino, Michel, 'New Insights into Harappan Town-Planning, Proportions and Units, with Special Reference to Dholavira', op. cit.
62. Varahamihira's *Brhat Samhita*, tr. Bhat, Ramakrishna M., Motilal Banarsidass, New Delhi, 1981, vol. 1, p. 642, 68.105.
63. Ibid., p. 556, 58.30.
64. Kak, Subhash, *The Astronomical Code of the Rgveda°*, pp. 101-02 & 124.

The exact ratio is 107.6 (the sun's average distance to the earth is 149.5 million kilometres while its diameter is 1.39 million kilometres).

65. Maula, Erkka, 'The Calendar Stones from Mohenjo-daro', in Jansen, M. & G. Urban, (eds), *Interim Reports on fieldwork carried out at Mohenjo-daro, Pakistan 1982–83*, German Research Project Mohenjo-daro, Aachen & Istituto Italiano Per Il Medio Ed Estremo Oriente, Roma, 1984, vol. I, pp. 159–170.

66. Balasubramaniam, R., 'On the Mathematical Significance of the Dimensions of the Delhi Iron Pillar', *Current Science*, vol. 95, no. 6, 25 September 2008, pp. 766–70. Balasubramaniam has extended this research to cave complexes of the Mauryan age and further to the Taj Mahal complex: 'New Insights on Metrology during the Mauryan Period', *Current Science*, vol. 97, no. 5, 10 September 2009, pp. 680–682, and 'New Insights on the Modular Planning of the Taj Mahal', *Current Science*, vol. 97, no. 1, 10 July 2009, pp. 42–49.

67. Mohan Pant and Shuji Funo wrote at least six papers on their research, beginning in 2000; the main papers for our purpose are: (1) 'Considerations on the Layout Pattern of Streets and Settlement Blocks of Thimi: A Study on the Planning Modules of Kathmandu Valley Towns', Part I, *Journal of Architecture, Planning and Environmental Engineering*, Architectural Institute of Japan, no. 574, December 2003, pp. 83–90. (2) 'The Grid and Modular Measures in the Town Planning of Mohenjodaro and Kathmandu Valley: A Study on Modular Measures in Block and Plot Divisions in the Planning of Mohenjodaro and Sirkap (Pakistan), and Thimi (Kathmandu Valley)', *Journal of Asian Architecture and Building Engineering*, vol. 4, May 2005, no. 1, pp. 51–59, available online at www.jstage.jst.go.jp/article/jaabe/4/1/51/_pdf (accessed 10 September 2008).

68. Pant, Mohan & Shuji Funo, 'The Grid and Modular Measures in the Town Planning of Mohenjodaro and Kathmandu Valley', op. cit., p. 57.

69. *Arthashastra* 2.20.18–19, see *The Kautilya Arthasastra*, tr. Kangle, R.P., op. cit., p. 139.

70. Pant, Mohan & Shuji Funo, 'The Grid and Modular Measures in the Town Planning of Mohenjodaro and Kathmandu Valley', op. cit., p. 54.

71. Ibid., p. 57.

72. Kenoyer, J.M., *Ancient Cities of the Indus Valley Civilization°*, p. 135.

73. E.g. Kenoyer, Jonathan Mark, Massimo Vidale & Kuldeep K. Bhan, 'Carnelian Bead Production in Khambat, India: An Ethnoarchaeological Study', in Bridget Allchin, (ed.), *Living Traditions: Studies in the Ethnoarchaeology of South Asia*, Oxford & IBH, New Delhi, 1994, pp. 281–306.

74. Lal, B.B., *The Sarasvati Flows On°*, ch. 4.

75. Ibid., pp. 132–35.

76. Mackay, E.J.H., *Further Excavations at Mohenjo-daro*, op. cit., vol. 1, pp. 273 & 538.

77. Ibid., p. 532–33.

78. Kenoyer, J.M., *Ancient Cities of the Indus Valley Civilization*, p. 44–45 & 186, also Jarrige, J.-F., *Les Cités oubliées de l'Indus°*, p. 87 (fig. 41) & 88 (fig. 42).

79. Casal, Jean-Marie, *La Civilisation de l'Indus et ses énigmes°*, p. 122.

80. Kenoyer, J.M., *Ancient Cities of the Indus Valley Civilization*, p. 90.
81. Kenoyer, J.M., 'The Indus Civilization', *Wisconsin Academy Review*, Madison, March 1987, p. 26.
82. Meadow, R.H. & J.M. Kenoyer, 'Recent Discoveries and Highlights from Excavations at Harappa: 1998–2000', online article at: www.harappa.com/indus4/print.html (accessed 15 September 2009).
83. Contrary to conventional histories, the first attested appearance of the Brāhmī script is not with Ashoka's edicts, but two centuries earlier at Anuradhapura in Sri Lanka: see Allchin, F.R., *Archaeology of Early Historic South Asia*°, pp. 176–179 & 209–211. Of course, evidence for a similar or even earlier date in the Ganges region cannot be ruled out and may emerge one day.
84. See Rao, S.R., *The Lost City of Dvaraka*, Aditya Prakashan, New Delhi, 1999, and Gaur, A.S., *Archaeology of Bet Dwarka Island*, Aryan Books International, New Delhi, 2005. For the dates, see ch. 2 of the latter book and *Current Science*, vol. 82, no. 11, 10 June 2002, pp. 1352–56.
85. For a discussion of the inscription (but within the framework of S.R. Rao's decipherment of the Indus script), see *The Lost City of Dvaraka*, op. cit., p. 115 ff.
86. Jayaswal, K.P., 'The Vikramkhol Inscription', *The Indian Antiquary*, 1933, vol. LXII, p. 60.
87. Lal, B.B., *The Earliest Civilization of South Asia*°, p. 157; Sali, S.A., 'The Extension of the Harappan Culture in the Deccan', in Joshi, J.P., (ed.), *Facets of Indian Civilization: Essays in Honour of Prof. B.B. Lal*, op. cit., p. 127; Agrawal, D.P., *L'archéologie de l'Inde*, Éditions du CNRS, Paris, 1986, pp. 266 & 269.
88. Sinha, B.P. & Sita Ram Roy, *Vaisali Excavations (1958–1962)*, Directorate of Archaeology and Museums, Patna, 1969, p. 121, Pl. XXX, no. 24. This find is commented on by Mahadevan, Iravatham, in ' "Murukan" in the Indus Script', *Journal of the Institute of Asian Studies*, March 1999, available online at http://murugan.org/research/mahadevan.htm (retrieved May 2008).
89. Mahadevan, Iravatham, ' "Murukan" in the Indus Script', op. cit.
90. Fabri, C.L., 'The punch-marked coins: a survival of the Indus civilization', *Journal of the Royal Asiatic Society*, 1935, p. 308. Fabri was not the first scholar to point to such parallels; he was preceded by Pran Nath in 1931 and Durga Prasad in 1933, see K.P. Jayaswal's note with the same title as Fabri's paper, in the same issue, pp. 720–21.
91. Ibid., p. 311.
92. Gonda, J., *Change and Continuity in Indian Religion*, Mouton & Co., The Hague, 1965, p. 26.
93. Sharma, Savita, *Early Indian Symbols: Numismatic Evidence*, Agam Kala Prakashan, Delhi, 1990, plates 10–13.
94. Langdon, Stephen, 'The Indus Script', in Marshall, John, (ed.), *Mohenjo-daro and the Indus Civilization*, Arthur Probsthain, London, 1931, 3 vols, several Indian reprints.

95. Hunter, G.R., PhD thesis of 1929 published in 1934, *The Script of Harappa and Mohenjo-daro and Its Connection with Other Scripts*; reprint Munshiram Manoharlal, New Delhi, 2003.

96. Kak, Subhash, 'On the Decipherment of the Indus Script: A Preliminary Study of its Connection with Brahmi', in *Indian Journal of History of Science*, no. 22, 1987, pp. 51-62; 'A Frequency Analysis of the Indus Script', *Cryptologia*, no. 12, 1988, pp. 129-143; 'Indus Writing', *Mankind Quarterly*, no. 30, 1989, pp. 113-118; 'Indus and Brahmi: Further Connections', *Cryptologia*, no. 14, 1990, pp. 169-183. The results of those four articles are summarized and updated in a 'Note on Harappan Writing', *Brahmavidya: The Adyar Library Bulletin*, vol. 66, 2002, pp. 79-85; I drew Table 9.4 from this last note.

97. Salomon, Richard, *Indian Epigraphy*, University of Texas, Austin, 1998, Indian reprint Munshiram Manoharlal, New Delhi, n.d., p. 29.

98. Chakrabarti, Dilip K., *India: An Archaeological History°*, p. 291.

99. Sircar, D.C., 'Inscriptions in Sanskritic and Dravidian Languages', *Ancient India*, no. 3, 1953, p. 215.

100. Jarrige, Jean-François, 'Du néolithique à la civilisation de l'Inde ancienne', op. cit., p. 30.

101. Agrawal, D.P., 'An Indocentric Corrective to History of Science', 2002, p. 5, online: www.infinityfoundation.com/indic_colloq/papers/paper_agrawal.pdf (accessed 15 September 2009).

10. The Intangible Heritage

1. For instance at Hastinapura, see Lal, B.B., 'Excavation at Hastinapura and other Explorations in the Upper Ganga and Sutlej Basins 1950-52', op. cit., p. 43. Fig. 10-1 shows swastikas from Rupar and Ahichchhatra, both from Sharma, Y.D., 'Explorations of Historical Sites', *Ancient India*, no. 9, 1953, pp. 129 & 139.

2. Sarkar, H. & B.M. Pande, *Symbols and Graphic Representations in Indian Inscriptions*, Aryan Books International, New Delhi, 1999, ch. 3; Sharma, Savita, *Early Indian Symbols*, op. cit., ch. 3.

3. From a copper plate of Dhruva II of Gujarat Rashtrakuta branch, 884 CE: see Sarkar, H. & B.M. Pande, *Symbols and Graphic Representations in Indian Inscriptions*, op. cit., plate IX, and also pp. 64, 128.

4. Chakrabarti, Dilip K., *India: An Archaeological History°*, p. 154.

5. Mahadevan, Iravatham, 'The Cult Object on Unicorn Seals: A Sacred Filter?', *Puratattva*, no. 13 & 14, 1981-83, pp. 165-186; 'The sacred filter standard facing the unicorn: more evidence', in Parpola, Asko & Petteri Koskikallio, (eds), *South Asian Archaeology 1993*, Suomalainen Tiedeakatemia, Helsinki, 1994, I.435-450.

6. See the second reference in the preceding note.

7. See for instance Ranade, H.G., *Illustrated Dictionary of Vedic Rituals°*, pp. 40, 95, 114, 143, 149.

8. Rig Veda, 1.135.8, 10.97.5. Many passages in Atharva Veda. In the Rig Veda, the sacred sticks (*arani*) which, rubbed together, produce Agni, are partly made of the *ashvattha*.

9. Reproduced in Sharma, Savita, *Early Indian Symbols: Numismatic Evidence*, op. cit., p. 110.

10. Aravamuthan, T.G., *Some Survivals of the Harappa Culture*, Karnatak Publishing House, Bombay, 1942, p. 46 ff (my thanks to Dr R. Nagaswamy for kindly procuring a copy of this book). More recently, also by Sharma, Savita, *Early Indian Symbols: Numismatic Evidence*, op. cit., p. 101.

11. Harappan female figurines with large earrings can be seen for instance in Mackay, E.J.H., *Further Excavations at Mohenjo-daro*, op. cit., vol. 2, plates LXXIII no. 6 & LXXIV no. 15.

12. E.g. Miller, Barbara Stoler, (ed.), *Exploring India's Sacred Art: selected writings of Stella Kramrisch*, Indira Gandhi National Centre for the Arts & Motilal Banarsidass, New Delhi, 1994, p. 72, and Kramrisch's endorsement of this survival (she calls it a 'spade-shaped head').

13. E.g. Franz, Heinrich Gerhard, (ed.), *L'Inde ancienne: histoire et civilisation*, Bordas, Paris, 1990, p. 356.

14. *Exploring India's Sacred Art: selected writings of Stella Kramrisch*, op. cit., p. 87.

15. Gonda, J., *Change and Continuity in Indian Religion*, op. cit., p. 26, with reference to Kramrisch, Stella, *Indian Sculpture*, Y.M.C.A. Publishing House, Calcutta & Oxford University Press, London, 1933, pp. 11 & 143.

16. Varenne, Jean, *L'art de l'Inde*, Flammarion, Paris, 1983, p. 105.

17. Rao, S.R., *Dawn and Devolution of the Indus Civilization*, p. 187. See a more detailed explanation in Lal, B.B., *India 1947–1997°*, pp. 88–91.

18. E.g. Kenoyer, J.M., *Ancient Cities of the Indus Valley Civilization°*, pp. 59 & 120.

19. See also parallels between Mohenjo-daro's Great Bath and the tanks of Modhera or Sravana-Belgola by Stietencron, Heinrich von, 'Les religions', in Franz, Heinrich Gerhard, (ed.), *L'Inde ancienne: histoire et civilisation*, op. cit., pp. 181 & 186.

20. E.g. Kenoyer, J.M., *Ancient Cities of the Indus Valley Civilization*, p. 83.

21. Ibid., pp. 119–120.

22. Marshall, John, (ed.), *Mohenjo-daro and the Indus Civilization*, op. cit., vol. 1, p. vi.

23. At Baghor (Madhya Pradesh). See Kenoyer, J.M., et al., 'An Upper Palaeolithic Shrine in India?' *Antiquity*, LVII, 1983, pp. 88–94, reproduced in Allchin, F.R. & Dilip K. Chakrabarti, (eds), *A Source-book of Indian Archaeology*, Munshiram Manoharlal, New Delhi, 2003, vol. III, pp. 49–54. Let us note that the excavators understood the significance of the triangular stone that symbolizes the mother goddess only after observing similar stones in several nearby tribal temples—over 10,000 years apart! In conclusion, the authors noted 'the remarkable continuity of religious beliefs and motifs in the Indian subcontinent'.

24. Rig Veda, 9.96.6.

25. See Krishna Yajur Veda, 1.8.22, 2.2.10, 2.2.11, 4.5.8, etc. (Verse numbers are from A.B. Keith's translation, which will also be used as a reference in further notes below.)
26. Hymn 6.74 of the Rig Veda is dedicated to 'Soma-Rudra' as a fused god. The fusion of gods is frequent in the Rig Veda (Heaven-Earth, Indra-Agni, Mitra-Varuna . . .), a reminder that all those gods and goddesses are merely different faces of the same divinity, as the famous hymn 1.164.46 explicitly states. The Rig-Vedic religion is not polytheism, but 'polymorphism'.
27. Shiva as a god appears in the Yajur Veda. European Sanskritists decided that the word *shiva* found in the *Rudra Prasna* of the Krishna Yajur Veda (ch. 24) is only an adjective (meaning 'good' or 'auspicious') and not a proper noun. But traditional Vedic scholars disagree: priest and poet Prof. Vishnu Narayan Namboodiri of Kerala, inheritor of a lineage that has orally transmitted the Krishna Yajur Veda for many centuries, explains (personal communication) that several of the eleven mentions of the word *shiva* in this text can only be proper nouns (capitalized in the following examples), appearing as they do next to the adjective *shiva*: *Mīdhushtama sivatama Shivo nah sumanā bhava* ('O Shiva, most auspicious one, give us your blessings and be gracious to us!') or *Namah Shivāya cha shivatarāya cha* ('Salutations to Shiva and to the most auspicious one!').
28. Kenoyer, J.M., *Ancient Cities of the Indus Valley Civilization°*, p. 114.
29. E.g. Rig Veda, 8.68.15; Krishna Yajur Veda, 4.7.15.w.
30. Rig Veda, 6.16.46, 10.115.9.
31. Ibid., 10.15.6.
32. Ibid., 6.1.6.
33. Ibid., 6.32.3.
34. Ibid., 7.95.4.
35. Except for the *gaur*'s human face (my own observation), the seal is so described by Allchin, Raymond & Bridget, in *Origins of a Civilization°*, p. 202. It is reproduced by Parpola, Asko, in *Deciphering the Indus Script°*, p. 256, after Mackay 1943, pl. 51:13.
36. Allchin, Raymond & Bridget, *Origins of a Civilization°*, p. 202.
37. Rig Veda, 1.160.2, 5.43.2, etc.
38. Ibid., 1.159, 1.160, 6.70, etc.
39. Ibid., 5.83.
40. Pusalker, A.D., 'The Indus Valley Civilization', ch. IX of *The Vedic Age*, vol. I in Majumdar, R.C., (ed.), *The History and Culture of the Indian People*, Bharatiya Vidya Bhavan, Bombay, 1951–88, p. 192.
41. *The Mahabharata of Krishna-Dwaipayana Vyasa*, op. cit., vol. IV, Santi Parva, XII.343, p. 166.
42. Rig Veda, 6.16.39 for Agni, 7.19.1 and 10.86.15 for Indra (the translation here is Griffith's). Also Yajur Veda, 2.6.11.r for Agni.
43. Rig Veda, 9.15.4 (Griffith's translation). Soma sharpens his horns again in 9.70.7.
44. Ibid., 10.103.01.

324   Notes to pp. 238–243

45. Ibid., 1.33.13.
46. Ibid., 1.55.1.
47. Ibid., 7.18.18.
48. Ibid., 8.85.5.
49. Ibid., 5.59.3 (Sri Aurobindo's translation).
50. Ibid., 1.80.6, 8.6.6, etc.
51. Bisht, R.S., 'Excavation at Banawali, District Hissar', in *Indian Archaeology 1988–87—A Review*, Archaeological Survey of India, New Delhi, 1992, p. 33.
52. The Vishwa Veda Sathram, Pañjal (Kerala), April 2002; my talk was on 'Indus Valley Civilization and Vedic Culture'. Some of the Vedic scholars present had taken part in the impressive 1975 re-creation of the Vedic fire ritual recorded by Indologist Frits Staal; see Staal, Frits, C.V. Somayajipad & M. Itti Ravi Nambudiri, (eds), *Agni: The Vedic Ritual of the Fire Altar°*.
53. On the cosmic, astronomical and inner significance of the fire altars, see Kak, Subhash, 'The Axis and the Perimeter of the Hindu Temple', *Mankind Quarterly*, vol. 46, 2006.
54. See Witzel, Michael, 'Autochthonous Aryans? The Evidence from Old Indian and Iranian Texts', *Electronic Journal of Vedic Studies*, vol. 7, no. 3, 25 May 2001, § 26.
55. B.B Lal, personal communication. The Kalibangan altars are described in detail in Lal, B.B., et al., *Excavations at Kalibangan*, Archaeological Survey of India, New Delhi, vol. 2, in press.
56. Allchin, F.R., 'The Legacy of the Indus Civilization', in Possehl, Gregory L., (ed.), *Harappan Civilization: A Recent Perspective*, op. cit., p. 388.
57. Rao, S.R., *Lothal: A Harappan Port Town*, Archaeological Survey of India, New Delhi, 1985, vol. I, p. 121 & 216.
58. Ibid., vol. I, p. 217 & vol. II, p. 499.
59. In the case of the square altar of the *Shulbasūtra*, the 'handle' is 80 *angula*s wide and the side 320 *angula*s long (see *The Sulbasutras*, op. cit., *Baudhāyana-Sulbasūtra* 17.3 & p. 220). Lothal's altar has a platform 65 cm wide for a side of 2.65 m, hence a ratio of 0.245 (measurements taken on the sketch of the altar, see Rao, S.R., *Lothal: A Harappan Port Town*, op. cit., vol. I, p. 97).
60. See Joshi, J.P., 'Religious and Burial Practices of Harappans: Indian Evidence', in Pande, G.C., (ed.), *The Dawn of Indian Civilization (up to c. 600 BC)*, Centre for Studies in Civilizations, New Delhi, 1999, p. 381, and his comments on the fire altars at Kalibangan and Lothal. See a similar treatment and additional details on Rakhigarhi in his *Harappan Architecture and Civil Engineering°*, ch. 7.
61. See a few examples in Possehl, Gregory L., *The Indus Civilization°*, p. 148 ff.
62. Ibid., p. 153.
63. McEvilley, T., 'An archaeology of yoga', *Res*, 1, 1981, pp. 44–77.
64. Dhyansky, Yan Y., 'The Indus Valley Origin of a Yoga Practice', *Artibus Asiae*, vol. 48, 1987, no. 1/2, pp. 89–108.
65. See examples in Lal, B.B., *The Saraswati Flows On°*, p. 127.

66. E.g. Jarrige, Jean-François, 'Du néolithique à la civilisation de l'Inde ancienne', op. cit., p. 12–14 & Possehl, Gregory L., *The Indus Civilization*°, pp. 114–17.

67. Chanda, Ramaprasad, *Survival of the Prehistoric Civilisation of the Indus Valley*, Archaeological Survey of India, 1929, p. 25.

68. Wheeler, Mortimer, *L'Inde avant l'histoire*, Sequoia-Elsevier, Paris-Bruxelles, 1967, p. 41. (I do not have access to the original English and have retranslated here from the French.)

69. Chakrabarti, Dilip K., *India: An Archaeological History*°, p. 197.

70. Rig Veda, 5.81.1 (Sri Aurobindo's translation).

71. Ibid., 1.51.10.

72. Ibid., 1.84.3.

73. Ibid., 5.2.6 (adapted from Sri Aurobindo's translation, *The Secret of the Veda*°, p. 368).

74. The best exposition of the spiritual experience enshrined in the Rig Veda remains, in my opinion, Sri Aurobindo's *Secret of the Veda*°.

75. Dhyansky, Yan Y., 'The Indus Valley Origin of a Yoga Practice', op. cit., p. 104.

76. Kosambi, Damodar Dharmanand, *Myth and Reality*, Popular Prakashan, Bombay, 1962; reprint 2005, p. 75. Kosambi assumes that Cemetary H is 'undoubtedly Aryan' (p. 74), but apart from the absurdity of such a racial label, it has recently been shown that there are 'clear continuities' between that phase and the earlier urban one: Meadow, R.H. & J.M. Kenoyer, 'Recent Discoveries and Highlights from Excavations at Harappa: 1998–2000', available online at www.harappa.com/indus4/print.html (accessed 15 September 2009); see also Kenoyer, J.M., *Ancient Cities of the Indus Valley Civilization*°, p. 175.

77. Rig Veda, 10.27.22, Griffith's translation.

78. Sharma, D.V., K.C. Nauriyal & V.N. Prabhakar, 'Excavations at Sanauli 2005–06: A Harappan Necropolis in the Upper Ganga-Yamuna Doab', *Puratattva*, no. 36, 2005–2006, pp. 166–79.

79. Kenoyer, Jonathan Mark, *Ancient Cities of the Indus Valley Civilization*°, p. 81.

80. Keller, Olivier, *La figure et le monde, une archéologie de la géométrie: peuples paysans sans écriture et premières civilisations*, Vuibert, Paris, 2006, p. 138.

81. For instance, *Manasara*, 35.18–20, Acharya, Prasanna Kumar, *Architecture of Manasara*, Munshiram Manoharlal, 1934; reprint New Delhi, 1994, p. 374.

82. See Kak, Subhash, 'Time, Space and Structure in Ancient India', paper presented at a conference on 'Sindhu-Sarasvati Valley Civilization: A Reappraisal', Loyola Marymount University, Los Angeles, 21 & 22 February 2009, available online at http://arxiv.org/pdf/0903.3252v2 (accessed 15 September 2009).

83. Apart from titles quoted earlier, see Parpola, Asko, *Deciphering the Indus Script*°; Sergent, Bernard, *Genèse de l'Inde*, Payot, Paris, 1997, p. 114 ff.; Feuerstein, Georg, Subhash Kak & David Frawley, *In Search of the Cradle of Civilization*°, ch. 4 & 7; Pathak, V.S., 'Buffalo-Horned Human Figure on the Harappan Jar at Padri: A Note', *Man and Environment*, vol. XVII, 1992, no. 1, pp. 87–89; Danino, Michel, 'The Harappan Heritage and the Aryan Problem', *Man and Environment*, vol. XXVIII, 2003, no. 1, pp. 21–32; and

various papers in Agrawal, Ashwini (ed.), *In Search of Vedic-Harappan Relationship°*.

84. Parpola, Asko, *Deciphering the Indus Script°*, p. 222.
85. Bisht, R.S., 'Dholavira Excavations: 1990–94' in Joshi, J.P., (ed.), *Facets of Indian Civilization: Essays in Honour of Prof. B.B. Lal*, op. cit., vol. I, pp. 111–112.
86. Bisht, R.S., 'Harappan and the Rgveda: Points of Convergence', in Pande, G.C., (ed.), *The Dawn of Indian Civilization (up to c. 600 BC)*, op. cit., p. 416.
87. Singh, Bhagwan, *Vedic Harappans°*, chapters VII–XI.
88. Lal, B.B., *India 1947–1997°*, p. 123.
89. See Suggested Further Reading, under the heading 'The Aryan Problem (in the Indian context)'.
90. Lal, B.B., *The Sarasvati Flows On°*, pp. ix–x.
91. Kenoyer, Jonathan Mark, 'Interaction Systems, Specialized Crafts and Cultural change', in George Erdosy, (ed.), *The Indo-Aryans of Ancient South Asia: Language, Material Culture and Ethnicity*, Walter de Gruyter, Berlin & New York, 1995, p. 234.
92. Kenoyer, Jonathan Mark, *Ancient Cities of the Indus Valley Civilization°*, p. 180.
93. Jarrige, Jean-François, 'Du néolithique à la civilisation de l'Inde ancienne', op. cit., p. 21.
94. Ibid., p. 28.
95. Shaffer, Jim G., 'The Indus Valley, Baluchistan, and Helmand Traditions: Neolithic through Bronze Age', in Ehrich, Robert W., (ed.), *Chronologies in Old World Archaeology*, third edn, The University of Chicago Press, Chicago & London, vol. I, p. 459.

11. The Sarasvatī's Testimony

1. Müller, F. Max, *Vedic Hymns*, op. cit., p. 60.
2. E.g. Misra, V.N., 'Climate, a Factor in the Rise and Fall of the Indus Civilization: Evidence from Rajasthan and Beyond', in Lal, B.B. & S.P. Gupta, (eds), *Frontiers of the Indus Civilization°*, p. 482.
3. Kenoyer, Jonathan Mark, *Ancient Cities of the Indus Valley Civilization°*, pp. 27–29.
4. See Chapter 2 for references to the Sarasvatī from books 2 to 7, widely accepted to be the Rig Veda's oldest *mandalas* (the so-called 'family books'; e.g. Renou, Louis & Jean Filliozat, *L'Inde classique: manuel des études indiennes*, op. cit., vol. 1, p. 272).
5. Allchin, Raymond & Bridget, *Origins of a Civilization*, p. 213.
6. Ibid., p. 24.
7. Possehl, Gregory L., *Indus Age: The Beginnings°*, p. 384.
8. Ibid., p. 363.
9. Ibid., p. 363.
10. Chakrabarti, Dilip K. & Sukhdev Saini, *The Problem of the Sarasvati River°*, p. 38.

11. Possehl, Gregory L., *Indus Age: The Beginnings*°, p. 382, Fig. 3.145.
12. Winternitz, Moritz, *A History of Indian Literature*°, vol. I, p. 288.
13. Winternitz, Moritz, *Some Problems of Indian Literature*, Bharatiya Book Corporation; reprinted Delhi, 1977, pp. 3–4.
14. Ghosh, B.K., 'The Origin of the Indo-Aryans', in Bhattacharya, K., (ed.), *The Cultural Heritage of India*, vol. I: *The Early Phases*, The Ramakrishna Mission Institute of Culture, Calcutta, 1958, p. 137.
15. Casal, Jean-Marie, *La Civilisation de l'Indus et ses énigmes*°, p. 205.
16. With the exception of some Bactrian styles or artefacts, but these only represent growing contacts between the two regions, not a 'Bactrian migration'. See Jarrige, Jean-François, 'Du néolithique à la civilisation de l'Inde ancienne', op. cit., p. 22.
17. Danino, Michel, 'Genetics and the Aryan Debate', *Puratattva*, New Delhi, no. 36, 2005–06, pp. 146–154.
18. Lal, B.B., *The Sarasvati Flows On*°, p. 75.
19. Danino, Michel, *The Elusive Aryans and the Dawn of Indian Civilization*°. See also Suggested Further Reading under 'The Aryan Problem', for a choice of studies and perspectives.
20. Thapar, Romila, 'Ideology and Interpretation of Early Indian History', in *Interpreting Early India*, Oxford University Press, New Delhi, 1992, p. 10. (The author states in her preface that this paper was written in 1974.)
21. Thapar, Romila, *Ancient India: A Textbook of History for Class VI*, National Council of Educational Research and Training, New Delhi, 1987, p. 38. (This textbook was reprinted thirteen times till January 2000.)
22. Thapar, Romila, *The Penguin History of Early India: From the Origins to AD 1300*, op. cit., p. 42.
23. Thomas, Edward, *The Rivers of the Vedas, and How the Aryans Entered India*, Stephen Austin & Sons, Hertford, 1883.
24. Ibid., p. 8.
25. Kochhar, Rajesh, *The Vedic People*°, p. 123.
26. Ibid., p. 126.
27. Witzel, Michael, 'Autochthonous Aryans? The Evidence from Old Indian and Iranian Texts', *Electronic Journal of Vedic Studies*, vol. 7, no. 3, 25 May 2001, §25.
28. Rig Veda, 3.33.10.
29. Kochhar, Rajesh, *The Vedic People*°, p. 127.
30. Witzel, Michael, 'Autochthonous Aryans? The Evidence from Old Indian and Iranian Texts', op. cit., §25.
31. *Imperial* Gazetteer, new edn, 1908, vol. 23, p. 179.
32. Wilhelmy, Herbert, 'The Shifting River: Studies in the History of the Indus Valley', *Universitas*, vol. 10, 1967, no. 1, p. 60.
33. Macdonell, A.A. & A.B. Keith, *Vedic Index*°, p. 301.
34. The Belgian Indologist Koenraad Elst has presented other arguments to refute Kochhar's thesis, which I do not repeat here. See his *Asterisk in Bharopiyasthan: Minor Writings on the Aryan Invasion Debate*°, ch. 2.

35. Kochhar, Rajesh, *The Vedic People°*, p. 127.
36. Ibid., p. 128.
37. Jansen, Michael, 'Settlement Networks of the Indus Civilization', op. cit., p. 118.
38. It is, to be precise, the 'Ravi aspect' of the Hakra phase. See Meadow, R.H. & J.M. Kenoyer, 'Recent Discoveries and Highlights from Excavations Harappa: 1998–2000', available online at www.harappa.com/indus4/print.html (accessed 15 September 2009).
39. Lal, B.B., et al., *Excavations at Kalibangan*, vol. 1, Archaeological Survey of India, New Delhi, 2003, p. 103.
40. Ibid., p. 30.
41. Shinde, Vasant, et al., 'Exploration in the Ghaggar Basin and Excavations at Girawad, Farmana (Rohtak District) and Mitathal (Bhiwani District), Haryana', in Osada, Toshiki & Akinori Uesugi, (eds), Occasional Paper 3, *Linguistics, Archaeology and the Human Past*, Research Institute for Humanity and Nature, Kyoto, 2008, pp. 77–158.
42. Rao, L.S., et al., 'New Light on the Excavation of Harappan Settlement at Bhirrana', *Puratattva*, no. 35, 2004–05, pp. 60–68.
43. Kochhar, Rajesh, *The Vedic People°*, p. 131.
44. Ibid., p. 209.
45. Ibid., p. 132.
46. Oldham, R.D., 'On Probable Changes in the Geography of the Panjab and its Rivers: An Historico-Geographical Study', *Journal of Asiatic Society of Bengal*, vol. 55, 1886, p. 341.
47. E.g. Talageri, Shrikant G., *The Rigveda: a Historical Analysis°*, pp. 120–124 (as regards fauna), and Lal, B.B., *The Homeland of the Aryans: Evidence of Rigvedic Flora and Fauna°*.
48. Witzel, Michael, 'Autochthonous Aryans? The Evidence from Old Indian and Iranian Texts', op. cit., §25.
49. Bhargava M.L., *The Geography of Rgvedic India*, The Upper India Publishing House, Lucknow, 1964, ch. 1: 'The Seas'.
50. Bhargava, P.L., *India in the Vedic Age°*, p. 85.
51. Frawley, David, *Gods, Sages and Kings°*, p. 45. See also his 'Geographical References: The Ocean and Soma', ch. 4 of *In Search of Vedic-Harappan Relationship°*.
52. Kazanas, Nicholas, 'Samudra and Sarasvatī in the Rig-Veda', *Quarterly Journal of the Mythic Society*, vol. 95, 2004, pp 90–104.
53. Rig Veda, 1.11.1, Griffith's translation.
54. Ibid., 1.174.9, 6.20.12.
55. Ibid., 7.33.8, Griffith's translation.
56. Ibid., 10.136.5.
57. Ibid., 1.169.3, 8.20.4.
58. Ibid., 7.68.7, 1.117.14, among others.
59. Ibid., 1.116.4, Griffith's translation.
60. Ibid., 1.116.5.

61. Ibid., 1.46.2.
62. Ibid., 1.71.7 (see also 1.190.7).
63. E.g., Rig Veda, 7.6.7, 3.22.3, 1.163.1.
64. Ibid., 2.34.12.
65. Ibid., 4.58.5.
66. Ibid., 9.73.1, Griffith's translation.
67. Müller, F. Max, *Vedic Hymns*, op. cit., p. 60.
68. Habib, Irfan, 'Imagining River Sarasvati: A Defence of Commonsense', *Proceedings of the Indian History Congress*, 61st session, Kolkata, 2000–01, pp. 67–92, reproduced in *Social Scientist*, V.29, nos 1–2, January–February 2001, #332–333, pp. 46 ff. All subsequent quotations from Habib in the rest of chapter 10 are from this paper; I have used the article's widely circulated Internet version: http://members.tripod.com/ahsaligarh/river.htm (accessed 15 August 2008).
69. Oldham, C.F., 'The Sarasvatī and the Lost River of the Indian Desert', *Journal of the Royal Asiatic Society*, vol. 34, 1893, p. 51.
70. Rig Veda, 3.23.4.
71. Shatapatha Brāhmana, V.3.4.1. See Eggeling, Julius, *The Satapatha Brāhmana°*, p. 73.
72. Wheeler, Mortimer, *L'Inde avant l'histoire*, Sequoia-Elsevier, Paris-Bruxelles, 1967, p. 30, where he states that Kalibangan overlooks the arid valley of the Ghaggar, 'the ancient Sarasvati'. (I do not have access to the English original.) See also his reference to 'the former Ghaggar or Sarasvatī', in Spear, Percival, (ed.), *The Oxford History of India*, Oxford University Press, fourth edn, Delhi, 1974–1998, p. 26. (Ch. 2, 'Prehistoric India', is by Mortimer Wheeler.)
73. Casal, Jean-Marie, *La Civilisation de l'Indus et ses énigmes°*, pp. 190 & 191.
74. Asko Parpola fully accepts the identification of the Ghaggar–Hakra with the Sarasvatī: see his *Deciphering the Indus Script°*, pp. 5 & 9.
75. Dani, Ahmad Hasan, in his foreword to Mughal, M.R., *Ancient Cholistan: Archaeology and Architecture°*, writes of the 'old, one-time flourishing river, such as a Sarasvati and Drishadvati, so well recorded in the Rigveda', a course of which is 'Hakra in Pakistan and Gagra (Ghaggar) in India' (p. 11, see also p. 12).
76. Personal communication (2006) from Dr S.P. Gupta, who was trying to obtain details from his Pakistani colleagues. Not having access to recent Pakistani papers, I am unable to provide a precise reference for those sites.
77. Stein, Aurel, 'A Survey of Ancient Sites along the "Lost" Sarasvatī River', op. cit., p. 181.
78. Possehl, Gregory. L, *Indus Age: The Beginnings°*, pp. 372–77.
79. Flam, Louis, 'The Prehistoric Indus River System and the Indus Civilization in Sindh', *Man and Environment*, vol. XXIV, 1999, no. 2, p. 58.
80. Flam, Louis, 'Ecology and Population Mobility in the Prehistoric Settlement of the Lower Indus Valley, Sindh, Pakistan', in Meadows, Azra & Peter S. Meadows, (eds), *The Indus River: Biodiversity, Resources, Humankind*, Oxford University Press, Karachi, 1999, pp. 315–17.

81. Adapted from Louis Flam's map in ibid., p. 315.
82. Mughal, M.R., *Ancient Cholistan: Archaeology and Architecture*°, p. 21.
83. Wilhelmy, Herbert, 'The Ancient River Valley on the Eastern Border of the Indus Plain and the Sarasvatī Problem', in *Vedic Sarasvatī*, p. 97.
84. Allchin, Bridget 'Some Questions of Environment and Prehistory in the Indus Valley from Palaeolithic to Urban Indus Times', in *The Indus River: Biodiversity, Resources, Humankind*, op. cit., 1999, p. 294.
85. Francfort, Henri-Paul, 'Evidence for Harappan Irrigation System in Haryana and Rajasthan', *The Eastern Anthropologist*, 1992, vol. 45, p. 91.
86. Ibid., p. 89.
87. Gentelle, Pierre, 'Paysages, environment et irrigation: hypothèses pour l'étude des 3ᵉ et 2ᵉ millénaires', in Francfort, Henri-Paul, (ed.), *Prospections archéologiques au nord-ouest de l'Inde: rapport préliminaire 1983–1984*, Éditions Recherches sur les Civilisations, Paris, mémoire 62, 1985, p. 41.
88. Francfort, H.-P., 'Distribution des sites', in ibid., p. 65.
89. Francfort, Henri-Paul, 'Evidence for Harappan Irrigation System in Haryana and Rajasthan', op. cit., p. 98.
90. Francfort, H.-P., 'Distribution des sites', *Prospections archéologiques au nord-ouest de l'Inde*, op. cit., p. 65.
91. Rig Veda, 7.96.2.
92. *The Mahabharata of Krishna-Dwaipayana Vyasa*, op. cit., vol. III, Salya Parva, IX.55, p. 151.
93. Tripathi, Jayant K., Barbara Bock, V. Rajamani & A. Eisenhauer, 'Is River Ghaggar, Saraswati? Geochemical constraints', *Current Science*, vol. 87, no. 8, 25 October 2004, pp. 1141–45.
94. Ibid., Fig. 1–b, p. 1142. According to the map's caption, samples were taken at 'Sirsa and Fatehabad on Ghaggar', but the dry bed is a few kilometres north of Sirsa and Fatehabad is some 20 km south of the Ghaggar.
    (Curiously, the map is actually based—without acknowledgements—on a scan of a map of mine, an earlier version of the map reproduced in Fig. 4.2 in this book; it is strange that the four scientists were unable to draw a map of their own on a scale suitable for showing the precise locations of their sampling sites. Even more curiously, after erasing most names from my map, the authors added the word 'Saraswati' and two big arrows pointing to the course I drew, which is the course of the Ghaggar–Hakra—even though the main point of their paper was to deny this identity!)
95. Courty, M.-A., 'Geoarchaeological Approach of Holocene Paleoenvironments in the Ghaggar Plains', *Man and Environment*, vol. X, 1986, p. 112.
96. Casal, Jean-Marie, *La Civilisation de l'Indus et ses énigmes*°, p. 7.
97. Erdosy, George, 'Prelude to Urbanization', in *Archaeology of Early Historic South Asia*°, p. 77.
98. Allchin, Raymond & Bridget, *Origins of a Civilization*°, p. 124.
99. Possehl, Gregory L., *Indus Age: The Beginnings*°, p. 356.
100. McIntosh, Jane R., *A Peaceful Realm*°, p. 46.
101. Kenoyer, J.M., *Ancient Cities of the Indus Valley Civilization*°, p. 27.

102. Sharma, Ram Sharan, *Advent of the Aryans in India*°, ch. 2.

103. Lal, B.B., *The Sarasvatī Flows On*°, p. 8 ff.

104. One such promising study recently published a preliminary report of exploration: Singh, R.N., et al., 'Settlements in Context: Reconnaissance in Western Uttar Pradesh and Haryana', *Man and Environment*, vol. XXXIII, no. 2, 2008, pp. 71–87.

12. Epilogue: Sarasvatī Turns Invisible

1. *The Mahabharata of Krishna-Dwaipayana Vyasa*, op. cit., Salya Parva, vol. III, IX.54, p. 149.

2. Ibid., p. 150.

3. O.P. Bharadwaj identifies Plakshaprāsravana with a location in the Nahan district of the Shivaliks, see 'The Rigvedic Sarasvatī', in *In Search of Vedic-Harappan Relationship*°, p. 16.

4. Valdiya, K.S., *Saraswati, the River That Disappeared*°, p. 26.

5. Ibid., p. 54.

6. Flam, Louis, 'The Prehistoric Indus River System and the Indus Civilization in Sindh', op. cit., p. 57 (emphasis in the original).

7. See Bharadwaj, O.P., 'Vinasana', *Journal of the Oriental Institute of Baroda*, vol. 33, 1983, nos 1–2, pp. 69–88. Bharadwaj, keen to identify *Vinashana* with Kalibangan, argues for a Sarasvatī–Drishadvatī confluence *above* Kalibangan, but this can hardly be accepted, as topographic studies and satellite imagery have made clear.

8. Bharadwaj, O.P., 'Vinashana', op. cit., p. 78.

9. *The Mahabharata of Krishna-Dwaipayana Vyasa*, op. cit., vol. III, Salya Parva, IX.42, p. 118.

10. Iyengar, R.N., 'Profile of a Natural Disaster in Ancient Sanskrit Literature', *Indian Journal of History of Science*, vol. 39, 2004, no. 1, pp. 11–49, available online at www.ifih.org/NaturalDisasterinAncientSanskritLiterature.htm (accessed 15 September 2009); 'On Some Comet Observations in Ancient India', *Journal of the Geological Society of India*, vol. 67, March 2006, pp. 289–94.

11. Chakrabarti, Dilip K., *The Oxford Companion to Indian Archaeology*°, pp. 209 & 211.

12. Mathur, U.B., 'Chronology of Harappan Port Towns of Gujarat in the Light of Sea Level Changes during the Holocene', *Man and Environment*, vol. XXVII, no. 2, 2002, pp. 61–67.

13. Kenoyer, J. Mark, 'New Perspectives on the Mauryan and Kushana Periods', in *Between the Empires: Society in India 300 BCE to 400 CE*, Oxford University Press, New York, 2006, pp. 34 & 46.

14. Joshi, J.P., Madhu Bala & Jassu Ram, 'The Indus Civilization: A Reconsideration on the Basis of Distribution Maps', in Lal, B.B. & S.P. Gupta, (eds), *Frontiers of the Indus Civilization*°, p. 516.

15. Shaffer, Jim G. & Diane A. Lichtenstein, 'The Concepts of "Cultural Tradition" and "Paleoethnicity" in South Asian Archaeology', in Erdosy, George,

(ed.), *The Indo-Aryans of Ancient South Asia*, op. cit., p. 139 (emphasis in the original).

16. Shaffer, Jim G., 'The Indus Valley, Baluchistan, and Helmand Traditions: Neolithic through Bronze Age', in *Chronologies in Old World Archaeology*, op. cit., p. 450.

17. Shatapatha Brāhmana, 1.4.1.10–19. See Eggeling, Julius, *The Satapatha Brāhmana°*, pp. 104–06.

18. *Lātyāyana Shrautasūtra*, 10.18.3, quoted in and translated by Burrow, Thomas, 'On the Word *Arma* or *Armaka* in Early Sanskrit Literature', in *Journal of Indian History*, vol. 41, 1963, pp. 159–166.

19. Burrow quotes the Rig Veda where '*armaka*', the word for 'ruin', occurs once in an unspecified context, and builds on it a conviction that it was 'the Aryans who were responsible for the overthrow of the Indus civilisation'. This view has been categorically rejected by archaeologists in recent decades.

20. Tewari, Rakesh, 'The Origins of Iron Working in India: New Evidence from the Central Ganga Plain and the Eastern Vindhyas', *Antiquity*, vol. 77, 2003, no. 297, pp. 536–544, available online at http://antiquity.ac.uk/ProjGall/tewari/tewari.pdf and www.archaeologyonline.net/artifacts/iron-ore.html (accessed 15 September 2009).

21. Tewari, Rakesh, 'The Myth of Dense Forests and Human Occupation in the Ganga Plain', *Man and Environment*, vol. XXIX, 2004, no. 2, pp. 102–116.

22. Darian, Steven, 'Gangā and Sarasvatī: An Incidence of Mythological Projection', *East and West*, vol. 26, 1976, nos 1–2, pp. 153–165.

23. *The Mahabharata of Krishna-Dwaipayana Vyasa*, op. cit., vol. III, Salya Parva, IX.42, p. 117 (slightly altered).

24. Rig Veda, 1.3.10–12. The translation is my adaptation of two different translations by Sri Aurobindo, *The Secret of the Veda°*, pp. 85 & 519.

Suggested Further Reading

The following titles are meant for those who wish to explore some of the unending ramifications glimpsed in this book. With a few exceptions, I have listed recent works accessible to a non-specialist public; they represent a broad spectrum of views. More scholarly or technical studies are found in Notes. I have retained a few French titles when those have no English translation.

I. India's Prehistory and Protohistory

Agrawal, D.P. & Kharakwal, J.S., *South Asian Prehistory: A Multi-disciplinary Study*, Aryan Books International, New Delhi, 2002

Agrawal, D.P. & Kharakwal, J.S., *Bronze and Iron Ages in South Asia*, Aryan Books International, New Delhi, 2003

Allchin, Bridget & Raymond, *The Rise of Civilization in India and Pakistan*, Cambridge University Press, New Delhi, 1996

Allchin, F.R., (ed.), *Archaeology of Early Historic South Asia: The Emergence of Cities and States*, Cambridge University Press, Cambridge, 1995

Chakrabarti, Dilip K., *The Archaeology of Ancient Indian Cities*, Oxford University Press, New Delhi, 1997

Chakrabarti, Dilip K., *India: An Archaeological History*, Oxford University Press, New Delhi, 1999

Chakrabarti, Dilip K., *The Oxford Companion to Indian Archaeology: The Archaeological Foundations of Ancient India*, Oxford University Press, New Delhi, 2006

Kennedy, K.A.R., *God-Apes and Fossil Men: Paleoanthropology in South Asia*, University of Michigan, Ann Arbor, 2000

Misra, V.N., *Rajasthan: Prehistoric and Early Historic Foundations*, Aryan Books International, New Delhi, 2007

Sankalia, H.D., *Prehistory of India*, Munshiram Manoharlal, New Delhi, 1977

Singh, Upinder, *The Discovery of Ancient India: Early Archaeologists and the Beginnings of Archaeology*, Permanent Black, New Delhi, 2004

II. The Indus–Sarasvatī Civilization

Agrawal, D.P., *The Indus Civilization: An Interdisciplinary Perspective*, Aryan Books International, New Delhi, 2006

Allchin, Raymond & Bridget, *Origins of a Civilization: The Prehistory and Early Archaeology of South Asia*, Viking, New Delhi, 1997

Casal, Jean-Marie, *La Civilisation de l'Indus et ses énigmes*, Fayard, Paris, 1969

Chakrabarti, Dilip K., *Indus Civilization Sites in India: New Discoveries*, Marg Publications, Mumbai, 2004

Dhavalikar, M.K., *Indian Protohistory*, Books & Books, New Delhi, 1997

Eltsov, Piotr Andreevich, *From Harappa to Hastinapura: A Study of the Earliest South Asian City and Civilization*, Brill Academic Publishers, Boston, Leiden, 2007

Gaur, A.S., Sundaresh & Vora, K.H., *Archaeology of Bet Dwarka Island*, Aryan Books International, New Delhi, & National Institute of Oceanography, Goa, 2005

Gupta, S.P., *The Indus–Sarasvatī Civilization: Origins, Problems and Issues*, Pratibha Prakashan, Delhi, 1996

Habib, Irfan, *The Indus Civilization*, vol. 2 in *A People's History of India*, Tulika Books, sec. edn, New Delhi, 2003

Jarrige, Jean-François, (ed.), *Les Cités oubliées de l'Indus: archéologie du Pakistan*, Association française d'action artistique & Musée national des Arts asiatiques Guimet, Paris, 1988

Joshi, Jagat Pati, *Harappan Architecture and Civil Engineering*, Rupa & Infinity Foundation, New Delhi, 2008

Kenoyer, Jonathan Mark, *Ancient Cities of the Indus Valley Civilization,*

Oxford University Press & American Institute of Pakistan Studies, Karachi & Islamabad, 1998

Lahiri, Nayanjot, (ed.), *The Decline and Fall of the Indus Civilization*, Permanent Black, New Delhi, 2000

Lahiri, Nayanjot, *Finding Forgotten Cities: How the Indus Civilization Was Discovered*, Permanent Black, New Delhi, 2005

Lal, B.B. & Gupta, S.P., (eds), *Frontiers of the Indus Civilization*, Books and Books, New Delhi, 1984

Lal, B.B., *The Earliest Civilization of South Asia*, Aryan Books International, New Delhi, 1997

Lal, B.B., *India 1947-1997: New Light on the Indus Civilization*, Aryan Books International, New Delhi, 1998

Lal, B.B., *How Deep Are the Roots of Indian Civilization? Archaeology Answers*, Aryan Books International, New Delhi, 2009

McIntosh, Jane R., *A Peaceful Realm: The Rise and Fall of the Indus Civilization*, Westview Press, Boulder, 2002

McIntosh, Jane R., *The Ancient Indus Valley: New Perspectives*, ABC-Clio, Santa Barbara, 2008

Mughal, Mohammad Rafique, *Ancient Cholistan: Archaeology and Architecture*, Ferozsons, Lahore, 1997

Possehl, Gregory L., *Indus Age: The Beginnings*, Oxford & IBH, New Delhi, 1999

Possehl, Gregory L., *The Indus Civilization: A Contemporary Perspective*, Altamira Press, Oxford, 2002; Indian edn, Vistaar, New Delhi, 2003

Rao, S.R., *Dawn and Devolution of the Indus Civilization*, Aditya Prakashan, New Delhi, 1991

Ratnagar, Shereen, *The End of the Great Harappan Tradition*, Manohar, New Delhi, 2000

Ratnagar, Shereen, *Understanding Harappa: Civilization in the Greater Indus Valley*, Tulika, New Delhi, 2006

Stein, Marc Aurel, *An Archaeological Tour along the Ghaggar–Hakra River*, Gupta, S.P., (ed.), Kusumanjali Prakashan, Meerut, 1989

Wheeler, R.E. Mortimer, *The Indus Civilization*, third edn, Cambridge University Press, Cambridge, 1968

Wright, Rita P., *The Ancient Indus: Urbanism, Economy, and Society*, Cambridge University Press, New York, 2010

III. The Sarasvatī River and Goddess

Airi, Raghunath, *Concept of Sarasvatī (in Vedic, Epic and Puranic Literature)*, The Rohtak Co-operative Printing and Publishing Society, Rohtak, 1977

Bhattacharyya, Kanailal, *Sarasvatī: A Study of her Concept and Iconography*, Saraswat Library, Calcutta, 1983

Chakrabarti, Dilip K. & Saini, Sukhdev, *The Problem of the Sarasvati River and Notes on the Archaeological Geography of Haryana and Indian Panjab*, Aryan Books International, New Delhi, 2009

Ghosh, Niranjan, *Srī Sarasvatī in Indian Art and Literature*, Sri Satguru, Delhi, 1984

Gonda, Jan, *Pūshan and Sarasvatī*, North-Holland Publishing Co., Amsterdam, 1985

Kalyanaraman, S., *Sarasvatī*, vols 2 (Rigveda) & 3 (River), Babasaheb Apte Smarak Samiti, Bangalore, 2003

Kalyanaraman, S., (ed.), *Vedic River Sarasvati and Hindu Civilization*, Aryan Books International, New Delhi, & Sarasvati Research and Education Trust, Chennai, 2008

Lal, B.B., *The Sarasvatī Flows On: The Continuity of Indian Culture*, Aryan Books International, New Delhi, 2002

Ludvik, Catherine, *Sarasvatī Riverine Goddess of Knowledge*, Brill, Leiden, Boston, 2007

Radhakrishna, B.P. & Merh, S.S., (eds), *Vedic Sarasvatī: Evolutionary History of a Lost River of Northwestern India*, Geological Society of India, Bangalore, 1999

Valdiya, K.S., *Saraswati, the River That Disappeared*, Indian Space Research Organization & Universities Press, Hyderabad, 2002

IV. The Indus Script

Joshi, Jagat Pati & Parpola, Asko, (eds), *Corpus of Indus Seals and Inscriptions: 1. Collections in India,* Suomalainen Tiedeakatemia, Helsinki, 1987 (see vol. 2 under 'Shah' below)

Kalyanaraman, S., *Sarasvatī*, vols 6 (Language) & 7 (Epigraphs), Babasaheb Apte Smarak Samiti, Bangalore, 2003

Mahadevan, Iravatham, *The Indus Script: Text, Concordance and Tables*, Archaeological Survey of India, New Delhi, 1977

Mitchiner, J.E, *Studies in the Indus Valley Inscriptions,* Oxford & IBH, New Delhi, 1978

Parpola, Asko, *Deciphering the Indus Script,* Cambridge University Press, 1994, Indian paperback edn, 2000

Possehl, Gregory L., *Indus Age: The Writing System,* Oxford & IBH, New Delhi, 1996

Shah, Sayid Ghulam Mustafa & Parpola, Asko, *Corpus of Indus Seals and Inscriptions: 2. Collections in Pakistan,* Suomalainen Tiedeakatemia, Helsinki, 1991, (see vol. 1 under 'Joshi')

V. The Aryan Problem (in the Indian context)

Agrawal, Ashvini, (ed.), *In Search of Vedic-Harappan Relationship,* Aryan Books International, New Delhi, 2005

Bhargava, P.L., *India in the Vedic Age: A History of Aryan Expansion in India,* D.K. Printworld, third edn, New Delhi, 2001

Bryant, Edwin, *The Quest for the Origins of Vedic Culture: The Indo-Aryan Migration Debate,* Oxford University Press, New York, 2001

Bryant, Edwin F. & Patton, Laurie L., (eds), *The Indo-Aryan Controversy: Evidence and Inference in Indian History,* Routledge, London & New York, 2005

Chakrabarti, Dilip K., *Colonial Indology: Sociopolitics of the Ancient Indian Past,* Munshiram Manoharlal, New Delhi, 1997

Chakrabarti, Dilip K., *The Battle for Ancient India, an Essay in the Sociopolitics of Indian Archaeology,* Aryan Books International, New Delhi, 2008

Danino, Michel, *L'Inde ou l'invasion de nulle part: Le Dernier Repaire du Mythe Aryen,* Les Belles Lettres, Paris, 2006

Danino, Michel, *The Dawn of Indian Civilization and the Elusive Aryans,* forthcoming

Dhavalikar, M.K., *The Aryans: Myth and Archaeology,* Munshiram Mahoharlal, New Delhi, 2007

Elst, Koenraad, *Update on the Aryan Invasion Debate,* Aditya Prakashan, New Delhi, 1999

Elst, Koenraad, *Asterisk in Bharopiyasthan: Minor Writings on the Aryan Invasion Debate,* Voice of India, New Delhi, 2007

Feuerstein, Georg, Kak, Subhash & Frawley, David, *In Search of the*

Cradle of Civilization, Quest Books, Wheaton, U.S.A, 1995 ; Indian edn, Motilal Banarsidass, Delhi, 1999

Frawley, David, *Gods, Sages and Kings: Vedic Secrets of Ancient Civilization*, Motilal Banarsidass, Delhi, 1993

Frawley, David, *The Rig Veda and the History of India*, Aditya Prakashan, New Delhi, 2001

Kochhar, Rajesh, *The Vedic People: Their History and Geography*, Orient Longman, Hyderabad, 2000

Lal, B.B., *The Homeland of the Aryans: Evidence of Rigvedic Flora and Fauna*, Aryan Books International, New Delhi, 2005

Rajaram, N.S. & Frawley, David, *Vedic Aryans and the Origins of Civilization: A Literary and Scientific Perspective*, Voice of India, third edn, New Delhi, 2001

Sethna, K.D., *The Problem of Aryan Origins*, Aditya Prakashan, sec. edn, New Delhi, 1992

Sharma, Ram Sharan, *Advent of the Aryans in India*, Manohar, New Delhi, 2001

Singh, Bhagwan, *The Vedic Harappans*, Aditya Prakashan, New Delhi, 1995

Thapar, Romila, et al., *India: Historical Beginnings and the Concept of the Aryan*, National Book Trust, New Delhi, 2006

Trautmann, Thomas R., *Aryans and British India*, Vistaar, New Delhi, 1997

Trautmann, Thomas R., (ed.), *The Aryan Debate*, Oxford University Press, New Delhi, 2005

Tripathi, D.N., (ed.), *A Discourse on Indo-European Languages and Culture*, Indian Council of Historical Research, New Delhi, 2005

VI. Vedic Texts and Studies

Aurobindo, Sri, *The Secret of the Veda*, Sri Aurobindo Ashram, Pondicherry, 1972

Bhattacharya, N.N., *A Cultural Index to Vedic Literature*, Manohar, New Delhi, 2007

Eggeling, Julius, *The Satapatha Brāhmana*, vol. 12 in *Sacred Books of the East*, 1882; republ. Motilal Banarsidass, Delhi, 2001

Gonda, Jan, *The Vision of the Vedic Poets*, Mouton, The Hague, 1963; Indian edn, Munshiram Manoharlal, New Delhi, 1984

Gonda, Jan, *Vedic Literature (Samhitās and Brāhmanas)*, Otto Harrassowitz, Wiesbaden, 1975

Griffith, Ralph T.H., (tr.), *The Hymns of the RgVeda,* sec. edn 1896; republ. Motilal Banarsidass, Delhi, 1973

Griffith, Ralph T.H., (tr.), *Hymns of the Atharvaveda,* 1884; republ. Munshiram Manoharlal, New Delhi, 2002

Kak, Subhash, *The Astronomical Code of the Rgveda,* sec. edn, Munshiram Mahoharlal, New Delhi, 2000

Kazanas, Nicholas, *Indo-Aryan Origins and Other Vedic Issues,* Aditya Prakashan, New Delhi, 2009

Keith, A.B., *A History of Sanskrit Literature,* 1928; reprinted Motilal Banarsidass, Delhi, 1993

Macdonell, A.A. & Keith, A.B., *Vedic Index of Names and Subjects,* 2 vols, 1912; reprinted Motilal Banarsidass, Delhi, 1958–2007

Miller, Jeanine, *The Vedas: Harmony, Meditation and Fulfilment,* Rider, London, 1974

Müller, F. Max, *A History of Ancient Sanskrit Literature,* Allahabad, 1859; reprint Asian Educational Services, New Delhi, 1993

Müller, F. Max, *Vedic Hymns,* part I, vol. 32 in *Sacred Books of the East,* 1882; reprint Motilal Banarsidass, Delhi, 2001

Ranade, H.G., *Illustrated Dictionary of Vedic Rituals,* Aryan Books International, New Delhi, 2006

Staal, Frits, et al., *AGNI: The Vedic Ritual of the Fire Altar,* Asian Humanities Press, Berkeley, 1983, 2 vols; reprinted Motilal Banarsidass, Delhi, 2001

Staal, Frits, *Discovering the Vedas,* Penguin Books, New Delhi, 2008

Talageri, Shrikant G., *The Rigveda: A Historical Analysis,* Aditya Prakashan, New Delhi, 2000

Talageri, Shrikant G., *The Rigveda and the Avesta: The Final Evidence,* Aditya Prakashan, New Delhi, 2008

Winternitz, M., *A History of Indian Literature,* 3 vols, 1907; reprinted Motilal Banarsidass, Delhi, 1981

Copyright Acknowledgements

Index

108 (sacred number), 207–209

Abhijñānashakuntalam, 45
Acharya, Prasanna Kumar, 325
Ad Badri, 18, 22; traditional source of the Sarasvatī, 48, 65, 252
Adarshana, 41, 44
Adi Badri (Chamoli district, Uttarakhand), 19
Afghanistan, 13, 26, 39, 110, 133, 260, 264; Harappan sites in, 91, 107
Africa, 181
Agarwal, Vishal, 298
Agni, 234, 237, 238, 245, 291
Agrawal, Ashvini, 326, 337
Agrawal, D.P., 302, 303, 304, 305, 308, 315, 320, 321, 333, 334; cultural continuity, 224; end of the Indus civilization, 187; Harappan metallurgy, 307; Harappan society, 119; satellite imagery of the Sarasvatī, 68; the Sarasvatī, 187
āhavanīya, 239
Ahichchhatra, 226
Airi, Raghunath, 336
Ajmer, 44
Akkad, 108
Alberuni, 49
Alexander the Great, 25, 27, 127
Allahabad, 44, 50
Allah's bund, 183
Allchin, Bridget, 97, 256, 271, 306, 307, 311, 312, 315, 317, 323, 326, 330, 333, 334; continuity between the

Ghaggar–Hakra and the Nara, 274; desiccation of the Sarasvatī, 153; floods in the Indus basin, 185; Harappan polity, 116–117; the Sarasvatī, 254–255; the Sarasvatī at Kalibangan, 153; Vedic-Harappan parallel, 237
Allchin, Raymond, 97, 256, 271, 306, 307, 311, 312, 315, 316, 320, 323, 324, 326, 330, 333, 334; Dholavira, 166; fire altars at Kalibangan, 241; floods in the Indus basin, 185; Harappan polity, 116–117; Harappan sites in the Sarasvatī basin, 153; the Sarasvatī, 153, 254–255; the Sarasvatī at Kalibangan, 153; Vedic-Harappan parallel, 237
Altyn Tepe, 110
Ambala, 10, *20*, 21, 55
Amri, 90
Amu Darya, 91
An, Cheng-Bang, 314
angula, 206–208. *See also danda, dhanus*
Anquetil-Duperron, A.H., 16
Anupgarh, 10, 14, 15, 61, 130, 149
Anuradhapura, 320
Āpayā, 270
Arabian Sea, 32, 114, 175
Aravalli Hills, 49, 50, 71, 291
Aravamuthan, T.G., 229, 322
Archaeological Survey of India, 46, 62, 84–87, 101, 122, 135, 204, 340
Arghandab river, 260
Aristobulus, 25

Page numbers in italics refer to figures.

341